The Phylaxis
COLLECTION ONE
January 1974 to September 1976

Phylaxis Imprint Book Publishing
PO Box 5675
Albuquerque, NM 87185-5675

ISBN: 978-1-948043-00-7

Copyright 2017. All rights reserved. No part of this work may be reproduced or transmitted in any form or by any means, electronic or mechanical, or stored in any retrieval system, without written permission from the publisher.

Printed in the United States

Dedication

We dedicate this volume to Joseph A. Walkes, Jr., founder and first president of The Phylaxis Society, and to John G. Lewis, patron of the Society.

Walkes

Lewis

From the President

Why do we need this collection? It has been said that The Phylaxis magazines are a gold mine of masonic information. Having put this first collection together, we say it is a gold mine with streaks of silver and platinum sprinkled with diamonds. We are a little biased, but we have come to believe that these magazines are awesome; we have to share them. We owe it to our masonic brothers to do it.

The information in The Phylaxis magazine is too valuable to remain scattered around the world in periodicals waiting to be tossed. Of course, I know members of the Phylaxis Society who claim they never toss their copies of The Phylaxis, an attitude that speaks to the quality of the magazine. This collection gives the wealth of information in our magazine new life and makes it available to a new generation of researchers.

Alex Smith
President

A gold mine with streaks of silver and platinum sprinkled with diamonds

Preface

This volume contains the first ten issues of *The Phylaxis* magazine—magazines that set the tone for a research, historical, and educational society that, at this writing, is in its fifth decade of research, history, and education. I have said publicly that freemasonry made me a better man, and I can now say that the Phylaxis Society made me a better mason. I wonder even now what the world would be if every man could be a mason, and how much better still if every mason could reap the benefits of a society such as this.

This compilation encapsulates the spirit upon which the Phylaxis Society was built and it should serve as encouragement and inspiration to any Prince Hall mason who studies it well. Take your time. This is not a task to be rushed. This compilation has the power to transform, and when you are transformed, as I think you will be, you owe it to those masons you love to help them with their transformation. This volume should be required reading for Prince Hall masons, but because this is no trivial task, your insistent encouragement will be needed to motivate your brothers to the effort.

> **Freemasonry made me a better man … the Phylaxis Society made me a better mason…**

We say we are seeking light, but more to the point we are seeking *truth*—that fundamental tenant of Freemasonry we call a divine attribute and the foundation of every virtue. Join with us. "You will know the truth, and the truth shall set you free."

Several articles in this collection justify the cost of this publication. The articles by Alexander Clark (volume 2, number 5, page 135) and Martin Delaney (volume 2, number 6, page 160) show why they are considered giants in Prince Hall masonry. The Delaney article is a

> **We say we are seeking light, but more to the point we are seeking truth…**

true work of art. One might take issue with details of its historical narrative, but for those inclined toward his point of view, Delaney makes a strong case for the African origin of Freemasonry (volume 2, number 6, page 160). The poetic voice of Alexander Clark shines brightly in the Masonic classic published in volume 2, number 5, page 135. The silver tongue of Alexander Clark might just be strong enough to convert a hostile audience to his point of view. Ira Holder became the first fellow of the Society, and his papers, featured frequently in early editions, prove him worthy of the honor. Then there are the papers of Joseph A. Walkes, Jr., the Society's second fellow, founder, and first president, who has an incredible sense of history. It is clearly his tireless investigation, examination, and exploration that allows him to discover the pearls of wisdom we find in this volume and to craft masterpieces of his own as he does time and time again. I call your attention to his address to the Conference of Grand Masters (volume 2, number 7, page 171), not for its artistry or historical significance, but because it sets out the way Prince Hall masons can benefit from an active association with the Phylaxis Society and the reason that Prince Hall masons should be strong supporters of the Society and its goals.

Please take your time with the collection. Get to know Prince Hall from his charges to African Lodge and from his letter book, all of which you will find within these pages. Get to know the early giants of masonic thought from their words. The more you study this volume, the more rewarding the experience will become. Then consider, there are a dozen more collections to come covering the period from 1977 to the present.

John B. Williams, FPS, Life
Editor

This volume should be required reading for Prince Hall masons

Table of Contents

Volume 1 Number 1 January 1974

3 A Word from the President Welcome to the Society. Describes the Phylaxis Emblem. Describes membership and fellowship policy.

3 What Does the Phylaxis Society Seek? Too much information about Prince Hall Masons is written by those who have little knowledge of the subject. Research into Prince Hall Masonry is needed.

3 The U.L.F. and the Phylaxis Society The United League of Freemasons is non-conducive to Prince Hall Masonry. The body is judged as clandestine by American Masonic bodies.

3 Prince Hall Masonry Discusses the three degrees of Masonry and attendant duties.

6 John Marrant, Brother Chaplain John Marrant was chaplain of African Lodge 459 under Prince Hall. Prince Hall describes him as "a black minister from back home, but last from "Brachtown, Nova Scotia."

7 Some Important Events in the Life of Prince Hall This article appeared in the Plumbline of the MWPHGL of Louisiana. Reveals known activities of Prince Hall, the man. (Relies heavily on Grimshaw.)

9 Prince Hall Public School The Prince Hall Elementary School is the first public school in American to be named after our founder, Prince Hall. It was opened on September 7, 1973 in the City of Philadelphia on 18th and Godfrey.

10 Roster of Grand Masters A listing of sitting grand masters.

10 Caucasian Prince Hall Lodge In 1871 there was a lodge of German Jews working in New York City under the jurisdiction of the Prince Hall Grand Lodge of New York.

12 PHA Masonic Structure An illustration of Masonic bodies to include the York and Scottish rites.

Volume 1 Number 2 May 1974

14 The Phylaxis Society and the Philalethes Society An editorial; how the Phylaxis Society was patterned after the Philalethes Society.

14 Hold Rites for Vern T. Watts, Grand Master Bio and obituary of deceased Grand Master Vern T. Watt of Kansas.

15 A Word from the President Plans for future articles, investigation of non-Prince Hall bodies. Early mention of the Northwest Chapter of the Phylaxis Society.

16 You Be the Judge??? Poses questions about the 1827 Declaration of Independence of African Lodge. Did it forever sever its connection with the Grand Lodge of England?

16 I am Freemasonry Musing about the Masonic Order. "I teach the lessons of life and of death, and the relationship of MAN to GOD and MAN to MAN."

17 Profile of a Non-Prince Hall Masonic Organization Presents a profile of a bogus grand lodge in New Orleans claiming to have drawn members from the Compact Grand Lodge. Refers to those groups as "Bogus" who claim to be masonic without legitimate masonic authority.

18 The Masonic Philosophy of Samuel W. Clark Samuel Clark is described as a voice crying in the wilderness during the dark days of our Masonic history. His appeal was for truth and justice before the world Masonic community against hypocrisy.

19 The Phylaxis Society Subscription Card Membership subscription form.

Volume1 Number 3 August 1974

22 Our Responsibility as Prince Hall Masons Many men joining bogus groups are lost to Prince Hall Masonry. We need a program of education for our members about their origins.

23 Profile of a Non-Prince Hall Masonic Organization Continued from the previous issue. Scottish Rite masons claim masonic lineage back to Mother Kilwinning Lodge No. 0 of Scotland.

24 Northwest Phylaxis Society Chapter Tacoma-Seattle Washington News about the activities of the Northwest Phylaxis Chapter. Roster of members.

25 O'Misawa Lodge #54 – O'Misawa, Japan Members of a lodge in Japan help to support a child abandoned by her African-American father and her Japanese mother.

26 Welcome to New Members A list of early Society members includes Sovereign Grand Commander Jno. G. Lewis and Charles H. Wesley.

26 Notice to Grand Master, Greetings An appeal for official publications of grand lodges and for other assistance.

26 Members of Northwest Chapter Phylaxis Society Photograph of the chapter members.

27 The Iowa Masonic Library The Society requested this article from the author so that the Prince Hall family would learn of the existence of the Iowa Masonic Library and freely use its facilities. "First, Best, and Biggest in the world."

28 Prince Hall Masonry and the Civil War - Part I, A Masterpiece. After issuing the Emancipation Proclamation, Lincoln reversed his earlier position and authorized the use of freed blacks in the Union Army. Prince Hall Masonic military lodges followed shortly thereafter.

Volume 2 Number 1 January 1975

34 A Word From the President Brother Walkes asks grand lodges to celebrate the Prince Hall bi-centennial this year and celebrate the American bi-centennial next July.

35 Welcome to New Members New members include William D. Green, soon be Financial Secretary.

35 Freemasonry Among Negroes and Whites in America: A Study in Masonic Legitimacy Comments relative to a book of the same title.

36 Notes, Queries and Information on items of Masonic Research A new column that addresses reader questions about (1) Primus Hall, (2) Prince Hall Bicentennial, (3) Interference, (4) Grimshaw, (5) Prince Hall Postage Stamp, (6) Prizes and Awards for Writing and Painting, and (7) Other Awards.

38 The Phylaxis Society and the Iowa Masonic Library An appeal to grand lodges to send material to the Iowa Masonic library and to use the resources of the library.

38 A Mason and a Man A poem submitted by Robert L. Hughes, Northwest Chapter Phylaxis Society.

39 The Northwest Chapter of the Phylaxis Society The three great lights.

39 Does the 'Prince Hall' Masonic Charter Exist? The author traveled to Boston where he was allowed to examine the charter and record books of African Lodge. He reports it to be in an excellent state of preservation.

41 The Significance of Brotherhood A Prince Hall Masonic Classic read before and printed under the auspices of Prince Hall Lodge No. 38, MWPHGL of New York, May 23, 1919. It urges black men to get back to that moral and intellectual excellence of the blacks of antiquity of whom Herodotus claims the Olympian gods called "faultless Ethiopians."

44 History of Prince Hall Masonry A paper read at the 64th anniversary of Frank J. Brown Lodge #80, St. Louis, Missouri. (Relies heavily on Grimshaw.)

45 Grand Master Gilliam of Mississippi Passes Obituary for deceased Grand Master Gilliam of Stringer Grand Lodge.

45 The Local Chapter - The key to Co-ordinate Activity in the Phylaxis Society Program A discussion on how local Phylaxis chapters are formed.

47 Prince Hall Masonry and the Civil War - Part II A Masterpiece continued from previous issue. Martin Delaney is commissioned a major in the army from civilian life. Governor Andrews presents to GM Lewis Hayden of Massachusetts a gavel made from a slave whipping post and a straw basket used to escape from slavery.

Volume 2 Number 2 March 1975

54 A Word from the President Facts about Prince Hall, Master of African Lodge and some of his challenges. This issue commemorates the two hundredth anniversary of the initiation of Prince Hall. It recounts a petition from Prince Hall about three Negro members of African Lodge kidnapped into slavery.

55 Prince Hall's Letter Book Upton gives a summary of the letter books of Prince Hall.

58 A Charge Delivered to the African Lodge Delivered June 24, 1797 at MEMOTOMY, MASS. by the Right Worshipful Prince Hall.

61 Congratulations Executive Secretary, Bro. James E. Herndon, was honored as Master Mason of the year. Other honors went to First Vice President Herbert Dailey and to Second Vice President Zellus Bailey.

61 The Phylaxis Society and the Prince Hall Confession of Faith Presents a credo espousing belief in freemasonry and belief in Prince Hall freemasonry.

62 Alexander Clark, P.G.M Known as the colored orator of Iowa. Past Grand Master of the Grand Lodge of Missouri, he was a man of national reputation and distinguished at home and abroad as such.

65 Vital Dimensions of Effective Power I. Intellectual Power, II. Economic Power, III Political Power, IV. The Power of Togetherness, V. Psychological Power, and VI. The Power of Faith.

69 The Storm that Produced Light on a Dark Subject In 1897 Gideon S. Bailey and Con A. Rideout, two Prince Hall masons, petitioned the Grand Lodge of Washington to engage in fraternal communication. The fraternal storm then ensued.

71 Recognized, Unrecognized, Clandestine I have read hundreds of discussions and opinions in Grand Lodge proceedings on this subject—among which are some of the most vitriolic attacks on Negroes and Negro Freemasonry. The white brethren have not added to their stature by their actions.

72 Whence Come You and Whither Are You Traveling? The first fellow of the Society (Holder) traces the origin of these terms through various masonic lecturers including Preston and Webb.

74 Notes, Queries and Information on Items of Masonic Research (8) Alexander G. Clarke historical site, (9) Tornado destroys Masonic Hall, (10) Qualification of petitioner, (11) Prince Hall military officer, (12) Compact lodges in New York

Volume 2 Number 3 September 1975

78 A Word from the President My aim is to preserve the memory of the things I love, to be truthful to them and therefore to write as well about them as I can. We plan to continue issuing special editions in March of each year in tribute to the Master, Prince Hall. Ira Holder has been made the first fellow of the Society

79 Prince Hall Masonry and the Civil War, Part Three The second Prince Hall military masonic lodge to serve in the Civil War was Phoenix Lodge No. 1. One can the workings of Prince Hall masonry and the African Methodist Episcopal Church both having played a major role in sustaining Black America.

83 Prince Hall's Letter Book, Part Two Upton's summary continues.

86 Whence Come You and Whither are You Traveling, Part Two Holder shows the requisites to advancement one must have: a mission to perform, determination perform that mission, and constant` travel toward one's objective.

88 John Pine Noted Masonic Engraver was Black John Pine engraved the frontis piece to Dr. James Anderson's Constitution of 1723 and again in 1738.

90 The Phylaxis, Phylalethes, and M.P.S. The Phylalethes objected to use of "M by the Phylaxis Society and suggested the society use PSM instead.

90 Prince Hall Bi-Centennial The writer suggests that Prince Hall masons should be about the business of building hospitals and universities of higher education

91 Bro. Kivie Kaplan Passes He was national president of the NAACP.

82 Welcome to New Members includes James A. Mingo of the District of Columbia.

92 Phylaxis Profile: Dr. William M Freeman Southern University professor and MPS named in Who's Who in the South and Southwest

93 The Membership Committee Goals This four member committee is the forerunner of the Council of Representatives.

94 Should Prince Hall Freemasonry Explore the Table Lodge? Lodges might know the "fourth degree" in which members mingle in an anteroom or dining room f after-meeting sandwich or meal. The table lodge is not mere banquet with entertainment; it is a special lodge ceremony with a ritual, formalities, and a special terminology which is of some interest.

95 The Ceremony of the Seven Toasts The ritual of the seven toasts.

95 Notes, Queries and Information on Items of Masonic Research (4) Grimshsaw, (2) Bi-Centennial, (13) Past Master's Degree, (14) 100 Most Influential Black Americans, (15) Non-Prince Hall Grand Masters, (16) Negro Masonry in the United States, (17) Universal League of Freemasonry (ULF), (8) PGM Alexander G. Clark

99 A Bright Mason A term usually applied to one who is well posted in the lectures of the various degrees, but the whole heart must be in whatever we do.

Volume 2 Number 4 December 1975

 102 A Word from the President The first meeting of the executive committee was held in Denver. President Walkes was awarded FPS for his masterpiece. Arthur H. Frederick and Charles H. Wesley were nominated as fellows.

 103 Those Magnificent Masonic Buffalo Soldiers Part One Little is known of Prince Hall military lodges because they failed to maintain minutes or report to their grand lodges. The first of the lodges was chartered by Texas and attached to the Tenth Cavalry: Baldwin Lodge No. 16.

 106 Stormy is the Road, A Masterpiece, Ira S. Holder, Sr. Follows Gideon S. Bailey and Con A. Rideout as they seek fraternal communication in the State of Washington.

111 Welcome to New Members

111 The Phylaxis Society and the Missouri Masonic Library Second Vice President Zellus Bailey assists in creating a new Masonic library in Missouri.

112 The Masonic Service Association of the United States The MSA is a voluntary association of masonic grand lodges.

113 Notes, Queries and Information on Items of Masonic Research (11) Prince Hall military officers, (18) Conference of Prince Hall grand masters, (8) PGM Alexander Clark, (18) Recognition, and (5) Prince Hall postage stamp.

Volume 2 Number 5 March 1976

 118 A Word from the President This issue pays homage to the Master, Prince Hall. The Phylaxis Society has begun to attract enemies!

119 America's Bi-Centennial While the country was at war with Britain, masonic meetings ceased in Boston. By 1777 both the white and black lodges were on the road to re-organizing.

120 Should Prince Hall Masons Celebrate the Bi-Centennial- Yes Jerry Marsengill, FPS (Philalethes Society), argues that, though the country is far from perfect, we do not need any group disassociation itself.

 121 Should Prince Hall Masons Celebrate the Bi-Centennial - No President Walkes suggests that some consider it a celebration of slavery.

 122 How Long is Your Cable Tow? FPS Holder traces the historical origin of the cable tow. He observes that the Masonic cable tow symbolically binds the candidate to darkness and ignorance.

126 Joseph G. Findel, Honorary Prince Hall Grand Master Findel was a German masonic writer and scholar, who believed the lodges of colored people were legally constituted.

131 Prince Hall: A Great Negro American In the proceedings of the 91st Congress, Hon Phillip Philbin says "Prince Hall stood in his great day and spoke out militantly for truth, humanity and freedom."

132 A Charge Delivered to African Lodge, June 24,1792 A charge delivered Prince Hall.

134 The Master's Sign A description of a Masonic token in flowery prose.

135 A Prince Hall Masonic Classic This well-crafted address by Alexander Clark, PGM of Iowa and Missouri, is rightly identified as an Masonic classic

138 Welcome New Members

139 Notes, Queries and Information on Items of Masonic Research: Pine's famous frontspiece, Dr. Charles Wesley, John W. Davis, Non-Prince Hall organizations.

140 Report from Wisconsin This distinguished committee headed by State Supreme Court Judge George Currie recommended that the Prince Hall Grand Lodge be recognized.

140 Masonic Duty A well-read mason is a rare thing.

141 The Phylaxis Society and the Prince Hall Confession of Masonic Faith A masonic credo.

142 Phylaxis Profile William E. Allen, Jr., MPS, was the first black radiologist receive a gold medal from the American College of Radiology.

143 The Lady Freemason The lady was Miss Elizabeth St. Leger. A decision to be made: put her to death, or make her a mason in due form.

Volume 2 Number 6 July 1976

146 A Word from the President President Walkes refers to the society as *international*. The annual executive meeting was held in Seattle, Washington Grand Master Jno. G. Lewis is acknowledged for his constant support and encouragement. This issue is dedicated to Martin Delaney.

147 The Power of Togetherness FPS Holder refers to the operative masons medieval times and to the formation of the Grand Lodge of 1717 to make point.

149 Notes, Queries and Information on Items of Masonic Research William Allan, Prince Hall masonic postage stamp, Alphonse Cerza, Philadelphia str named for Prince Hall mason (Richard Allen), Schomburg Center, Transactions of the Phylaxis Society, John W. Davis, Asa B. Sampson, Prince Hall Masonic Yearbook, *Prince Hall Life and Legacy*.

150 Martin R. Delaney Militant Master Mason This short, stocky black militant attended Harvard until prejudice forced him out. His hatred of racism led him to consider use of force and resettlement in Africa as solutions.

154 Executive Meeting Held James Herndon was named a fellow. Two Caucasian masons, Keith Arrington and Jerry Marsengill, were named honorary fellow.

154 The Real Mason A poem.

155 Planning for Spiritual Growth This is the keynote address given by the Executive Secretary of the Masonic Services Association, Conrad Hahn, at the Grand Lodge of Michigan.

158 L. Sherman Brooks, Masonic Calligrapher A professional scribe, he did the back cover for this issue.

158 The Lady Freemason, How She Came to be Initiated Continues from the previous issue.

159 Welcome New Members

160 The Origin and Objects of Ancient Freemasonry: Its Introduction into the United States, and Legitimacy Among Colored Men. A treatise delivered before St. Cyprian Lodge No. 13, June 24, 1853 by Martin R. Delaney.

Volume 2 Number 7 September 1976

166 A Word from the President Increasing the membership of the Phylaxis Society must be a result of the effort of all the members.

166 Herndon and Holder Retire Charter members step down.

167 Two Blacks Inadvertently Disrupt White America FPS Holden addresses the disruptions in the State of Washington resulting from the activity of Gideon S. Bailey and Con A. Rideout in 1897.

170 57th Conference of Grand Masters Group photograph.

171 A Speech by Joseph A. Walkes, F.P.S. Presented to the Conference of Grand Masters in 1976. My purpose is to attempt to explain the role of a small body of Prince Hall Freemasons who have organized themselves into a research society and their relationship to you.

173 Notes, Queries and Information on Items of Masonic Research Drew Sales, Jno. G. Lewis Testimonial, Deceased members honored in New Orleans, Middle Class Blacks in a White Society, Conference of Grand Master's schedule, Back Issues of magazines, Prince Hall Masonic yearbook, GM Lewis listed in *Who's Who*,

174 Report of the Caucasian Grand Lodge F.&A.M. of Wisconsin The final report concerning the question whether the Grand Lodge of Prince Hall Masons of Wisconsin shall be recognized by the Grand Lodge of Wisconsin.

176 The Origin and Objects of Ancient Freemasonry Continued from previous issue. Delaney creates an intricate theory showing how Freemasonry evolved from mysteries of African origin.

179 Welcome New Members

Introduction

The Phylaxis Society was organized by Prince Hall Freemasons for those who seek Masonic light and those who have light to share. It has since opened membership to all regular Freemasons and has become international in its support.

Our Magazine. The Phylaxis magazine has been its principle means of communicating with its members. It has become the most respected publication in Prince Hall masonry and one of the most important publications, we think, in all of Freemasonry. A close review of this first collection of magazines will give the reader an idea of why this is and how it came about.

Our Patron. A turning point in the growth of the Society occurred when it attracted the attention of John G. Lewis, one of the most influential black masons of his day, being grand master in Louisiana, Chairman of the Conference of Grand Masters, and Sovereign Grand Commander of the Southern Jurisdiction of the Ancient and Accepted Scottish Rite of Freemasonry. The importance of his support was recognized by the Phylaxis Society when it named its highest honor, the Jno G. Lewis Medal of Honor, in his memory. The Society also attracted the support of important masonic historians, men like Charles Wesley, an early fellow of the Society and Harry Williamson, whose writings are featured in the magazine. Ira Holder, who became the first fellow of the Society is featured prominently in this collection of magazines, and the reader will see why he was selected for this honor.

Our Dedication. The Phylaxis Society is an international historical, literary research organization dedicated to perpetuating the memory of Prince Hall who became the first African-American Freemason in Colonial America, the founder of the first black Masonic lodge and the leader of the first black interstate organization in America.

Our Goals. The Society is incorporated under the laws of the State of Kansas and is a not-for-profit corporation the nature of whose business is for charitable and educational purposes. The goals of the Society are: To advance the knowledge of the history, culture, and ethical standards of Prince Hall Freemasonry by publishing a magazine, holding seminars, conducting research, and providing other educational activities; To provide a fraternity-wide center for the collection of Masonic news, arranging for educational speakers, and for the dissemination of information about Prince Hall Freemasonry; To provide periodic meetings to allow Masonic authors to share their findings with the members of the Society; To promote the social services available to members and disseminate information on programs available to the widows and orphans of deceased members of the Prince Hall Masonic fraternity; To encourage the development of books, papers, art and other cultural heritage that will increase the knowledge about black people in general in American society; and to do all additional things necessary to support the above goals of the Society. The motto of the Society is, "A Society for Prince Hall Freemasons who seek more light and who have light to impart."

Our Members. If you are a Prince Hall Freemason (PHA), if you are a Freemason in a grand lodge in amity with a Prince Hall grand lodge, or if you are a Freemason in a grand lodge in amity with the United Grand Lodge of England, you may participate in the annual membership meeting (March 6th) by asking to become a member. You must subscribe to the magazine to become a member, but you can subscribe to the magazine without becoming a member if you want to. The easiest way to join or to subscribe is to do so on our website, but you can also mail in a membership form downloaded from the website.

Visit our web site to learn more about the Society:

http://thephylaxis.org

THE PHYLAXIS

JANUARY 1974

Volume 1   Number 1

**A SOCIETY FOR PRINCE HALL
FREEMASONS WHO SEEK MORE
LIGHT AND WHO HAVE LIGHT TO
IMPART**

THE PHYLAXIS
Published at Jefferson City, Mo., by
THE PHYLAXIS SOCIETY

Arthur H. Frederick M.P.S. .... Editor
Box 43, Roxbury, Massachusetts 02119

OFFICERS

Joseph A. Walkes, Jr, M.P.S. .... President
P. O. Box 3151, Ft. Leavenworth, Kansas 66027

Herbert Dailey, M.P.S. .... First Vice President
1616 South Cedar, Tacoma, Washington 98405

Zellus Bailey, M.P.S. .... Second Vice President
7039 Dover Court, St. Louis, Missouri 63130

James E. Herndon, M.P.S. .... Executive Secretary
1574 Ivanhoe Street, Denver, Colorado 80220

Alonzo D. Foote, Sr., M.P.S. .... Treasurer
P. O. Box 3139, Tacoma, Washington 98405

SUBSCRIPTION RATE: FOR ONE YEAR, $5.00

The Phylaxis Magazine is the official publication of the Phylaxis Society. Any article appearing in this publication expresses only the opinion of the writer, and does not become the official pronouncement of the Phylaxis Society. No advertising of any form is solicited or accepted. All communication relative to the magazine should be addressed to the Editor. Inquiries relative to membership must be addressed to the Executive Secretary. Membership is by invitation and recommendation only. The joining fee is $3.00. Dues are $5.00 per year in advance, which amount includes a subscription to the "Phylaxis" magazine for one year.

All rights reserved. No part of this work may be reproduced or transmitted in any form or by any means, electrical or mechanical, or retrival system, without written permission from the publisher.

INDEX

A Word From the President,
Joseph A. Walkes, Jr.,
M.P.S. 2
What Does the Phylaxis
Society Seek? 3
The U.L.F.
and the Phylaxis Society 3
Prince Hall Masonry,
by Arthur H. Frederick,
M.P.S. 3
John Marrant, Brother Chaplain
by Joseph A. Walkes, Jr.,
M.P.S. 6
Some Important Events
in the Life of Prince Hall
by William M. Freeman 7
Prince Hall Public School 9
Roster of Grand Masters 10
Caucasian Prince Hall Lodge
by Joseph A. Walkes, Jr.,
M.P.S. 10
PHA Masonic Structure 11

A WORD FROM THE PRESIDENT

"As Negro Masons, we need expect no recognition from organized White American Masons; I plead for none; I care for none at the sacrifice of honor and dignity. I stand as just, as true, as pure a Free Mason as ever trod God's green earth. My title is as perfect as that of the Prince of Wales or the President of the United States; as he who travels with the caravan over the desert or he who dwells on the plains of the far west. Where ever he may be upon the continents of the land or the islands of the sea, if he be a Free Mason he is my brother and cannot deny if he would."

Samuel W. G. Clark
50th Annual Communication
of the M.W.P.H.G.L. of
Ohio.

I would like to welcome all of our readers to this, the first issue of "THE PHYLAXIS" magazine.

The Phylaxis Society is a national body, composed of dedicated Prince Hall Freemasons, writers and editors. It has no special creed or dogma, and its members will express their individual opinions only. It has as its purpose the binding together of those who are anxious to help make Prince Hall Masonic journalism and literature more efficient, and to encourage Prince Hall Masonic writers around the world in their quest for truth and light in Masonry.

We have chosen as our emblem, The Book of Truth, the Square and Compass, which are well known Masonic emblems, and are understood by all Freemasons where ever dispatched around the globe. The number fifteen are the honored Fellows, Prince Hall and the fourteen free men of color initiated March 6, 1775. All members of the Phylaxis Society should strive for this honored title. The Lamp of Knowledge symbolizes the goals of the Society; the search for knowledge, more light in Masonry.

The Society does not seek members, they being chosen by the nomination of a Masonic writer who is already a member. This nomination is passed on by the four members of the Executive Committee. If the nomination is approved and elected by a majority of this committee, he is admitted without further formality. He is then notified of this unsolicited honor.

The Fellowship is limited to fifteen. When vacancies occur new Fellows are elected from the "Members" who are expected to write a "masterpiece" of not less than five hundred words on some subject, dealing with Prince Hall Masonry, and will be subsequently published in the PHYLAXIS MAGAZINE.

JOSEPH A. WALKES, JR, M.P.S.

WHAT DOES THE PHYLAXIS SOCIETY SEEK?

Too often information concerning Prince Hall Masonry is written by those who have little knowledge of Masonry in general and Prince Hall Masonry in particular. This leaves the written work in most cases un-masonic in nature, and often not worthy of consideration, or seriousness. We often review the official organs of many of the Prince Hall Grand Lodges that publish newspapers and magazines for their individual jurisdictions, and needless to say, they leave much room for improvement.

It is the official position of the Phylaxis Society that research into all phases of Prince Hall Masonry is truely needed, and that the true history of Prince Hall Masonry must be written by Prince Hall Masons themselves. It is my honest belief, and a statement that I can prove, that the history of Prince Hall Masonry is also a history of the Black man in America.

Prince Hall Masons want true facts. Facts that are undeniable. We want to learn the Masonic histories of those great Masonic Black heroes, like Bro James Forten of the Revolutionary war, Bro Prince Sanders, Bro Richard Allen the founder and first bishop of the AME church, Bro Absolom Jones, Bro Arthur A. Schomberg, Bro Dr. Peter W. Ray, Bro Martin R. Delaney, Bro Phillip Randolph, Bro Thurgood Marshall. We want to know of the Masonic history of Bro John Trusty, Bro John Milton Turner, Bro Charles H. Wesley. We want to read about our Lodges that were stations for the Underground Railroad, we want to learn about our Lodges that were used as the first schools for Black children, we want to learn about those schools like Lincoln University in Missouri that Prince Hall Masons helped build. We want to learn about those brave Black military units, the 29th Conn., the 54th and 55th Mass, the 9th and 10th Cav Buffalo Soldiers, the 24th and 25th Inf, and those Prince Hall Military Lodges that were attached to them. We want to learn the truth about the two "Prince Hall" Grand Lodges in Florida, and why they have refused to merge, since both come from the same source. We want to learn about Grand Master Prince Hall, not the Grimshaw stories, but the truth. In a word, we of the Phylaxis Society want to learn what we can learn about Prince Hall Masonry. We are seekers of LIGHT!

I believe that a method for which to seek this Masonic knowledge, research and study, is with the PHYLAXIS SOCIETY. A Society composed of Prince Hall editors, writers, students and thinkers, those who are truly seeking more LIGHT!

THE U.L.F. AND THE PHYLAXIS SOCIETY

It is the official position of the Phylaxis Society as stated in our Newsletter, that the United League of Freemasons is "Non-conducive" to Prince Hall Masonry. History has clearly showed us our mistakes in forming the National Grand Lodge or Compact, and it has cost us dearly, as this disbanded body invades our jurisdictions with their clandestine Lodges.

It has come to our attention that a Past Grand Master from the Most Worshipful Prince Hall Grand Lodge of Michigan has been appointed as National Deputy of the U.L.F. replacing a "Deputy" who was forced to withdraw his membership by the Grand Master of California.

We cannot understand, why this P.G.M., would accept such a position, nor why he would join an organization that has been judged by American Masonic bodies, as Clandestine. The Phylaxis Society will not brand this organization as such, but we maintain that it is non-conducive to Prince Hall Masonry. The U.L.F. has shown by its newsletters to have an understanding attitude towards Prince Hall Masonry, and it has defended P.H.A. against racially motivated attacks from Caucasian Masonic bodies, but, the mere fact that it accepts, "regular," irregular and clandestine "Masons" into its ranks is cause for the Phylaxis Society to take the stand that it does.

PRINCE HALL MASONRY
BY
ARTHUR H. FREDERICK M.P.S. (MASSACHUSETTS)

INTRODUCTION — I

There never has been an institution framed by man since the beginning of time that can boast of the long life of the Masonic Order, nor is there any organization that has exhibited purer or better principles than the Most Worshipful Prince Hall Free and Accepted Masons; it has triumphed over ignorance and superstition, and has overcome all the evil desires which envy and malice have given birth to, by the mild and peaceful doctrines which its precepts teaches, and it has come down to us, thus purified in the fire of persecution, a gem which is a rich inheritance to its possessor, dissolving by its warm and animating beams all those corroding passions which infect the moral system and which are opposite to every virtuous principle.

Many are the attempts which have been made to destroy the Most Worshipful Prince Hall Free and Accepted Masons by torture, lies, and inquisition. By lies and by dissemination of falsehood through the medium of publications of various kinds. Many deceptions made their appearance and will continue to make their appearance but deception cannot and will not last long when the mark of the beast is plainly stamped upon its features. It may rise, but it will never fall, leaving the admirers in mental darkness.

Yes, the foes of this affiliation draw their swords in vain being baffled in their attempts, cutting the empty air.

ENTERED APPRENTICE

As an E.P. you are taught how to stand upright like a man.

You are taught three great duties: To God, neighbor and yourself. A zealous attachment to these principles will ensure public and private esteem.

Although your frequent appearance at your regular meetings is earnestly solicited, yet it is not meant that Masonry should interfere with your necessary vocations; for these are on no account to be neglected; neither are you to suffer your zeal for the institution to lead you into arguments with those, who, through ignorance, may ridicule or cause the fraternity embarrassment. At your leisure hours, that you may improve in masonic knowledge, you are to converse with well-informed lecturers and Brethren. Finally, keep sacred and inviolable the mysteries of the Order, these distinguish you from the rest of the community, and marks you as a Mason. Most important, if in your circle of friends you find a person desirous of being initiated into Masonry, be particularly not attentive not to recommend him, unless you are convinced he will conform to all our acient rules and regulations; that the honor, glory, and reputation of the Prince Hall will not be tarnished. Masons will not be damaged by an unworthy person and the world-at-large will be further convinced of the good work of our fraternity.

According to some masonic scholars, an E.P. who completely learns and understands all sections of the First Degree, knows more of Masonry than most Royal Arch Masons. A Mason who learns and understands the second section of the second and third degree has an education equal to that of a Bachelor of Arts Degree.

The obligation of secrecy, one of the most notable features of free masonry, the veil of mystery — that awful secrecy — behind which it moves and acts.

The first obligation of a Mason is that of silence and secrecy and is the most confused part because some Masons use it to shield their ignorance of the Order beyond the ritual.

Secrecy has a unifying factor; harmony, and strength can be secured thereby, which cannot be obtained in any other way. Secrecy has a mystic, binding, almost supernatural force. The possession of a secret by a considerable number, produces a family-feeling. Two people with a secret can never forget each other, as long as they keep the secret, they are bound to each other.

What is a Masonic secrecy? The answer is the ritual and all related work even to another Mason until you have found him so to be. The problem is when we are asked a question we do not have answer to, we say the answer is secret. For example, should a non-mason ask what is the initiation fee, some say that's secret to the potential candidate. The truth might be — he does not know, therefore, he cannot tell. The potential candidate might need to know so he can get his finances together to request further of our Order.

Each Mason for himself must decide at the time he is asked whether or not he should give the requested information. An appropriate answer for all occasions is "Why do you seek this information?" On the answer to that question, it should be your answer to his question.

Be careful when in the Temple. More restraint should be observed here than any other place. I can personally testify to the loseness in the Temple.

FELLOWCRAFT DEGREE

In the obligation the Fellowcraft takes upon himself obligations not entrusted to an E.P.

Any summons sent to a Fellowcraft, he must attend.

4

The most important part of this degree is the "Cable-Tow" How long is a cable tow? Thousands have asked the question and few have attempted to reply.

In early days it was three miles; that was when a brother was expected to attend lodge whether he wanted to or not. Today, we have learned there is no merit in attendance that comes from fear or compulsion. Free Masonry is not unreasonable. It does not make impossible demands. What is easy for one may be hard for another. To one brother, three miles away might mean extreme difficulty to answer a summons; to another thousands of miles away — who owns an airplane — it could be very easy.

The cable-tow for all brothers is equal in length, but it is the degree of how much a brother can do that varies. Therefore, a general rule to follow is this, the cable-tow is "the scope or amount of a brother's reasonable ability to do or give." Such a length all brothers may take to heart. No Brother is compelled against his will, each must determine for himself what is just, right, and reasonable — and brotherly.

In the Fellowcraft Degree, we find the word Hele, hail, heel, this is often confusing. However you spell or pronounce it in Masonry, it means the same thing "To conceal." In old English a "healer" or "heler" is one who covers roofs with tiles or slates. The word is sometimes confused with "Tiles" one who puts on the tiles or slates. Generally, the tiler goes to work after the heler has finished. In the same way a plasterer goes to work after a carpenter has built a wall.

From the working tools the Fellowcraft learns to carry the Square of Virtue in his breast and build no art, no matter how small, which does not fit within its right angle.

Omar the poet wrote, "The moving finger writes, and having writ, moves on." The poet Oxenham phrased it, "No man travels twice the great highway, which winds through darkness up to light, through night, to day."

The Freemason can never unbuild that which is erected on the level of time; once gone, the opportunity is gone forever.

The fellowcraft should judge his work by his own Plumbline and not by anothers. Judge not that ye may not also be judged.

The wages of a Fellowcraft are symbols of sacrifice, of the fruits of labor, of wages earned. To receive your wages you must labor. You must till the fields of your heart or build the temple of your own house not made with hands, you must give labor to your brother, carry stones for your Brothers or give labor to your neighbor. If he does his part for the Lodge, takes his place for Freemasonry, he will receive his wages. For it is true "in the sweat of thy face thou shall eat bread."

Finally, the letter "G." Every Mason will say "But that is secret." Aye, the ritual is secret. One can no more keep secret the idea that God is the essence of all life. Take God out of Freemasonry and nothing is left.

Secret? Let a man who loves his wife and child try to explain to anyone how much he loves them. All the world may know he loves them, and that he does love them, but no words can tell the degree of love he has in his heart for them.

All the world may know that the symbol of Deity shines in the East of a Masonic Lodge; only the true Mason, who is actually a Mason in his heart, as well as in his mind, may know just how and in what way the Great Architect is the very essence and substance of our Ancient Craft.

MASTER MASON

This degree delves into the deepest recesses of a man's nature, it probes into the Holy of Holiest of his heart.

This degree teaches no creed, no dogma, no religion, only there is a hope of immorality; there is a Great Architect by whose mercy we may live again; leaving each brother to interpret for himself what he may read of the Great Beyond.

It teaches the power — the powerlessness — of evil.

The ceremony is not of the earth, but of that land of the inner life, that home of the Spirit where each man thinks the secret thoughts he never, never tells.

The Legend of Hiram Abif is at once the tragedy and the hope of man; it is virtue struck down by error, evil, and sin, and raised again by truth, goodness and mercy. The legend is the glory of Freemasonry. Many a Mason and Masonic scholar have attempted to show the legend is incorrect; some have said that it is not a part of the degree, all have failed and some have ended up in insane asylums.

Is there a Santa Claus? To a child, yes, because he believes. For his elders it means telling a beautiful truth. If truth means "containing a great truth" then both the mysteries of Santa Claus and of the Master Builder are true in the most real sense.

Here is the shock, the surprise, and the glory of the third Degree. It presents us with eternity in the midst of life. It pushes back the confines of our own little world, our own tiny measurements of time, our small comprehension of space and shows us that we enter eternity at neither birth nor death. Misguided men, assassins, tried to kill the Master Builder but they were powerless against the might and right of Freemasonry. Each of us is born, lives his little life, wears his little white apron, and goes where thousands have gone before him.

A Master Mason's wages are paid in coin of the heart, not of the mint. They are earned by what a Mason does with his mind, not his hand.

In Masonry a Master builds into his own spiritual temple as many perfect ashlars as he can and receives for his labor uncounted coins of happiness, satisfaction, knowledge, understanding, and spiritual uplift.

For those attending this workshop, you have a choice of two things: You can hear this and be satisfied, or you may see this lecture only as an introduction, a gateway, a sign pointing out the path and read and study and ponder until it has earned you a handful of pennies, each penny a thought, each thought a blessing, making life easier to live.

The Master Mason builds. Let him who would receive all that Freemasonry has to offer dig deeply into the symbolism, the history, the philosophy, the jurisprudence, and the spiritual meanings of the Ancient Craft.

So, and only so will you become a true Master Mason. So mote it be.

Bibliography:

Proceedings of the Annual and Special Communications of the Most Worshipful Prince Hall Grand Lodge, Robert R. Teamok, 1910

Negro Masonry in the United States, 1972, by Arthur H. Frederick

JOHN MARRANT, BROTHER CHAPLAIN

JOSEPH A. WALKES.

BY

JOSEPH A. WALKES, JR, M.P.S. (KANSAS)

In the early days of Prince Hall Masonry, there was an extraordinary Black man who is recorded in the history of the Black race in America, as bringing a spiritual influence to the North American Indian. We are indebted to the research efforts of our dear Caucasian Brother and friend, William H. Upton, P.G.M. of the Caucasian Grand Lodge of Washington, author of *"Negro Masonry, being a Critical Examination among the Negroes of America"* (1902), for a brief glimpse of the Masonic life of John Marrant, Brother Chaplain.

In the printed transactions of the Ars Quatuor Coronati Lodge Number 2076, Volume XIII for January 1900, under the title of *"The Prince Hall Letter Book"* and listed as entry number 21, is a copy of a letter from Prince Hall to R. Holt, Deputy Grand Master of the Grand Lodge of England and dated June 4, 1789.

> "Received into the Lodge since August, two members namely John Bean and John Marrant, a Black minister from home, but last from Brachtown, Nova Scotia."[1]

There is also under entry number 27, Prince Hall's letter to Lady Huntington[2] to "convey his humble thanks for the labors of John Marrant," and, "We, the members of African Lodge, have made him a member of that honourable society, and Chaplain of the same which will be a great help to him in his travels, and may do a great deal of good to society."[3]

It is recorded that Brother Marrant preached a sermon before African Lodge 459, on June 4th, 1787,[4] and from a journal privately printed in London by J. Taylor and Company at the Royal Exchange, ciria 1788, it is written by Marrant that he had been helped by "Mr. Prince Hall at whose house, I lodged, one of the most respectable characters in Bostontown."

Brother John Marrant, Chaplain of African Lodge No. 459, a Prince Hall Mason, whose name is placed high in the annals of service like the Jesuits of old, who spread the seed of Christianity among the American Indians before the birth of the American Republic,[5] "right on the soil where they had been born and reared in plain view of the cruilties and sufferings melted out to their African forbears."[6]

On June 15, 1765, there was born in New York City, (no place specifically mentioned) a boy who was named John Marrant.[7] The Reverend Mr. Aldridge, the biographer of Marrant states he was taken by his mother when five years old to Saint Augustine where he was sent to school, "and taught to read and spell." From listening to sermons preached by Missionaries, Marrant received inspiration, and devoted his life to Christianity. By constant and patient study, he became an itinerant preacher among his fellow Blacks. His biographer records that an Indian hunter befriended him and taught him to speak his Indian language. With this, he became welcome among the Indian tribes around the state of New York where he converted to Christianity the King of the Cherokee nation and his daughter. When the American Revolution came, Brother Marrant had carried the Gospel into the ranks of the Cherokees, Creeks, Catawar and Housaw Indians.[8]

He fought against the Colonists, by joining the English as a sailor on board the *"Princess Amelia"* and participated in an engagement off Dogger Bank on the 5th of August 1781. He served six years and eleven months with the British navy.

He was ordained on May 15, 1785, in London, England, six months before the Reverend Lemuel Haynes, whom many believed to be the first ordained of the race of North America (who became a pastor of a Caucasian Congregation in Torrington, Conn., later in 1785).

Not much more is known of Brother Marrant after his famous sermon to African Lodge, but history has judged this Prince Hall Mason as truly an extraordinary man.

He is listed on the Roster of African Lodge No. 459 1775-1809 (compiled from the old Ledger of African Lodge 459 and appears in the Proceedings of the Prince Hall Grand Lodge of Massachusetts, 1901), as "Rev'd John Morant."

FOOTNOTES

1. William H. Upton, Transactions of the Ars Coronati Lodge No. 2070, Vol. XIII, Jan, 1900, "*Prince Hall Letter Book*" (London) p. 54.

2. Selina, Countess of Huntingdon, born 1707, died 1791, was head of a sect of Calvinistic Methodists who became known as "The Countess of Huntingdon's Connections."

3. Upton, *op. city.*, p. 5..

4. John Marrant, (Brother Chaplain) A sermon preached on the 24th day of June 1789, being the Festival of St. John the Baptist, etc., at the request of the R. W. Grand Master Prince Hall, 1789, Boston.

5. John Marrant, Sermon (Reprinted for private circulation, edited by Arthur A. Schomburg, (Past Grand Secretary, M. W. Prince Hall Grand Lodge of New York), New York, 1920) cited by the *Journal of Negro History*, Vol. 21, 1936, p. 400.

6. *Ibid*, p. 394-395

7. Rev. William Aldridge, *"A Narrative of the Lord's Wonderful Dealings with John Marrant, A Black"* (now going to preach the Gospel in Nova Scotia) etc. (London, 1785) 4th Edition, p. 40 cited in *Journal of Negro History*, Vol. 21, 1936, p. 395.

8. *Ibid*, 397.

BIBLIOGRAPHY

Katz, William Laren, *Eyewitness: The Negro in American History*, New York: Pitman Publishing Corp., 1967.

Davis, Harry E., *A History of Freemasonry Among Negroes in America*, 1946.

Some Important Events in The Life of Prince Hall
A RESEARCH STUDY MADE BY BRO. WILLIAM M. FREEMAN

"The following article appeared in 'The Plumb Line' The Official Organ of the Prince Hall Grand Lodge of Louisiana, in August 1972, and is herein printed by permission of Bro Freeman, and who in April 1973, was kind enought to send a copy of his manuscript to The Phylaxis Society. Bro Freeman is not a member of the Society at this time. He is a Professor of Education at Southern University, and a 33rd degree Prince Hall Mason.

Prince Hall was the son of Thomas Prince Hall an Englishman, a leather merchant, whose wife was a free Negro woman of French descent. Born in Barbadoes, British West Indies in 1748, young Prince Hall left the West Indies at the early age of 17 and settled in the city of Boston in the Massachusetts Colony. He took a very prominent part in both the religious and civic affairs of the Negroes in the colony. In fact, such reports as are extant indicate him to have been the recognized leader of his race upon numerous and important occasions. Little is known about his occupation, but it is clear that at times he followed catering. With little money and few books, he worked hard and studied hard and became a trained minister in the Methodist Church.

In 1775 he made application to the Committee for Safety in Boston for permission to recruit some of the slaves in the colony for the Revolutionary Army, but in reply the Committee declared that none but free men could be enlisted as soldiers. He himself enlisted sometime during the month of February 1776 and was placed in Captain Benjamin Dillingham's Company and later in Captain Joshua Welboro's Company and finally in Thacker's Regiment. Through an order issued by General George Washington and prompt action of the Continental Congress, other free Negroes enlisted in the army at that time.

On January 13, 1777, Prince Hall, together with several others, addressed a petition protesting against the existence of slavery in the colony. This was forwarded to the Massachusetts Legislature, but no action was taken on it. They later submitted a petition to the Massachusetts Legislature protesting against the kidnapping and subsequent sale into slavery of a number of Negroes who had been taken away from Boston in a sailing vessel by force. This petition was submitted on February 27, 1788, and produced wholesome results. The men were returned to Boston after being detained by the Governor of Maine who complied with the request of the Governor of Massachusetts to release them.

Prince hall was the first black man to be initiated into the Masonic Order in the American Colonies. On March 6, 1775, Hall and 14 other free Negroes were made freemasons in Lodge No. 441, which was a Military Lodge working under the Grand Lodge of Ireland and attached to one of the regiments in the army under the command of General Gage. (Some wrtiers are inclined to think that Hall was initiated in the same year but one or two lodge meetings prior to the 14 other free Negroes.) One year later, in 1776, Hall organized the first Negro lodge in America. In due course, Lodge No. 441 was removed from the vicinity of Boston to New York State and became one of the lodges which participated in the formation of the first Caucasian grand lodge of that state. Brother J. B. Batt, Master of Lodge No. 441, left the Negro lodge with a permit which allowed it to operate and which proved to be the only credential it had for a long time. Hall submitted at least three petitions for a charter from the Caucasian jurisdiction of Massachusetts, but first one problem and another caused several years of delay and the charter was never issued. Soon after the Negro lodge had received the permit from its mother lodge, the brethren petitioned Provincial Grand Master, Joseph Warren, for Masonic recognition and charter from the Caucasian jurisdiction of Massachusetts and the petition had been favorably received, but before any action could be taken, Joseph Warren was killed in the Battle of Bunker Hill. From then on the possibility of securing the charter worsened. Growing impatient with this, Hall applied to the Grand Lodge of England for a charter and after much delay it arrived in Boston on April 29, 1787, naming the Negro lodge "African Lodge No. 459."

After some other Negro lodges were established in the area a grand lodge was organized, and Prince Hall was made Grand Master of the first Grand Lodge of Negroes in the United States. It was named the African Grand Lodge of North America and formed in Boston, June 24, 1791. Thus Prince Hall gave us the privilege of exercising ourselves freely in all of the pursuits of freemasonry without being suppressed or repressed by the Caucasian power structure. Two facts are outstanding in the history of Prince Hall Masonry. The Fraternity is indebted to two foreign Grand Lodges for its origin. It was through the Grand Lodge of Ireland that men of color in America first obtained the degrees of Freemasonry, and it was through the Grand Lodge of England that organized Freemasonry, for them, became a reality.

Most Worshipful Brother Prince Hall passed into the Great Beyond in Boston, Massachusetts, on December 7, 1807. He was buried in Copp's Hill Cemetery in Boston and a large monument has been erected to his memory and upon regular occasions the various grand bodies throughout the nation make pilgrimages thereto. As recently as the middle of August 1970, such a pilgrimage was made in connection with the 51st

Annual Conference of Grand Masters in Boston, and many of our brethren from Louisiana were in that pilgrimage.

The year after the death of Prince Hall the title of the Negro Grand Lodge of which Hall was Grand Master was changed from African Grand Lodge of North America to its present title of Prince Hall Grand Lodge, F. & A. M. of Massachusetts in his honor, and Deputy Grand Master Nero Prince was made Grand Master in Prince Hall's stead.

This information was gathered and compiled from the following sources:

1. Davis, Harry E., **A History of Freemasonry Among Negroes in America**

2. Grimshaw, William H., **History of Freemasonry Among Colored People of North America**, pp. 74-98

3. Mackey, Albert G. and E. R. Johnston, **Masonry Defined**, Revised, Shreveport, La.: National Masonic Press, Inc., 1939

4. Peterson, William O. (Editor), Masonic Quiz Book, Chicago: The Charles T. Powner Co., 1969

5. Upton, William H., **Light On A Dark Subject** and **Prince Hall's Letter Book**

6. Voorhis, Harold V. B., **Negro Masonry in the United States**, and **Masonic Organizations**

7. Williamson, Harry A., **The Prince Hall Primer**, Revised Edition, Richmond, Va.: McCoy Publishing and Masonic Supply Co., Inc., 1956

PRINCE HALL PUBLIC SCHOOL

"FIRST SCHOOL IN AMERICA NAMED AFTER OUR ILLUSTRIOUS FOUNDER"

"The Prince Hall Elementary School, 18th and Godfrey, Philadelphia, Pennsylvania, opened on Friday, September 7, 1973. This is the first school in the United States to be named after PRINCE HALL, the Illustrious Founder of the Most Worshipful Prince Hall Grand Lodge, Free and Accepted Masons in the United States and one of the largest and oldest Fraternal Organizations in this country. The Prince Hall School, under the Principalship of Ms. Martha Young, is an ultra modern structure with a remarkable innovative motivation program designed to produce ingenious new warp to affect education."

Opening ceremonies on Friday, September 21, 1973, at 7:30 P.M. Prince Hall Masons participated in the opening ceremonies and a bust and portrait of PRINCE HALL were unveiled during the ceremonial program.

"Because PRINCE HALL is an individual of Historical Salute, he is a definite part of the heritage of Black children and early American History. This school will be ranked among the Masonic Shrines of our Nation, thus it should be historically significant that all of us as PRINCE HALL MASONS give our utmost support to such a worthy cause to a Brother who believed profoundly in Thy Creator."

PRINCE HALL SCHOOL was built at the request of the Community. The Ad Hoc Committee chaired by Mrs. Virginia Lee got the school reinstated in the Capital Budget. This committee also is responsible for getting the school name changed from the West Oak Lane School to PRINCE HALL.

Mrs. Martha Young, Principal, states that one of the aims of the school is that the Elementary school will be a tribute to Prince Hall. "The underlying objective of PRINCE HALL SCHOOL is to tailor the educational program to fit the needs and interests as well as background of the learners." Our goal is an individualization of instruction.

The school will have selfcontained classrooms, some areas will have operable walls, two areas will be completely open.

The staff underwent a development program to insure smooth operation.

DIRECTORY
Roster of Grand Masters

Alabama: S. J. Bennett, 1720 Center Street, So., Birmingham 35205

Alaska: Richard J. Watts, Sr., P. O. Box 1371, Anchorage 99501

Arizona: Douglas M. Nelson, 4017 W. Palo Verde Drive, Phoenix 85019

Arkansas: Dr. L. W. Williamson, P. O. Box 117, Washington 71862

Bahamas: Kenneth L. Moss, P. O. Box 418, Marsh Harbor

California: Roy M. Moore, 3685 Crenshaw Blvd., Los Angeles 90016

Canada: Robert M. Foster, 12 Woodlawn Drive, Crimsby, Ont.

Colorado: Ernest O. Davis, 891 Constitution Drive, Foster City, California 94404

Delaware: Courtney P. Houston, Jr., 59 No. McKee Road, Dover 19901

Connecticut: Madison Boulden, 2 Hickory Lane, Bloomfield

District of Columbia: Henry A. Dove, 1722 D Street, N.E., Washington 20002

Florida: Rudolph Bradley, 2965 N.W. 52nd Street, Miami 33142

Georgia: X. L. Neal, 330 Auburn Avenue, N.E., Atlanta 30303

Illinois: Rufus Starks, 206 N. 62nd St., East St. Louis 62203

Indiana: Clarence W. Foster, 3039 W. Cross St., Anderson 46102

Iowa: Vernon H. Baker, 320 So. 6th St., Burlington

Kansas: See article in this issue of the passing of Grand Master Watts

Kentucky: John W. Delaney, 30 West 15th St., Covington 41011

Louisiana: Jno. G. Lewis, Jr., P. O. Box 2974, Baton Rouge 70821

Liberia: E. Jonathan Goodridge, Masonic Temple, West Benson St., Monrovia

Maryland: Samuel T. Daniels, 6116 Benhurst Road, Baltimore 21209

Massachusetts: Richard W. Richardson, Masonic Temple, 1095 Tremont Street, Boston 02120

Michigan: Peyton J. Thomas, 3100 Gratiot Ave., Detroit 48207

Minnesota: Robert H. Johnson, 729 Sheridan Ave., North, Minneapolis 55411

Mississippi: James C. Gilliam, 516 Paul Edwards Avenue, Clarksdale 38614

Missouri: A. Cleveland Compton, 4625 Farlin, St. Louis 63121

Nebraska: James Manese, 2703 Sprague St., Omaha 68111

New Mexico: Elijah J. Johnson, 423 Maryland Ave., Alomoryorda 88310

New Jersey: Charles W. Campbell, 60 Thorntown Lane, Bordentown 08505

New York: Vincent E. Best, 4 Dunbar St., Amityville 11701

North Carolina: Clark S. Brown, 727 N. Patterson, Winston-Salem 27101

Ohio: Curvis F. Rhyne, 1029 East Noble St., Alliance 44601

Oklahoma: Herman E. Duncan, P. O. Box 1588, Muskogee 74401

Oregon: Elijah Graham, 5310 N. E. Rodney Ave., Portland 97211

Pennsylvania: Alvin H. Swiggett, 930 Central Avenue, Chester 19013

Rhode Island: William T. Jackson, 9 Caleb Earl St., Newport 02840

South Carolina: R. H. Foster, P. O. Box 157, Gaffney 29340

Tennessee: Charles F. Williams, 253 Parkway West, Memphis 38109

Texas: I. H. Clayborn, 1227 Serenade Lane, Dallas 75241

Virginia: J. Luvelle Taylor, 1301 Chatham Hill Rd., N.W., Roanoke

Washington: James E. Chase, E. 3811 Upriver Dr., Spokane 99207

West Virginia: J. Hobart Hale, P. O. Box 78, Boomer 25031

Wisconsin: Herman Smith, Jr., 6561 W. County Line Rd., Milwaukee 53223

CAUCASIAN PRINCE HALL LODGE
BY
JOSEPH A. WALKES, JR, M.P.S. (KANSAS)

Portions of this article were taken from "A Chronological History of Prince Hall Masonry 1788-1932" by Harry A. Williamson, by per- *mission of the "Schomburg Center for Research in Black Culture, The New York Public Library, Astor, Lenox and Tilden Foundations." Bro*

Walkes thanks the foundation for allowing him to use portions of the material for the "Phylaxis."

One of the most interesting facts to come to light, is to be found in the minute book of the Most Worshipful Prince Hall Grand Lodge of New York, under the proceedings for the year 1871. Here is to be found a Lodge of German Jews working under the authority of this Prince Hall Grand Lodge.

This Lodge, sometimes designated as both "Downshire" and "Progress" No. 12, was located in New York City and warranted February 3, 1870. Its members were all Hebrews of German extraction. The only American born Black member was Brother Albert Wilson, its Secretary, and who at the same time was Secretary to the Grand Lodge.

It is recorded that from February to December of 1870, that this Lodge held twelve regular communications. The well-known Prince Hall Masonic scholar, Bro Harry E. Davis, of the Most Worshipful Prince Hall Grand Lodge of Ohio, and author of "A History of Freemasonry Among Negroes in America," states that the warrant was recalled, as these Brethren returned to Europe at the time of the Franco-Prussian War. Bro Harry A. Williamson in his "A Chronological History of Prince Hall Masonry 1784-1932" adds that those members remaining ultimately transferred their membership to the Caucasian Grand Lodge of that state. In support of this statement, Bro Williamson records the proceedings of the Prince Hall Grand Lodge for 1874 as:

> "Progress Lodge No. 12, New York City changed to Shakespear Lodge No. 750 under the Jurisdiction of the New York Grand Lodge (white)."

Bro Williamson and Bro Davis quotes that in a further record pertaining to the above statement, information was obtained in 1910, through one of these members, a Bro B. Le Vene, who was then a member of Wm. McKinley Lodge 840, under the jurisdiction of the Caucasian Grand Lodge of New York. He stated that he had been a member of the Prince Hall Lodge and that the first two degrees were re-conferred on him when he transferred his membership to the Caucasian body, but not the third as his raising under the Prince Hall Jurisdiction was deemed sufficient.

Bro Williamson states that the records of Downshire No. 12, as noted in the minutes of the Prince Hall Grand Lodge reads:

"Downshire Lodge No. 12, organized February 3rd (Thursday), 1870. We are in possession of reports from this Lodge under dates of November 30, 1870, September, October, and December, 1871. An appeal addressed to the Grand Lodge September 7, 1870, is signed in the handwriting of the following Brethren:

W. M. Abraham Levy
S. W. D. Jones
J. W. Acting, Julius Cohn

In the Williamson Prince Hall Masonic collection housed in the New York Public Library, is a report sheet submitted to the Prince Hall Grand Lodge in 1870, showing the following named members:

1. Abraham Levy
2. Dramin Jones
3. Abram Newfeldt
4. Tobias Cohen
5. Herman Holzwasser
6. Davis Cerciwitz
7. Jacob Goldfarb
8. Henry Rosenthal
9. Marcus Rosenthal
10. Zundel Hebstein
11. Morris Isaacs
12. Max Levy
13. Abraham Newmark
14. Samuel Lener
15. John Delvert
16. Simon Goldstein
17. Solomon Goldstein
18. Morris Goldstein
19. Henry Levy
20. Julius Cohn
21. Sol. Alexander
22. Moritz Brookman
23. Meyer Rosenthal
24. Ossac Wasseioug
25. John Brown

Additional facts from the records read as follows:

> "Twelve (12) regular communications, three (3) initiations, two (2) crafting - one raised. Rejected one (1) - Mr. Nathan Isreal. Reinstated two (2) Bros Sol. Goldstein and John Cooper. Affiliated one (1) Bro John Bowles, initiated Bros Aaron Oppenheim, William Rosenthal, Jacob Levy. Buried one (1) Samuel Laner."

The above statistics are from the report of the Most Worshipful Prince Hall Grand Lodge of New York of September 1, 1871, and is without parallel in the annals of Prince Hall Masonic history.

It is also interesting to note that in the history of the Most Worshipful Prince Hall Grand Lodge of Georgia, that the first Lodge established in that state of Prince Hall origan was Eureka Lodge No. 11, located in Savannah and warranted February 4th, 1866, and that occupying the position of Junior Steward was a Brother "Miller Max" who was reputed to a Caucasian Freemason, a resident of Savannah of long standing and likewise a member in good standing at the time in one of the Lodges operating under the Jurisdiction of the Caucasian branch of the Fraternity in that state.

11

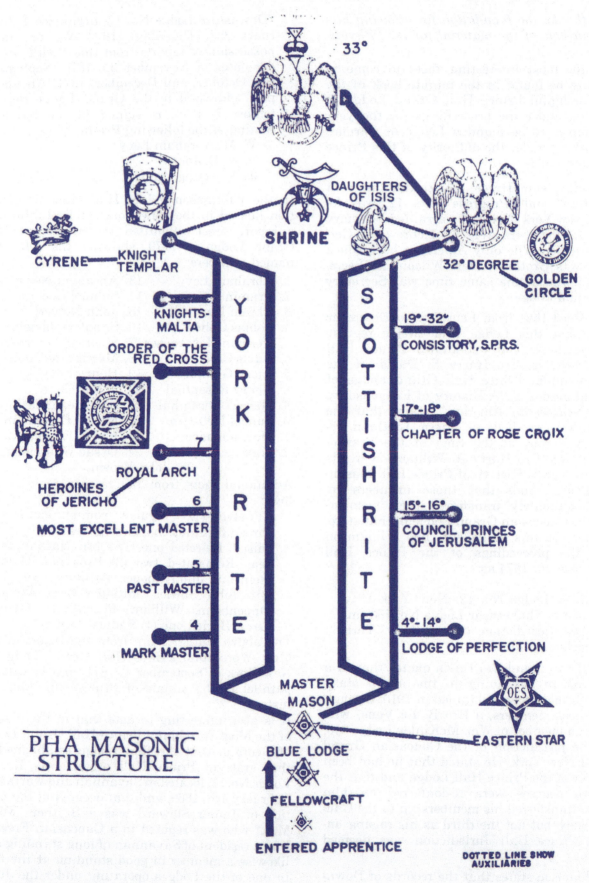

THE PHYLAXIS

MAY 1974

Volume I   Number 2

**A SOCIETY FOR PRINCE HALL
FREEMASONS WHO SEEK MORE
LIGHT AND WHO HAVE LIGHT TO
IMPART**

THE PHYLAXIS
Published at Jefferson City, Mo., by
THE PHYLAXIS SOCIETY

Arthur H. Frederick M.P.S. .... Editor
Box 43, Roxbury, Massachusetts 02119

OFFICERS

Joseph A. Walkes, Jr, M.P.S. .... President
P. O. Box 3151, Ft. Leavenworth, Kansas 66027

Herbert Dailey, M.P.S. .... First Vice President
1616 South Cedar, Tacoma, Washington 98405

Zellus Bailey, M.P.S. .... Second Vice President
7039 Dover Court, St. Louis, Missouri 63130

James E. Herndon, M.P.S. .... Executive Secretary
1574 Ivanhoe Street, Denver, Colorado 80220

Alonzo D. Foote, Sr., M.P.S. .... Treasurer
P. O. Box 3139, Tacoma, Washington 98405

SUBSCRIPTION RATE: FOR ONE YEAR, $5.00

The Phylaxis Magazine is the official publication of the Phylaxis Society. Any article appearing in this publication expresses only the opinion of the writer, and does not become the official pronouncement of the Phylaxis Society. No advertising of any form is solicited or accepted. All communication relative to the magazine should be addressed to the Editor. Inquiries relative to membership must be addressed to the Executive Secretary. Membership is by invitation and recommendation only. The joining fee is $3.00. Dues are $5.00 per year in advance, which amount includes a subscription to the "Phylaxis" magazine for one year.

All rights reserved. No part of this work may be reproduced or transmitted in any form or by any means, electrical or mechanical, or retrival system, without written permission from the publisher.

INDEX

The Phylaxis Society and The
    Philalethes Society 14

Hold Rites for Vern T. Watts,
    Grand Master 14

A Word From The
    President 15

You Be The Judge??? 16

I Am Freemasonry 16

Profile of a Non-Prince Hall
    Masonic Organization 17

The Masonic Philosophy
    of Samuel W. Clark 18

The Phylaxis Society
    Subscription Card 19

Reference 20

Editorial

THE PHYLAXIS SOCIETY AND THE PHILALETHES SOCIETY

When one desires to form a organization, irregardless of the nature of the organization, he first looks around to locate others who have similar views as his; second, he searches to find a organization to pattern after. And such was the case of the *"Phylaxis Society"* which pattern itself after the *"Philalethes Society."* Our emblem, Constitution and By-laws, and our organizational structure is quite similar, likewise our goals and purpose, i.e., *"more light in Masonry!"*

The *"Philalethes Society"* was organized October 1, 1928 by George Imbrie, Editor of the Masonic Light, Kansas City, Missouri (not to be confused with the Masonic Light of the Prince Hall Grand Lodge of Missouri), Robert Clegg, world famous revisor and editor of Mackey's Encyclopedia of Freemasonry, Harold V. B. Voorhis, author of *"Negro Masonry in the United States"* (later withdrawn from the market), and others formulated the plans for this Caucasian Masonic society in Cedar Rapids, Iowa. Its highly respected magazine *"The Philalethes"* began publishing March 1946, and is published six times a year.

The *"Phylaxis Society"* wishes the best for our Caucasian counterpart.

HOLD RITES FOR VERN T. WATTS, GRAND MASTER

Vern T. Watts, Grand Master of the Most Worshipful Prince Hall Grand Lodge F. and A. M., of Kansas and Jurisdiction, died Sunday, at the North hospital, Hutchinson, Kans., after being confined three days. He was elected to the office of Grand Master, July 8, 1973, after the death of P. G. Porter, Olathe, who held that office for 26 years, before his death.

Mr. Watts was born April 11, 1893, in Ellsberry, Mo., and moved to Hutchinson at an early age. He attended public schools in Hutchinson and graduated from high school there. He attended Kansas University, Lawrence, for two years and entered the U. S. Postal Service in Hutchinson as a mail carrier and retired in 1963 after 41 years of service.

He was a member of the Second Baptist church, Hutchinson, where he served as a deacon for many years. He was a 50-year member of D. G. Lett Lodge No. 30, F. and A. M., Hutchinson and had served as secretary, treasurer and was a Past Worshipful Master. He and his wife, Mrs. Watts, the former Viola Cornelius Saunders, observed their Golden wedding anniversary in 1967 in Hutchinson, and Mrs. Watts preceded him in death in September, 1971.

They have two children, a son, Vern T. Watts, Wichita; and a daughter, Mrs. Joan Hailstalk, Washington, D.C.

In 1940, he was elected Grand Lecturer of Prince Hall Grand Lodge — Kansas and served this office for 19 years. In 1959, he was elected Deputy Grand Master in the city of Salina, Kans., and served this office until his advance to Grand Master last summer.

During the Council of Deliberation held in Hutchinson, October 24, 1973, he was elected a candidate to receive the 33rd degree and was to be crowned an Inspector General in the city of Philadelphia, Pa., May, 1974, at the United Supreme Council Ancient Accepted Scottish Rites. He was a member of Western Star Consistory No. 18, Wichita, Order of Eastern Star, Hutchinson and was given the degree of Past Grand Patron during the 1973 Grand Chapter Order of Eastern Star in Junction City, Kans., by Mrs. Maudella T. Brooks, Worthy Grand Matron of Kansas City, Kans.

Other surviving relatives are a granddaughter, Cynthia Watts, Wichita; brother, Bert Watts, Milwaukee, Wis.; sister, Mrs. Bessie Harrison, Hutchinson, and other relatives.

Scottish Rites and Eastern Star services were conducted Wednesday night at Johnson Funeral parlor, Hutchinson. Church services were held in the chapel Thursday morning. Final Masonic rites were rendered at graveside in Fair Lawn cemetery, Hutchinson.

From "THE CALL" Kansas City, Mo., week of Jan. 18 to Jan. 24, 1974.

A WORD FROM THE PRESIDENT

"Just the other day in the office of the Executive Director of our Conference, (The Late) Most Worshipful Amos T. Hall, I noticed the series of books lately published giving the story of the Negro in America. His trials, his tribulation, his sorrows, his successes and his leaders. At no point did I find a chronicle of the work and influence of the Masonic institution or the part it played, in giving a struggling race direction, as it trudged laboriously up freedoms road. Many of Masonry's illustrious sons were mentioned but no mention or thought given to the institution that sustained them and bore them safely over their periods of depression and frustration. If this night brings and end to that traditional silence, then SO MOTE IT BE!"

Jno G. Lewis, S.G.C.
given at a banquet in honor
of Bro Thurgood Marshall

When these words were spoken by Bro Lewis, the *"Phylaxis Society"* wasn't even a dream, but today it is a reality, and we plan to break that *"traditional silence"* that Bro Lewis spoke of. In future issues of the *"Phylaxis,"* we plan to present such articles of Masonic interest to the Prince Hall Mason as, *"Martin R. Delaney — Free Mason," "Arthur Schomberg — Craftsman," "The Masonic Philosphy of Lewis Hayden," "Harry E. Williamson — Prince Hall Scholar,"* and one article that will be quite controversal, *"Masonic Misinformation,"* a story of a gold chain that was presented to the Most Worshipful Prince Hall Grand Lodge of Massachusetts.

Our various committees will be making a number of reports also. Our Second Vice President Zellus Bailey, M.P.S. (Missouri) has been gathering information on "Non Prince Hall" bodies operating throughout the various jurisdictions, and will present a state by state breakdown on these organizations. Most Grand Jurisdictions within the Prince Hall family has received letters from Bro Bailey and his committee requesting their assistance. With the publications of this list, our magazine will also serve as a handy guide to keep tables of just who is invading our individual Masonic jurisdictions.

In the Seattle/Tacoma area, the *"Northwest Chapter"* of the Phylaxis Society is operating under the leadership of our First Vice President Herbert Dailey, M.P.S. (Washington), and are exploring many areas of interest for the members of the Phylaxis Society.

I would like to thank the many brethren of the Craft, and the individual members of the Society for the many kind letters they sent concerning the first issue of the *"Phylaxis."*

JOSEPH A. WALKES, JR., M.P.S.

YOU BE THE JUDGE???

On March 6, 1775 Prince Hall and fourteen others received their degrees, and met as a Lodge without any warrant or authority, until May, 1787.

In 1784, Prince Hall petitioned the Grand Lodge of England for a Charter and the Charter was granted and received by Prince Hall in 1787.

In 1797, Prince Hall established a Lodge in Philadelphia, Pennsylvania.

In 1799, Prince Hall established a Lodge in Providence, Rhode Island.

In 1808, the three above lodges organized into a Grand Lodge, then further organized Lodges in other states.

In 1827, John T. Hilton, R.W.G.M.; Thomas Dalton, G.S.W.; Lewis York, G.J.W.; and J. H. Purran, G. Secretary had published in a Boston newspaper the following statement, taken from context. In the next issue of the Phylaxis Magazine the full statement will appear. However, here is the section we want you to review.

"It is now, however, with great pleasure we state that the present age has arrived to that degree of proficiency in the art, that we can at any time select from among us many whose capacity to govern enables them to preside with as much good order, dignity, and propriety as any other Lodge within our knowledge. This fact can be proved by gentlemen of respectibility, whose knowledge of Masonry would not be questioned by any one well acquainted with the art. Since the rise of the Lodge to this degree of proficiency, we concluded it was best and proper to make it known to the Most Worshipful Grand Lodge of England from whence we derive our charter . . . yet we have never received a single line or reply from that Hon. Society. We do, therefore, . . . publicly declare ourselves free and independent of any Lodge from this day, and that we will not be tributary, or be governed by any Grand Lodge than that of our own."

Now You be the Judge???

1. By the above statement did the Prince Hall Grand Lodge forever severe its connection with the Grand Lodge of England?

2. Does the statement change any of the conditions of the charter that was issued to Prince Hall?

3. Is the Prince Hall Grand Lodge just as bound to the Grand Lodge of England today as it was when the Charter was issued irregardless to what was written in a newspaper?

Answers in next issue of Phylaxis Magazine.

Bibliography:

The History of Freemasonry by:
   Albert C. Mackey, M.D. 33°
   William R. Singleton, 33°
   William James Hughan, P.S.G.D. of G. L. of England
   Volume #6

I AM FREEMASONRY
BY
HERBERT DAILEY M.P.S. (WASHINGTON)

I was born in antiquity, in the ancient days when men first dreamed of GOD. I have been tried through the ages, and found TRUE. The crossroads of the world bear the imprint of my feet, and the Cathedrals of all nations mark the skill of my hands. I strive for beauty and for symmetry. In my heart is Wisdom and Strength and Courage for those who ask. Upon my Altars is the Book of Holy Writ, and my prayers are to the One Omnipotent GOD. My sons work and pray together, without rank or discord, in the public mart and in the inner Chamber. By signs and symbols I teach the lessons of life and of death, and the relationship of MAN with GOD and MAN with MAN. My arms are widespread to receive those of lawful age and good report who seek me of their own free will. I accept them and teach them to use my tools in the building of MEN, and thereby, find direction in their quest for perfection, so much desired and so difficult to attain. I lift up the fallen and shelter the sick. I hark to the orphan's cry, the widow's tears, the pains of the old and destituted. I am not church, nor party, nor school, yet my sons bear a full share of responsibility to GOD, to Country, to neighbor and themselves. THEY ARE FREEMEN, tenacious of their liberties and alert to lirking danger. At the end I commit them as each one undertakes the journey beyond the vale into the glory of everlasting life. I ponder the sand within the glass and think how small is a single life in the eternal universe. Always have I taught immortality, and even as I raise men from DARKNESS into LIGHT, I am a way of life.

"I AM FREEMASONRY"

PROFILE OF A NON-PRINCE HALL MASONIC ORGANIZATION

RESEARCH PAPER BY
ZELLUS BAILEY, M.P.S. (MISSOURI)

Phylaxis Society's Committee
On Non-Prince Hall Masonry
March 31, 1974

It is not possible to find reference to Negro (Black) unrecognized Masonic bodies in reputable literature, my objective is to compile subjective information on these groups and point out areas of demarcation. These groups or organizations have and are succeeding in securing as members men who desire to become Masons but do not know which group is legitimate and which are irregular or "bogus." In many cases the degree peddlers move into a new community and exploit the less informed.

Substantial activities on the part of unrecognized or "bogus" masonic groups and or organizations, who claim to be masonic, uses masonic designations, titles, emblems, and insignia all without legitimate masonic authority.

The Ancient and Accepted Scottish Rite of Free Masonry, The Supreme Council Of The Most Illustrious Soverign Grand Inspector General of the Ancient and Accepted, Scottish Rite of Free Masonry. Mother Council in the United States for the Ancient and Accepted Scottish Rite of Freemasonry. In all of the degrees from the first through the Thirty-third. Sitting in the Valley of New Orleans, State of Louisiana. This organization is the first of a series, I will give a complete profile as to its orgin, history and masonic lineage. This National Supreme Council for North America derives it authority from the Grand Orient of France. In the early years of development it allegedly drew candidates from the Compact Grand Lodges subordinates. During this period "Dr. Peter D. Ray, M.D., served as the Most Powerful Soverign Grand Commander of the National Supreme Council A. and A. Scottish Rite Masons from 1865 to 1889."[1]

It is the opinion of this writer that the name of the Compact Grand Lodge is used out of text. There are facts to substantiate that this National Compact Grand Lodge was brought into existence by the Regular Grand Lodge of Negro (Black) Masons then in existence. It was created in 1847 and abolished in 1877. It is unfortunate that men today are interested in misleading people into fraudulent lodges by capitalizing on the statement that the National Compact had it origin in France, or that it originated with the Scottish Rite.

On the 17th of October, 1839, the M . . Ill . . B. B. . . de Santangelo, (1) Rocoa de Santi Pietri, (2) J. J. Conti, (3) F. Burtheau and R. E. de David-Perdreauville, all soverign Grand Inspectors, held a meeting and organized a Supreme Council for the United States of America. The reason for which they took this title is found in that the "United Supreme Council for the Western Hemisphere," which in 1836 existed in the City of New York, under the Grand Commandership of T. . . M. . . Ill. . . Elias Hicks, was then slumbering and there was no recognized authority for the Scottish Rite in the United States.

The officers of the first Supreme Council sitting in New Orleans were: Orazio de Attelis, Marquis de Santangelo — Grand Commander; Jean Jacques Conte — Lieutenant Grand Commander; Rene Elizabeth de David-Perdreauville — Grand Secretary; Francois Frederic Burtheau — Guard of the Seal and Archives; Jose Antonio Roca de Santi Pietri — Grand Treasurer; Guillaume Alfred Montmain — Grand Master of Ceremonies; Jean Francois Connonge — Grand Expert; Louis Feraud — Grand Captain of the Guard.

This Supreme Council for the United States of America became the Supreme Council of Louisiana by an act of incorporation March 16, 1870, granted at an extra session of the legislature of Louisiana. The act of incorporation took place under the Grand Commandership of the M. . . Ill. . . B. . . Eugene Chassaignac.[2]

(1) Orazio de Attellis de Santangelo was created a 33rd in the Valley of New York, on the 16th of November 1827 by then the M. . . Ill. . . B. . . Joseph Cerneau, then most powerful Grand Commander of the same Supreme Council over which the M. . . Ill. . . B. . . Elias Hicks presided in 1836, and which was known in the masonic world under the name of the "United Supreme Council for the Western Hemisphere" in accordance with the title given it by the treaty of alliance of 1834."[1]

(2) Jose Antonio Roca de Santi Pietri was created 33rd, on the 10th of April, 1832, by the National Supreme Council of Spain.[2]

(3) J. J. Conte was created a 33rd by the Supreme Council of France on the 20th of May, 1822.[3]

(Continued in Next Issue)

17

THE MASONIC PHILOSOPHY OF SAMUEL W. CLARK

BY
JOSEPH A. WALKES, JR., M.P.S. (KANSAS)

"One of the saddest things about controversy is that it frequently obscures every other element concerning a topic except the point controverted. Colored Masonry has suffered much from this blight of controversy. In Masonic, as well as in political history, the Negro has been the vortex around which a veritable torrent of passion has whirled. In the midst of these tempests men do not take time to assemble and analyze simple facts, the scientific pose is lost, the historian is superseded by the advocate, and a wealth of information is neglected."[1]

Throughout the history of the Black man in America, Masonic as well as political, has appeared on the stage, some of the most eloquent spokesmen this country has ever produced. Not only eloquent, but dedicated Prince Hall Freemasons, whose only weapons, were words, and the justness of their cause. Words placed on paper so many years ago, are yet still alive, passionate words to combat the prejudice and racism of the past, as well as the present. Their names are held in reverence, and deep respect by Masonic scholars around the world, Prince Hall, Lewis Hayden, Martin R. Delany, John T. Hilton, Harry A. Williamson, Arthur A. Schomburg, Harry E. Davis and scores of others.

No voice was more eloquent or more forceful than the Masonic writings and philosophy of Samuel Wilcox Clark. Of him could be truthfully said "his was a voice of one crying in the wilderness during the dark days of our Masonic history."[2]

His work, *"Negro Masonry in Equity,"* and his memorable words are worthy to be remembered throughout the Prince Hall fraternity.

The subject of this article was born in Cincinnati, Ohio, July 25th, 1846. Initiated and raised in 1870 in True American Lodge No. 2, in Cincinnati, and serving that Prince Hall Jurisdiction as Grand Master from 1879 to 1888, and again from 1898 to 1902.[3]

It was in 1886, that the then Grand Master Clark published in the proceedings of the Grand Lodge his *"Negro Masonry in Equity"* which was later published as a pamphlet. Grand Master Barnes of Michigan praised Clark and this work by saying, "few jurisdictions have produced his equal in Masonic knowledge and untiring devotion to the fraternity. His name will live as long as Masonry exists among Colored Men!"[4]

His legacy can be found in his philosophy, and his attacks upon the White Masonic power structure of his day. His appeal was for truth and justice before the world Masonic community, against hypocrisy.

"The time is full at hand when we must no longer depend upon our friends to do battle for us. The fight must be our own. Neither must it be a defensive one, we must be aggressive, we must assert ourselves, we must tear away the flimsy mask behind which the White American Mason takes refuge from the penetrating eye of truth and justice. Let us turn upon him the fierce light of recorded history, thereby disclosing to the open gaze of the world the false, unjust, and un-Masonic position which he assumes."[5]

His appeals stand as meaningful today, as when they were first penned.

"Masons of the World, wheresoever dispersed, the Negro Mason of America stands before you today as a just and upright Mason, and as such demands that you shall try him by the Square of Virture, and having tried him and found him just and true, he further demands that you deny him not, but that you receive him and accept him, and accord unto him all of the rights that may belong to him. He does not make this demand because he is a Negro, neither does he ask that you do this as a favor, but he demands it because he is a Mason as you are, and because his right to the title of Free and Accepted Mason is equal to yours — no more, no less!"[6]

While American Masonry praised Albert Pike, the negrophobic Confederate General, author of *"Morals and Dogma,"* classed as the most profound Masonic work written in the United States, which should be judged as the writings of a hypocritical prejudiced Mason who in September 14, 1875, wrote "When I have to accept negroes as brothers or leave Masonry, I shall leave it!"[7]

Of him, Clark asked "What think you of a man professing to be a Mason uttering such sentiments as these . . ." "God pity Brother Pike and the thousands of canting hypocrites like him."[8]

"While, we know there are large numbers of White Masons, who acknowledge the justness of our claims, and stand ready and willing to try us and not deny us, we, also, feel and know that there is a vaster and a mightier number who, knowing all these things to be true, yet reject us and deny us. You ask what motive can impel these men — Men whose eloquent utterance, in chaste and beautiful language, have bid the world to pause and gaze upon the matchless symmetry of our grand and noble institution, and contemplate in awe the grandeur and sublimity of its principles — to reject the truth? Is it that slimy coated and cold-blooded serpent of prejudice against the Negro. You see it in every feeble and tottering imbecile and in the little, prattling child, wherever you turn the monster, with his ever-open, glassy eye, is staring at you. No place is secure from his intrusion, go to the halls of justice and you will find him there, and even within the sacred portals of God's tabernacles does he stealthily crawl, not even sparing the alter where the humble Christian kneels to take the consecrated emblems of our Lord and Saviour. This is why we are denied, this is why we are rejected, this is why we are termed clandestine, illegal and irregular!"[9]

"The general ignorance of the great mass of American Masons concerning (Prince Hall) origin and history, the bitter prejudice, which seems many Americans have against the Negro. This prejudice, which seems to be almost inherent, if not wholly so, renders them unfit to do justice to the Negro Mason!"[10]

And of the false claims of Caucasian Masonic historians, Clark wrote, "The White Masonic historians, knowing of the many irregularities of their early organization, seek many ways to find excuses and make apologies for them!"[11] And of the greatest offender of them all, Clark scoffs, "What a commentary here upon the attitude of the Grand Lodge of Massachusetts towards the Negro Masons of America, who can show by the very records brought to light by her, a clearer and better title to legitimacy than either Massachusetts or New Hampshire. Does it need a seer to tell the reason of this unjust discrimination? Shame! Shame! Shame!!!"[12]

"They either refuse to examine the records of history for fear they may discover that the Negroes right is equal to theirs, or, knowing the facts, they endeavor to subvert them by misstatements and false reasoning!"[13]

Above all, Clark remained the realist, "but we say to him, your professions are not sustained by words, and that you do give the lie to your words when you say you believe in the Brotherhood of Man!"[14]

THE PHYLAXIS SOCIETY SUBSCRIPTION CARD

Subscription rate: $5.00/Yr.

Mail to: James E. Herndon, MPS
Executive Secretary
1574 Ivanhoe Street
Denver, Colo. 80220

Gentlemen:

Enclosed is my subscription the the Phylaxis Magazine.

_____ Check Enclosed _____ amount payable to Phylaxis Magazine

Name: _____

Address: _____

City: _____ State: _____ Zip Code: _____

A SOCIETY FOR PRINCE HALL FREEMASONS WHO SEEK MORE LIGHT AND WHO HAVE LIGHT TO IMPART

19

And to Clark must be said above all, he was a proud Mason, "As Negro Masons, we need expect no recognition from organized White American Masons, I plead for none; I care for none at the sacrifice of honor and dignity. I stand as just, as true, as pure a Free Mason as ever trod God's green earth. My title is as perfect as that of the Prince of Wales, or the President of the United States, as he who travels with the caravan over the desert or he who dwells on the plains of the far west. Wherever he may be upon the continents of the land or the islands of the sea, if he be a Free Mason he is my brother and cannot deny me if he would!"[15]

Upon the death of this scholary Prince Hall Mason the following resolution was submitted at the 1903 Grand Lodge Session by Joseph L. Jones and adopted:

WHEREAS: This M. W. Grand Lodge having authorized the publication of the second edition of "The Negro Mason in Equity," written by our lamented M. W. Past Grand Master, Samuel W. Clark.

BE IT RESOLVED: That we recommend that there be added to this work the funeral oration as delivered by R. W. Bro. Alexander Morris, Grand Orator, the two being combined, printed and sold for the purpose of placing a Masonic monument upon the grave of our distinguished brother, as a mark of the esteem in which he was held by the Craft."

In concluding an address to the Prince Hall Grand Lodge of Ohio, Grand Master Clark declined a further re-election and used these words "There is a very beautiful story told in one of the books of an eminent author, in which he describes an angel as coming down from heaven to see "what men live by." After a sojourn of more than two years upon the earth and an association with all grades of society, the angel discovered that "men live by love." They may have wealth, station, reputation, and renown, but unless their lives and their communion with their fellow men be crowned with love, they live in vain."[16] What better way to end this article. This writer believes that the greatest monument befitting the memory of Bro. Clark, would be the mandatory reading of his classic, *"The Negro Mason in Equity"* by each and every Prince Hall Freemason. Not to glorify this splendid work, as it can stand on its own merit, but to educate the mass of the fraternity to their history, and to *"Render unto Caesar the things which are Caesar's."*

REFERENCE

[1]Harry E. Davis, 33°, *A History of Freemasonry Among Negroes in America* (United Supreme Council, A.A.S.R., Northern Jurisdiction, U.S.A., Prince Hall Affiliation, Inc., 1946) p. 5.

[2]Address of Grand Master Robert C. Barnes 39th Annual Communication of the Prince Hall Grand Lodge of Michigan, Battle Creek, Tuesday, January 26th, 1904.

[3]Charles H. Wesley, *The History of the Prince Hall Grand Lodge of Free and Accepted Masons of the State of Ohio 1849-1960* (Wilberforce Ohio: Central State College Press 1961) p. 90, 91.

[4]Barnes, *op. cit*.

[5]Samuel W. Clark, *The Negro Mason in Equity* (M. W. Grand Lodge of Free and Accepted Masons for the State of Ohio 1886) p. 3.

[6]*Ibid.*, p. 68.

[7]Views of General Albert Pike, Sovereign Grand Commander, A.&A. Scottish Rite letter to John D. Caldwell, 13th September 1875 cited by John D. Caldwell, *"New Day — New Duty"* Reports, Memorials, etc. to the M. W. Grand Lodge of Ohio, relative to Colored Grand Lodge F & A.M. of Ohio, (Cincinnati, 1875) p. 50 and William H. Upton, *Negro Masonry being a Critical Examination* (Cambridge, 1902) p. 214 and others.

[8]Clark, *op. cit.* p. 62.

[9]*Ibid.*, p. 60.

[10]*Ibid.*, p. 4.

[11]*Ibid.*, p. 23.

[12]*Ibid.*, p. 38.

[13]*Ibid.*, p. 4.

[14]*Ibid.*, p. 11.

[15]Address of Grand Master Samuel W. G. Clark, 50th Annual Communication of the Prince Hall Grand Lodge of Ohio, 1899.

[16]Address of Grand Master Samuel W. G. Clark, August 22nd, 1888, M. W. Prince Hall Grand Lodge of Ohio.

THE PHYLAXIS

AUGUST 1974

Volume I   Number 3

A SOCIETY FOR PRINCE HALL FREEMASONS WHO SEEK MORE LIGHT AND WHO HAVE LIGHT TO IMPART

THE PHYLAXIS
Published at Jefferson City, Mo., by
THE PHYLAXIS SOCIETY

Arthur H. Frederick M.P.S. .... Editor
Box 43, Roxbury, Massachusetts 02119

OFFICERS

Joseph A. Walkes, Jr, M.P.S. .... President
P. O. Box 3151, Ft. Leavenworth, Kansas 66027

Herbert Dailey, M.P.S. .... First Vice President
1616 South Cedar, Tacoma, Washington 98405

Zellus Bailey, M.P.S. .... Second Vice President
7039 Dover Court, St. Louis, Missouri 63130

James E. Herndon, M.P.S. .... Executive Secretary
1574 Ivanhoe Street, Denver, Colorado 80220

Alonzo D. Foote, Sr., M.P.S. .... Treasurer
P.O. Box 99601, Tacoma, Washington 98499

SUBSCRIPTION RATE: FOR ONE YEAR, $5.00

The Phylaxis Magazine is the official publication of the Phylaxis Society. Any article appearing in this publication expresses only the opinion of the writer, and does not become the official pronouncement of the Phylaxis Society. No advertising of any form is solicited or accepted. All communication relative to the magazine should be addressed to the Editor. Inquiries relative to membership must be addressed to the Executive Secretary. Membership is by invitation and recommendation only. The joining fee is $3.00. Dues are $5.00 per year in advance, which amount includes a subscription to the "Phylaxis" magazine for one year.

All rights reserved. No part of this work may be reproduced or transmitted in any form or by any means, electrical or mechanical, or retrival system, without written permission from the publisher.

INDEX

Our Responsibility 22
Profile of a Non-Prince Hall Masonic
   Organization 23
Northwest Phylaxis Society Chapter,
   Tacoma-Seattle Washington 24
O'Misawa Lodge #54 25
Notice to Grand Master, Greetings 26
Iowa Masonic Library 27
Prince Hall Masonry and the Civil War 28

22

EDITORIAL

The Phylaxis Society is made up of Prince Hall Freemasons who seek more light and who have light to impart. Membership in the Society is by application.

The Phylaxis Magazine is the official publication of the Phylaxis Society.

Any member of the Prince Hall family, or other writers may send an article or manuscript to the Editor for publication in the magazine. The subject must be in good Masonic taste and be in the rules of journalistic good conduct.

Letters to the Editor are welcomed and may criticize, in a positive way, any article that is in the magazine.

Material from local Lodges, Auxiliaries, Grand Lodges, or any other Masonic Body are welcome.

It has been said many times and many ways before but here it is again, "We may not agree with what you say but we respect your right of free speech."

"OUR RESPONSIBILITY AS PRINCE HALL MASONS"

BY
IRA S. HOLDER, SR., M.P.S.
(New York)

Throughout the length and breadth of the United States, there are literally hundreds of Non-Prince Hall Grand and Subordinate Lodges whose combined membership runs into thousands of unsuspecting young men who unwittingly find themselves caught like flies in a spider's web. Seldom do any of these unfortunate victims (for such they are) realize their predicament until they find themselves within the ranks of these various groups, through no fault of theirs other than that of not knowing which Masonic Fraternity to chose.

I must point out, that after many of these unsuspecting victims realize their big mistake, not only do they become dissolutioned and lose all interest in the masonic order, but seldom, if ever, do they try to correct their grave mistake by once more seeking membership in Regular Masonic Lodges; and therefore must be considered lost to the Prince Hall Fraternity.

I do not have at my finger tips, nor do I know if any Research has ever been made as to the overall membership of these irregular groups scattered over the United States. If such statistics are not available, every effort should be made to acquire this important information, which I am sure will stagger our wildest imagination.

In view of this tragic situation, for such it is, it becomes the direct responsibility of the Prince Hall Fraternity as a whole, to institute an Educational and Publicity Program through its Grand and Subordinate Lodges. First, by starting a comprehensive Program aimed at informing the Craft at large, not only on Ritualistic Work, which is necessary, but on knowing something of their origin as Prince Hall Masons; so that in their contact with members of these Non-Prince Hall groups, they may be able to defend themselves against the opposition which many of these groups are amply prepared to present, so as to discredit Prince Hall Masonry. It is alarming to find the number of Prince Hall Masons, who can recite the Ritual from cover to cover, yet are totally ignorant of the historical background of our Order. This situation must be corrected through an Educational approach. Outline some of the many court cases won by several of the Prince Hall Grand Lodges against Non-Prince Hall groups; along with letting the public at large know of the rich heritage of the Prince Hall Fraternity. Let them know something about the noble and honorable efforts of Prince Hall — our Patron Saint; not only in the Masonic field, but of his efforts in trying to gain the freedom of many slaves during the Revolutionary War by seeking to have the State of Massachusetts permit them to serve in the Revolutionary Army, and thus gain their freedom. Tell them, how although encountering overwhelming odds at times, this dedicated leader continued to fight for what he thought was just and right. This great man, for such he was, was not only a great Masonic Leader, but an avid supporter of human dignity; whose main concern was to gain and preserve the Civil Rights of every individual. Tell the public, let them know everything about our precious Charter which was issued to Prince Hall by the Grand Lodge of England on September 29, 1784. Tell them that this precious document is now in safe keeping in one of the vaults of a bank in Boston, Mass. Tell them of the fitting memorial to this great Masonic Leader — our Patron Saint, Prince Hall, erected after his passing in 1808, where he was laid to rest in Cobbs Hill Cemetery; where many of his followers travel from all parts of the world to pay homage to this outstanding leader.

Yes, my Brothers, we have quite a lot to tell them about Prince Hall Masonry. I know — because I was once one of those unsuspecting victims, who fell into the net; not once, but twice during a period of 31 yrs. Today, after only 15 years in the Prince Hall Family, I can truthfully say: I HAVE SEEN THE LIGHT.

PROFILE OF A NON-PRINCE HALL MASONIC ORGANIZATION
by Zellus Bailey M.P.S. (Missouri)
Continued From Issue #2

WHERE DO THEY GET THEIR AUTHORITY TO WORK THE ANCIENT AND ACCEPTED SCOTTISH RITE?

This Scottish Rite body get their authority from four directions or in four ways. First by their Masonic lineage, heritage and historical connections; secondly be charter rights; thirdly, by the general rules and regulations of the order; and finally, by their act of incorporation.

Their Masonic lineage, heritage and masonic connections date back to Mother Kilwinning Lodge No. 0 of Scotland, established in the little town of Kilwinning more than nine hundred years ago. Mother Kilwinning Lodge No. 0 of Scotland established the mother lodge of Marseilles, France, about the year 1400. The Mother Lodge of France granted a provisional charter to Polar Star Lodge in New Orleans in 1794. Later in 1804 the Grand Orient of France granted a charter to Polar Star Lodge.

In 1812 a treaty of Masonic Union, Alliance, and Confederation was concluded in Paris, France by representatives of the Supreme Councils of New York, France, the Empire of Brazil, and Brussels creating the United Supreme Council for the Western Hemisphere sitting in New York City. The official representatives for the Supreme Council of New York were the Count St. Laurent, and Marquis Lafayette.

The United Supreme Council for the Western Hemisphere granted a charter for the establishment of a Grand Consistory in New Orleans in 1813.

Their charter rights stem from the original charter granted by the Mother Lodge at Marseilles, France to Polar Star Lodge in New Orleans in 1794, and later in 1804 from the charter granted the same Lodge by the Grand Orient of France, and from the charter from the United Supreme Council of the Western Hemisphere for the Grand Consistory in New Orleans.

The General Regulations of the order provide for the establishment of a supreme Council in any country, state, nation, or territory where no such authority exist. Three Inspector Generals regularly created thirty-third degree Masons may come together and organize a Supreme Council for the government of the Rite.

The Supreme Council for the United States of America became the Supreme Council of Louisiana by an act of incorporation dated March 16, 1870, and granted at an extra session of the Legislature of Louisiana.

Their Masonic lineage, heritage, and historical connections, charter rights, the provisions of the General Regulation of the order for the organization of a supreme council, and act of incorporation, give them their regularity, constitutionality, and genuineness.[3]

[1]Souvenir Journal, The anniversary of our Scottish Rite Bodies, New York, 1954.

[2]*The Perfect Ashlar,* (Supreme Council of Louisiana, A.A.S.R. F.M.) New Orleans, Louisiana, 1954, P.1.

[3]*The Perfect Ashlar,* (Supreme Council of Louisiana, A.A.S.R.F.M.) New Orleans, Louisiana, 1954. P.3.

1. ibid, P.1
2. ibid, P.1
3. ibid, P.1

BIBLIOGRAPHY

The Perfect Ashlar, Supreme Council of Louisiana, A.A.S.R.F.M., New Orleans, Louisiana, 1954.

Souvenir Journal, The Anniversary of our Scottish Rite Bodies in New York, 1954.

Regular, Irregular and Clandestine Grand Lodges, Ray V. Denslow, P.G.M., The Masonic Service Association, Washington 1, D.C., February 23, 1956.

The Invasion of our Jurisdiction, Grand Master Fred W. Dabney, Sixteenth Annual Communication M. W. Prince Hall Grand Lodge of Missouri, Kansas City, Missouri 1926.

NORTHWEST PHYLAXIS SOCIETY CHAPTER, TACOMA-SEATTLE WASHINGTON

The Northwest Phylaxis Society Chapter members have been very busy in the area for the past three months. During that time three briefing was given Prince Hall Masons of Tacoma and Seattle. The subject "Prince Hall and the Military." The briefing was prepared by the President Bro Joseph A. Walkes Jr., of Kansas along with a tape.

The first briefing was given in Tacoma, Washington at the Masonic Hall, the next one was at the Grand Lodge Northwest Conference held at the Sea-Tac Motor Inn in Seattle. On the 22nd of March the members travel to Seattle for a briefing at the Masonic Hall of that city. Each of these briefing was very well accepted and caused many questions from those present.

At these meetings we stated that we want to give some information that will cause each of them to want to know more. To inform them from whence they came and be proud of it. To be better informed so that he may talk to any NON-PRINCE HALL Mason and may be the cause or reason that he will become a Prince Hall Mason. Telling the truth and facts about Prince Hall Masons and enlighting its members is our GOAL.

The Northwest Phylaxis Society Chapter extends to each of the other area Chapters greeting and much success in your undertaking. For the success of the National Chapter depends on the membership. Moreso upon the officers and their willingness to serve and support the goals. It is ones heart that must be happy and not the pocket. The returns are the wages of a mason and not the amount of funds he has spent. We must always remember that within our masonic ties, Lodges — Consistory — OES Chapter and any other organization we are to give not only of our time but our funds also. Therefore when we became a member we wanted to and in turn we say we have the time and funds to do what is needed to be done on our part. It is not what the organization can do for you. WHAT CAN YOU DO FOR THE ORGANIZATION?

THINK

Inter-happiness — I have done the most that I can — I am pleased to be a part — Look at what we have done — I am a member of — I am happy to have my name on the rolls — I know where for I was there — I do support the goals.

ROSTER
Northwest Phylaxis Society Chapter

1. Troy Graham
2. Jimmy Robinson
3. Fidencio A. Perez
4. Armoid Apple
5. Roosevelt Shorter
6. Robert Hughes
7. Irvin Hawkins
8. John W. Porter
9. Aaron D. Ruth

Herbert Dailey
1st Vice President

Alonzo D. Foote, Sr.
Treasurer

O'MISAWA CRAFT

Some of the Officers and Members of O'Misawa Lodge #54, 6th District, Misawa, Japan. Seated left to right are: Bro. A. L. Sherman, S.W.; Bro. D. Roland, Worshipful Master; Bro. E. Coleman, J.W. Standing second row: Bro. I. Harris, S.D.; Bro. H. Haugerbrook, J.S.; Bro. C. Rowe, TY; Bro. H. Rembert; Bro. O. Moore, P.M.; Bro. R. Walker Secretary; and Bro. R. Smith, J.D. Back row: Bro. M. Knight, Chaplin; Bro. F. Denkins, Marshall; and Bro. J. Edmond, Asst. Secretary.

O'MISAWA LODGE #54
O'MISAWA, JAPAN

Gerald Kenneth Holloway, a male of Japanese and Negroid descent, was born on January 12, 1958, to Toshiko (Kudo) Holloway and Staff Sergeant Robert Roy Holloway at Chitose, Japan. Upon Sergeant Holloway's return to the United States in 1961, his wife and son did not accompany him. The mother being unable to support herself and the child later took him to a relative. From there he was placed in a Catholic Orphanage after all attempts to contact the mother and father failed.

The Holloway Case, as it became known, was brought to the attention of O'Misawa Lodge #54 in O'Misawa, Japan, in April 1971, through Past Master Ollie Moore. In June 1971 at a regular communication of the Lodge the Holloway Case was introduced to the members of the Craft. The Craft voted to accept the case as a major project of the Lodge. Since then the Lodge, each year, has contributed to the welfare and education of Gerald Kenneth Holloway.

GERALD KENNETH HOLLOWAY
A major project of the Lodge, is helping others to help themselves.

CHARITABLE WORK APPRECIATED

Sisters of St. Mary's Orphanage in Amori, Japan, present a plaque to the Brothers of O'Misawa Lodge #54 in appreciation for their support on behalf of Gerald Kenneth Holloway (standing between the Sisters). Receiving the plaque for the Lodge is Past Master Ollie Moore who also received personal recognition for his individual efforts.

25

WELCOME TO NEW MEMBERS

Oscar Roberts, Imperial Deputy Marshall, A.E.A.O.N.M.S. (PHA), 326 Dakots St., Leavenworth, Kansas 66048

Aaron D. Ruth, North-West Phylaxis Chapter, 1810 Madrona Drive, Seattle, Washington 98122

John Wilbert Porter, North-West Phylaxis Chapter, 3010 S. W. Kenny, Seattle, Washington 98126

Charles A. Method, Editor, The Lamp, M.W.P.H.G.L. of Ohio, 415 Merryhill Dr., Columbus, Ohio 43219

Robert L. Hughes, North-West Phylaxis Chapter, 4406 S. 7th St., Tacoma, Washington 98405

George L. Harris, North-West Phylaxis Chapter, 5929 A. Ohio Ave., Fort Lewis, Washington 98433

Ira S. Holder, Sr., Grand Historian Emeritus, M.W.P.H.G.L. of N.Y., Co-Author of the Complete History of Widow's Son Lodge No. 11, 21st St. James Place, Brooklyn, New York 11205

Jno. G. Lewis, Jr., Grand Master, Louisiana, Soverign Grand Commander, A.A.S.R. Southern Jurisdiction, USA PHA, Box 2974, Baton Rouge, Louisiana 70807

William M. Freeman, C.C.F.C., M.W.P.H.G.L. of Louisiana, 1755 79th Ave., Baton Rouge, Louisiana 70807

Eugene Hendrix, North-West Phylaxis Chapter, 6434-F Cooper Drive, Old Hilside, Ft. Lewis, Wash. 98433

Melvin Errons, North-West Phylaxis Chapter, 8614 Beachwood, Fort Lewis, Wash. 98433

Raymond A. Mark I, Grand Historian, M.W.P.H.G.L. of N.Y., 801-19 Tilden St., Bronx, N.Y. 10467

Albert J. Briscoe, Sr., Recorder, Fezzan Temple No. 26, 1639 Sheridan Ave. North, Minneapolis, Minnesota 55411

Charles H. Wesley, Grand Prior, A. & A.S.R., Southern Jurisdiction, Author, History of the M.W. Prince Hall Grand Lodge of Ohio, 1824 Taylor St., N.W., Washington, D.C. 20011

Charles D. Stubblefield, North-West Phylaxis Chapter, 5002 So. Cushman, Tacoma, Washington 98405

M.W. Patrick E. Knight, Grand Master Grand Lodge of Massachusetts, 24 Washington St., Boston, Massachusetts

NOTICE TO GRAND MASTER, GREETINGS:

We need your assistance in the following ways:

1. Please mail to us any publications of your Grand Lodge.

2. Please send us a list of names and addresses of your Grand Lodge officers and all Lodges within your Jurisdiction.

3. Appoint, if possible, a person who would send us news of your Jurisdiction.

4. Very shortly we will mail you some brochures of the Society requesting subscriptions. Please send them to your Lodges and membership urging their support.

5. If within your Grand Lodge or your Jurisdiction there are individuals interested in the Society to encourage membership which is $8.50 and should be mailed to the Executive Secretary.

6. During our present incipient stages we would appreciate any direct donations in lieu of subscriptions or memberships.

7. If you have any questions about the Society, please ask them without any hesitation or mental reservation.

Fraternally yours,
Arthur H. Frederick, M.P.S.
Editor, Phylaxis Magazine

MEMBERS OF NORTHWEST PHYLAXIS SOCIETY CHAPTER
Tacoma — Seattle

Herbert Dailey, James Faircloth, Fidencio A. Perez, Troy Graham, Arnold Apple, George Harris and Alonzo Foote, Sr.

Not Shown
Robert L. Hughes, Irvin Hawkins, John W. Porter, Aaron D. Ruth, Jimmy Robinson, Roosevelt Shorter and Eugene Hendrix.

THE IOWA MASONIC LIBRARY

BY
JERRY MARSENGILL
Guest Writer

(EDITOR'S NOTE: Jerry Marsengill is a well known Caucasian Masonic Writer from the Grand Lodge of Iowa A.F. & A.M., a member of Research Lodge No. 2, and author of *"Negro Masonry in Iowa."* The Phylaxis Society invited Bro Marsengill to write an article on the Masonic Library in Cedar Rapids, so the Prince Hall Family would learn of its existence and will freely use its facilities.)

First, Biggest,
and
Best in the World

There is an old adage, but one which is always true, that any institution is but the lengthened shadow of one man. In the case of the Iowa Masonic Library, the one man was our first Grand Secretary, Theodore Sutton Parvin. Parvin was the founder, not only of the Iowa Masonic Library but of the State Library and the Library of the University of Iowa. Parvin was a lifelong collector of books, but unlike many who had the same hobby, he didn't collect books merely for his own use but to make them available to others.

Nest to acquiring good friends, the best acquisition is that of good books.

The Iowa Masonic Library was founded with one book which the Grand Secretary contributed. This one volume was presented to him by a young lady in Muscatine. While Parvin was courting her, he became engrossed in the book and, seeing that his interest was elsewhere, she presented him the book and showed him the door all in the same motion.

At the Grand Lodge session in 1845, the Grand Master, Oliver Cock, stated in his address: "It has been suggested to me that if a certain amount of the funds of the Grand Lodge should be set apart each year, for the purpose of procuring books for the Grand Lodge, a very respectable Masonic Library might be thus collected without the amount expended being felt by the Grand Lodge. This seems to me a subject worthy of your consideration."

Although no record was made of who made the suggestion, we find in 1850, as if we could not have guessed, that the recommendation came from the Grand Secretary, T. S. Parvin.

In conformity with a resolution made at the time, the Grand Master appointed a committee for three to whom were referred the idea of forming a library. When the committee reported at a later time, they were in favor of forming a library but did not think that the funds of the Grand Lodge would permit extensive purchases. However, they did suggest that a small appropriation should be made and suggested an appropriation of $5.00 (five dollars) for the purchase of books.

Library Erected in 1884.

When the Grand Secretary reported back to the Grand Lodge the next year he stated that he had purchased a "Book of Constitutions" for two dollars a copy of the Trestle Board for fifty cents, a book of Masonic Melodies for fifty cents and a subscription to the Freemason's magazine for two dollars. At this communication the committee reported and the Grand Lodge voted him ten dollars ($10.00) for the ensuing year. This state of affairs continued for some five years and each year Parvin bought more and more material and the need for housing the library was becoming apparant. For the first forty years the library was in charge of Parvin, first at Iowa City, then at Davenport, and then again at Iowa City where it remained until 1884 when the building to house the library was completed. The Masonic Library remained from 1884 until 1944 in the building which Parvin saw erected at Cedar Rapids.

For a number of years problems had plagued the Grand Lodge due to the library builing. In 1944, the Centennial year of the Grand Lodge, there was appropriated the sum of $10,000.00 for repairs and improvements of the building and the grounds. This amount, along with $20,000.00 in surplus funds, was invested in securities for a Library improvement fund. In 1946, Grand Master William L. Perkins suggested the erection of a new building and that $10 of each initiation fee be allocated to a Grand Lodge Building Fund. Since this amount had previously been alloted to the Grand Charity Fund, this caused some problems. Finally it was decided to split the fee with $5.00 going the the Charity Fund and $5.00 to the Building Fund. To complete the funding of the new building the Grand Lodge voted in 1953 that each Iowa member should contribute $1.00 per year to the fund. The new building cost just over $1,000,000.00. The corner stone was laid on October 10, 1953, with Grand Master Charles B. Hayes presiding.

The building, while beautiful, while important to Iowa Masonry, since it contains all of our Grand Lodge offices, pales in importance when we consider what is contained in it. The official estimate was, for a long time, 60,000 volumes but more recent estimates place the contents of the library at 100,000 books. In Iowa we think a library exists only to be used. Except for rare and costly volumes which would be impossible to replace and single volumes which can be purchased only in complete sets, nearly every book in our library can be borrowed for a period of three weeks. We support a clipping bureau which consists of thousands of clippings taken from all types of Masonic magazines and periodicals. These items are loaned on request and afford a great deal of information, much of which has never been published in book form.

Proceedings of most of the research societies and lodges are available as are Proceedings of most of the Grand Lodges, and of the York and Scottish Rite bodies and the Eastern Star, etc. The library is deficient in their collection of Prince Hall proceedings but this is being remedied as quickly as proceedings are available.

The Iowa Masonic Library has never set any restrictive lending policy wherein books are loaned only to Masons or to certain individuals. Anyone, whether Mason or not, whether Iowan or not, may borrow books from our library. Some of these Masonic libraries, whose entire book collection consists of two books (one of them already colored) set policies wherein a man's entire pedigree must be examined before he is allowed to use their facilities. In our Iowa Masonic Library the students of Mount Mercy College, a Cedar Rapids Catholic School, use the Masonic Library exclusively for historical research and many favorable comments have been received from both students and faculty. When the Prince Hall Grand Lodge of Iowa rewrote its code, much of the research was done through the facilities of the Iowa Masonic Library.

An institution is but the lengthened shadow of one man, and we are thankful that our first Grand Secretary cast a long one.

THEODORE SUTTON PARVIN
Founder of the Library
Grand Secretary from 1844; Grand Secretary and Librarian 1845 to 1851, and again from 1853 until his death in 1901.

PRINCE HALL MASONRY AND THE CIVIL WAR
JOSEPH A. WALKES, JR., M.P.S.
(Kansas)
A MASTERPIECE

PART I

"Live and Act as Masons, that we may die as Masons"
Prince Hall
Charge to African Lodge
June 24, 1797

In the beginning of the Civil War, it was made quite clear, that President Lincoln was very reluctant to the use of Negroes in the armed services, and that the War Department had no intentions of using Negroes as soldiers.[1]

But by the close of 1862, the military situation was very discouraging. The Union troops had been beaten at Fredericksburg and Vicksburg, and Lincoln was forced to reverse his stand. He issued his long awaited Emancipation Proclamation, on January 1, 1863.[2] And even in this, Lincoln indicated little enthusiasm for the wide spread use of Negro soldiers.

The proclamation merely stated that Blacks would be used only for garrison duty and to man ships.[3]

John Albion Andrew, was inaugurated Governor of the Commonwealth of Massachusetts on the 5th of January 1861. Long a zealous abolitionist and a friend of Lewis Hayden, Grand Master of the Prince Hall Grand Lodge of Massachusetts, and who had first suggested to Andrew, that he run for governor.[4]

In 1862, events were taking shape that would play a major role in the history of the nation and also Prince Hall Masonry. Governor Andrew would visit Grand Master Hayden for a Thanksgiving Dinner at his residence at 66 Phillips Street. Grand Master Hayden was a remarkable man. The first Grand Secretary of the Prince Hall Grand Lodge of New York, a leader of the Boston Vigilance Committee, whose very house was a station of the Underground Railroad,[5] also where John Brown, during one of his last trips to Boston, stayed.[6]

At friendly get togethers such as these the Grand Master may have put the Governor in touch with many prominent Prince Hall Masons from New York, Pennsylvania, Ohio, Rhode Island and Massachusetts.[7]

In 1863, the Governor, armed with authority from the Secretary of War, began to seek Black volunteers to fill the 54th Regiment of that State, which would become the first all Black regiment from the North. Realizing that the Black population of Massachusetts was too small to fill the necessary quota, he chose, as recruiting agents, the most well known Negroes of the day. Among the Brethren of the Craft who aided this project by speeches or as agents was Martin R. Delaney.[8] Bro. Delaney was a Past Master of St. Cyprian Lodge No. 13 of Pittsburg, Pennsylvania, a District Deputy of the Western District for the National Grand Lodge,[9] and, who also had the distinction, one among many, of writing the first printed work on Negro Freemasonry, *"The Origin and Objects of Freemasonry, its Introduction into the United States and Legitimacy Among Colored Men."*[10] Delaney would later become the first Black Major in the U. S. Army, appointed to this rank by President Lincoln. A Black nationalist, author and orator. One of the most outstanding leaders in Black history. He saw the war as a means for the slaves to escape their bondage and return back to mother Africa. Delaney had little respect for the Caucasian race, and little liking for America. Unlike Grand Master Hayden, Delaney had never been a slave.

Also aiding Governor Andrew was John Mercer Langston, thought to have been a Prince Hall Mason, whose father, Charles M. Langston, was one of the organizers and first Worshipful Master of St. Marks Lodge No. 7, Columbus, Ohio,[11] both who assisted David Jenkins, who would become the 17th Grand Master of Ohio, in the Underground Railroad movement.[12]

William Schouler, Adjutant-General of Massachusetts states, "Lewis Hayden, formerly a slave in Kentucky but who had been for many years employed in the office of the Secretary of State, entered warmly into the business of recruiting colored soldiers for Massachusetts, and visited Pennsylvania and other states to advance that interest."[13]

Though no conclusions can be drawn from this statement, it opens the doors to several possibilities. Grand Master Hayden, who was traveling to these several states may have been also making official visits to these areas as a leader of the Underground Railroad, as many of the Prince Hall Lodge halls as well as the homes of its members were stations for the Underground Railroad, and was using the occassions also to recruit volunteers.

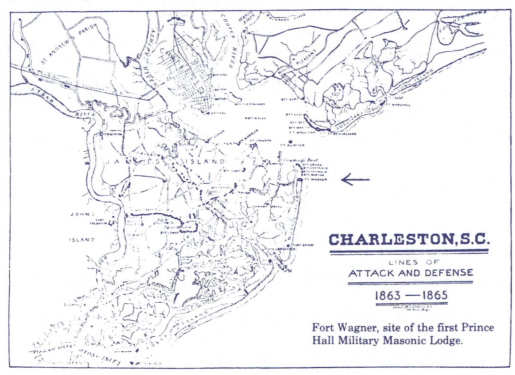

CHARLESTON, S.C.
LINES OF ATTACK AND DEFENSE
1863—1865

Fort Wagner, site of the first Prince Hall Military Masonic Lodge.

In a letter to him while he was in Pennsylvania, Governor Andrew wrote, "I do not favor recruiting for Massachusetts in that State, and I do not wish to be understood to favor it. But if, by work in Pennsylvania, you can help those fleeing from slavery through that state to reach Massachusetts, where they will be received into all the rights and advantages of our own citizens, I shall be glad. I do not want either to speculate out of the blood or courage of colored men, but I rejoice in having been instrumental in giving them a chance to vindicate their manhood, and to strike a telling blow for their own race, and the freedom of all their posterity. Every race has fought for liberty, and its own progress. The colored race will create its own future, by its own brain, hearts, and hands. If Southern slavery should fall by the crushing of the Rebellion, and colored men have no hand, and play no conspicous part, in the task, the result would leave the colored man a mere helot; the freedmen a poor, despised, subordinate body of human beings, neither strangers nor citizens, but "contrabands," who had lost their masters, but not found a country. All the prejudices, jealousies and political wishes of narrow, ignorant men and demagogues would have full force and the black man would be a helpless victim of a policy which would give him no peace short of his own banishment. The day that made a colored man a soldier of the Union, made him a power in the land. It admitted him to all the future of glory, and to all the advantages of an honorable fame, which pertained to men who belonged to the category of heroes. No one can ever deny the rights of citizenship in a country to those who have helped to create it or to save it."[14]

There has been many speculations as to the presence of a Prince Hall Military Lodge during the Civil War.[15] And in most cases the Masonic scholars and writers have been wrong in their selection of the military unit. The first Prince Hall Masonic lodge attached to a military unit was assigned to the 54th Massachusetts Volunteer Infantry.

Captain Luis F. Emilio, a Caucasian officer serving with this unit, writes, "First Sergeant Gray of Company C had received a Masonic Charter and organized a Lodge on Morris Island. The meeting place was a dry spot in the marsh near our camp, where boards were set up to shelter the members."[16] (See Illustration.) Truly an historical milestone in Prince Hall Masonic fraternalism.

Bro (LT) Peter Vogelsang
Member of the First Prince Hall
Masonic Military Lodge

There is an air of mystery concerning the early Black Masonic Lodges, due to the fact that only a handful of Black writers have written the history of these early Black units; leaving this mostly in the hands of their white officers. George Williams,[17] and Joseph T. Wilson are the exceptions to the rule, and even in their works, there is no mention of any Black Military Masonic Lodges.

THE PHYLAXIS SOCIETY SUBSCRIPTION CARD

Subscription rate: $5.00/Yr.

Mail to: James E. Herndon, MPS
Executive Secretary
1574 Ivanhoe Street
Denver, Colo. 80220

Gentlemen:

Enclosed is my subscription the the Phylaxis Magazine.

_____ Check Enclosed _____ amount payable to Phylaxis Magazine

Name: _____

Address: _____

City: _____ State: _____ Zip Code: _____

A SOCIETY FOR PRINCE HALL FREEMASONS WHO SEEK MORE LIGHT AND WHO HAVE LIGHT TO IMPART

What adds to the mystery for this writer is that all attempts to learn the identity of this Lodge and who actually authorized it, has so far escaped me. But, on these two subjects I will present my own views and reasons for it.

But during this time in the Black man's struggle for freedom from the bondage of slavery, to consider that a handful of Prince Hall Masons would be meeting and practicing the Royal Art is fantastic and should make all Prince Hall Freemasons proud to be a part of this truly great institution.

First Sergeant William H. W. Gray, 38 years old, married, occupation listed as a seaman. Enlisted at New Bedford, Massachusetts on the 14th of February 1863, and was mustered out on the 20th of August 1865, receiving $50 for his service. His military record shows that on September 22, 1863, Sergeant Gray was on furlough and received $3.50 for transportation from New York to New Bedford, Massachusetts, from the Quartermaster Office.[17]

It was during this trip, and the only furlough he had during his military service, that in all probability that Sergeant Gray picked up the Charter for this Lodge from the Prince Hall Grand Lodge of Massachusetts.

Lewis Hayden in his address before the Prince Hall Grand Lodge of Massachusetts, on December 27, 1865, St. John's Day, and three months after the unit was mustered out states, "It was the spirit of Love to God and man that caused the Grand Lodge to establish a Lodge in South Carolina, and that at Charleston, S.C., has been duly warranted and constituted under the name of "Hayden Lodge No. 8."[19]

Also in Haydens petition to the Caucasian Grand Lodge of Massachusetts in 1868, he wrote, "Hayden Lodge No. 8, Charleston, S.C., withdrawn October 1868, and with other Lodges formed a Grand Lodge for the State of South Carolina."[20] Harry A. Williamson, the noted Prince Hall Historian wrote "Sometime during the early portion of the year 1867, the New Jersey Jurisdiction established Hayden Lodge at Charleston."[21] This statement was of course incorrect. While William H. Grimshaw wrote that the Grand Lodge of Massachusetts established a Lodge in Charleston, S.C.[22]

Though there is no concrete proof, this writer believes that this Lodge either evolved from the Military Lodge attached to the 54th Massachusetts, or was in fact the same Lodge of 1863, but re-warranted in 1865 when the 54th left Charleston to be mustered out in August of 1865.

Captain Emilio in his history of the 54th records that, "In Charleston the Masonic Lodge organized on Morris Island, of which First Sergeant Gray of Company C was the Master, met in the third story of a house just across from the Citadel. Sergeants Vogelsang, Alexander Johnson, and Hemmingway were among the members, who numbered some twenty-five or thirty. It is thought that the Charter of this Lodge was surrendered ultimately to Prince Hall Lodge of Boston whence it came."[23]

This statement by the historian Emilio, an eye witness, further shed's light on this Lodge and makes it quite clear that the Lodge was functioning, and obviously quite healthy considering the war-time conditions in which it met.

Of the names mentioned by Emilio, we find that there were two Alexander Johnson's listed on the roster of the 54th. One though was only 16 years of age, so it is very doubtful that he was the one mentioned. The other was a Private from Company F. He was 34 years old, single, with an occupation listed as a laborer. His home was Elmira, New York, and he enlisted on the 8th of April 1863.[24]

Also from Company F, was First Sergeant A. F. Hemmenway. 28 years old, married, occupation listed as a barber. His home was Worcester, Massachusetts.[25]

Of the Masonic Brethren named, one of the most interesting is First Lieutenant Peter Vogelsang (see photo). A Quartermaster Officer. His date of birth was the 21st of August 1815, and his home was New York. He entered service in Brooklyn, New York, and was assigned to Company H on the 17th of April 1863, as a Quartermaster Sergeant. He was promoted to Second Lieutenant on the 28th of April, then a few weeks later, promoted to First Lieutenant on the 20th of June 1865. According to the roster, he was wounded the 16th of July 1863, at James Island, South Carolina, and died on the 4th of April 1887, in New York.[26]

CONTINUED IN NEXT ISSUE

REFERENCE TO PART I

[1] John Hope Franklin, *The Emancipation Proclamation*, (Garden City, N.Y., Doubleday & Co., Inc., 1963) p. 14.

[2] *Ibid*, p. 96.

[3] *The War Of The Rebellion, Official Records of the Union and Confederate Armies*, 128 Vols., (Washington, 1880-1902) 3 sets, I, 77, 78, 159, cited by Dudley Taylor Cornish, *The Sable Arm*. (New York, London, Toronto, Longmans, Green and Co., 1956) p. 96.

[4] Benjamin Quarles, *The Negro in the Civil War*. (Boston, Little Brown and Company, 1953) p. 101.

[5] William Loren Katz, *Eyewitness: The Negro in American History*. (New York, Toronto, London, Pitman Publishing Corporation, 1967) p. 189.

[6] Quarles, *Op Cit.*, p. 101.

[7] "If the friend of our race, the friend of humanity everywhere, whether in America, Europe or Africa, that man who knew no distinctions, save merit and virtue, and from whose inspiring counsel the widow, the orphan, the outcast, and even the slave, in his gloomiest hours found comfort and support, (we allude to John A. Andrews, who was never dressed in that now so much dishonored garb, *a white apron*) yet, whose natural love for, and recognition of, the Brotherhood of Man was prompted by the three tenets of our profession as Masons, Brotherly Love, Relief, and Truth, as shown by these memorable words: 'I know not what record of sin awaits me in the other world, but this I do know, that I never was so mean as to despise any man, because he was poor, because he was ignorant, or because he was Black' — and who as Governor, was the first, in his official capacity to recognize us as a Grand Lodge of Masons as he did in 1864." Lewis Hayden, *Grand Lodge Jurisdictional Claim or, War of Races*. (Boston, Edward S. Coombs, 1868) p. 43.

[8] Luis F. Emilio, *A History of the Fifty-Fourth Regiment of Massachusetts Volunteer Infantry 1863-1865* (Boston; The Boston Book Company, 1891) p. 12.

[9] Harry E. Davis, *A History of Freemasonry Among Negroes in America*, (Chicago, Charles T. Powner Co., 1946) p. 272.

[10] Harold Van Buren Voorhis, *Negro Masonry in the United States* (New York City, Henry Emmerson, 1940) P. x, Davis *Op Cit.*, p. 195.

[11] Charles H. Wesley, *The History of the Prince Hall Grand Lodge of Free and Accepted Masons of the State of Ohio, 1849-1960* (Wilberforce, Ohio, Central State College Press, 1961) p. 44.

[12] William Hartwell Parham and Jeremiah Arthur Brown, *An Official History of the Most Worshipful Grand Lodge of Free and Accepted Masons for the State of Ohio* (1906) p. 267.

[13] William Schouler, *A History of Massachusetts in the Civil War* (Boston, E. P. Dutton & Co., Publishers, 1868) p. 509.

[14] *Ibid*, p. 509.

[15] Voorhis, *op. cit.*, p. 42, Daivs, *op. cit.*, p. 185-186, and John Black Vrooman and Allen E. Roberts, *Sword and Trowel* (Fulton, Missouri; The Ovid Bell Press, 1964) p. 100.

[16] Emilio, *op. cit.*, p. 129.

[17] On September 29, 1884, on the occasion of the 100th Anniversary of the granting of Warrant No. 459 to African Lodge, George H. Williams presented an oration to the Prince Hall Grand Lodge of Massachusetts.

[18] Military Service Records, National Archives, Wash., D.C.

[19] Lewis Hayden, *Caste Among Masons*, (Boston, Edward S. Coombes & Company, 1866) p. 6-7.

[20] Proceedings of the Caucasian Grand Lodge of Massachusetts of September 13, 1876.

[21] Harry A. Williamson, *A Chronological History Prince Hall Masonry* (Published in the New York Ag 1934) p. 90.

[22] William H. Grimshaw, *Official History of Freemasonry Among the Colored People in North America* (New York, Macoy Publishing & Masonic Supply Co., 1903) p. 26

[23] Emilio, *op. cit.*, p. 313.

[24] *Ibid*, p. 365.

[25] *Ibid*, p. 365.

[26] *Ibid*, p. 330.

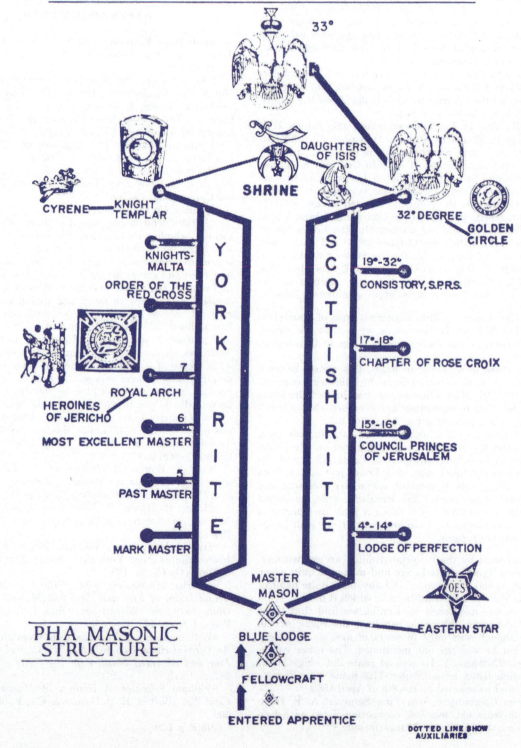

PHA MASONIC STRUCTURE

DESIGNED BY: ALLAN S. JUNIER 33°

DOTTED LINE SHOW AUXILIARIES

THE PHYLAXIS

January 1975

Volume II　　　　　Number 1

**A SOCIETY FOR PRINCE HALL
FREEMASONS WHO SEEK MORE
LIGHT AND WHO HAVE LIGHT TO
IMPART**

THE PHYLAXIS
Published at Jefferson City, Mo., by
THE PHYLAXIS SOCIETY

Arthur H. Frederick M.P.S. .... Editor
Box 43, Roxbury, Massachusetts 02119

OFFICERS

Joseph A. Walkes, Jr, M.P.S. .... President
P. O. Box 3151, Ft. Leavenworth, Kansas 66027

Herbert Dailey, M.P.S. .... First Vice President
1616 South Cedar, Tacoma, Washington 98405

Zellus Bailey, M.P.S. .... Second Vice President
7039 Dover Court, St. Louis, Missouri 63130

James E. Herndon, M.P.S. .... Executive Secretary
1574 Ivanhoe Street, Denver, Colorado 80220

Alonzo D. Foote, Sr., M.P.S. .... Treasurer
P.O. Box 99601, Tacoma, Washington 98499

SUBSCRIPTION RATE: FOR ONE YEAR, $5.00

The Phylaxis Magazine is the official publication of the Phylaxis Society. Any article appearing in this publication expresses only the opinion of the writer, and does not become the official pronouncement of the Phylaxis Society. No advertising of any form is solicited or accepted. All communication relative to the magazine should be addressed to the Editor. Inquiries relative to membership must be addressed to the Executive Secretary. Membership is by invitation and recommendation only. The joining fee is $3.00. Dues are $5.00 per year in advance, which amount includes a subscription to the "Phylaxis" magazine for one year.

All rights reserved. No part of this work may be reproduced or transmitted in any form or by any means, electrical or mechanical, or retrival system, without written permission from the publisher.

INDEX

President's Message	Page 34
Freemasonry Among Negroes and Whites	Page 35
Items of Masonic Research	Page 36
Phylaxis Society and Iowa Masonic Library	Page 38
The Northwest Chapter	Page 39
Does the Prince Hall Charter Exist?	Page 39
The Significance of Brotherhood	Page 41
Story of Prince Hall Masonry	Page 44
The Key to Co-ordinate Activity in the Phylaxis Society Program	Page 45
Prince Hall Masonry and the Civil War	Page 47

COMING MARCH 6, 1975, A SPECIAL ISSUE OF THE *PHYLAXIS* TO COMMEMORATE THE 200TH ANNIVERSARY OF THE RAISING OF OUR PATRON, PRINCE HALL.

BE SURE TO RECEIVE YOUR SPECIAL ISSUE OF THE *PHYLAXIS*. DUE OUT MARCH 6, 1975, THE 200th ANNIVERSARY OF THE RAISING OF PRINCE HALL.

A Word From The President

As we know, the United States of America is preparing to celebrate its Bi-Centennial, the 200th birthday of the founding of this country.

As Prince Hall Freemasons we must not forget the role played by our Patron Saint, Prince Hall, and those other gallant Prince Hall Masons who served the nation, the race, and the fraternity. Cyrus Forbes, George Middleton, Boston Smith, Thomas Sanderson, John Morrant to name but a few.

It is time for us to review, reproduce and display those historical documents that are a part of our Masonic heritage. The earliest recorded speech by a Black man in the United States was Prince Hall's charge to African Lodge in Charlestown, June 25, 1792. John Morrant's famous speech also to the Lodge, Prince Hall's petitions to the Massachusetts House of Representatives, and the historic Prince Hall Letter Book.

We should likewise remember the role of those Caucasians who assisted our brethren, J. B. (or John) Batt, whose tradition has it, raised Prince Hall in 1775; William Moody, Master of Brotherly Love Lodge No. 55, London, England; Captain James Scott; Dr. Belknap, the famed historian, St. Andrews Lodge; and the many others, who extended the hand of Brotherly Love and fellowship during the Colonial period.

The *Phylaxis Society* encourages each of our Prince Hall Masonic Jurisdictions to give thought to forming a Prince Hall Bi-Centennial Committee within their respective Grand Lodges and Jurisdictions, so that a proper celebration can be performed March 6th, 1975, and July 4th, 1976.

The *Phylaxis Society* will work with all Jurisdictions, in furnishing research data. In this we only ask that you write us, as we maintain one of the worlds largest Prince Hall Masonic libraries.

JOSEPH A. WALKES, JR, M.P.S.
President

Welcome to New Members

Shelly Porter, 6990th Scty Box 29206, APO S.F. 96239

Roosevelt Huggins, 1st Cav Div, A Troop 1/9 Cav' Fort Hood, Texas 74556

Milton Jacobs, 4531 Carrie, Apt B, St. Louis, Missouri 63108, Gateway Phylaxis Chapter

Randolph Boykin, 4219 College Avenue, St. Louis, Missouri 63107, Gateway Phylaxis Chapter

Lavelle Douglas, 5873 9th Street, Fort Lewis, Washington, 98433, Northwest Phylaxis Chapter

James Walker, 4909 Highland, St. Louis, Missouri 63113, Northwest Phylaxis Chapter

Irvin Hawkins, 1111 23rd Avenue South, Seattle, Washington 98144, Northwest Phylaxis Chapter

Arnold R. Apple, HHC, 1st Bde, Ft. Lewis, Washington 98433, Northwest Phylaxis Chapter

Jimmie L. Robinson, 11513 108th S. W., Tacoma, Washington, Northwest Phylaxis Chapter

Troy E. Graham, 7410 S. Montgomery Ave., Tacoma, Washington, Northwest Phylaxis Chapter

Fidencio A. Perez, HHB, 1st Bn 44th ADA, APO S.F. 96370

Frank S. Sport, 86 Timson Street, Lynn, Massachusetts 01902

Harry E. Heard, 2321 South Melrose, Tacoma, Washington 98405, Northwest Phylaxis Chapter

Esteban Castillo, 104-32-209th St., Queen Village, N.Y. 11429

John W. Eley, 2510 A, Ft. Lewis, Washington 98433, Northwest Phylaxis Chapter

Marshall L. Whiting, P.O. Box R, APO N.Y. 09141

Hiram A. Ransom, 3536 E. Roosevelt Ave., Tacoma, Washington 98404, Northwest Phylaxis Chapter

William D. Green, 1612 East 63rd St., Tacoma, Washington 98404, Northwest Phylaxis Chapter

Eddie Finney, 14576 Northlawn, Detroit, Michigan 48207

Sylvester Mitchell, 110 Glenway St., Dorchester, Mass. 02121

Luther C. Joyner, 144 Ruthven St., Roxbury, Mass. 02121

Maurice C. Davis, 5414 Swope Parkway, Kansas City, Mo. 64130

R. Irving Boone, 605 Eagle Road, Kinston, North Carolina 28501, Editor, Masonic Journal, M.W.P.H.G.L. of N.C.

William H. Baum, 27 Summer St., New London, Conn. 06320

Allan Husband, 138 Angus, La Salle, Quebec, Canada.

Freemasonry Among Negroes And White In America

A Study in Masonic Legitimacy
by HARVEY NEWTON BROWN

(EDITOR'S NOTE: Harvey Newton Brown is the Secretary of the U. S. Group of the Universal League of Freemasons, Editor of its Newsletter, and author of *Freemasonry Among Negroes and Whites in America*, A Study in Masonic Legitimacy.

The Phylaxis Society invited Bro. Brown to submit an article for publication, that would be of interest to our members.)

The action of the Grand Lodge of Massachusetts in 1947, in recognizing the legitimacy of origin of Prince Hall Masonry in that Commonwealth, caused a furor of excitement in American Masonic circles, both colored and white. Under the leadership of M. W. Bro. Thomas J. Harkins, P. G. M. (1940) of North Carolina, and the then Sovereign Grand Inspector General of the Scottish Rite (Southern Jurisdiction) in that state, later Sovereign Grand Commander, 1952-1955, a deliberate and coordinated

35

attack was made on the G. L. of Mass., resulting in the withdrawal of recognition by several grand lodges, and the threat of it by others. As a result, Massachusetts capitulated, and rescinded its 1947 action, although the "recognition" had been of a special and provisional nature only, in that it had excluded the right of intervisitation of members. At the present time (1966), the question of the recognition of P. H. Masonry is again being actively discussed in Massachusetts.

It would appear that there has been a feeling among at least some white and colored Brethren that the concept of "parallel lines," advanced in 1944, was a step forward, in that it would lead to the next step of intervisitation, and possible and eventual grand lodge "Union," thus advancing both Masonic ideals and race relations. That the entire question is the most important question in U. S. Masonry today seems indisputable, for three lodges in New York have taken in colored petitioners, as have three in Massachusetts. The G. M. of New Jersey appointed a colored Grand Chaplain from Alpha Lodge No. 116, of Newark, and as a result, the G. L. of Mississippi has withdrawn recognition from both N.J. and N.Y., and the G. L. of the State of Tamaulipas of Mexico has withdrawn recognition from Mississippi.

Bro. Harkins gave a series of lectures in N.C. Lodges after the 1947 action of Mass., and these were republished in 1962, for some reason, probably because the late Bro. George E. Bushnell, then S. G. C. of the Northern Jurisdiction had appeared in a civil suite of a P. H. Grand Lodge against a so-called "clandestine" G. L. of negroes, and there testified that in his opinion P. H. Masonry was legitimate. The republished pamphlet of lectures showed no publisher's or printer's name, nor was the work copyrighted, but it was available free of charge upon application to the Supreme Council, Southern Jurisdiction, 1733 16th St., N. W., Washington, D.C., 20009. Being a member 32°, the undersigned wrote the S. C. for a copy, and received one by mail, with an accompanying letter signed by Bro. Claude F. Young, Grand Secretary General.

Upon reading the Harkins pamphlet, it was observed immediately that it was full of all sorts of errors: historical, doctrinal and legal. Actually, it is almost incredible that the Supreme Council would sponsor the publication of such inferior work.

The writer, being firmly of the opinion that the Harkins pamphlet was a discredit to U. S. Masonry, has prepared a detailed answer. All of the contentions advanced by Bro. Harkins have been dealt with. The historical background of the Harkins pamphlet was so garbled that it was found necessary to prepare a special chapter dealing with early Masonic history in Massachusetts.

Since its circulation in the fall of 1965, the author has received some comments which may be of interest. Dr. Winthrop Wetherbee, Past Master of the Lodge of St. Andrew, Boston, wrote: ". . . your book . . . is a magnificent rebuttal of the claims made in the Harkins pamphlet, and one which is long overdue. In fact, if it had only been published in 1948 . . . it might well have had the effect of preventing the ill-advised action taken by that body (the G. L. of Massachusetts) in 1949." Professor William J. Whalen of Perdue University, the leading Roman Catholic authority on Masonry in the U. S. A. wrote: "You, demolished Bro. Harkins." Bro. Harold A. Wilson, Grand Historian of the Grand Lodge of New York, Prince Hall Affiliation, wrote: "About a month ago your book was handed to me. I find it excellent! You have my sincere congratulations. Please be advised that it is my sober and sane opinion that your book should receive Prince Hall consumption."

The book contains 101 pages, 23 of which are the two Harkins lectures in their entirety. The price is $3.00, post-paid, from the author, 2800 Tyler Avenue, El Paso, Tx. 79930.

Notes, Queries and Information on Items of Masonic Research

THE NUMBER OF LETTERS CONTAINING QUESTIONS which relate to matters of fact in Prince Hall Masonic history, biography and tradition justify their treatment in a column apart from other portions of the magazine.

Our readers and members are invited to send such material appropriate for use in this column, and especially information concerning research currently underway.

It must be noted however, that this page is for EXCHANGE of information and opinion, and does not pretend to provide the final answer to any query.

1. PRINCE HALL'S SON: Bro Randolph Boykin, M.P.S., 4219 College Avenue, St. Louis, Missouri 63107, ask's if Prince Hall had a son named Primus Hall?

Primus Hall, also known as Primus Trask, often claimed that he was the son of Prince Hall, but as far as it is known this was not true. Revolutionary War pension claim states that Primus Hall the son of PRINCE, a freeman of color and Delia, who was a servant in the family of a Mr. Walker, was born February 29, 1756, at the home of said Walker, on Beacon Street, Boston, Massachusetts. The Masonic Prince Hall was born between 1735 and 1737, which would have placed him between 20 or 22 at the time of Primus Hall's birth, certainly old enough to father a child, but the first recorded marriage of Grand Master Prince Hall was in 1763 (Grimshaw states 1784 in his "official history," page 83) but this is quite wrong. None of the wives of Prince Hall was named Delia. There is at this time, no proof uncovered that Primus Hall was Grand Master Hall's son, also the name Prince Hall was very common during that period among Blacks, and the fact that the above document states that Primus Hall's father was "a freeman of color" raised other questions and doubts, as there are documents showing that *maybe* the Masonic Prince Hall was set free in 1770. This is a debatable point, and easily verified, but it has no Masonic bearing whatsoever. Also in the document submitted to the Massachusetts Senate and House of Representatives on the 27th of Feb. 1788, and signed by Prince Hall, the signature of Primus Hall also appears, together with the names of members of African Lodge. Prince Hall was a leader of the Black community in his day, and he died broke, Primus Hall, was a Revolutionary War hero, a big business man, who died quite well off, in many cases many historians have confused the two men.

2. BI-CENTENNIAL: Research into the life and times of Grand Master Prince Hall has been launched by the United Supreme Council 33°, Ancient & Accepted Scottish Rite of Freemasonry, Southern Jurisdiction, U.S.A., Prince Hall Affiliation, John G. Lewis, Jr., M.P.S., Soverign Grand Commander, has commissioned Charles H. Wesley, M.P.S., Grand Prior to begin the task. Bro Wesley, is the author of the *History of the Prince Hall Grand Lodge of Ohio 1849 to 1960, Richard Allen, Apostle of Freedom, Negro Americans in the Civil War, From Slavery to Citizenship*, and scores of other works on Black History, a major contributor to the *Journal of Negro History* and member of *The Association for the Study of Negro Life and History, Inc.* The Phylaxis Society is working with Bro Wesley, and making research data from the Walkes Masonic library available.

3. INTERFERENCE: The Constitution and By-laws of the Phylaxis Society makes it quite clear that the "Society shall concern itself with nothing other than its purposes, and particularly shall make not so much as a suggestion concerning the legislative and ritualistic affairs of any Masonic body.

4. GRIMSHAW: Numerous readers have requested information on P.G.M. William Henry Grimshaw, and where they could purchase a copy of his *Official History of Freemasonry Among The Colored People In North America*, which is now out of print. A copy can be purchased from Books For Libraries, 1 Dupoint St., Plainview, New York 11803. Order number is LC#74-157370 ISBN 8808-6, the cost is $16.50. Bro. Grimshaw was a member of Social Lodge No. 1, in Washington, D.C., 1874 to 75, and Grand Master of that Prince Hall Jurisdiction in 1907. Recent research into the life of Prince Hall does not support the things that Grimshaw wrote, and this book must be viewed in that light.

5. PRINCE HALL MASONIC POSTAGE STAMP. Bro. Ira S. Holder Sr., M.P.S., Grand Historian Emeritus of the New York Jurisdiction informs us that the Bi-Centennial Celebration Committee are planning to have a 10 cent Postage Stamp issued with a likeness of Grand Master Prince Hall. Postage stamps were issued in connection with the Centennial celebration of the Celestial-Hiram Prince Hall Masonic Lodge in 1926. The stamps were used on first class mail for a limited period with the permission of the U.S. Government. The New York Jurisdiction expect to begin the celebration from October 1974 leading up to March 6, 1975. What is your jurisdiction doing?

6. PRIZES AND AWARDS FOR WRITING AND PAINTING. A motion picture producer and publisher of Masonic books are searching for articles and paintings suitable for a script for a youth oriented motion picture, to show young people that Freemasonry's teachings have what they are seeking.

What does Freemasonry offer the youth of today? Are its principles, teachings, and precepts what they are seeking? If you believe the answer is "Yes" — and can put it into dramatic form — you may win an award of from $10 to $100. If your writing is published in any form, the award will be duplicated, and your name will appear as author.

Articles should be about 2,500 words in length, typewritten, and double spaced. Those submitted become the property of Imagination Unlimited! A panel of judges from the staff of

Macoy Publishing and Masonic Supply Company and the Masonic Service Association will determine the awards. The contest will close June 30, 1975.

Also needed are original paintings of historical, Masonic, or religious subjects that can be used in books and documentary films. If suitable for publication, they will be purchased for $5 to $25 and will be eligible for an additional award of up to $100. These may be used immediately in a documentary film being produced for The Masonic Service Association.

Send all entries, or inquiries, to: Imagination Unlimited! Drawer 70-A, Highland Springs, Va. 23075. Attention: Allen E. Roberts.

7. NEW AWARDS. We note with some pride in the latest issue of *The Journal of Negro History* (Vol. LIX, No. 4, Oct 74) that the Association for the Study of Negro Life and History, Inc. has established *The Charles H. Wesley Award* of $100 annually for the best article published in the *Journal* on African History. Bro. Wesley is a member of the Phylaxis Society and the author of *The History of the Prince Hall Grand Lodge of the State of Ohio 1849-1960, Richard Allen, Apostle of Freedom,* AND Co-author of *Negro Americans in the Civil War, from slavery to Citizenship,* and many fine articles. Many of the lives that Bro. Wesley writes about, were like Richard Allen, a Prince Hall Mason.

The Phylaxis Society and the Iowa Masonic Library

One of the areas, that has been sadly neglected by the Prince Hall Fraternity, is its literature and its history.

The world's largest collection of Masonic material representing Prince Hall Masonry is the Harry Albro Williamson Masonic Collection housed in the New York Public Library, West 135th Street Branch, also several individual Grand Lodges maintain libraries for their jurisdictions use, New York and Ohio for example, but as far as we can tell these libraries are small and insignificant, in so far as serving the needs of the entire Prince Hall fraternity.

The world's largest Masonic library is located at Cedar Rapids, Iowa, and is owned and operated by that States Caucasian Grand Lodge.

The *Phylaxis Society* has an excellent working relationship with the library and has even featured an article concerning its history and the services that it renders to the entire Craft, in the last issue of the *Phylaxis* magazine.

38

A MASON AND A MAN

My Brother, Masonry means much more
    Than the wearing of a pin
Or carrying a paid up dues receipt
    So the Lodge will let you in

You may wear an emblem on your coat
    From your finger flash a ring
But if you're not sincere at heart
    This doesn't mean a thing

It's merely an outward sign to show
    The world that you belong
To this fraternal Brotherhood
    That teaches right from wrong

What really counts lies buried deep
    Within the human breast
Til Masonic teachings brings it out
    And puts it to the test

If you can practice out of Lodge
    The things you learn within
Be just and upright to yourself
    And to your fellowman

Console a brother when he's sick
    Or assist him when in need
Without a thought of personal gain
    for any act or deed

Walk and act in such a way
    That the world without can see
That none but the best
    can meet the test
Laid down by Masonry

Always live up to your trust
    And do the best you can
Then you can proudly tell the world
    You're a Mason and a Man

ROBERT L. HUGHES
President
The Northwest Chapter of the
    Phylaxis Society
Tacoma-Seattle, Washington

We have also encouraged the entire Prince Hall fraternity to utilize its facilities, while on the other hand, we have urged the library to broaden its collection on Prince Hall Masonry, by diligently seeking and procuring more material on our literature and history, i.e., items written by the Prince Hall Mason himself.

Towards this goal, we have urged all Prince Hall Grand Lodges that publish official organs, Grand Lodge Proceedings, histories and general masonic literature to send copies to this library where it can be permanently stored and preserved, and available for those who desire to research the labors of our fraternity.

A good example of this recently, was the Prince Hall Grand Lodge of Missouri which had been unsuccessfully searching more than thirty years for its Grand Lodge Proceedings, covering the period from 1865 to 1900, finally discovered copies on file at this library, and with the help of the staff at the library, these proceedings are in the hands of the Prince Hall Grand Lodge.

The *Phylaxis Society* therefore continues to stress not only the need for Prince Hall Masonic input to the Iowa Masonic library but the Harry Williamson Collection as well.

The Northwest Chapter of the Phylaxis Society

by
HARRY E. HEARD

Three of the greatest tools you have in masonry are the Holy Bible, Square and Compass. If you are troubled and do not know which way to turn, you can always turn to the Bible and seek comfort. As a young mason or an old mason, your Bible is where you will find your answer. Masonically, the Bible is one of the furnishings of our lodge which points out the past that leads to happiness, and of course, dedicated to GOD. It is also the rule and guide of Faith.

The Square is an indispensable tool used by carpenters in the building of houses, bridges, temples and etc. Masonically, we are reminded by the Square to square our action before GOD and MAN and most especially to our masonic brothers. It is also one of the furnishings of our lodge which teaches us to regulate our conduct by the principles of Morality and Virtue and is dedicated to the Master.

A good craftsman is at a loss without his COMPASS. For it is employed to transfer certain measurements from one place to another or utilized to scribe arcs and circles. A good mason becomes lost if he overlooks what his compass teaches him masonically. We should control our passion at all times and be ready to render a helping hand to another brother mason if needed to keep him within due bounds. The Compass is one of the furnishings of the lodge and teaches us to limit our desires in every station and is dedicated to the craft.

Does the "Prince Hall" Masonic Charter Exist?

by
HAROLD V. B. VOORHIS
Guest Writer

This article by Harold Van Buren Voorhis, Fellow of the American Lodge of Research F & A.M., and originally published in the TRANSACTIONS of the Lodge — Volume I - Number 1 (July 1930 - February 1932).

(PHYLAXIS NOTE: Bro. Voorhis is a Caucasian Masonic Scholar known throughout the world Masonic community. He is a member of numerous Lodges of Research, including Quatuor Coronati Lodge No. 2076, London, England; American Lodge of Research, New York, New York, of which he is a Past Master; North Carolina Lodge of Research No. 666, the Philalethes Society of which he is a Fellow, and the exclusive organization for Masonic writers, The Society of Blue Friars, of which he is Grand Abbott. His Masonic affiliation, awards, and books would take up an entire page.

In 1940 he published *Negro Masonry in the United States*. He later withdrew his book from circulation. Asked why by the *PHYLAXIS*, Bro. Voorhis wrote that he based his book on the writings of Grimshaw, which he had taken for being *OFFICIAL*, but new research, disclosed that many of the statements published by Grimshaw were found to be without fact, and with new facts unearthed, he decided that it would be best to withdraw the book.

He also published *Our Colored Brethren, The Story of Alpha Lodge of New Jersey*. (Alpha No. 116 F & A.M. a Black lodge, chartered by the Caucasian Grand Lodge of New Jersey, in which Bro. Voorhis is an Honorary Member.

39

The following were on the Prince Hall Committee when Bro. Voorhis saw the Charter: Dr. Alfred P. Russell, Jr., who made the arrangements; William Lloyd Marshall of Newtonville, Mass.; and Benjamin C. Hazel, P.G.M. and Grand Secretary, of Cambridge, Mass.

At the request of Bro. Voorhis certain deletions and additions have been made from the original article to bring it up to date.

There is no more certain method to start a discussion among Masonic students than to bring up the question used in the title of this article. For ten years I have heard this topic commented upon publicly and privately, orally and in writing, but we have gotten further and further away from the answer. My conclusion reached as a result of these talks, was that no one positively knew. At least, no one ever gave an answer worthy of the name. Of opinions there have been and are many, but like the answers they were of no value in solving the question.

In October 1931, I resolved to determine, if physically possible, if the Charter is in existence and thus settle the matter. I got in touch with persons whom I believed could properly direct my quest, and while at Washington, D.C., received a letter of introduction to a colored dentist in Boston, Massachusetts. Upon my arrival in Boston I was assured that the following day I might meet the Chairman on Archives of the Prince Hall Grand Lodge.

Such was my privilege, and after a pleasing and lengthy conversation arrangements were completed to meet with the Committee at the vault of one of Boston's oldest Trust Companies.

An oaken chest, about 4x2x2 feet, labeled "Prince Hall Grand Lodge" was produced. The seals were examined and broken and the tapes removed.

The entire contents were taken from the chest and I examined the original minutes and records of "African" and "Prince Hall" Lodge and Grand Lodge, all in perfect order and excellent condition.

I was then granted the very unusual privilege of holding and examining the original Charter of "African Lodge," listed on the roll of the Grand Lodge of England as No. 459 (see Freemason's Calendar for 1785 listing 1874 Lodges. "No. 459, Boston, New England," etc., as given on page 96 in "Handy Book to the Lists of Lodges" by John Lane.

The Charter is kept in a round metal tube-container. It is on heavy parchment and is folded once, then rolled in order that it may be inserted into the tube. From its long rest in this position it is difficult to spread out, but with care this was accomplished and I examined it most carefully, contents, signatures, seal and condition.

Its text has been printed in several works on Negro Masonry and may be passed by, as it is not my purpose to discuss the contents of the document in any way. Having replicas or copies of the signatures and seal said to have been thereon, I compared them with those on the warrant and found them duplicates.

The entire document is preserved with the exception of a small spot near the center of the right hand edge which had been charred in a fire that destroyed the room in which it was kept for many years, but all of the writing is perfectly legible excepting one word at this charred spot.

In short, the document is in an excellent state of preservation. Having been granted in 1784, it is close to 190 years old.

Besides, the Prince Hall Grand Lodge is in possession of an original "seal press" or "stamp" of the Grand Lodge of England. This was delivered to the Lodge at the same time as the Charter, as was the custom of the Grand Lodge of England to provide its subordinate bodies with its seal.

In all there were six persons (excluding the safe deposit vault attendants) involved in making possible my view of the document. The original man written to; the man from whom he secured the address of the writer of my letter of introduction (both of New York City); the writer of the introductory letter (a famous Negro bibliophie); the Negro dentist of Boston; and the two members of the Committee on Archives of Prince Hall Grand Lodge.

I am in possession of the names and addresses of all of these persons, as well as of the trust company in Boston, but I am purposely withholding them from print that they may not be annoyed by unauthorized or unscrupulous persons or curiosity seekers. I will, however, be glad to supply them to any member of the American Lodge of Research upon request.

The chest containing the archives of the Prince Hall Grand Lodge has not been opened for any purpose for two years as shown by the date on the seal, and I was informed that few living men of any race had ever seen its contents. Fewer had seen the Charter and that no living White man has before held it in his hands.

From my detailed examination I affirm that the question, "Does the Prince Hall Masonic Charter Exist?" had been positively answered by the simple word, "Yes."

THE SIGNIFICANCE OF BROTHERHOOD

BY: BRO. JOHN E. BRUCE

Read before and Printed under the auspices of PRINCE HALL LODGE NO. 38 F. & A.M. OF NEW YORK, May 1919

A PRINCE HALL MASONIC CLASSIC

THE PHYLAXIS SOCIETY takes pride in reproducing this Masonic Classic, and by so doing, we hope that it will find its way into Masonic libraries around the world. Prince Hall Masonry has over the years produced masterpieces of masonic literature, and this work must be classed as one.

May 23rd 1919.
NEW YORK CITY

Worshipful Master, Visiting Brothers, and Brethren of Prince Hall Lodge:

I felicitate Prince Hall Lodge upon having established a custom such as this, which makes possible the gathering together in social and fraternal alliance the brethren of the Craft, for the mutual exchange of ideas, and for such other benefits and advantages as may result from fraternal contact and converse.

It connotes that the Negro Mason is really beginning to understand that masonry means progress, and that progress cannot be made without agitation. It is on occasions such as this that the LIGHT of Masonry expands and illuminates the minds and clarifies the vision of those who under the guidance and direction of the Master builders seek more light and a more comprehensive interpretation of the Master's word. Also they will learn what Brotherhood, as defined and taught by Master Masons, means — what it signifies when used by Masons, and whether all Masons who employ it, really grasp its meaning and practice what it means and teaches. Words are nothing unless supported by deeds. An Eastern Philosopher, Firdausi, says: — The man who talketh much and never acteth, will not be held in reputation by any one.

We are met tonight for the purpose of conferring upon a number of brethren fore gathered with us here, the Sublime degree of Master Masons, a ceremony as beautiful as it is instructive and sacred. These brethren who are to receive this degree will better understand its significance and importance if they have made themselves familiar with the story of David and Jonathan, as recorded in the 18 Chapter of I Samuel, 1st verse: "And it came to pass when he had made an end to speaking unto Saul. The soul of Jonathan was knit with the soul of David, and Jonathan loved him as his own soul." Herein is the essence of freemasonry the knitting together of the souls of men, in the bonds of love and brotherhood. To show how this bond when once used correctly formed grips and binds, let me cite a passage from the prophet Zechariah, XI-14; "Then I cut asunder mine other staff even Bands that I might break the brotherhood between Judah and Israel." Judah and Israel were bound so closely together in the bonds of brotherhood that they excited envy. The bands or binder which held them together were mutual respect, and confidence; faith in each other's integrity and love, such as had knitted together the souls of David and Jonathan. It is hard to break asunder such bands, when once they have been formed into a compact as a band of brothers conscious of the sacredness of that compact, the binders which hold us together are invulnerable and invisible, and cannot be broken if we remain faithful to masonic usage and tradition.

"True Masons honor all men, love the brethren; fear God, and honor the King."

St. Paul says: "But as touching brotherly love ye need not that I write you, for ye yourselves are taught of God, to love one another." This is of the essences of brotherhood, and epitomizes what Robert Burns (see note) Scotch poet, sang almost a century ago:

A man's a man, for a' that and a' that.

And Cowper's famous lines:

    Fleecy locks and dark complexion
    Cannot alter nature's claim,
    Skins may differ, but affection
    Dwells in white and black the same.

The Negro Mason and his white brothers are as wide apart as the poles on the question of brotherhood. They are like Jews and Samaritans. They do not mingle nore taste salt together.

If there is anything that Masonry is not, it is that it is not an exclusive organization form-

41

ed for the use and benefit of one particular race only.

The Master Masons, Artificers and Apprentices working under the direction of Hiran Abiff, in the construction of the great temple whose ruins may still be located, were representative of every race; they were a band of brothers who worked in sympathy and harmony with each other, and with intelligence and precision.

Negro Masons ought to be the most friendly and brotherly of men, because they belong to a race which has for centuries been more ostracized and proscribed than any other race except the Jewish race. Unlike the Jewish race the Negro's have never been driven by wholesale out of any country on account of their race, but they have suffered as much physically and mentally as their kinsmen, the Jews. The memory of the horrors of the black night, of slavery in the Americas, the West Indies, in England, and Spain, and wherever on this globe the greed, and avarice of the white man found it possible to establish slavery and impose his domineering and dominating will upon our helpless race, and the more recent and shameless lynchings and burnings of our people in this country, in the light and blaze and glory of the XXth Century, ought to be sufficient to drive us closer together as a race and bind us to each other with hooks of steel in a bond of brotherhood as strong and real and enduring as the between Damon and Phythias, or Israel and Judah, or Jonathan and David.

I once was the guest of Mr. Frederick Douglass, when I lived in Washington, D.C., and one afternoon, we together strolled over his beautiful estate at Anacostial, and talked of many things. He had only recently arrived on a leave of absence from his post in Hayti, where he was U.S. Minister. President Harrison had appointed a white man commissioner extraordinary, Admiral Gherardi, to proceed to Hayti and negotiate with that Government on the session of Mole St. Nicholas for a U.S. Coaling Station. This was clearly a matter which came within and was one of the duties of the Minister accredited to that Government, but Mr. Douglass was a man of color, not a white man, and the President, and Mr. Blaine, then Secretary of State, assuming that the blacks of Hayti would pay more attention to this white man than to the minister gave him a war vessel and a commission with power to act independent of the Minister, in efforts to bring about the granting of this concession. It was of this matter that Mr. Douglass any myself talked as we strolled through the grounds at Anacostia. And there was one thing he said about the loyalty of the Haytians which I can never forget, and it was this: Mr. Bruce, those Haytians were quick to see and to understand the significance of the slight put upon me by my own government in sending a white man to carry out its wishes in a matter of such delicacy and which came within the purview of the duties of the Minister sent there to represent it, and they resented it. Mr. Firmin, the Haytian Secretary of State, and my good friend, intimated to me that the Haytian Government would deal with the American Minister only in this matter, as it had full confidence in his ability to handle this question as ably as the white commissioner. Then said Mr. Douglass, I knew I was among my brothers, men who were bone of my bone, and flesh of my flesh. Throughout the discussion of this matter, they stood as firm as the rock of Gibraltar. The essence of brotherhood was in their blood, and they gave proof of their loyalty by standing firmly by me and the Constitution of Hayti. Oh, said he, how I wished that we American Negroes, could imbibe some of the spirit of those Haytians?

This brethren is the spirit which ought to prevail among Negro Masons, and Negroes generally. It is the spirit that actuated Moses to slay the Egyptian in the way — the spirit that actuates white men today in misunderstandings between white men and black men, to go to the relief of white men.

The white race is organized on the family principal, no matter what their religious or political differences or social status, they are one people with one aim, one purpose, one destiny. We have seen this spirit of brotherhood made manifest in the various war drives within the past three or four years when they have sounded the tocsin of alarm, called the household together and raised billions of dollars, and we, influenced by the psychology and enthusiasm of the moment, have fallen in line and done our bit as subscribers to their various funds, but only as Negroes. When the enthusiasm has waned we have found ourselves face to face with the same problems and still as we ever shall be — Negroes. We cannot fuse with this people because our destinies are not coordinate. God in his infinite wisdom, has made us Different, but the difference does not necessarily imply inferiority. The black race is the race expectant, and its future is big with promise. We should have a more general knowledge of its mighty achievements, of its vast contributions to the sum of human knowledge, of its intimate and honored relations to the son of God, to whom it once acted as host, when all

42

the other races sought his life. When Joseph and Mary journeyed into Egypt with the young child Jesus that was not an accident it was one of the purposes of the Almighty which we only can aid in unfolding and making clear by right living by loving mercy, dealing justly and walking uprightly before Him who has said through His prophet Amos: "Are ye not as the children of the Ethiopians unto me O children of Israel, saith the Lord. Have not I brought Israel out of the land of Egypt, and the Philistines from Capthor and the Syrians from Kir?" If you will notice this Verse in Amos 9-7 you will observe that the Ethiopians precede the Israelites in the order of God's love for them.

He compares his love for the Israelites to that which he held for the Ethiopians. The incentive, then to brotherhood should be obvious to every Negro Mason.

"We as black men should strive to get back to that moral and intellectual excellence of the blacks of antiquity of whom Herodotus wrote: 'The Olympian gods who made yearly pilgrimages to these blacks declared them to be the only fit company for them.'" These "blameless Ethiopians." They were brothers, these scholarly blacks, and it is they, their predecessors and successors to whom the world is today indebted for more than it is willing to admit.

As a band of brothers imbued with a sincere desire to place Negro Masonry in the forefront among fraternal organizations of the world we could if we possessed the zeal, race pride, and the spirit of the whiteman for excelling, make a drive in this city among Negro Masons and their friends for $50,000 or $100,000 for the erection of a Negro Masonic Temple that would reflect everlasting credit upon us and upon the race generally. If we are true brothers we will do something like this and thus prove our right to the title Master Masons. It is a serious reflection upon us as men and masons to be compilled to hold our meetings in a hall like this, which, clearly, is not adapted to the purposes of a masonic gathering of this character. The Solomonic idea of a Temple is shown in the magnificent structure he erected costing millions of dollars, and on the site of which, now stands the Mosque of Omar, in Jerusalem. The mighty blacks of antiquity were a proud race. The magnificence and grandeur in which they lived and with which they did things was shown in the oriental splendor of King Solomon's temple.

We Negroes can build fine churches and fine houses, now let Negro masons think seriously about building the finest masonic temple in the great city of New York — the future metropolis of the world. When we will have done this we may well lay claim to being Master Masons and master builders of the great Masonic brotherhood, the germ of which had its birth in Africa's hot sands, and all that it teaches of the Sciences, Music, Harmony, Geometry, etc., etc., where first taught and practiced by Black men like ourselves to whom the early Greeks, and Romans made annual pilgrimages and sat at the feet of the black philosophers and sages to drink in wisdom.

In conclusion permit me to add one more thought. Brotherhood in the present state of public sentiment toward the Negro, due largely to his progress materially and intellectually, is one of our essential needs, and can be made one of our strongest weapons in fighting race caste and race prejudice. We should and we must unite in the same way, and for the same objects that the dominant race is united against us, and we must do it now; without the flourish of trumpets of the blare of brass bands, or press notices. The world is now undergoing a process of reconstruction and if we are not ready when the reconstructors arrive, we shall find ourselves in the position of the five foolish Virgins who had no oil for their lamps. Let us then, oil up our intellects. Cultivate brotherly love and endeavor to make Negro Masonry the medium through which to give the right direction to the thought and policy which is to govern and control our race in the fateful years ahead of us. I thank you.

(NOTE: Bro. John E. Bruce, better known to the public as "Bruce Grit," was born in Piscataway, Maryland, February 22, 1856. In the *Colored American* of February 16, 1901, he was described as "The Prince of Negro newspaper correspondents, having for the past twenty-six years represented papers in the West Indies, Africa and various sections of America." Bro. Bruce was the author of many pamphlets dealing with the problems of his people, including *The Blood Record* a review of lynchings in the United States "by civilized white man." His papers are available in the (Bro.) Schomburg library in New York City, Folder No. 7, John E. Bruce Collection, Schomburg, Collection, New York Public Library, West 135th Street Branch.

Bro. Robert Burns was made a Mason in 1781, and by 1784 was Deputy Master of St. James' Lodge, at Tarbolton, to which he afterwards wrote "Farewell to the Brethren." He became known as the Poet-Laureate of Masonry, before his death at the age of thirty-six years.

History of Prince Hall Masonry

by
JAMES WALKER, M.P.S.
(Missouri)

(A paper read at the 64th Anniversary of Frank J. Brown Lodge #80 F & A.M. in St. Louis, Missouri.)

Prince Hall, the first Worshipful Master and Grand Master of Masons among Negroes in America, was born at Bridgetown, Barbados, British West Indies, about September 12, 1748. He was free born. His father, Thomas Prince Hall, was an Englishman, and his mother a free colored woman of French extraction.

In 1865, at the age of 17, he worked his passage on a ship to Boston, where he worked as a leather worker, the trade learned from his father. Eight years later he had acquired real estate and was qualified to vote.

On March 6, 1775, Prince Hall and fourteen other free Negroes of Boston were made Master Masons by Master J. B. Batts, in an Army Lodge of white masons attached to one of General Gage's regiments, then stationed near Boston.

This lodge granted Prince Hall and his brethren authority to meet as a lodge, to walk in processions on St. John's Day, and as a Lodge to bury their dead; but they could not confer degrees nor perform any other Masonic "work."

It was on July 3, 1776, when African Lodge No. 1 was formally organized, with Prince Hall as Master, the first organized body of colored Masons in America. On June 30, 1784, Prince Hall formally petitioned the Grand Lodge of England for a Charter or Warrant, empowering him and his associates to work according to the Ancient Usages and Customs of Freemasonry. His petition was granted and a Charter issued on September 29, 1784, which was delivered to Prince Hall on April 29, 1787, by Captain James Scott, a brother-in-law of John Hancock, one of the signers of the Declaration of Independence.

On May 6, 1787, African Lodge No. 1, formally began to work under Charter No. 459, with Prince Hall as Master, as granted by the Grand Lodge of England.

On June 24, 1791, on call by Prince Hall, a general assembly of the Craft was held in Masons Hall, in Boston, and African Grand Lodge formed, Prince Hall being chosen Grand Master, which office he held until his death in December, 1807.

In order to erect a perpetual memorial to the memory of Prince Hall, African Grand Lodge met on June 24, 1808, and changed her title to the M.W.P.H. Grand Lodge, F. & A.M., Jurisdiction of Massachusetts, as it is today.

Today, there are 38 Masonic Grand Lodges among Black Masons in the United States, all direct descendants from the M.W.P.H. Grand Lodge of Massachusetts.

We move from Massachusetts to Pennsylvania where the first charter was issued to African Independent No. 1. On September 22, 1797, Prince Hall and his wardens installed the officers of this Lodge in Philadelphia. Later, warrants were issued by the Massachusetts body to: Union No. 2 in 1810, Laurel No. 5 in 1811, and Phoenix No. 6 in 1814.

In accordance with the ancient custom, these four lodges formed a Grand Body in 1815 which was named the "First African Independent Grand Lodge of North America for Pennsylvania. In 1882, the name was changed to the "M.W. Grand Lodge, F&AM of the State of Pennsylvania." Finally in 1945, in honor of the founder of Negro Masonry in America, its name was changed to "The M.W.P.H. Grand Lodge, F&AM of Pennsylvania.

From the Grand Lodge of Pennsylvania, we move to the organization of the Grand Lodge of Ohio on May 3, 1849, and incorporated in 1871. The organization was composed of Corinthian Lodge No. 1, True American No. 2, and St. John's No. 3, each of which held warrants granted by the first African Independent Grand Lodge of Pennsylvania.

By virtue of, and by authority of the Grand Lodge of Ohio, our M.W. Grand Lodge, AF&AM for the State of Missouri and the Masonic Jurisdiction organized in 1865 at St. Louis, was formally organized and instituted December 20, 1866. The first lodge established was Prince Hall No. 10 in 1858. The second was Lone Star No. 22 in 1860, and the third was H. McGee Alexander No. 8 in 1860. All of these lodges were warranted by and under the Jurisdiction of the Grand Lodge of Ohio. They are now registered as Prince Hall No. 1, Lone Star

No. 2, and H. McGee Alexander No. 3 and under the M.W.P.H. Grand Lodge, F&AM of the State of Missouri and Jurisdiction. These lodges withdrew from the Ohio Jurisdiction in July, 1865, and through Bro. H. McGee Alexander, a petition was presented to the Grand Lodge of Ohio under the date of June, 1865, praying for the formation of a Grand Lodge in Missouri. This petition was granted and the Grand Lodge formed June 24, 1865, with the following as the first Grand Lodge Officers of the new body:

H. McGee Alexander .... Grand Master
John Sexton .... R.W. Senior Grand Warden
George Phillips .... R.W. Junior Grand Warden
Wm. P. Brooks .... R.W. Grand Treasurer
Wm. Robertson .... R.W. Grand Secretary

The first session of the Grand Lodge, at which time it was formally instituted, was held December 30, 1866. This Grand Lodge was incorporated under the laws of the State of Missouri, December 21, 1881. By Pro Former Decree issued April 19, 1945, at Jefferson City, Missouri, the first incorporated name was changed to read and continues to read, "Most Worshipful Prince Hall Grand Lodge of Free and Accepted Masons of the State of Missouri and Jurisdiction." Most Jurisdictions changed their corporate names to include Prince Hall in honor of the Father of Masonry among Colored People of the United States and for Masonic unity. And from the seed of Prince Hall, planted on March 6, 1775, came forth a mighty tree, able to withstand the wind and rains building on a solid rock, of brotherly love, relief and truth. Beginning in Boston, Massachusetts, moving forward to Pennsylvania, and then into the state of Ohio, from Ohio to the high hills and low valleys of the state of Missouri. Being industrial as a Queen Bee, and from such a Grand Missouri Lodge, came a subordinate Lodge called J. Q. Johnson Lodge which is where the man Frank James Brown received his Blue House Degrees. He also was a Grand Lodge Officer. And held the Grand Senior Warden Station, until his health became very poor. He was a 32° Mason and also Past Potentate of Medinah Temple #39. Frank J. Brown established Frank J. Brown Lodge #80 some 64 years ago. Whereby he made it a point to visit such lodge before his death. Yes, Frank J. Brown Lodge #80 lives on today, because Prince Hall lived yesterday.

GRAND MASTER GILLIAM OF MISSISSIPPI PASSES

Funeral Services were held for Bro. James C. Gilliam, Grand Master of the Most Worshipful Stringer Grand Lodge (Prince Hall Affiliation), on Sunday, September 15, 1974, 2:00 P.M., at Friendship A.M.E. Church, Clarksdale, Mississippi.

He passed in Detroit, Michigan, on September 10th, after a prolonged illness. Masonic rites were held at the Masonic Temple in Jackson on Saturday, September 14th, at 5:30 P.M., which included the Eastern Star, Heroines of Jericho, Shriners, Consistory and Master Masons.

Sovereign Grand Commander Jno. G. Lewis, Jr., M.P.S., gave remarks at the services on Sunday, representing the United Supreme Council of which the deceased was an active member.

Grand Master Gilliam had served as head of the Mississippi Prince Hall Masons since 1946 and initiated many worthy programs and projects for the Grand Lodge, including an annual scholarship program, contributions to the Legal Defense Fund of the N.A.A.C.P. and the March of Dimes, and the erection of the Masonic Temple in Jackson.

He was the recipient of numerous honors and awards, and was a senior member of the Grand Masters conference. He was the first Black ever elected as a delegate to the National Democratic Convention from Mississippi in 1968. He was a member of Phi Beta Sigma Fraternity and was named "Sigma Man of the Year" in 1963. An honor of which he was especially proud was bestowed upon him by his Alma Mater, Alcorn State University, when he was named "Alumnus of the Year," and in reality, the "Alumnus of the Century" since the occasion was the centennial observance of the institution.

He is survived by one son, Dr. J. C. Gilliam of Detroit, Michigan; three daughters, Mrs. Adelle Mitchess of Greenwood, Mississippi; Mrs. Odessa Davis, Detroit, Michigan; Mrs. George Brown of Institute, West Virginia; eight grandchildren; four great grandchildren; two sisters, Mrs. Cozetta Cooper, and Mrs. Nellie Mabry of Clarksdale, Mississippi; nephews; nieces; and a host of relatives and friends.

The Local Chapter - The Key to Co-ordinate Activity in the Phylaxis Society Program

One of the most important functions of the Phylaxis Society is that of making Prince Hall Freemasonry and its history more realistic, more understandable and more applicable to the problems of every day life.

More particularly is the Society, through its publication the *Phylaxis* magazine, making a most important contribution to be better knowledgable and understanding with the *Symbolic Lodge*.

As the Phylaxis Society proudly proclaims it is *"A Society for Prince Hall Freemasons who seek more Light, and who have Light to impart,"* so may we add that there is no higher attainment for a Prince Hall Freemason than to be an intelligent Blue Lodge member. With this in mind we feel that all other degrees, houses, orders and Masonic systems do — or should — illustrate and simplify the teachings of the Symbolic Lodge. The Blue Lodge is the basis of all Freemasonry, and ought to be better understood to be used and appreciated.

It can be truthfully said that the greatest activity and power of the Phylaxis Society is to be found in its individual members, and that gathering these members together in *Local Chapters* of the Society in every city and town where there are three or more members, it is possible to meet, enjoy fellowship, lay designs on the Trestle Board and promote the plan of a united activity by which the true principles of Freemasonry may be practiced.

How then, are Local Chapters activated? What is the purpose? How do they function? With inquiries being received as to how Local groups can engage themselves in our work, the following suggestions are offered for those who desire to bring the Phylaxis Society to a local level.

Those interested in forming a local Chapter of the Phylaxis should get together and discuss details of organization, go over prospective members, outline a plan of procedures, pick officers to be elected, and lay the ground work for the permanent organization.

Simplicity should be the keynote of the group. A short meeting, a minimum of officers, a planned program of activity, a long range plan by which interest could be stimulated, and best of all, a lot of enthusiastic discussion of the projected Chapter.

When the final plans have been laid, it would be well to arrange a meeting — a "Dutch Treat" dinner meeting would be good — at which all interested parties would be present. A temporary Chairman and a temporary Secretary, together with a Chaplain to open the meeting.

Again, simplicity and a lack of bogging detail, will make the objective best attained. After the meal and good fellowship, the temporary Chairman would have the objects of the Society and the proposed Chapter intelligently and adequately outlined.

A President, Secretary and Chaplain should be elected, and it should be determined how many meetings are proposed for the work of the group, etc.

Great emphasis should be placed on the fact, first that the local Chapter is, with other groups, a part of the national organization and receives an authorization to become a Chapter, and that, while it carries on its programs locally, must not interfere in the workings of any Masonic body.

Taking the example of the St. Louis, "Gateway" Chapter, upon their initial meeting they determined they would begin research into the history of the Prince Hall Grand Lodge of Missouri's Annual May Day parade. The largest of our Chapters, the Tacoma/Seattle "Northwest" Chapter began presenting seminars to the Prince Hall Grand Lodge of Washington and local Lodges in the area. They presented slides and lectures on Prince Hall Masonry, and the Military, and a tape recording of the History of Prince Hall Masonry, both furnished by the National Organization. Such meetings not only stimulate interest in the Phylaxis Society, but also gives greater essence to closer Masonic cooperation with Masonic bodies whose objectives and activities are similar in nature — especially Blue Lodges and/or Scottish or York Rite bodies.

A supply of brochures outlining the aims, purposes, and special programs of the Society, together with a supply of application blanks should be provided. To better illustrate the activities of the Society, copies of various issues of the *Phylaxis* magazine should be handy.

As the final step in organizing a local Chapter of the Phylaxis Society, it is suggested that a good program should be arranged to be the "meat" of the meeting.

This program should be a Masonic Program!!

A paper, written by a competent and interested Prince Hall Brother on a live, interesting and practical Masonic topic, not long, and certainly not more than ten or fifteen minutes in length, followed by an all out audience participation can leave a taste of good Freemasonry in the minds of all those who attend the meeting, and will certainly stimulate interest for further activities. In this, the National Organization will work with any member in preparing a lecture on any Masonic subject.

Some have said that membership in the Phylaxis Society is for *literary people* only. This is absolutely not so, for any Prince Hall Freemason who is interested in Prince Hall Freemasonry, its application to civic life and who wants to have a better understanding of the principles, background and understanding of the Craft is welcome.

Essentially, there are three types of Freemasons — first, the leaders, who with a keen knowledge of Freemasonry, can direct and lead us to a better understanding of its aims. Next, there are the workers in Freemasonry, who follow the leader or the pilot in putting into action these principles, and finally, there are those who have joined Freemasonry because of a deep belief in its teachings, a desire to be associated with progressive actions, but who, for many reasons, are unable to participate in its work.

Each of these classes has a place in our society. The leader so desperately needed to guide our activities, the workers to carry on, and the ordinary member, whose dues help pay the way, whose enthusiasm helps us get the enthusiasm to meet our objectives, and whose silent support is so needed to bring us to understanding. We can do without none of these members, and to each we bring something that will be helpful.

To the leader we bring ideas by which to lay out our work and make our dreams, to the worker we give a plan of action to put into execution, and to the common member we offer a variety of activities, interests, hobbies and contacts which will be pleasant, helpful and satisfying. Let us never underestimate the potential of our society, or the value of the local association and contact.

There is something valuable in the activities of the Phylaxis Society, and especially in the local Chapter, for each member. There are several very important activities and phases of the society for the particular interest of each member.

On a page of every issue of the *Phylaxis* magazine will be the department known as *Notes and Queries on Masonic Information*, which will be conducted by our President, Joseph A. Walkes, M.P.S., and his private masonic library, called the *"Worlds largest Privately Owned Prince Hall Masonic Library."* Here questions of special interest on topics of unusual Masonic quality are submitted, and through it, contacts can be made with other members of the society with like interests. Not only does this give contact for research, but life-long friendships have been formed through such contact.

Look through the pages of the *Phylaxis* magazine! In it you will find something that will fill your needs for joining a local Chapter or organizing a Local Chapter of the Phylaxis Society.

PRINCE HALL MASONRY AND THE CIVIL WAR

PART II

BY

JOSEPH A. WALKES, JR., M.P.S.
A MASTERPIECE

"Query, Whether at that day, when there was an African church, and perhaps the largest Christian church on earth, whether there was no African of that order; or whether, if they were all whites, they would refuse to accept them as their fellow Christians and brother Masons; or whether there were any so weak, or rather to foolish, as to say, because they were Blacks, that would make their lodge or army too common or too cheap? Sure this was not our conduct in the late war; for then they marched shoulder to shoulder, brother soldier and brother soldier, to the field of battle; let who will answer, he that despises a Black man for the sake of his colour, reproacheth his Maker.***

A Charge to the brethren of African Lodge, Charlestown, Massachusetts, 25th of June, 1792 by the Right Worshipful Master PRINCE HALL.

What is of interest concerning Bro. Vogelsang, is the fact that his name is mentioned in a number of books. In Bro. Charles H. Wesley's *Richard Allen — Apostle of Freedom*[27] he is mentioned as having signed a circular in 1830 for the African Methodist Episcopal Church which was founded by another Prince Hall Mason, Bro. Richard Allen. His name is also mentioned in Benjamin Quarles, *Black Abolitionists* as having been a member of the Phoenix Society, a Negro self-improvement organization founded in New York in 1833, and also as a member of the Committee for Superintending the Application for Funds for the College for Colored Youth.[28] His name is also mentioned in the book *The Life and Public Services of Martin R. Delaney* in which Bro. Delaney states "Brave Vogelsang, the intripid lennox."[29]

Bro. Delaney (see photo) mentioned earlier was a Prince Hall Masonic Brethren of many first,[30] one being the first Black to achieve the rank of Major in the Service of the United States, appointed to this rank from civilian life with the approval of President Lincoln, and by the direction of the Secretary of War. He was mustered into service February 27, 1865 as *"Major, United States Colored Troops,"* and assigned to the 104th United States Colored Troops on detached service to the Freedman Bureau in South Carolina.[31] Here the Masonic lines may have crossed.

The mere mention of Delaney's words of *"Brave Vogelsang"* can not be taken lightly, as everything Delaney said had a purpose, as this, which is well recorded, when Bro. Delaney addressed an outdoor meeting of 600 ex-slaves on St. Helena Island, South Carolina, he exclaimed, "As before the whole South depended upon you. I give you advice how to get along.

47

Get up a community and get all the lands you can, if you can not get any singly. Now you understand that I want you to be the producers of this country. It is the wish of the Government for you to be so. We will send friends to you, who will further instruct you how to come to the end of our wishes. You see that by so adhering to our views you will become a wealthy and powerful population. Now I look around me and notice a man, barefooted, covered with rags and dirty. Now I ask, what is that man doing, for whom is he working. I hear the words that he works for that and that farmer " *for 30 cents a day,*" I tell you that must not be. That would be slavery over agin. I will not have it, the Government will not have it, and the Government shall hear about it. I will tell the Government. I tell you slavery is over, and shall never return again. We have now 200,000 of our men well drilled in arms and used to warfare and I tell you it is with you and them, that slavery shall not come back again, and if you are determined it will not return again."³²

So, the mention of the name "Vogelsang" by Bro. Delaney, leads this writer to wonder, if Delaney, a Past Master and District Deputy was not only aware of the presence of this Lodge, and if infact, actually attending its meetings? One can only speculate.

There could not have been to much concern about Black man practicing Masonry at the time from the Caucasian branch of American Masonry, as Governor Andrews a non-mason was, making presentations to the Prince Hall Grand Lodge of Massachusetts, and this was well known. His letter to Grand Master Lewis Hayden of the 21st of December 1864 is of interest.

"I send you with this note, for presentation to the Prince Hall Grand Lodge a gavel, made from a piece of the shipping-post at Hampton, Va. The gentleman who sent it to me say, "This post or tree stood directly in the rear of the old court-house, and in front of the jail. While I was cutting it about twenty colored men and women bore testimony to me that it was the identical post or tree that they had been tied to and had their backs lacerated with the whip." I also place in your hands, for the same purpose, a rude boat of straw, made in the woods by a poor refugee from slavery, Jack Flowers, who after a protracted journey through the forest, tracked by blood-hounds, reached a stream, down which he floated past the rebel pickets, till he reached a point guarded by the Union Army, where he landed a free man. A copy of his narrative will be given you for presentation with this interesting relic." (The straw boat, here spoken of, attracted much attention at the State House; and the wonder was, how, so frail a bark could float a man from slavery to Freedom. The narrative of Jack Flowers was furnished the Governor by a gentleman of the name of Judd, and tells a terrible tale of the sufferings and wrongs of this poor man. It is too long to quote entire. He was a slave in South Carolina, and escaped by means of his straw boat. Through the rebel pickets, and landed safely at Hilton Head. Jack says that he made several attempts to pass the rebel picket line, but failed. We now quote from his narrative.

"So when I found it was no use to get over that way, I concluded to try another. Uncle lent me his axe and knife, and I cut a lot of brushes, and a tough oak-tree for splints, and went to work in the woods, and made this basket. It took me two days to weave it, after the stuff was all ready; the pitch I got by cutting into a tree, and catching the gum, which I boiled in a kettle of my sister's. The old shutter came from Dr. Fuller's house. It was three miles to the water, and I carried the basket along on my head in the dark night, for fear of the pickets. It was so late in the night when I got all ready to start in the creek, that I did not get down to the coosa till day clear, so I landed on a little hammock close by the mouth of the

Past Master, Past District Deputy Grand Master

creek, and hid the boat and myself for another day. But before nine o'clock the next night, I put out and paddled over to Port Royal, too glad to get away. The Yankee picket wasn't asleep, but challenged me before I got near the shore, and I told him right off, that I was a runaway nigger coming ashore for freedom. The Rebel picket heard me, and after I got up the bank he hailed across "Yanks, who have you got?" Yankee say, "One of your fellows." "What you going to do with him?" "Don't know, what do you think best?" "Cut him up for fish-bait, he ain't good for nothing else!"³³

48

"I know of no place more fitting for the preservation of these memorials of the barbarous institution that is now tottering with its rapidly approaching fall, then the association of free colored citizens of Massachusetts over which you preside. Some among you may be reminded by them of the suffering and bondage from which the hands of God has delivered you, while others, whose happier lot it has been to be born and reared as free men in a free state, as they look upon these things, will thank Him that He has been graciously pleased that their lines should fall in more pleasant places; and to those who shall come after you let the sight of these things be a perpetual memorial of God's favor to their fathers, in delivering them from their oppressors, as well as the victorious power which will one day right every wrong and justify every manful, dutiful, and sincere effort in behalf of truth, honor, and humanity.

I am faithfully yours, etc.
John A. Andrew[34]

The Prince Hall Grand Lodge answered:

Boston, Jan. 20, 1865

To His Excellency, John A. Andrew, Governor of the Commonwealth of Massachusetts.

Sir, at a communication of Prince Hall Grand Lodge, held on the 27th day of December last, your interesting letter, presenting a gavel made from a piece of the whipping-post torn down by the Union soldiers near the Court House at Hampton, Va., and the basket-boat in which the refugee-hero Jack Flowers made his escape from slavery, was read by M.W. D.G.M., Robert Morris. The undersigned were charged with the pleasant duty of tendering you the sincere thanks of Prince Hall Grand Lodge for these valuable relics, and the kind and sympathizing expressions contained in your letter.

The fraternity of which we are members is one of the most excellent and time honored institutions existing among civilized men. The Charter under which we exist, as a Lodge, is one of the most ancient in our country. The principles of our Order are universal, and its duties and obligations imperative and absolute. Nevertheless, the pernicious influence of slavery has caused our white brethren to remove an "ancient landmark;" to foster an unchristian and unmasonic caste which makes them forgetful of their great duties and obligations to us, which we, as brethren, can never fail to practice toward them; and for this Christian spirit which thus animates us, we devoutly thank the Great Architect of the Universe.

The possession of the boat affords us the liveliest pleasure and satisfaction. Hereafter, we shall call it our ark. We can well understand the feelings of Jack Flowers, when, after making his escape from slavery, pursued by cruel and savage men, accompanied by bloodhounds, scarcely less merciless than their masters, baffling the keen scent of the dogs and the vigilance of the men, tired, worn, and weary, he sat down in the dense woods and con-

structed this rude and frail ark. Surely as the God of our fathers guided Moses as he led the children of Israel through the Red Sea to their promised Canaan, so was He with this poor fugitive, tenderly guiding him in his flight from slavery to freedom.

The manufacture of this gavel from a piece of that relic of barbarism, the old whipping-post, a tool so Masonically significant, was a most happy conception of your excellency. It will constantly remind us of the difference between obedience wrung from an oppressed race by power and might, with thumb-screws, whipping posts, branding irons, and the lash, and that obedience so willingly rendered by us as freemen to those in authority, where the rights of the poor and most humble citizen are sacred and protected by law.

We avail ourselves of this opportunity to thank you for the disinterted and real friendship always manifested by you for our race; for your kind and sincere sympathy in our misfortunes; for your determined efforts in private and public life in favor of immediate emancipation, and in behalf of civil and political rights. Especially do we thank you, as governor of our good old Commonwealth, for your noble and successful efforts in raising the Fifty-Fourth and Fifty-Fifth Regiments of Massachusetts Volunteers, the first two colored regiments sent into the service; thus setting an example to the other States, as patriotic as it has proved successful. Surely it must be a source of great happiness to your excellency to know that the conduct of these troops has been such as to force the general government to adopt your policy, and that today three hundred thousand colored soldiers are in the field fighting nobly for the salvation of the United States of America.

In behalf of Prince Hall Grand Lodge, and for ourselves, we are, very repsectfully,

Your excellency's obliged and humble servants,

           Robert Morris
           Thomas Dalton
           Francis P. Clary[35]

There can be little doubt that the Caucasian officers of the 54th was aware that this Prince Hall Masonic Military Lodge was attached to this unit, and many of these officers were members of the Craft themselve's.[36]

Captain Emilo in his book mentions that "Dr. Albert G. Mackey, and other citizens appeared, and representing that the Rebel rear guard was still in the place, begged protection, and assistance in quelling the flames, which threatened the total distruction of the City."[37]

Dr. Albert Gallatine Mackey, known for his History of Freemasonry, Jurisprudence, Symbolism, and Encyclopedia of Freemasonry, was a collector of the Port of Charleston,[38] and was as Harry Williamson, the Prince Hall Masonic scholar records, "unfavorable to the Freemasonry of the Negro."[39]

His having to beg for protection to the Black troops of the 54th Massachusetts may have been the cause.

The sister unit of the 54th, the 55th Masachusetts, first Black officer, Chaplain John H. Bowles, years later would become the Grand Historian of the Prince Hall Grand Lodge of Ohio.[40] It is this writers opinion that the membership of this initial Prince Hall Military Lodge was composed of members of both units, but more research is needed. Not until the records of those individual Grand Lodges that were involved are made available to those who are willing to explore the Masonic past, the complete story may be a long time in reaching light.

In support of my belief that Hayden Lodge No. 8 of Charleston, South Carolina, was either this military Lodge attached to the 54th or evolved from it is the fact that Grand Master Lewis Hayden, had leveled a bitter attack on President Andrew Johnson, himself a Freemason, who, on October 24, 1864 had addressed the Blacks of Nashville and denounced slavery and the "damnable aristocracy" which had profited from human bondage, and expressed the belief that only loyal men, white and Black, should have a voice in the reconstruction of the seceded states. Johnson ventured the hope that, "as in the days of old," "a Moses might arise" to lead them safely to their Promised Land of freedom and happiness." The Blacks thereupon cried, "you are our Moses!" Johnson responded "Humble and unworthy as I am, if no better shall be found, I will indeed be your Moses, and lead you through the Red Sea of War and bondage to a fairer future of liberty and peace. But when Grand Master Hayden visited this very Lodge in South Carolina, he found the man who had promised to become a "new Moses" was instrumental in assisting the former slave owners to return the freedom to a status resembling slavery.

In a bitter attack on President Johnson before the Prince Hall Grand Lodge at the Festival of St. John the Evangelist, December 27, 1865, Grand Master Hayden mentions his visit. This speech was presented only a few months after the 54th left Charleston.[41]

It would seem to suggest that he may have visited the military traveling Lodge and rewarranted it as a regular non-military Lodge.

CONT'D IN NEXT ISSUE: PART III — THE SECOND MILITARY LODGE

REFERENCES TO PART II

[27]Charles H. Wesley, *Richard Allen — Apostle of Freedom* (Washington, D.C., The Associated Publishers, Inc., 1935) P. 235.

[28]Benjamin Quarles, *Black Abolitionists* (London, Oxford, New York, Oxford University Press, 1969) P. 102 & 107.

[29]Frank A. Rollins, *Life and Public Services of Martin R. Delany* (New York, Arno Press & New York Times, 1969) P. 153.

[30]Daniel A. Payne, *Recollections of Seventy Years* (New York, Arno Press & New York Times 1969) P. 160. Payne records "The Major was a man of fine talents and more than ordinary attainments. He traveled much, and traveled with eyes and ears wide open. Therefore he knew much of men and things in Africa, England, Scotland, and America and in Canada as well as in the United States. He studied medicine at Harvard University, and would have been rich if he had practiced it as a profession for life. But he was too much of a cosmopolitan to stick to it. His oratory was powerful, at times

magnetic. If he had studied law, made it his profession, kept an even course, and settled down in South Carolina, he would have reached the Senate-Chamber of that proud state. But he was too intensely African to be popular, and therefore multiplied enemies where he could have mulitpled friends by the thousands. Had his love for humanity been as great as his love for his race, he might have rendered his personal influence co-extensive with that of Samuel R. Ward in his palmiest days, or that of Frederick Douglass at the present time. The Major was a great admirer of ancient heroes, especially those of Hamitic extraction. Therefore he named all of his six children after the Toussaint L' Ouverture, Alexander Dumas, St. Cyprian (Also the name of his Lodge.), Soulouque, Faustin, and Ethiopia are the names of his five sons and one daughter.

[31] Military Service Records, National Archives, Washington, D.C.

[32] Report of LT. Edward M. Stoeber, Washinton, D.C., National Archives, July 24, 1865, Record Group 94, cited by William Loren Katz, Eye-witness: *The Negro In American History*, Op Cit, P. 252-253.

[33] William Schouler, Op City, P. 585.

[34] Lewis Hayden, *Caste Among Masons*, an Address at the Festival of St. John the Evangelist, December 27, 1865 (Boston, Edward S. Coombs & Company, 1866) P. 70-71.

[35] Ibid. P. 71-72.

[36] Emilio, Op Cit., P. 252.

[37] Ibid, P. 282.

[38] Ibid, P. 312.

[39] Harry A. Williamson, The Prince Hall Primer (New York, Macoy Publishing & Masonic Supply Co., 1925) P. 21. Mackey, years later would write that racial prejudice existed in American Masonry, but it would be unjust to charge the organized Masonic institution because of the personal prejudice of some of its members. And that the Prince Hall Lodge of Boston, whether originally legal or not, certainly lost its legality, subsequently, if it ever had it. And whether legal or not, as a particular Lodge, it could, under no law of Masonry recognized in this country, assume of its own violation the functions of a Grand Lodge. Therefore all subordinate Lodges formed under its obedience are irregular and their members clandestine. (Voice of Masonry Volume 14, 1878, page 423). While on the other hand, he refrains from a like declaration of clandestinism when he records that the Kilwinning Lodge (Scotland) seceded from the Grand Lodge and established itself as an independent body. It organized Lodges in Scotland, and several instances are on record of its issuing Charters as Mother Kilwinning Lodge to Lodges in foreign countries. Thus, it granted one to a Lodge in Virginia in 1758. (Page 518, Encyclopedia of Freemasonry, by Albert Mackey; (New York, Macoy Publishing and Masonic Supply Co., 1950) Or on the subject of German Lodges, he records that "a curious feature of the growth of the Craft in Germany is the number of independent Masonic bodies which, with or without special authority, excercises control over other lodges. There are also several independent Lodges in existence. The first of these Grand Lodges was probably the Zu den drei Weltkugeln (Three Globes) Lodge, opened in Berlin by the comand of Frederick, who afterwards assumed the position of Grand Master as often as his military duties permitted. (Mackey, Op Cit. P. 402).

But yet, Mackey would state that "there is a well known maxim of the law which says *Omnis innovatis plus novitate perturbat quam utilitate prodest*, that is, every innovation occasions more harm and disarrangement by its novelty than benefit by its acutal utility. This maxim is peculiarily applicable to Freemasonry, whose system is opposed to all innovations of the American system of so called exclusive territorial jurisdiction. This leaves this writer to dismiss Mackey.

[40] Charles Bernard Fox, *Record of the Service of the 55th Regiment of Massachusetts Volunteer Infantry*. (Printed for the Regimental Association by John Wilson & Son, 1868) P. 25., and William Hartwell Parham and Jeremiah Arthur Brown, *History of Ohio Grand Lodge* (P.H.A.) Op Cit., P. 28)

[41] Lewis Hayden, Caste Among Masons, Op Cit., P. 7 "That at Charleston, S.C., has been duly warranted and constituted under the name of "Hayden Lodge, No. 8." Its master is Brother Robert S. Lord.". . .I found in Charleston, S.C., a still higher class of people, even, than at Petersburg, as regards general education, the mechanical arts, and all the elements which tend to make a first class society. In proof of this, I have brought with me a list of applications for initiations to their Lodges, the signers of which will compare favorably with the members of any Masonic Lodge, either white or black, in the United States, whether we take into consideration proficiency in the mechanical arts, or social and mental endowments. Of the people of Charleston whether in the Order or not, I am constrained to say, that the many acts of kindness and the generous hospitality received at their hands, during my sojourn among them, have made an impression upon my heart, which neither time nor changing fortune can ever efface. The Atlantic Monthly would report that . . . a branch of the Masonic brotherhood, which has a few sickly subordinate Lodges and a state lodge; for this a charter was obtained, I am informed, from the state of Massachusetts. These colored Masons are not recognized by the white Lodges or grand body of the State" (South Carolina Society, June 1877, P. 683, The Atlantic Monthly.)

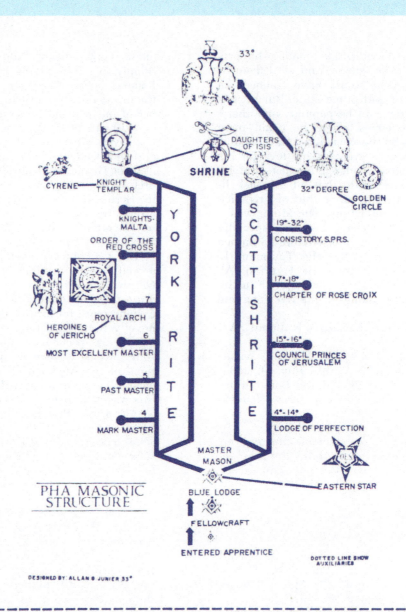

THE PHYLAXIS SOCIETY SUBSCRIPTION CARD

Subscription rate: $5.00/Yr.

Mail to: James E. Herndon, MPS
Executive Secretary
1574 Ivanhoe Street
Denver, Colo. 80220

Gentlemen:

Enclosed is my subscription the the Phylaxis Magazine.

_____ Check Enclosed _____ amount payable to Phylaxis Magazine

Name: _____

Address: _____

City: _____ State: _____ Zip Code: _____

A SOCIETY FOR PRINCE HALL FREEMASONS WHO SEEK MORE LIGHT AND WHO HAVE LIGHT TO IMPART

THE PHYLAXIS

MARCH 1975

Volume II   Number 2

"SPECIAL ISSUE"
IN COMMEMORATION
OF THE 200th
ANNIVERSARY OF THE
INITIATION OF
PRINCE HALL —
MARCH 6th, 1775."

A SOCIETY FOR PRINCE HALL
FREEMASONS WHO SEEK MORE
LIGHT AND WHO HAVE LIGHT TO
IMPART

THE PHYLAXIS
Published at Jefferson City, Mo., by
THE PHYLAXIS SOCIETY

Arthur H. Frederick M.P.S. .... Editor
Box 43, Roxbury, Massachusetts 02119

OFFICERS

Joseph A. Walkes, Jr, M.P.S. .... President
P. O. Box 3151, Ft. Leavenworth, Kansas 66027

Herbert Dailey, M.P.S. .... First Vice President
1616 South Cedar, Tacoma, Washington 98405

Zellus Bailey, M.P.S. .... Second Vice President
7039 Dover Court, St. Louis, Missouri 63130

James E. Herndon, M.P.S. .... Executive Secretary
1574 Ivanhoe Street, Denver, Colorado 80220

Alonzo D. Foote, Sr., M.P.S. .... Treasurer
P.O. Box 99601, Tacoma, Washington 98499

SUBSCRIPTION RATE: FOR ONE YEAR, $5.00

The Phylaxis Magazine is the official publication of the Phylaxis Society. Any article appearing in this publication expresses only the opinion of the writer, and does not become the official pronouncement of the Phylaxis Society. No advertising of any form is solicited or accepted. All communication relative to the magazine should be addressed to the Editor. Inquiries relative to membership must be addressed to the Executive Secretary. Membership is by invitation and recommendation only. The joining fee is $3.00. Dues are $5.00 per year in advance, which amount includes a subscription to the "Phylaxis" magazine for one year.

All rights reserved. No part of this work may be reproduced or transmitted in any form or by any means, electrical or mechanical, or retrival system, without written permission from the publisher.

1975 DUES
ALL 1974 MEMBERS ARE
REQUESTED TO FORWARD THEIR
1975 DUES ($5.00) TO THE
EXECUTIVE SECRETARY.

INDEX

A Word from the President	54
Prince Hall's Letter Book	55
A Charge Delivered to the African Lodge, June 24, 1797	58
Congratulations	61
The Phylaxis Society and the Prince Hall Confession of Masonic Faith	
Alexander Clark, P.G.M.	62
Vital Dimensions of Effective Power	65
The Storm that Produced Light on a Dark Subject	69
Recognized, Unrecognized, Clandestine	71
The Masonic Addresses and Writings of IRA S. HOLDER, Sr., M.P.S.	72
Notes, Queries and Information on Items of Masonic Research	74

A WORD FROM THE PRESIDENT

Perhaps it may be more agreeable to transcribe what was given me in answer to this query by the aforesaid Prince Hall. "Harmony in general (says he) prevails between us as citizens, for the good law of the land does oblige every one to live peaceably with all his fellow citizens, let them be black or white. We stand on a level, therefore no pre-eminence can be claimed on either side. As to our associating, there is here a great number of worthy good men and good citizens, that are not ashamed to take an African by the hand; but yet there are to be seen the weeds of pride, envy, tyranny, and scorn, in this garden of peace, liberty and equality."

Having once and again mentioned this person, I must inform you that he is Grand Master of a Lodge of freemasons, composed wholly of blacks, and distinguished by the name of the "African Lodge." It was begun in 1775, while this town was garrisoned by British troops; some of whom held a lodge, and initiated a number of negroes. After the peace, they sent to England and procured a charter under the authority of the Duke of Cumberland, and signed by the late Earl of Effingham. The lodge at present consists of thirty persons; and care is taken that none but those of good moral character are admitted.

Queries Respecting the Slavery and Emancipation of Negroes in Massachusetts, proposed by the HON. Judge Tucker of Virginia, and answered by the Rev. Dr. Jeremy Belknapp, April 21, 1975.

With this issue of the *Phylaxis Magazine,* we commemorate the 200th Anniversary of the initiation of *"The Master"* — Prince Hall, into Masonry.

Prince Hall was truly one of the most outstanding Black men of his day, and the words recorded by the famed historian Jeremy Bel-

54

knapp has left us glimpses of "The Master." "The negroes of sufficient property vote in townmeetings. Prince Hall — Grand Master of the Black Lodge constantly votes for Governour and Representatives (P. 12 the Belknapp Papers, 1788).

And the case of three kidnapped Negroes, one a member of African Lodge, sent into slavery to the West Indies, Belknapp recorded, "The negroes themselves have been put on preferring a petition to the same purpose. I read it last evening. It is a truly original and curious performance, written by the Grand Master of the Black Lodge. (P. 22, 2 March 1788).

To the Honorable, The Senate and House of Representatives of the Commonwealth of Massachusetts in General Court assembled, on the 27th February 1788;

The Petition of a great number of Blacks, freeman of this Commonwealth, humbly showeth:

That your petitioners are justly alarmed at the inhuman and cruel treatment that three of our brethren, free citizens of the town of Boston, lately received. The Captain, under pretense that his vessel was in distress on an Island below in this harbor, having got them on board, put them in irons, and carried them off from their wives and children, to be sold for slaves. This being the unhappy state of these poor men, what can your petitioners expect but to be treated in the same manner by the same sort of men?

What, then are our lives and liberties worth, if they may be taken away in such a cruel and unjust manner as this? May it please your Honors, we are not insensible that the good laws of this State forbid all such bad actions; notwithstanding we can assure your Honors, that many of our free Blacks that have entered on board of vessels as seamen, have been sold as slaves, and some of them we have heard from, but know not who carried them away. Hence, it is, that many of us, who are good seamen, are obliged to stay at home through fear, and one-half of our time loiter if they were protected in that lawful calling, they might get a handsome livelihood for themselves and theirs, which in the situation they are now in, they cannot. One thing more we would beg leave to hint, that is, that your petitioners have for some time past, beheld with grief, ships cleared out of this harbor for Africa, and they either steal our brothers and sisters, fill their ship-holds full of unhappy men and women, crowed together, then set out for the best market to sell them there, like sheep for slaughter, and then return here like honest men, after having sported with the lives and liberty of their fellow-men, and at the same time call themselves Christians. Blush, O Heavens at this! These, our weighty grievances, we cheerfully submit to your Honors, without dictating in the least, knowing by experience that your Honors have, and we trust ever will, in your wisdom, do us that justice that our present condition requires, as God and the good laws of this Commonwealth shall dictate to you.

As in duty bound, your petitioners shall ever pray (signed) PRINCE HALL, Primus Hall, Brittion Balch, Cyrus Forbes, etc.

The Phylaxis Society takes pride in publishing this Special Edition, and reproducing Prince Hall's Letter Book, and his charge to the members of African Lodge. Therefore, this edition is dedicated not only to the memory of *"The Master"* Prince Hall, but to all Prince Hall Master Masons where-so-ever dispatched around the globe.

JOSEPH A. WALKES, JR M.P.S
President

PRINCE HALL'S LETTER BOOK
by

WILLIAM H. UPTON, P.G.M.
(Cau. Grand Lodge of Washington as published in the Transaction of the Quatuor Coronati Lodge of London, England)

(PHYLAXIS NOTE: In commerating the 200th Anniversary of the initation of Prince Hall into Masonry we the Phylaxis Society take pride in reproducing his letter book, which is one of our most sacred documents, we also take pride in the fact that the first class of graduates of the *Prince Hall Elementary School* located at 18th and Godfrey Ave., Philadelphia, Pennsylvania, and as reported in *The Light* of the Most Worshipful Prince Hall Grand Lodge of Pennsylvania, took place June 24th, 1974.)

Any unpublished document more than a century-old, having any relation to Masonry, can hardly be wholly without interest to the student of our institution; and this seems to me especially true of a document relating to a subject which gives promise of being a cause of more or less discord within the Craft until the views in regard to it now en-

55

tertained by the vast majority of American Masons are entirely changed. Hence I deem it worth while to report that one of the results of the interest in the subject of Masonry among the negroes of America excited by the declarations of the Grand Lodge of Washington in 1898 and 1899, practically recognizing the legitimacy of that Masonry from an historical standpoint, has been the unearthing of three manuscripts, of considerable antiquity, which shed some additional light on Negro Masonry, and which it is the purpose of this paper to attempt to describe with sufficient fulness to preserve their more important contents in the attempt to describe with sufficient fulness to preserve their more important contents in the not improbable event that the originals again became lost.

These three documents may be designated as (1) Minutes of African Lodge, Boston, 1779-1787; (2) Prince Hall's Letter Book; and (3) Minute Book of African Lodge, Philadelphia, 1797-1800. They were found, with a number of the old records of Celestial Lodge — to be mentioned hereafter, — in May, 1899, in the possession of members of the John T. Hilton Lodge of Lynn, Massachusetts, a constituent of the Prince Hall Grand Lodge. No question exists as to their genuineness. A word in regard to Prince Hall and his sodality may be almost essential to make what follows intelligible to readers to whom Negro Masonry is a new subject.

PRINCE HALL

Prince Hall was a negro, residing during the latter half of his life at Boston, Massachusetts. His birthplace is unknown. Negro Masons in Maryland have claimed him — on what authority, if any, I know not — as a son of that colony; and a single word in one of this own letters (No. 21 below) might lead some to look to England for his nativity. The date of his birth is equally uncertain, — 1738, 1742 and 1748 having all been mentioned as the year. Of these, the earliest seems the best authenticated, although John D. Caldwell, (white) Grand Secretary of Ohio, appears to cite W. S. Gardner, (white) P.G.M. of Massachusetts, as fixing the date as November 9th, 1742. He died December 7th, 1807.

He and fourteen other negroes were initiated, May 6th, 1775, in an army Lodge attached to one of the British regiments under General Gage, stationed in or near Boston. Hall served in the American army during the war for independence, which began just before his initiation; but his mother Lodge, in the army of the enemy, exemplified the catholicity of Masonry by issuing to their black brethren — in accordance with a not unusual practice of that day[1] — a permit to meet as a Lodge, but with very limited powers (see item 2 below). Under this permit, Hall and his followers met — but conferred no degrees — from 1776 until 1787. In the latter year they were regularly organized as African Lodge No. 459, under a warrant granted them by the Grand Master of England ("Moderns") in 1784, but not received until 1787. As we shall presently see, a Lodge was organized in Philadelphia in 1797 by negroes who had been initiated in England and Ireland. A third negro Lodge was subsequently formed in Providence, Rhode Island — in accordance with an old usage, the validity of which had then but recently been affirmed by the Grand Lodge of Scotland[2] — for the accommodation of members of No. 459 who resided there; and in 1808.

Origin of the Negro Lodges.

These three formed the African Grand Lodge, a body which in 1847 changed its name to Prince Hall Grand Lodge of Massachusetts. From these sources the light of Masonry gradually spread among the negroes, until now they have Lodges and Grand Lodges in most of the States, and in Canada and Liberia. African Lodge No. 459 continued to work until at least as late as 1846[1]; and I am credibly informed that the present Celestial Lodge, Boston, is really Lodge 459 under another name, and that but one brother who belonged to the Lodge before the change of names still survives, John J. Smith, an aged resident of Jamaica Plain. Why or when the change was made, I have not learned.

Before proceeding to describe the three documents, I wish to acknowledge my indebtedness for almost all the material for this paper to W. Bro. Frederic S. Monroe, Master of Union Lodge, New Bedford, Mass., Committee on Correspondence of Prince Hall Grand Lodge, and one of the best informed and most accurate of New England Masons.

MINUTES OF AFRICAN LODGE, BOSTON.

As this is the most ancient of our three documents, it might be expected to be the most interesting. I regret to say it is not, and I fear it is of little value. It consists of a few tattered sheets of paper, upon which are written rough minutes of African Lodge from 1779 to 1787. They do not appear to be pages from a minute book, but rather, rough notes from which the minutes were to be written up, taken down upon scraps torn for that purpose from an old bank book: They are not the records described by Bro. Jacob Norton, some years ago, as examined by him. The ink is badly faded, the writing very poor and largely undecipherable, and the matters noted of very little interest, — often being no more than that the Lodge met at the date named. The following are samples of some of the more complete entries:

"Boston, November 13, 1787
"The Lodge No. 459 has met, where the business was carried to the Constitution, where the new members is expected of James Hicks, Prince Clary, Geo. Miller, Joseph Hicks."

"Boston, December 13, 1787
"A list of the brethren that has paid towards the feast of St. John's Day— Mr. Sanderson 4 shillings each brother is to pay — Br. Middleton 4"

Then follow fourteen other names, without prefixes, with "3" opposite one of them, and "4" opposite each of the others. Among them are Hicks and Gregory, and Sanderson again; but Hall, Forbes, Spooner, Prince, and others with whom we shall become familiar, were not on the list. Opposite the names, is written:

	D	S	
"Paid for the R…	10	3	
Cooking them	10	3	11"

PRINCE HALL'S LETTER BOOK.

Our second document is of much greater interest. It is a record book of about 300 foolscap pages, pasteboard bound, covered with sheepskin, and lettered on the outside, "Prince Hall's Sermons, 1787." It is nearly filled with matter of which I shall attempt to give a digest below, written throughout in the handwriting of Prince Hall. As a rule it is quite legible: on a number of pages the ink is nearly bleached out, while on others it is as black as when first written. The spelling is often phonetic, the capitalization that of the last century; and of punctuation or paragraphing there is practically none. I have seen no advantage in retaining these peculiarities in the extracts quoted below, save in a few instances. I have indicated by a dotted line (. . .) illegible letters and have placed within square brackets all words not found in the original. The volume is badly smoked and water-stained, probably indicating that it went through the fire which destroyed the temple and some of the records of Prince Hall Grand Lodge in 1869[2], at which time Grand Master Kendall saved the ancient warrant of African Lodge — of which much more, presently, — at the risk of his life. That Grand Lodge possessing no fire-proof vault, the volume was probably passed from one Grand Secretary to another until it found its way into John T. Hilton Lodge. I will now give an epitome of its contents, arranged chronologically and numbered for the sake of convenience, with occasional comments but avoiding remarks of a controversial nature as far as possible.

(1) "A paragraph inserted in the Boston paper, viz. Draper and Folsom of Monday. December 31, 1782.

"On Friday, last, 27th, the Feast of St. John the Evangelist, was celebrated by St. Black's Lodge of Free and Accepted Masons, who went in procession preceded by a band of music, dressed in their aprons and jewels from Brother G. . .pions up State Street and thro Cornhill to the House of the Right Worshipful Grand Master in Water Street, where an elegant and splendid entertainment was given upon the occasion.

"The Master's answer to the above sketch:
"Mr. Willis,

"Sir: Observing a sketch in Monday's paper painted by Mess. Draper and Folsom, relative to the celebration of the feast of St. John the Evangelist by the African Lodge, the Master of said Lodge being possessed of a charitable disposition to all manking, does therefore hope the publisher of the said sketch meant to give a candid description of the procession —c. Therefore with due submission to the public, our title is not St. Black's Lodge; neither do we aspire after high titles. But our only desire is that the Great Architect of the Universe would diffuse in our hearts the true spirit of masonry, which is love to God and universal love to all mankind. These I humbly conceive to be the two grand pillars of masonry. Instead of a splendid entertainment, we had an agreeable one in brotherly love.

"With humble submission to the above publishers and the public, I beg leave to subscribe myself, your humble servant.
                Prince Hall
                Master of African Lodge
                  No. 1,
                    Dedicated to St. John."

This was before the warrant was granted, and while the Lodge was meeting under the "Permit" mentioned in the letter following:

African Lodge, under Dispensation.
(2) *Prince Hall to William Moody,* of London, Dated March 2nd, 1784.

Addressed to "Mr. Moody." "Most Worshipful Sir." Thanks him and "the Wardens and Rest of the Brethern of our Lodge without his warrant, and signed in manner and form as B'Reed."

"Dear Brother I would inform you that this Lodge hath been founded almost eight years and we have had only a Permit to Walk on St. John's Day and to Bury our Dead in manner and form. We have had no opportunity to apply for a Warrant before now, though we have been importuned to send to France for one, yet we thought it best to send to the Fountain from whence we received the Light, for a Warrant: and now Dear Br. we must make you our advocate at the Grand Lodge, hoping you will be so good (in our name and Stead) to Lay this Before the Royal Grand Master and the Grand Wardens and the rest of the Grand Lodge, who we hope will not deny us nor treat us Beneath the rest of our fellowmen, although Poor yet Sincere Brethren of the Craft."

The letter is printed in full, with some slight errors, in my "Critical Examination" and elsewhere. Its date, which has been printed sometimes as "March 1," "March 6," and "March 7," is "Boston, March 2, 1784." Caldwell supposed it was addressed to the Grand Secretary; and the Massachusetts writers (white) say it accompanied the petition for a warrant. The "Permit" mentioned, or as we should now say "dispensation," was doubtless from the military Lodge in which these brethren had been initiated, and restricted their powers. The word "B'Reed" is plainly written. I have taken it for an error for "D'Reed" — "directed" — thinking it likely that Moody, when aiding some of these brethren when stranded in London, had told them that they ought to have diplomas or certificates, properly signed, and had "directed" them how to sign; but a more capable brother suggests to read, "Brother Received." Some account of Moody's Lodge connection is given under Nos. 6 and 11 below.

Warrant granted.
(3) *Prince Spooner to Hall.* London, April 8th, 1784 [*recte* 1785].

Calls attention to the fact that the warrant for Affican Lodge was lying in the Grand Secretary's office. "Brother Gregory hath been for the charter of our Lodge" but had not taken it away. The writer thinks "it will be a discredit to us," if they fail to pay the fees and take it away.

Spooner was at the time a member of African Lodge. The warrant issued, by the premier Grand Lodge of the world, to Prince Hall and others as "African Lodge No. 459," bears date 20th September, 1784, and is in the possession of Prince Hall Grand Lodge. It has been often printed.

(4) *Hall to Spooner.* Not dated.

Regrets delay in taking out warrant; would have sent the money before, if written to. "But as I knew there were on the spot three brothers, I had not the least thought but that they would have paid for it." Has sent by Mr. Hartfield £6-0-8, which "with your one part, will pay for the whole charges of the charter." The Lodge send their hearty thanks to Mr. Moody.

(5) *Hall to* [evidently H.R.H. Henry Frederick, Duke of Cumberland, Grand Master.] Dated, "— 12th, 1785."

Thanks him for granting the warrant, and declares that that act will make manifest, not only "to us, but to the whole world that the true spirit of Masonry hath its foundation from the spirit of our ever blessed Grand Master Jesus Christ who though he is styled King of Kings and Lord of Lords, yet is not ashamed to call and to own the meanest (whom men call mean), if sincere, his beloved brethren of the Fraternity." "I shall in all my lectures endeavor to advance the things as, by the blessing of God, may redound to the honour of the Craft, and also use that discipline in the Lodge as shall make the guilty tremble, and at the same time establish the true honest brother."

(6) *Moody to "The Right Worshipful Master, Wardness and Brethren of the African Lodge, Boston, New England."* June 21st, 1785.

Written in the third person, quite formally, not to say stiffly, requesting them to take up the "constitution" before November, he having obtained it for them

57

"in consequence of a letter from the above Lodge, signed by the then Master, Prince Hall, and the rest of the officers." "The expense is 5 guineas and a half. Viz. 4 for the constitution, 1 for the enrollment in the list of Lodges, and one half for the under Secretary."[1] Signed, "William Moody, No. 4 Hanway Street, near Oxford Street, near Soho, "Brotherly Love Lodge."

Brotherly Love Lodge appears on the Lists, 1781-1791, as No. "55 Lodge of Brotherly Love, King's Head Tav. Holborn," which Gould ("The Four Old Lodges," 69) appears to identify with the Lodge given on Cole's engraved List of 1770 as "71 The Star, Coleman St.," constituted "Dec. 21, 1736."

(7) *Hall to Moody.* August 12th, 1785.

Acknowledges receipt of No. 6, "by the hands of Captain Washington;" thanks him warmly for getting the "constitution;" regrets Gregory's negligence; explains that Gregory had agreed to attend to it, "and so made ourselves easy" until Spooner notified them o the neglect; "Immediately I called the Lodge together and collected twenty dollars, and Captain Scott was to sail soon, I had not time to get but a few together and [was] obliged to send only . . . with order for our Brother Spooner to pay whatever more might be due to the Secretary. But as he has come away before Captain Scott arrived," asks Moody to send the warrant and promises to remit "if Mr. Hatfield doth not pay you." Signed, "Prince Hall,
  "Master of the African Lodge
  "at the Golden Fleece in Water
   Street, Boston."

Spooner, Gregory and others were probably mariners, sailing back and forth between Boston and London. In his Correspondence Report for 1873, Lewis Hayden printed a letter from Hall to Moody, of this same date, relating to the same subject and of the same general import; but evidently not a version of this letter. **Continued on Page 75**

A CHARGE
Delivered to the

AFRICAN LODGE
June 24, 1797
At MEMOTOMY, MASS.

By the Right Worshipful
PRINCE HALL

Published by the Desire of the Members of Said
LODGE 1797.

PRINCE HALL
Our Patron and Founder, Born Sept. 12th, 1748 in Barbados, died in Boston, Dec. 7th, 1807.

A CHARGE
Beloved Brethren of the African Lodge.

'Tis now five years since I deliver'd a Charge to you on some parts and points of Masonry. As one branch or superstructure on the foundation when I endeavored to shew you the duty of a Mason to a Mason, the charity or love to all manking, as the mark and image of the great God, and the Father of the human race.

I shall now attempt to shew you, that it is our duty to sympathise with our fellow men under their troubles; the families of our brethren who are gone: we hope to the Grand Lodge above, here to return no more. But the cheerfulness that you have ever had to relieve them, and ease their burdens, under their sorrows, will never be forgotten by them; and in this manner you will never by weary in doing good.

But my brethren, although we are to begin here, we must not end here; for only look around you and you will see and hear of numbers of our fellow men crying out with holy Job, Have pity on me, O my friends, for the hand of the Lord hath touched me. And this is not to be confined to parties or colours; not to towns or states; not to a kingdom, but to the kingdom of the whole earth, over whom Christ the kind is head and grand master.

Among these numerous sons and daughters of distress, I shall begin with our friends and brethren; and first, let us see them dragg'd from their native country, by the iron hand of tyranny and oppression, from their dear friends and connections, with weeping eyes and aching hearts, to a strange land and strange people, whose tender mercies are cruel; and there to bear the iron yoke of slavery & cruelty till death as a friend shall relieve them. And must not the unhappy condition of these our fellow men draw forth our hearty prayer and wishes for their deliverance from these merchants and traders, whose characters you have in the xviii chap. of the Revelations, 11, 12, — 13 verses, and who knows but these same sort of traders may in a short time, in the like manner, bewail the loss of the African traffick, to their shame and confusion; and if I mistake not, it now begins to dawn in some of the West-Indie islands; which puts me in mind of a nation (that I have somewhere read of) called Ethiopeans, that cannot change their skin: But God can and will change their conditions, and their hearts, too; and Let Boston and the world know, that He hath no respect of persons; and that that bulwark of envy, pride, scorn and contempt, which is too visible to be seen in some and felt, shall fall, to rise no more.

When we hear of the bloody wars which are now in the world, and thousands of our fellow men slain; fathers and mothers bewailing the loss of their sons; wives for the loss of their husbands; towns and cities burnt and destroyed; what must be the heart-felt sorrow and distress of these poor and unhappy people? Though we cannot help them, the distance being too great, yet we may sympathize with them in their troubles, and mingle a tear of sorrow with them, and do as we are exhorted to — weep with those that weep.

Thus, my brethren, we see what a chequered world we live in. Sometimes happy in having our wives and children like olive branches about our tables; receiving the bounties of our great Benefactor. The next year, or month, or week, we may be deprived of some of them, and we go mourning about the streets; so in societies; we are this day to celebrate this Feast of St. John's, and the next week we might be called upon to attend a funeral of someone here, as we have experienced since our last in this Lodge. So in common affairs of life we sometimes enjoy health and prosperity; at another time sickness and adversity, crosses and disappointments.

So in states and kingdoms; sometimes in tranqulity; then wars and tumults; rich to-day, and poor tomorrow; which shews that there is not an independent mortal on earth; but dependent one upon the other, from the king to the beggar.

The great law-giver, Moses, who instructed by his father-in-law, Jethro, and Ethiopean, how to regulate his courts of justice, and what sort of men to choose for the different offices; hear now my words, said he, I will give you counsel, and God shall be with you; be thou for the people to Godward, that thou mayest bring the causes unto the way wherein they must walk; and the work that they must do: moreover thou shall provide out of all the people, able men, such as fear God, men of truth, hating covetousness, and place such over them, to be rulers of thousands, or hundreds and of tens.

So Moses hearkened to the voice of his father-in-law, and did all that he said — Exodus xviii, 22-24.

This is the first and grandest lecture that Moses ever received from the mouth of man; for Jethro understood geometry as well as laws that a Mason may plainly see; so a little captive servant maid by whose advice Nomen, the great general of Syria's army, was healed of his leprosy; and by a servant his proud spirit was brought down: 2 Kings, v, 3-14. The feelings of this little captive, for this great man, her captor, was so great that she forgot her fate of captivity, and felt for the distress of her enemy. Would to God (said she to her mistress) my lord were with the prophets in Samaria, he should be healed of his leprosy. So after he went to the prophet, his proud host was so haughty that he not only disdain'd the prophet's direction, but derided the good old prophet; and had it not been for his servant, he would have gone to his grave, with a double leprosy, the outward and the inward, in the heart, which is the worst of leprosies; a black heart is worse than a white leprosy.

How unlike was this great general's behaviour to that of as grand a character, and as well beloved by his prince as he was; I mean Obadiah, to a like prophet. See for this 1st Kings, sviii, from 7 to 16th.

And as Obadiah was in the way, behold Elijah met him, and he knew him, Yea, go and tell they Lord, behold Elijah is here; and so on to the 16th verse. Thus we see, that great and good men have, and always will have, a respect for ministers and servants of God. Another instance of this is in Acts viii, 27 to 31, of the European Eunuch, a man of great authority, to Philip, the apostle; here is mutual love and friendship between them. This minister of Jesus Christ did not think himself too good to receive the hand, and ride in a chariot with a black man in the face of day; neither did this great monarch (for so he was) think it beneath him to take a poor servant of the Lord by the hand, and invite him into his carriage, though but with a staff, one coat and no money in his pocket. So our Grand Master, Solomon, was not asham'd to take the Queen of Sheba by the hand, and lead her into his court, at the hour of high twelve, and there converse with her on points of masonry (for if ever there was a female mason in the world she was one) and other curious matters; and gratified her by shewing her all his riches and curious pieces of architecture in the temple, and in his house: After some time staying with her, he loaded her with much rich presents: he gave her the right hand of affection and parted in love.

I hope that no one will dare openly (tho' in fact the behaviour of some implies as much) to say, as our Lord said on another occasion. Behold a greater than Solomon is here. But yet let them consider that our Grand Master Solomon did not divide the living child, whatever he might do with the dead one, neither did he prentend to make a law, to forbid the parties from having free intercourse with one another without the fear of censure, or be turned out of the synagogue.

Now, my brethren, as we see and experience, that all things here are frail and changeable and nothing here to be depended upon: Let us seek those things which are above, which are sure and steadfast, and unchangeable, and at the same time let us pray to Almighty God, while we remain in the tabernacle, that he would give us the grace of patience and strength to bear up under all our troubles, which at this day God knows we have our share. Patience, I say, for were we not possess'd of a great measure of it you could not bear up under the daily insults you meet with in the streets of Boston; much more on public days of recreation, how are you shamefully abus'd, and that at such a degree, that you may truly be said to carry your lives in your hands; and the arrows of death are flying about your heads; helpless old women have their clothes torn off their backs, even to the exposing of their nakedness; and by whom are these disgraceful and abusive actions committed, not by the men born and bred in Boston, for they are better bred; but by a mob or horde of shameless, low-lived, envious, spiteful persons, some of them not long since servants in gentlemen's kitchens, scouring knives, tending horses, and driving chaise. 'Twas said by a gentleman who saw that filthy behaviour in the common, that in all the places he had been in, he never saw so cruel behaviour in all his life, and that a slave in the West-Indies, on Sunday or holidays enjoys himself and friends without molestation. Not only this man, but many in town who hath seen their behaviour to you, and that without any provocations, twenty or thirty cowards fall upon one man, have wonder'd at the patience of the Blacks: 'tis not for want of courage in you, for they know that they dare not face you man for man, but in a mob, which we despise, and had rather suffer wrong than to do wrong, to the disturbance of the community and the disgrace of our reputation: for every good citizen doth honor to the laws of the State here he resides.

My brethren, let us not be cast down under these any many other abuses we at present labour under: for the darkest is before the break of day: My brethren, let us remember what a dark day it was with our African brethren six years ago, in the French West Indies. Nothing but the snap of the whip was heard from morning to evening; hanging, broken on the wheel, burning, and all manner of torture inflicted on those unhappy people, for nothing else but to gratify their master's pride, wantonness and cruelty: but blessed be God, the scene is changed; they now confess that God hath no respect of persons, and therefore receive them as their friends, and treat them as brothers. Thus doth Ethiopia begin to stretch forth her hand, from a sink of slavery to freedom and equality.

Although you are deprived of the means of education; yet you are not deprived of the means of meditation; by which I mean thinking, hearing and weighing matters, men and things in your own mind, and making that judgment of them as you think reasonable to satisfy your minds and give an answer to those who may ask you a question. This nature hath furnished you with, without letter learning; and some have made great progress therein, some of those I have heard repeat psalms and hymns, and a great part of a sermon only by hearing it read or preached, and why not in other things in nature; how many of this class of our brethren that follow the seas, can foretell a storm some days before it comes; whether it will be a heavy or light, a long or short one; foretell a hurricane, whether it be destructive or moderate; without any other means than observation and consideration.

So in the observation of the heavenly bodies, this same class without a telescope or other apparatus have through a smoak'd glass observed the eclipse of the sun: One being ask'd what he saw through his smoaked glass? said, Saw, saw, de clipsy, or de clipseys; — and what do you think of it? — stop. dere be two; — right, and what do they look like — Look like, why if I tell you, they look like two ships sailing, one bigger than tother; so they sail by one another, and make no noise. As simple as the answers are they have a meaning and shew, that God can out of the mouth of babes and Africans shew forth his glory; let us then love and adore him as the God who defens us and supports us and will support us under our pressures, let them be ever

59

so heavy and pressing. Let us by the blessing of God, in whatsoever state we are, or may be in, to be content; for clouds and darkness are about him; but justice and truth is his habitation; who hath said, Vengeance is mine and I willl repay it, therefore let us kiss the rod and be still, and see the works of the Lord.

Another thing I would warn you against, is the slavish fear of man, which bringest a snare, saith Solomon. This passion of fear, like pride and envy, hath slain its thousands. — What but this makes so many perjure themselves; for fear of offending them at home they are a little depending on, for some trifles: A man that is under a panic of fear, is afraid to be alone; you cannot hear of a robbery or house broke open or set on fire, but he hath an accomplice with him, who must share the spoil with him; whereas if he was truly bold, and void of fear, he would keep the whole plunder to himself; so when either of them is dected and not the other, he may be call'd to oath to keep it secret, but through fear (and that passion is so strong) he will not confess, still the fatal cord is put on his neck, then death will deliver him from the fear of man, and he will confess the truth when it will not be of any good to himself or the community: nor is this passion of fear only to be found in this class of men, but among the great.

What was the reason that our African kings and princes have plunged themselves and their peaceable kingdoms into bloody wars, to the destroying of towns and kingdoms, but the fear of the report of a great gun or the glittering of arms and swords, which struck these kings near the seaports with such a panic of fear as not only to destroy the peace and happiness of their inland brethren, but plung'd millions of their fellow countrymen into slavery and cruel bondage.

So in other countries; see Felix trembling on his throne. How many Emperors and kings have left their kingdoms and best friends at the fight of a handful of men in arms; how many have we seen that have left their estates and their friends and ran over to the stronger side as they thought: all through fear of the man; who is but a worm, and hath no more power to hurt his fellow worm, without the permission of God, than a real worm.

Thus we may see, my brethren, what a miserable condition it is to be under the slavish fear of men; it is of such a destructive nature to mankind, that the scriptures everywhere from Genesis to the Revelations warn us against it; and even our blessed Savior himself forbids us from this slavish fear of man, in his sermon on the mount; and the only way to avoid it is to be in the fear of God: let a man consider the greatness of his power, as the maker and upholder of all things here below, and that in Him we live, and move, and have our being, the giver of the mercies we enjoy here from day to day, and that our lives are in his hands, and that he made the heavens the sun, moon and stars to move in their various orders; let us thus view the greatness of God, and then turn our eyes on mortal man, a worm, a shade, a wafer, and see whether he is an object of fear or not; on the contrary, you will think him in his best estate, to be but vanity, feeble and a dependent mortal, and stands in need of your help, and cannot do without your assistance, in some way or other; and yet some of these poor mortals will try to make you believe they are Gods, but worship them not. My brethren, let us pay all due respect to all whom God hath put in places of honor over us: do justly and be faithful to them that hire you, and treat them with that respect they may deserve; but worship no man. Worship God, this much is your duty as Christians and as Masons.

We see then how necessary it is to have a fellow feeling for our distress'd brethren of the human race, in their troubles, both spiritual and temporal — How refreshing it is to a sick man, to see his sympathizing friends around his bed, ready to administer all the relief in their power; although they can't relieve his bodily pain yet they may ease his mind by good instructions and cheer his heart by their company.

How doth it cheer up the heart of a man when his house is on fire, to see a number of friends coming to his relief; he has so transported that he almost forgets his loss and his danger, and fills him with love and gratitude; and their joys and sorrows are mutual.

So a man wreck'd at sea, how must it revive his drooping heart to see a ship bearing down for his relief.

How doth it rejoice the heart of a stranger in a strange land to see the people cheerful and pleasant and are ready to help him. How did it, think you, cheer the heart of those our unhappy African brethren to see a ship commissioned from God, and from a nation that without flattery faith, that all men are free and are brethren; I say to see them in an instant deliver such a number from their cruel bolts and galling chains, and to be fed like men, and treated like men. Where is the man that has the least spark of humanity, that will not rejoice with them; and bless a righteous God who knows how and when to relieve the oppressed, as we see he did in the deliverance of the captives among the Algerines; how sudden were they delivered by the sympathizing members of the Congress of the United States, who now enjoy the free air of peace and liberty, to their great joy and surprise, to them and their friends. Here we see the hand of God in various ways, bringing about his own glory for the good of mankind, by the mutual help of their fellow men; which ought to teach us in all our straits, be they what they may, to put our trust in him, firmly believing that he is able and will deliver us against our enemies; and that no weapon from'd against us shall prosper; only let us be steady and uniform in our walks, speech and behaviour; always doing to all men as we wish and desire they would do to us in the like cases and circumstances.

Live and act as Masons, that you may die as Masons; let those despisers see, altho' many of us cannot read, yet by our searches and researches into men and things, we have supplied that defect, and if they will let us we shall call ourselves a charter'd lodge, of just and lawful Masons; be always ready to give an answer to those that ask you a question; give the right hand of affection and fellowship to whom it justly belongs, let their colour and complexion be what it will: let their nation be what it may, for they are our brethren, and it is your indispensable duty so to do; let them as Masons deny this, and we and the world know what to think of them be they ever so grand: for we know this was Solomon's creed. Solomon's creed did I say, it is the decree of the Almighty, and all Masons have learnt it: plain marked language and plain and true facts need no apologies.

I shall now conclude with an old poem I found among some papers:

Let blind admirers handsome faces praise,
And graceful features to great honor raise,
The glories of the red and white express,
I know no beauty but in holiness;
If God of beauty be the uncreate
Perfect idea, in this lower state.
The greatest beauties of an human mould
Who most resemble Him we justly hold;
Whom we resemble not in flesh and blood,
But being pure and holy, just and good:
May such a beauty fall but to my share,
For curious shape or face I'll never care.

*Obtained through the courtesy of
Bro. Augustus C. Fleet from H. E. Pickersgill
and printed by
Arthur A. Schomburg, Grand Secretary*

CONGRATULATIONS

Executive Secretary, James E. Herndon, M.P.S.

The *Phylaxis Society* is quite blessed, as its leadership which is controlled by the Executive Committee, has truly dedicated Prince Hall Masons.

Our Executive Secretary, Bro. James E. Herndon, was honored as *"Master Mason of the Year"* by Centennill Lodge #4 in Denver, Colorado. A honor which clearly reflects his dedication to the Prince Hall fraternity. Bro. Herndon, a retired US Army First Sergeant besides being the Executive Secretary of the *Phylaxis Society,* is the Junior Deacon of his Lodge. A Past Patron of Bathsheba Chapter #14, Fort Leonard Wood, Missouri, and Queen of the South Chapter #11, OES in Denver. He is also the Commander-in-Chief of Mountain Plains Consistory #33 and the Recorder of Syrian Temple #49.

The *Phylaxis Society* considers Bro. Herndon, not only Master Mason of the Year, but Mr. Prince Hall Masonry. Congratulations Jim.

Our hat also goes off to our First Vice President, Bro. Herbert Dailey. From a paper read before Prince Hall Military Lodge #21, in Seoul, Korea by the President of the *Phylaxis Society*, Joseph A. Walkes in 1971 and appeared in the Missouri *Masonic Light* under title *Profile of a Traveling Man,* that among the giants of Prince Hall Masonry was Bro. Herbert Dailey.

We quote from the article. After becoming a Mason, he was sent to Korea. While there he helped organize a Masonic Study Club. He left Korea in 1958 heading for the State of Washington, where he became active in Cassia Lodge #5, in Tacoma. He received his 32° in Consistory #67 in Seattle and became President of the Triangle Club #2 in Tacoma. This being composed of 32nd degree Prince Hall Masons. During his military career, he help the Baumholder Military Study Club under the Prince Hall Military Lodge at Frankfurt, Germany and had the honor as serving as Commander-in-Chief for the first class of 92 Master Masons which became Prince Hall Military Consistory #304. He would later become involved in Pike Lodge #5 in Colorado Springs, Colorado, King Solomon Lodge #15, Fort Leonard Wood, Missouri and the Bumble Bee Masonic Study Club in Lang Bin, South Viet Nam. A truly dedicated Prince Hall Freemason.

Our Second Vice President, Bro. Zellus Bailey can be truly called a *"Master Mason's, Master Mason."* Bro. Zellus Bailey formed the first Prince Hall Lodge in the Canal Zone, Prince Hall Military Lodge #174, in Panama, and today this Prince Hall Masonic Lodge help birth a second Lodge and has now become a Masonic District of the Most Worshipful Prince Hall Grand Lodge of Missouri.

This is only a part of the Executive Committee of the Phylaxis Society, but truly the best that Prince Hall Masonry has to offer.

THE PHYLAXIS SOCIETY AND THE PRINCE HALL CONFESSION OF MASONIC FAITH

In this declaration of the Principals of *Phylaxis Society* we call upon the words of Bro. George W. Crawford, from his book *Prince Hall and His Followers* (1914).

So far from lamenting the absolute disassociation of Negro Masonry from the white Masonry of this country, our attitude towards that fact should be that of serene indifference. Because of what it is meant to imply, and because of its usual accompaniment of degradation, the Negro people frequently find themselves complled to oppose the separation of the races. This fact is often seized upon by detractors, both within and without the ranks, as evidence of our lack of proper racial self-esteem. More is the reason, therefore, that on those occasions when it does not hurt to be by ourselves, we ought to be conspicuous in our contentment to have it so.

THE FOLLOWERS OF PRINCE HALL ARE REGULAR MASONS. Why should they crave "recognition" from those whose Masonic divestment has left them still clothed in all the pettiness and prejudice of the profane; and to whom the word brother is a designation of a social status rather than of the universal kinship of men?

THE FOLLOWERS OF PRINCE HALL BELIEVE IN THE UNIVERSALITY OF MASONRY. Shall they feel aggrieved at being denied affiliation with those whose Masonry is of such sort that they halt the worthy candidate at the porch of the Temple to inquire if he be Aryan, or Finn, or Hottentot?

THE FOLLOWERS OF PRINCE HALL ARE PROUD OF THEIR MASONRY. Shall they therefore aspire to assume Masonic offices for those who would deem it a condescension to accept the same? Or shall they desire to take their distress to those who would consider any proffered relief not the charity of a Mason but the alms of a profane?

The only recognition which Negro Masons could ever accept without self-stultification would be recognition coupled with union with them under the wide baldachin of universal Masonry, from which the white brethren have drawn themselves aprt. As to recognition on any other basis — a fig!

* * * * CREDO * * * *

I BELIEVE IN GOD, GRAND ARCHITECT OF THE UNIVERSE, THE ALPHA OF THE UNRECKONED YESTERDAYS, THE OMEGA OF THE IMPENETRABLE TOMORROWS, THE BEGINNING AND THE ENDING.

I BELIEVE IN MAN, POTENTIALLY GOD'S OTHER SELF, OFTEN FALTERING ON HIS WAY UPWARD BUT IRREPRESSIBLE IN THE URGE TO SCALE THE SPIRITUAL ANNAPURNAS.

I BELIEVE IN FREEMASONRY — THAT CORPORATE ADVENTURE IN UNIVERSAL BROTHERHOOD, DESPISING KINSHIP WITH NO CHILD OF THE ALL-FATHER.

I BELIEVE IN PRINCE HALL MASONRY, A DOOR OF BENEVOLENCE, SECURELY TILED AGAINST THE UNWORTHY, BUT OPENED WIDE TO MEN OF GOOD REPORT, WHETHER ARYAN OR HOTTENTOT.

I BELIEVE IN MASONIC VOWS — THE TROTHS OF TRUE MEN PLIGHTED IN THEIR BETTER SELVES.

The *Phylaxis Society* stands behind these words, and declares it before the entire Masonic world, where-so-ever-a-Freemason be dispatched. And to those who are the enemies of Prince Hall Masonry — TAKE DUE AND TIMELY NOTICE, and govern yourself accordingly.

ALEXANDER CLARK, P.G.M.

Of the Most Worshipful Grand Lodge of Free and Accepted Masons (colored) for the State of Missouri and its jurisdiction, popularly known as colored orator of Iowa, was born in Washington county, Pennsylvania, on the 25th day of February, 1826, his parents being John Clark and Rebecca, nee Darnes. His father was born a slave, yet the son of his master, an Irishman, who emancipated both him and his mother, who was a bulatto. The mother of Alexander Clark died May 7th, 1887, at the age of ninety. She was purely Africo-American. Consequently our subject is two-thirds African and one-third Irish. To his relationship to the first named nationality is due in a great measure the genius and brilliancy which adorns his character, and which has led to his success. On his mother's side he comes from a robust and long-lived stock. His grandfather, Geo. Darnes, died at the age of seventy-three, and his grandmother, Lettice, lived to the age of one hundred and one, and her sister, Penda, lived to the age of one hundred and four. Alexander received but a limited education in the common schools of his native village, but he was a bright, intelligent lad, and seemed to learn by intuition. He read men and books and was continually absorbing from everything around him. At the age of thirteen he removed to Cincinnati, Ohio, where he learned the barbering business with his uncle, William Darnes, who also sent him to school for about a year at different periods, where he made considerable proficiency in grammar, arithmetic, geography and natural philosophy. In 1841 he left Cincinnati and went south on the steamer George Washington as bartender. In May, 1842, he settled in Muscatine, Iowa, which has since been his home. Here he conducted a barbershop till 1868, when failing health, resulting from the confinement incident to the business, compelled him to seek a more active occupation. Having, by industry and frugality accumulated some capital, he invested in real estate, boughr some timber land in the neighborhood of Muscatine, obtained contracts for the furnishing of wood to steamboats, did some speculating, which proved successful; and the result is the accumulation of a competence on which he lives in ease. In 1851 he became a member of the Masonic order by joining Prince Hall Lodge, No. 10, of St. Louis, Missouri, then operating under a charter from the Grand Lodge (colored) of Ohio, but which is now No. 1, under the Grand Lodge of Missouri (colored) of Free and Accepted Ancient Masons. In 1868 he was arched and knighted and elected deputy grand master of the Grand Lodge, H. McGee Alexander being grand master. The latter dying on the 20th of April, 1868, our subject became grand master in his stead and fulfilled his unexpired term. The jurisdiction then extended over Missouri, Iowa, Minnesota, Tennessee, Arkansas and Mississippi. He organized most all the subordinate lodges in the last three states and assisted in organizing their grand lodges. At the next annual meeting of the Grand Lodge of Missouri he was elected grand treasurer and appointed a delegate to the Most Worshipful National Grand Compact of Masons (colored) for the United States, held at Wilmington, Delaware, on the 9th of October, 1868. In June, 1869, he was elected grand master and held the distinguished office for three consecutive years. In 1872 he was elected grand secretary, and in 1873 was appointed chairman of the committee on foreign correspondence. In 1874 he was again called to the position of grand master and annually re-elected to the same position up to 1877. His jurisdiction now extended over the States of Missouri, Iowa, Minnesota and Colorado, and embraced eighty-seven lodges and twenty-seven hundred members. He is said to be one of the most accomplished ritualists, and among the most able and successful executive officers. In politics he is a Republican, and one of the most eloquent and pungent orators of the nation. It will readily be conceded that he exercises a controlling influence upon his brethren wherever he is brought in contact with them. In 1863 he enlisted in the First Iowa Colored Volunteer Infantry and received the appointment of sergeant major, but was refused muster on account of physical disability in left ankle. In 1869 he was appointed by the colored state convention of Iowa a delegate to the colored national convention which met that year at Washington, and by that organization he was appointed chairman of the committee to bring before the proper committee of the Senate and House of Representatives the claims of colored soldiers and seamen to an equality with their white copatriots in the matter of bounties and pensions. He was also appointed a member of the committee from the same convention to wait upon President Grant and Vice President Colfax to tender to them the congratulations of the colored people of the United States upon their election to the highest offices in the gift of the American people, and on the first occasion was the mouthpiece of the committee. In 1869 he was a member and vice president of the Iowa Republican State convention, and took a prominent part in its deliberations. In the following year he was also a delegate to the state convention and a member of the committee on resolutions, and on each occasion addressed the convention with such power, enthusiasm and effect as secured for him the title of "Colored orator of the West," and it is generally conceded that in this regard he is second only to the redoubtable Fred Douglass. He "stumped" the State of Iowa as well as most of the Southern States, and is recognized as one of the most powerful, eloquent and sapient orators of the country. In 1872 he was appointed by the Republican State convention of Iowa one of the delegates at large to the National convention at Philadelphia, which nominated Grant and Wilson for President and Vice President. In 1873 he was appointed by President Grant consul to Aux Cayes, Hayti, but refused the position owing to the smallness of the salary. In January, 1876, he was appointed by a colored convention of Iowa a delegate the Centennial Exposition at Philadelphia, for the purpose of preparing statistics and gathering useful information for the colored race. Later in the same year he was appointed an alternate delegate by the Iowa State Republican convention to the National convention at Cincinnati, Ohio, which nominated Hayes and Wheeler. It will thus be seen that Mr. Clark, like the great apostles of freedom, Sumner, Goodell, Garrison, Phillips and Fred. Douglass, he has struggled manfully for the emancipation and elevation of his race. He had undying faith from the earliest of reason that he would live to see the extirpation of slavery from the United States if not from the world and he has not lived and labored in vain. The names of Brown, Lincoln, Lovejoy and Grant are indelibly written upon his heart and should be cherished as talismanic by the African race for all time to come. On the 9th of October, 1848, at Iowa City, he married Miss Catherine Griffin, of African and Indian origin, born in slavery, but manumitted at the age of three years. She was a woman in every way suited to his companionship and worthy of her husband, and was highly esteemed for her Christian character by all who knew her. She bore him five children, two boys and three girls, of whom two, John and Ellen, died in infancy. The survivors, Rebecca J., Susan V. and Alexander G., all inherit their father's intellectual endowments; all severally graduates of the high school of Muscatine, and give promise of useful and honorable lives. Alexander is a printer, having learned the same in the office of the Muscatine Journal, he also graduated in 1869 from the law department of the Iowa State University, L.L.B. Rebecca is the wife of G. W. Appleton, of Muscatine, Iowa. Susan is the wife of the Rev. Richard Holley, a minister in the African M. Episcopal Church. Our subject became a member of the African Methodist Episcopal Church in 1850, and continues in fellowship. He was superintendent of the Sabbath school of the church of that denomination in Muscatine for twenty-five years, and is also one of the trustees of said church, to the support of which he is the largest contributor. He is also generous with his means

63

for the support of charities and benevolent institutions of the city of his adoption, and is, in short, one of the best citizens of the place. Alexander Clark is a man of unquestioned ability. His Masonic addresses bespeak the soundest judgment and the clearest intellect, besides thorough research and acquaintance with the most ancient history, rivaling in many regards the orations of the most famous craftsmen of the order, often ranging high in the regions of the poetic and sublime. As a political orator he is clear, prompt and strong, and has the rare merit of stopping when he is through, and while he is uncompromising in his principles, yet he says things so straight, and in a manner so cautious as to excite no ill-will from anyone; he is, in short, a valuable citizen of whom the State of Iowa feels proud. His leading characteristic is a philosophic turn of mind, by which he analyzes everything claiming his attention with reference to its usefulness. If a matter will not contribute to his own good or the good of his fellow men he will have nothing to do with it. As already mentioned he is a Republican from gratitude. He appreciates fully the boon of emancipation and enfranchisement not because it has been of special benefit to him but because of its numerous blessings to others. Striving as he has done all his life against the prejudice of color, he longs to see the time when a man will be esteemed at his true worth without regard to circumstances of race or birth, hence he never was a sympathizer with the principles of the Know Nothings or Native American party. Although he is a Methodist both in principle and practice, he cultivates a feeling of liberality toward, all other creeds. He is at the same time frank and outspoken in his own opinions. In all departments of thought and action he believes that honesty is the best policy, hence he is never in favor of restoring to any expedient or to doubtful means in order to insure a temporary triumph, or even a permanent success; he will not do evil that good may come; he has more faith in being and doing than in mere belief, although he believes the latter to be essential. His friendships are slow in their formation, but when once formed they are enduring; indeed, he has never been known to desert a friend. His feelings of sympathy are easily enlisted, though in matters of charity he exercises the same caution that he does in his own business affairs, and is seldom deceived. Many a poor, helpless one, especially of his own race, has reason to thank God from the heart for the existence of such a man as Alexander Clark.

The foregoing we copied from the United States Biographical Dictionary of Eminent and Self-made Men, Iowa volume of date of 1878, and we continue a brief history of Mr. Clark from 1878 to date.

One of the most important positions assigned our subject, was his appointment by the General Conference of the African M. E. Church, in 1880, one of its twelve delegates to the Ecumenical Conference of Methodists which convened in City Road Wesleyan chapel, London, England, September 7th, 1881, continued its session until the 20th. The conference represented twenty-eight different denominations. The conference was the largest and most scholarly Christian by ever convened upon the continent of earth. It was represented by delegates from all parts of the world, England, Ireland, Scotland, France, Germany, Italy, Norway, Sweden, Switzerland, Polynesia, Africa, India, China, Japan, Australia, New Zealand, the United States, South America, Canada and the West Indies, and be it said to the credit of the African M. E. Church that its delegates compared favorably with the most learned representatives of that grand body of scholars. The twelve delegates of said church, viz: Bishops D. A. Payne, D.D., LL.D., Rev. James, A. Shorter, John M. Brown, D.D., D.C.L., Wm. F. Dickerson, D.D., Elders B. F. Lee, D.D., James M. Townsend, D.D., A. T. Carr and J. C. Embry, D.D., laymen, Prof. J. P. Shorter, A. M., Mr. H. T. Gant, Prof. Joseph Morris, and our subject, Alexander Clark, LL.B.

In 1884 he organized Hiram Grand Lodge (colored) of Iowa, and was elected to the Grand East three consecutive years. There being another Grand Lodge (colored) holding concurrent jurisdiction, our subject, with that masterly hand and strong intellect, having hold upon the affections of both grand bodies, assisted by that prince of Masons, G. H. Cleggett, Grand Master of African Grand Lodge, he succeeded in uniting the two into one body to be known and styled United Grand Lodge (colored) of Iowa. He was made president of the convention that united the two into one. In this act Mr. Clark displayed nerve, tact and parliamentary ability, forcing the belligerent elements to yield to the right, making the needful concessions on both sides. For which he has the esteem of all true Masons.

In the National Masonic convention in Chicago, held on the 4th, 5th and 6th days of September, 1877, our subject displayed that sound and logical knowledge of Masonic law and jurisprudence, and by his eloquence, after a hard two days' debate, secured the passage of a resolution upon the subject of concurrent jurisdiction, which put to flight the strong hold of the American Saxon Masons' prejudice against the African brother Masons. (See Clark's resolution, minutes of said convention.)

Whilst in London, attending the Ecumenical conference he visited France and Switzerland. Interviewed the Grand Orient of France, and on Sabbath was the guest of the Grand Secretary. They were driven to Marseilles, there visiting the turning on of the waters, which is a grand sight and occurs once a month, and always comes on Sunday, as France has no Sabbath. His interviewing the record of the Grand Lodge of England developed the facts of the legality of Masonry among colored men in this country. His Letters from Paris, London and Geneva portrayed that power of mind to analyze men and things closely.

In 1884 our subject, at the age of fifty-five entered the Iowa State University law department, graduating with the title of LL.B. The banquet given him by the Muscatine bar, on his return home, speaks of the esteem he is held in by the people of his home for the past forty years.

In December, 1882, he bought the Chicago Conservator, a colored journal owned published by A. T. Bradley, a colored man of ability, but a Bourbon Democrat. Mr. Clark, on buying the paper, associated his son, Alex. G. and Mr. F. L. Barnett in copartnership, wheeling the paper into the ranks of a true radical Republican paper. After two years the paper became unsustaining, he bought out his son and Mr. Barnett, paid off all the debts and conducted it successfully for two and a half years as sole owner, editor and proprietor, bringing its circuation to 1,200 copies issued weekly. Sold the paper out on the 15th of March last so as to save himself. As an editor he was and now is held in high esteem by the colored press, and at the National Press Association, at its sitting at Atlantic City, New Jersey, 1886, was elected Treasurer and appointed chairman of the Executive Committee. He prepared the programme for the National sitting held at Louisville, Ky., August 9th, 1887, and there and then by his clear and logical talk enlisted the favorable criticism of the entire white and colored press of said city. His speech in response to the welcoming address by Prof. Simmons, President of the association, so impressed the convention that they refused to let him retire from office and membership although not now nor then in active newspaper business. A tintype in the Louisville papers presented the stern face of our subject. Thus it will readily be conceded, as said his biography from which we largely copied, that Mr. Clark is a man of broad and well cultured mind, with commanding influence whenever he comes in contact with his fellow-citizens, both white and colored, holding a place in the hearts of his race incased in letters of gold indellible. His letter in the A. M. E. Church Review on Socialism, July, 1886, elicited much favorable comment by some of the ablest journals of the country. The Chicago Inter-Ocean gave a column in its editorial page, pronouncing it one of the ablest articles written on that subject.

At the reception of the Right Honorable the Lord Mayor of London (W. McArthur, Esq., M. P.,) and Lady Mayoress, given at the great Mansion House on Wednesday eve., Sept. 7th, to the delegates attending the conference and ministers in London and other distinguished guests numbering over nine hundred persons, our subject was present as one of the delegates of the conference, and had the honor of being presented to the Lady Mayoress' youngest sister, who, by her brother, by Dr. Arthur, invited him to accompany her to the large drawing-room, to hear her Italian band discourse some of the finest pieces. Thus it will be seen, as before mentioned, that Alexander Clark, P.G.M., of the Grand Lodge of Missouri, is a man of National reputation, and distinguished at home and abroad as such.

VITAL DIMENSIONS OF EFFECTIVE POWER

We are living at a time of strange contradictions, conflicting ideologies, confused issues, and baffling inconsistencies! The ugly state of confusion and strange paradoxes in our today's society are reminiscent of the social temper described by Charles Dickens, in his **Tale of Two Cities,** some one hundred years ago, in 1859, when he wrote:

"It was the best of times, and the worst of times; it was an age of wisdom an age of foolishness; it was an epoch of belief, and an epoch of skepticism; it was a season of light, and a season of darkness! it was a springtime of hope and wintertime of despair; everything was before us, and nothing was before us."

Thus wrote Charles Dickens, 110 years ago.

I submit that this paradoxical and inconsistent state of affairs, as described by Dickens in 1859 is clearly characteristic of our own times. Ours, too, is a time of strange contradictions, conflicting philopsophies, baffling confusions, and ugly paradoxes. On the one hand, we have the best; on the other hand, we are plagued with the worst. On the one hand, there is light-hearted jubilation; on the other hand, there is frightful frustration. On the one hand — in this our day — there is abounding wealth; on the other hand there is wretched poverty. On the one hand, there is excessive luxury; on the other hand, there is ghastly starvation. Ours is a time, when billions of dollars can be found for fantastic trips to the moon; and a time, when not enough money can be found to feed the hungry, and clean up the slums. Ours is a time of great schools and colleges and universities; and a time when ignorance is rampant, and when crime is at an all-time high.

These are times when the gospel of peace and love and brotherhood is proclaimed from thousands of churches and synagouges; while, at the same time, hatred and violence and war are eroding human hearts and destroying human lives. These, indeed, are times of strange and baffling contradictions; times of unparelelled inconsistencies!

In the midst of this global confusion; in the midst of these vicious paradoxes, a bewildered and frustrated minority — long denied the fruits of democracy; long denied the promises enunciated in the organic law of the land; long oppressed and intimidated; this struggling minority, is rightly demanding its place in the sun, and rightly clamoring for a proprotionate share of power. These demands are the normal expressions of normal men and women, emerging forth in the day-dawn of a new era.

The urge for power — for total involvement and participation in every facet of contemporary life — is fitting and proper and imperative. Power in itself, is all right; it's the goal of every society; it's the dynamics which turn the wheels of progress! it's the undergirding of our economy, and the juglar vein of our society. Power, in itself, is a normal human urge; and the aquisition of power is basic to human progress. But, keep in mind the fact that effective power transcends all superficial labels of race, color, or nationality. Effective power, by its very nature, is fully capable of commanding respect and demanding its rightful recognition.

Effective power is such as was exhibited by Socrates, when he called around himself the young men of Greece, and — in the face of rebuffs — explained to them the essence of democracy. It is such as was exhibited by Frederick Douglass — that great American statesman of other years — when, against terrific odds, he took his stand for justice, and equality for a down-trodden race. It is such as was shown by Booker T. Washington, when, through sheer ability, he inaugurated a system of education, which revolutionized the American economy. Effective power is such as was exhibited by Mahatma Ghandi, whose program of non-violence brought emancipation to 400 million natives of India. It is such as was demonstrated by that prophet in our own day, the late Dr. Martin Luther King, Jr., when, throughout this nation, he advocated a philosophy of love and Christian brotherhood, and courageously expounded a program of equity and human rights for the oppressed and disinherited. Effective power is such as was exemplified by the Man of Galilee, when, on the brow of Olivet — following the tragedy of Golgotha, and the triumph of the Resurrection — He declared, "You shall have power after you have received the spirit of God . . ."

In this context, I would discuss a few specific and **vital dimensions** of **effective power**.

I. Intellectual Power. "Knowledge is power." More than ever, is this an undeniable fact. In this day of technological advances, and of rigid competition, education is an absolute necessity. Whether we like it or not, it is simply one of the stern realities that, "those who **know** will continue to be the masters of those who know **not**. Those who know **not** — be they black or white — will continue to occupy inferior roles. This fact suggests the inescapable conclusion that, more and more, we should march to the centers of learning; march to the sources of knowledge. If we are to have effective power, instead of "burn, baby, burn," our motto should be, "learn, baby, learn." The so-called Afro haircuts, and beards and beads are perfectly all right — for those who like such; but unless under that bush, there is some **gray matter** and some know-how, we will be miserably wanting, and will not be able to command much power!

Let the word go out — clearly and unmistakably — that "the apparel does not make the man;" and the color of one's skin — be further established that basic in this whole matter of our quest for rightful recognition and for our rightful place on the American scene is this vitally important dimension of **intellectual power!**

II. Economic Power. Effective power is economic power. In our search for power, it is highly imperative that we recognize the importance of an economic base. Undergirding our entire social structure is this matter of economics; this matter of ownership. A "beggar race" is not in position to exert much power. One of the sure ways of entering the main stream of the American life, and attaining effective power is through strong economic resources. A certain business enterprise — worth over a hundred million dollars — owned, and operated by Negroes: that's power! In a certain city, a chain of some forty substantial businesses — owned and operated by blacks; that's power! A certain city-wide bus line — the only one in a city of 150,000 population — owned and operated by Negroes; that's power! In another city, a certain black citizen, with holdings of over $8,000,000 that's power; that's real power; effective power!

III. Political Power. Another dimension of power which deserves major consideration is that of political power; the power of the ballot. It has been said, again and again — through the press and from many platforms — and we might as well get this fact well in mind, that "a voteless people is a helpless people," Remember, too, that our active interest in the political area must be more than a once-a-year, at-election-time, spasmodic-type of interest. Political power — in order to be fully effective and productive — must be a year-round concern; a year-round program of action.

The men and women of color in the United States Congress; the scores of our racila group in the various state legislatures; the over forty Negro mayors — many of whom are in some of our largest cities — and the hundreds of other elected officials, including sheriffs, city councilmen, county commissioners, members of boards of education — all of whom are viable forces in the power structure — acquired their respective roles through the instrument of the ballot. If we, as a race, would move forward, continually; if we would give substance and real meaning to our cry for "black power," there must be a concentration, increasingly, on this matter of the **ballot;** there must be increased emphasis on **political** action! Herein is one of the sure avenues to effective power — on the American scene.

IV. The Power of Togetherness. Effective power is the power of togetherness; the power of united action. Of late, there has been noticeable agitation by certain segments of our racial group for a so-called "separate society;" the concept of separatism. I submit that this sort of movement is both dangerous and disintegrating. Be it known that black racism is just as bad as white racism, and both are the ways of futility. One sure way to dissipate our strength and to retard our progress is through a splintering of our forces. "Whom the gods would destroy, the first divide."

Effective power will come through **togetherness** — both, as a race and as a nation. As a race, our resources are insufficient for us to indulge the "luxury" of internal scisms; and, as a nation, we cannot hope to endure through a "division of our ranks. As a people, we are, in truth, **one nation.** We the 23 million men and women of color, are a very real part of the American heritage. The labors and sacrifices and spilled blood of our forefathers felled the forests, forded the canals, manned the industries, cultivated the soil, and built the cities. This, indeed, is the land where **our** fathers died, and "gave their last full measure of devotion." Let no one deceive you! This is **our** country; our native land; our flag! Let us continue to stand **together**, and press our rightful claim, until, "from every mountainside freedom **shall** ring; from every mountain-side, and from every plane; from the clay hills of Alabama; from the sand dunes of Mississippi; from the slum-ridden ghettos of every city, freedom and justice shall ring!

V. Psychological Power. Another vital dimension of power is that of psychological power. By this I mean the power which is derived from a proper sense of identity; the proper evaluation and appreciation of our own history; a proper understanding of our contribution to American culture and to world civilization.

It is an undeniable fact that one of America's most brutal acts of injustice and inhumanity against the Negro has been the brazen attempt to deny him his rightful place in history, and make it appear that his past is totally barren, and unworthy of historic recognition. Nothing can be further from the truth; and, I submit that it we would enjoy effective power, we must guard against this vicious distortion; we must give the "lie" to this contemptuous fallacy. We must inform ourselves and our children of the true facts of history — as they are. We must inform ourselves of the undeniable fact that, across the years, the black man has played a major role in the march of progress — both in the United States and in the world.

Before there was an America; before there was a Europe; before the British Armada sailed the Seven Seas, black men, on the banks of the Nile and Euphrates, were creating a mighty nation, and presiding as rulers and administrators of a flourishing empire. Before the emergence of modern technology, men of color were artisians and architects and builders of distinction and renown; they were the designers and builders of the mighty pyramids of Egypt, one of the seven wonders of the world. Moreover, fully documented facts reveal that, across the years, men of color have been in the vanguard of progress in every facet of human endeavor. It was a Negro, Crispus Attucks, who was the first man to give his life for American independence; it happened at Bunker's Hill. It is opportune, at this time and place, to point to the fact that this very city in which we now meet — our nation's capital — is enternally indebted to a black man for its beginnings; for, indeed, it was a Negro, Benjamin Banneker, a distinguished mathematician and surveyor, who helped to draw the plan and survey the site for this beautiful metropolis on the banks of the Potomac; and, by the way, it was this same black man, Benjamin Banneker, who invented America's first clock, and published one of the first almanacs. I could go on and on, citing outstanding instances, but I shall mention, here, just one more significant example. Here of

67

late, a great deal has been said about the scientific achievements of a certain surgeon by the name of Christian Barnard of South Africa, and of his experiments in transplanting human hearts — a scientific feat, which is still very questionable; but I would remind you that, long before there was a Dr. Barnard; long before his surgical efforts, a black man, by the name of Daniel Hale Williams of Pennsylvania, in the year of 1893, performed the first successful operation on the human heart and through his scientific genius, opened the way for all subsequent heart surgery.

In sceince, in statesmanship, on the battlefields, in invention, in discovery and exploration, in literature and the arts, and in every phase of endeavor, men and women of color have played well their parts in the unfolding drama of human progress. Let no one deceive you; we have been a very real part of this nation's upward strides in every national venture; and we have been a significant part of her bulwark in every crisis. We were there, when Columbus sailed the Atlantic; we were there, when Washington crossed the Deleware; we were there, when Grant fought back the advancing Confederates; and we were instrumental in helping Lincoln defend Old Glory and preserve this Nation. We've been there in every struggle — from the rock-ribbed heights of Bunker's Hill to the germ-infested swamps of Vietnam, and in each crisis, men of color have performed with valor, and fidelity, and heroism — unexcelled! This fact, we must always keep in focus — as an important psychological dimension of power.

VI. The Power of Faith. Finally, still another vital dimension of power is the power or **faith;** that internal, spiritual resource which enables one to stand firm and unfaltering, in the midst of threatening dangers and terrifying crises; that inward, spiritual ingredient which enables one to "mount up with wings, as eagles; to run and not be weary; to walk and not faint." This is the clarion challenge; this is the urgent need — the dimension of **faith!**

We must have faith in ourselves and in our own possibilities, with the sure conviction that if we qualify for the opportunities at hand, and if our cause is just, there is no force on earth that can stay our progress. We must have firm and uncompromising faith in ourselves, — with the full realization that, in the divine economy of God, each individual is a sacred entity, in whose bosom burn the fires of the eternal!

Have faith in our fellowmen! Our society today is plagued with **distrust, suspicion,** and **lack of confidence** — each in the other. We must always keep in mind that, notwithstanding the legions of "undesirables," in our society; notwithstanding the thousands of extremists and the racists and the enemies of justice which infest our land, there are millions of men and women — both black and white — who stand firmly on the eternal doctrine of the fatherhood of God and the brotherhood of man, and who are fully resolved to defend to the utmost that which is **right** — whatever the cost!

Have faith! — faith in America! — faith in our Native Land! We know, for a fact that there are many wrinkles in our national garment; many flaws in our national government. But the good citizen is one who dedicates his energies — positively and vigorously — toward correcting these faults. It is not one who engages in a campaign of destruction; but it is one who employs his talents in constructive efforts and creative endeavors for mutual betterment and for the good of all, and it is one who has faith in our Nation: faith that, one day, in the not distant future, America will rise to its true stature, throw off all sham and hyprocrisy, and as "one nation, indivisible," live its own **noble creed,** under the banner of the immortal proclamation that, "all men are created equal, and that they are endowed by their Creator with certain inalienable rights, and that among these are life, liberty, and the pursuit of happiness."

Have faith — unconditional faith in the Enternal God! faith which is grounded in the assurance that God still moves in history, and still determines the destinies of men and nations; faith which knows that, under God, a better day is already dawning, and a brighter tomorrow is sure to come. This is the faith of our fathers, who, even in the darkest hours, would not grow weary; in the midst of persecutions, would not despair; but, out of the depths of their souls, sang triumphantly, "I'm so glad trouble don't last always." This, mind you, was a song of faith; this was a song of prophecy and of triumph!

Effective power involves the element of faith! — faith in the Eternal, All-sufficient, Never-Failing God; faith that He still lives, and reigns and rules; that He is still Lord of lords and King of kings, that He is still fully able to liberate those who are in bondage and set the captives free!

Through the power of faith, one envisions the time, when the superficial labels of race and color and nationality will "fade into thin air," and every individual will be judged on his merit, and recognized on the basis of his character and his service to mankind.

This dimension of faith gives one the assurance that one day "every valley will be exhalted; every mountain and hill will be made low; the crooked ways made straight, and the rough places plain and the glory of the Lord will be revealed, and all flesh — the black, the white, the brown, the yellow — all flesh, shall see it together, for the mouth of the Lord has spoken it..."

This power of faith enables one to share with James Russell Lowell the stirring sentiments of those prophetic and immortal lines:

"Right forever on the scaffold; wrong forever on the throne; But the scaffold sways the future, and behind the dim unknown — Standeth God, within the shadow, keeping watch above His own..."

THE STORM THAT PRODUCED LIGHT ON A DARK SUBJECT
by
JOSEPH A. WALKES, JR., M.P.S.
(Kansas)

In the context of the Negro problems neither whites nor blacks, for excellent reasons of their own, have the faintest desire to look back, but I think that the past is all that makes the present coherent, and further, that the past will remain horrible for exactly as long as we refuse to assess it honestly.

JAMES BALDWIN

By the beginning of the twentieth century, the Caucasian Grand Lodge of Washington would stretch forth a hand of friendship to Prince Hall Masonry, and would find itself swirling in a sea of passion, controversy and hostility the likes never before witnessed in Freed Masonry.

A period of masonic history so disgraceful and shameful, that the great light's so brilliant in its symbolic beauty would become veiled in shame upon the alters of Masonry, and its "sons of Light" would become the sons of hate.

In 1897, two Prince Hall Masons, Bro.'s Gideon S. Bailey and Con A. Rideout, both residing in the State of Washington, petitioned the Caucasian Grand Lodge of that State to "devise some way" whereby they might be "brought into communication with" members of the Craft in the State.

The petition was referred to a committee of three; Thomas M. Reed, James E. Edmiston and William H. Upton, two being Past Grand Masters.[1]

The committee made a year long exhaustive study and submitted their report to the Grand Lodge at its communication in 1898, and the report was approved by a practically unanimous vote.[2]

1. Asserted the right of its subordinates to recognize all Negroes made in Lodges descended from Prince Hall.

2. It declared African Grand Lodge, and the two Black Grand Lodges in Pennsylvania, legitimate Grand bodies.

3. Stated Prince Hall Lodges and Grand Lodges established in the State of Washington would not be deemed an invasion of its jurisdiction.

4. Extend its sympathy to Prince Hall Masons.

5. Declared that race or color were not proper tests to apply to a candidate.[3]

Between October 1898 and June 1899, sixteen Caucasian Grand Lodges would declare "non-intercourse" with this Grand Lodge and some would even dare attack its very soverignity.

The Caucasian Grand Lodge of Florida meeting at its 70th Annual Communication, would brazenly declare that the Grand Lodge of Washington was "invading on its rights and territory."[4]

At the 82nd Annual Communication of the Caucasian Grand Lodge of Indiana, held in Indianapolis, May 23, 1899, the Grand Master appointed a special committee, which reported that the Grand Lodge of Washington was ill advised, that its actions was uncalled for, and resolved in very forcible language to sever fraternal intercourse with said Grand Lodge.[5]

On the 6th of June 1899, Iowa, meeting in its 56th Annual Communication in Mason City, a city originally known as Shibbolethe and later as Masonic Grove, a city founded by a number of Freemasons[6], likewise formed a special committee which reported in part: "Sincerely regretting the action of Washington in renewing the agitation, and regarded such action as ill advised and well calculated to disturb the harmony of the fraternity."[7]

The Caucasian Grand Lodge of Alabama, meeting in Montgomery in its 78th Annual Communication, Dec. 6th, 1898, stated that "Masonry being pre-eminently social, the social equality of the whites and blacks is imperiously asserted by the former."[8]

69

While Arizona, at its 17th Annual Communication, held in the City of Glove, Nov. 15th, 1898, called the actions of Washington "unwarranted because it trangresses an unwritten law."

But none would reach the baseness of the Caucasian Grand Lodge of Kentucky, meeting in its 99th Annual Session in Louisville, Oct. 18th, 1898, declared the action to be "undignified and unmasonic, revolutionary and uncalled for!" This remark was made by Grand Master H. R. Thompson [9]

The matter was brought before a special committee for final action. The report was read by the Grand Secretary who disgracefully stated that "your committee shall as have other Masonic writers refrain from commenting upon any remarks made by Grand Master Thompson, for the reason that since they were made, he has in all probability joined Prince Hall, in the Grand Lodge above, where it is to be presumed that even Kentuckians associate with Negroes."[10]

A quote from a Prince Hall Grand Master while speaking of a negrophobic Masonic Confederate General would be most appropriate. "What think you of a man professing to be a Mason uttering such sentiments as these. . ." God pity Bro. . . . and the thousands of canting hypocrites like him."[11]

Louisiana, at its 78th Annual Communication, held in New Orleans, Feb. 13th, 1899, the subject was given little attention and referred to a special committee as a matter of form as the Constitution of this Grand Lodge reads, "A candidate for the Degrees of Freemasonry must be a White Man!"[12]

As the printed proceedings from Washingtons other sister Grand Lodges became available, it became evident that they presumed to sit in judgement without any adequate study of the question. In most cases they showed a complete ignorance of Masonic law and Prince Hall Masonic history.

From the unmasonic attacks and criticism heaped upon it, the Grand Lodge of Washington compelled it to justify itself in the eyes of reasonable Masons at home and abroad. They printed in pamphlet form simultaneously with a report of its Committee on Correspondence under the title, *Light On a Dark Subject.*

This pamphlet would evolve into *Negro Masonry a Critical Examination* by William H. Upton.

While the bitter attacks were being leveled at Washington the M. W. Prince Hall Grand Lodge of Massachusetts meeting in Boston, Dec. 21, 1899, would take note of the growing storm, and Grand Master Fred M. Douglass would write, "There, was nothing in the character of these resolutions to warrant the abuse and denunciation which followed. They were cautious and conserative, with greater negative than positive strength, and however liberally the spirit of them might have been interpreted that spirit would have been denied expression outside of the State of Washington. But a hu and cry was raised and under the dominating strength of bitter, unreasoning prejudice, by the time the Annual Communication of 1899 more than a score of professedly Masonic American Grand Lodges had declared non intercourse, and six others . . . has threatened it unless the action was repealed.

At the Annual Communication of 1899 it wa referred to a committee of seven Past Grand Masters as follows . . . The report which wa accepted with but two dissenting votes, rea firms the first resolution and in pointed word calls attention to the un-Masonic character o those Grand Lodges which by direct legisla tion have excluded men because of the color o their skin; repeals the second resolution an then addes that their relations with the Unite Grand Lodge of England have been and are o such a fraternal nature that they can not wit courtesy to that Grand Lodge refuse to allow their constitutency to continue to recognize a legitimate Masons, men initiated in lodges ex isting by authority originally derived from th Grand Lodge of England (Modern), the Gran Lodge of England (Ancient), or the United Gran Lodge formed by the union of these two in 1813 so long as the regularity of such initiation continue to be recognized by the United Grand Lodge of England. This simply removes th claim of colored Masons to legitmacy from the American Lodge to the Grand Lodge o England.

The third resolution was repeated withou comment and does not pledge the Grand Lodg to hostile legislation should colored Mason enter the jurisdiction. The situation, so fa as colored Masons are concerned, is practic ally unchanged.

"The direct recognition of colored Mason is rescinded and a report has been adopted i its stead under cover of which colored Mason receive whatever of benefit was conferred b the acts of 1898. The attack of these Grand Lodges upon the Grand Lodge of Washington adds one more to the many blows aimed at th life of the Law of exclusive Grand Lodge ter ritorial jurisdiction. Under this law a Grand Lodge is supposed to be supreme and inde pendent of all authority, save the Landmark and its own constitution, within its jurisdiction But their action says the legislation of a Gran Lodge within its jurisdiction is to be subjected to the will and pleasure of Grand Lodges with out. Our white brethren may not have had a Na tional Grand Lodge at any time in their history but when they invoked the concerted action o a majority of the American Grand Lodges t coerce the Grand Lodge of Washington, the certainly employed National Grand Lodge pow ers!"¹³

When knowledge of the declaration by Washington reached the Caucasian Grand Lodge of Massachusetts, it was among the simular committee appointed to investigate the subject of Prince Hall Masonry in Massachusetts coincided with the Washington report adopted in 1898, to such an extent that the average Masonic student may well consider them in agreement.¹⁴

The depth and intensity of P.G.M. Utpon's feelings are examplified by a provision in his will that no monument be erected over his grave until both white and black Masons could stand beside it as brothers. The day has yet to come.

Bro. Upton generously turned over the rights to the publication of his famous *"Negro Masonry"* to the Most Worshipful Prince Hall Grand Lodge of Massachusetts.

And another chapter in American Masonry would close, but not be settled.

REFERENCES

1. William H. Upton, *Negro Masonry Being a Critical Examination* (Cambridge, Mass., The M.W. Prince Hall Grand Lodge of Massachusetts, 1902) Chapter 1.
2. *Ibid*, P. 2
3. Harry E. Davis, *A History of Freemasonry Among Negroes in America* (United Supreme Council, A.A.S.R. Northern Jurisdiction, USA, P.H.A., Inc., 1946) P. 156, and Proceedings of the Grand Lodge of Washington, 1898, P. 60.
4. The Proceedings of the M.W. Prince Hall Grand Lodge of Missouri, 1900, P. 137. henceforth cited as Proceedings of Mo.
5. *Ibid*, p. 138
6. Harold V. B. Voorhis, *Facts for Freemasons,* (New York, Macoy, 1951) P. 201.
7. Proceedings of Mo., P. 138.
8. *Ibid*, P. 138.
9. Proceedings of the Grand Lodge of Kentucky, 1898, P. 7.
10. Proceedings of Mo., P. 140.
11. Samuel W. Clark, *The Negro Mason in Equity* (M.W. Grand Lodge of Free and Accepted Masons for the State of Ohio, 1886) P. 62.
12. Proceedings of Mo., P. 140
13. *Ibid*, P. 118
14. *Negro Masonry in America*, a paper by Marshall E. Gordon, issued by Walter F. Meirer Lodge of Research No. 281, F & A.M., Seattle, Washington. Approved for publication Sept. 1964, P. 267.

1975 DUES
ALL 1974 MEMBERS ARE REQUESTED TO FORWARD THEIR 1975 DUES ($5.00) TO THE EXECUTIVE SECRETARY.

RECOGNIZED, UNRECOGNIZED, CLANDESTINE
by HAROLD VAN BUREN VOORHIS

(PHYLAXIS NOTE: The following is the "Foreword" to Part One, of Negro Masonry in the United States (1940) and is printed herein by permission of the author. The subject, should be of interest to all Prince Hall Freemasons, and should be food for thought.)

The subject is one about which the white Freemason is not even vaguely familiar. In a general way the Negro Freemason knows something of his history, just as the white Freemason knows the general facts connected with his. But, because this subject is replete with comparisons between "recognized" and "unrecognized" Freemasonry, the task of presenting the picture clearly is not simple.

The first difficulty is to determine what to include and what to leave out without affecting the true picture. To this is added the necessity of going into jurisprudence angles which are not common knowledge on the part of the Master Mason. Aside and beyond these things, there is the element of difference of opinion, which so largely enters into this story.

The whole idea of this book, as mentioned in the Preface, is to give the facts in such a manner that they may be easily understood and profitably read. But it becomes necessary in certain places to record some rather intricate and, without a doubt, some confusing things — from the laymen's point of view. It is regrettable that recourse to these intricate and confusing points must be had, but there seems no other way to give a full picture of the situation. If a review of the rise of Negro Freemasonry were given without referring to or comparing it with "recognized" Freemasonry, the final picture would be but a bare sketch without the background or shading to complete it.

Freemasonry is divided into two groups — Recognized and Unrecognized Freemasonry. Under the first grouping are those bodies which "recognize" each other, Masonically, and often described as "Regular" bodies. To this group belong the state Grand Lodges of white Freemasons in the United States. The second group is composed of "unrecognized and irregular or clandestine" bodies — two distinct classes. It has become a habit, by usage, to consider the terms "irregular" and "clandestine" as synonymous — and often Masonic legislation has been written on this basis.

Because the fact has been lost sight of that an "unrecognized" Masonic body may be perfectly "regular," and not be "recognized" (as were all which are now in the "recognized" group — before recognition), the "unrecognized," though "regular" part of the second group of Freemasons, has come to be considered in the same category as those that are irregular or clandestine.

A clandestine Masonic body is one that has been set up since organiz Grand Lodge Freemasonry was formed, without any authority of any kind, by individuals grouping themselves into such a body. They may or may not have been Freemason previously.

An irregular Masonic boyd is one whose "working" was once recognized, but because of some Masonic impropriety, is no longer recognized, no matter how regular it once was.

Both classes may, under certain conditions, become recognized by "healing," changing or removing their offending reasons for non-recognition, etc., etc.

There remains a much larger group — those whose Masonic regularity is quite normal, and yet who have not been "recognized." In this group are the Negro brethren.

To understand what follows, it is necessary to bear this difference of classification in mind and to remember that regularity and recognition are not the same thing.

It becomes necessary, also, to caution the reader that in those places where a "tearing apart" of statements of "historians" of the last century is resorted to, it is not in any way saying, in effect, that "recognized" Freemasonry is not within its province when it continues its non-recognition of Negro Masonry. It is the illogical and frequently unfair methods used by some of our white brethren in trying to "explain" the situation, which are exposed. Too often writers have failed to look at both sides of the matter and have frequently extracted material to prove this or that point which, if completely used, would mullify the very objective of their attack. The nearest approach to reason for such tactics seems to be that in these instances prejudice is the blinding force — for these same wirters on other subjects are peers in their field. This gives undue credulousness to their opinions on Negro Freemasonry and, by the unsuspecting, their statements are absorbed *in toto*.

Over a period of many years I have read hundreds of discussions and opinions in Grand Lodge proceedings on this subject — among which are some of the most vitriolic attacks on Negroes and Negro Freemasonry. Yet, during the times when these attacks were in especially full bloom, was well as during periods of quiescence, there is only the evidence of our Negro brethren facing the issue very calmly as gentlemen. As I now look back upon the picture I cannot but feel that the white brethren have not added to their stature by their actions. The mountains builded out of molehills have not withstood the elements of careful scrutiny and are being leveled by the plumb of reason and the square of honest judgement. Have fewer oral stones been thrown many more glass houses might now be standing.

THE MASONIC ADDRESSES AND WRITINGS OF
IRA S. HOLDER, SR., M.P.S.
(NEW YORK)

"Whence Come You!"

and

Whither Are You

Travelling?"

(PHYLAXIS NOTE: Bro. Ira S. Holder Sr., M.P.S. is the Grand Historian Emeritus of the Prince Hall Grand Lodge of New York, and with Bro. Courtney L. Wiltshire is the co-author of the *"History of Widow's Son Lodge No. 11 F — A.M. of Brooklyn, NY"* his mother Lodge. He has been nominated by the President to become the first "Fellow" of the Phylaxis Society and to receive the first *"Certificate of Literature"* presented by the Phylaxis Society. The nomination goes before the "Committee of Fellows chaired by Arthur H. Frederick, Editor of the Phylaxis Society.

Wednesday, October 3, 1962

Worshipful Master,
Grand Lodge Officers (Past & Present)
Past Masters,
Senior & Junior Wardens,
Visiting Brethren of the Craft,
Members of Sampson Lodge #65.

Good evening:

In looking around, I recognize the faces of several members of this distinguished lodge whom it has been my good fortune and pleasure to have previously met, and whose friendship I cherish. Having therefore that "At Home Feeling" I can now relax, confident in the fact that I am not in your midst as a stranger, but as a brother.

The subject I have chosen for this evening is a very familiar one; one that undoubtedly has been asked and answered by all of us at some time or another:

"Whence Come You? and Whither Are You Travelling?"

Before going into the body of my subject matter however, I deem it not only necessary, but important that I give you a brief outline of the source of this most important question. In doing so, I earnestly crave not only your attention but also your indulgence. My brief remarks are humbly directed to all members of the craft gathered here, especially the younger and less experienced brethren on whom so much depends.

Masonic History tells us that in the year 1730, Martin Clare an English school-master and Masonic Lecturer, very active in his lodge and also the Grand Lodge of England, introduced the following from: "FROM WHENCE CAME YOU?" in one of his series of lectures. It supplimented James Anderson's test question or Lecture which was in use at that time. It must be understood that a long time elapsed before there was a standardization of Lectures such as we have today. The standardization of these Lectures however, became a reality through the efforts of William Preston, who was born in Edinburgh, Scotland. His father was an attorney, and saw to it that his son was given a thorough education. Young Preston for a long time was employed by an outstanding linguist of great reputation, Thomas Ruddiman. With this affiliation he became quite proficient himself. It was this added advantage that enabled him to make a study of all phases of Freemasonry, even in foreign countries; specializing in Ritualistic Work. It was he who changed it to read:

"From Whence Come You? And Whither Are You Bound?"

At this point I think it important that I give you a brief historical background of the mason who did much for Freemasonry the world over, especially in this hemisphere, through his modification of Preston's Masonic Lectures. His name is Thos. Smith Webb. He was born in Boston, Mass., in 1771. After completing his trade as a printer and book-binder, he moved to Keene, New Hampshire where he continued to pursue his trade. He became interested in Freemasonry, and was initiated into Rising Sun Lodge in that State on December 24, 1790. On March 7, 1792 he withdrew from Rising Sun Lodge and moved to Albany, N.Y. where he became a Charter Member and Second Master of Temple Lodge now #14. He had received the lower degrees of the Royal Arch Chapter at some unknown time and place, for he was recorded as a sojourner in Harmony Chapter #52 where he received the Royal Arch Degree, May 18, 1796. At Albany, Webb met an English Freemason named John Hanmer, well skilled in Lodge Rituals, expecially the Prestionian System. With Hanmer's assistance, he promptly set about condensing and rearranging this work for practical use; and the result was, "Freemason's Monitor" & "Illustrations of Freemasonry," published in 1797, which was the first Masonic work of its kind in this country. It was in this year that our subject:

"Whence Come You? & Whither Are You Travelling?"

was changed to the form we now use.

Once again we find Webb on the move, this time to Providence, R.I., where he engaged in manufacturing. He affiliated with St. John's Lodge #2, becoming Junior Grand Warden of the Grand Lodge in 1801, Senior Grand Warden in 1804 and Grand Master in 1813-15.

It is interesting to note some of the changes and modifications made on Preston's Lectures by this worthy brother and scholar, namely:

1. The 1st. Degree was considered too lenghty, and was reduced from 6 parts to 3.
2. The 2nd Degree from 4 parts to 2.
3. The 3rd Degree from 4 parts to 3.

These my brethren, are some of the outstanding accomplishments of this Illustrious Masonic Scholar and Lecturer, which are best summed up by Enoch T. Carson, founder of the Masonic Archeological Society who referred to him as the (and I quote) "ablest Masonic Ritualist of his day — the very Prince of Masonic Workmen." (end of quote) As members of this noble brotherhood and fraternity of masons, we owe much to this outstanding Pillar of Wisdom, both for his constructive Ritualistic efforts, and being the first American to contribute so much to the craft the wold over. All things must sooner or later come to an end, so it was in this respect: the Grand Architect of the Universe dimmed the brightness of the star that illuminated the Masonic Firmament, by calling our most distinguished brother from this labors to rest, in Cleveland, Ohio on July 6, 1819; thus ending the many accomplishments of so brilliant a career and writing the final chapter that will forever be indelibly inscribed on the pages of Masonic History.

Continued in Next Issue

> 1975 DUES
> ALL 1974 MEMBERS ARE REQUESTED TO FORWARD THEIR 1975 DUES ($5.00) TO THE EXECUTIVE SECRETARY.

NOTES, QUERIES AND INFORMATION ON ITEMS OF MASONIC RESEARCH

THE NUMBER OF LETTERS CONTAINING QUESTIONS which relate to matters of fact in Prince Hall Masonic history, biography and tradition justify their treatment in a column apart from other portions of the magazine.

Our readers and members are invited to send such material appropriate for use in this column, and especially information concerning research currently underway.

It must be noted however, that his page is for EXCHANGE of information and opinion and does not pretend to provide the final answer to any query.

8. The Jan. 9th issue of JET quotes: "The fate of the Alexander G. Clark (Sr. P.G.M. of Missouri and Iowa), is in the hands of the Cedar Rapids (Iowa) chapter of LINKS Inc., a Black women's civic group. This 19th Century two-story structure, which qualifies for the national registry for historical sites was the home of Alexander G. Clark, the most prominent Black man in Iowa during the 19th century.

Clark parlayed his small barber business into a thriving timber supply business for steamship companies. He was instrumental in an Iowa Supreme Court decision enabling all children, regardless of race to be entitled to attend public school in Iowa. In 1890, Clark was appointed minister and counsel-general to Liberia by President, Benjamin Harrison.

The house will be demolished by the city after Jan. 25th (this date has been extended into March), to make room for a low-rent housing project for the elderly unless the LINKS can raise the $40,000 needed to relocate the house, according to Mrs. Burtine W. Motley, President of the Cedar Rapids LINKS.

Donations can be sent to: Alexander Clark Memorial Fund, Merchants National Bank, Cedar Rapids, Iowa 52401.

For further information, contact: Mrs. Burtine W. Motley, 1920 Fifth Avenue, S.E., Cedar Rapids, Iowa 52403.

THE PHYLAXIS SOCIETY is proud to produce a biography of this truly dedicated Prince Hall Mason elsewhere in this issue.

9. CROWLEY TORNADO DESTROY MASONIC HALL. A massive tornado struck Crowley, Louisiana, October 29, 1974 and destroyed the Masonic Hall of C. F. Ladd Lodge No. 48, of the M.W. Prince Hall Grand Lodge of Louisiana. The Lodge is appealing for aid and donations. All donations should be sent to Prince Hall Grand Lodge, P.O. Box 2974, Baton Rouge, La. 70821.

10. QUALIFICATIONS OF A PETITIONER. We could not help but note the following which appeared in the Grand Lodge Bulletin of the Caucasian Grand Lodge of Iowa. "Because of a number of request we have had regarding the right of the Lodge to act on a petition presented by a member of a minority group. We print below a rather concise statement issued by Past Grand Master Joseph Z. Marks in an October 26, 1973 letter.

"I am in receipt of your letter of October 22, 1973. You are apparently the recipient of some false information."

"The Masonic Code of Iowa has no restrictions for qualifications of its members because of race, color, creed or religion."

"Anyone who would blackball a petitioner because of his race, color, creed or religion would be guilty of un-Masonic conduct."

With 514 Lodges and a membership of 76,452, it would be interesting to learn how many members are Black?

11. PRINCE HALL MILITARY OFFICERS: Interest was created by the January issue of the *Phylaxis* with the photograph of Bro. Martin R. Delaney, a Past Master and District Deputy, as well as the first Black Major in the U.S. Army. What would Bro. Delaney have thought if he learned that today, Major General Harry Brooks, Jr., is a Prince Hall Mason and Shriner. A member of Menes Temple No. 32, Lawton, Oklahoma. Anyone having information on other Prince Hall Military leaders, past and present, please forward them to the President, P.O. Box 3151, Ft. Leavenworth, Kansas 66027.

12. COMPACT LODGES UNDER THE JURISDICTION OF NEW YORK: Bro. Ira S. Holder, Sr., M.P.S., 21 St. James Place, Brooklyn, New York 11205 is trying to obtain a listing of the subordinate lodges of the National Grand Lodge (Compact).

Boyer Grand Lodge (named after the famous Haitian General) was formed March 14, 1845. The National Grand Lodge was formed in 1847. Boyer was re-organized Oct. 13, 1848 as the United Grand Lodge of F & A.M. of N.Y. The two consolidated Dec. 27, 1877 and became the Grand Lodge of N.Y. F & A.M. The phrase Prince Hall was added in 1920. The title was changed in June 1944 to the Most Worshipful Prince Hall Grand Lodge of the Most Ancient and Honorable Fraternity of Free and Accepted Masons, State of New York, which was in accordance with an understanding reached at the Session of the Grand Masters Conference held at Hot Springs, Arkansas, January 1944.

There was a clandestine Grand Lodge named Saint Phillips Grand Lodge of the State of New York formed in 1841, and very little information is available on this group. In 1858 there existed Oscris Electric Grand Lodge of North America, and the Philanthropic Grand Lodge of North America, both quite irregular.

5. PRINCE HALL MASONIC POSTAGE STAMP. The Prince Hall Grand Lodge of Missouri has announced the formation of a Bi-Centennial Celebration Committee and plans to seek the printing of a Postage Stamp issued with a likeness of Grand Master Prince Hall. The PHYLAXIS SOCIETY salutes this Grand Lodge, and ask what is your Jurisdiction doing?

The significance of Brotherhood by Bro. John E. Bruce, printed in the January 1975 issue, page 41, was printed by permission of *The Schomburg Center for Research in Black Culture*, **The New York Public Library, Astor, Lenox and Tilden Foundations.** *The Phylaxis Society* would like to thank Mrs. Jean Blackwell Hutson, Curator, Schomburg Center for Research in Black Culture, 103 West 135th St., New York 10030 and Ms. Faye Simkin, Executive Officer of the New York Public Library for their assistance to us.

The Masterpiece "Prince Hall Masonry and the Civil War, Part III" Will be continued in the next issue of the Phylaxis.

FELLOWS WRITE MASTERPIECES

The election of a member of the Phylaxis Society as a *fellow*, brings him, according to the Philalethes Magazine, to ancient custom, to the task of writing a *Masterpiece,* imitating the ancient guildsmen, who required the apprentices, to submit the masterpiece for approval before being admitted to the higher rank in the order.

Continued from Page 58

A Lodge as Soldiers.
(8) November 26th, 1786. *Memorial* to His Excellency James Bowdoin, [Governor of Massachusetts.]
Offering the services of the members of African Lodge as a military force to aid in suppressing insurrection growing out of the Shay Rebellion.
"Shay's Rebellion" is a well known incident in American history.

(9) *Hall to Moody.* December 16th, 1786.
States that Capt Scott will advance the money "sent by me in his ship two years ago by his stewrd Hartfield" and anything more that might be necessary and asks Moody to explain the matter to the Grand Lodge. "Sir, I would be glad if you would procure me the last constitution and the Mason's Mmoneke."

Mnemonics
"Last constitution," I take to mean the last edition of the Book of Constitutions; but others might read *"lost constitution"* and think the warrant was meant. The letters of the word "Mmoneke" seem clear: Quaere, Was "Mnemonics" intended.

(10) *Moody to Hall.* Golden Square, London . . . 23rd, 1786.
"I received your kind letter and am much obliged to you for sending me that money; but I have not got it yet." Capt. Scott has gone to Boston. "The last time I saw Mr. Hartfield I asked him if he saw any body belonging to us and he told me no." "You desired me to ask Mrs. Hartfield to advance me some money, but she told me she had no orders to do it. I have sent you an almanac." "My wife joins me in love to you."
The mention of Mrs. Hartfield indicates the existence of another letter, of which we have no trace.

(11) *Moody to Hall.* March 10th, 1787.
Money received; charter taken from Grand Lodge and delivered to Capt. Scott; Moody had had Book of Constitutions bound, instead of sending in sheets; some good advice as to how to conduct his Lodge. "I have sent you an excellent book which I have taken a deal of time in perusing and find it a very useful book as it contains many very useful remarks and information. Therefore I send it to you for your perusal and acceptand." Commends his special attention to the "four cardinal virtues," Temperance, Fortitude, Prudence and Justice; "with the three religious virtues, Faith, Hope and Charity, in conjunction with the grand principle on which Masonry is founded, Brotherly Love, Friendship and Truth."
Signed, William Moody,
      "Present Master of the Prezuvence
      Lodge,
      "held at the Fleece,
      New Pullice Yard,
      "Westruins."
"N.B. I have the pleasure to inform you that His Royal Highness, the Prince of Wales, has been initiated into Masonry at the Britcher Lodge, Pell Mell."

The "excellent book" may have been Preston's "Illustrations" or Calcott's "Candid Disquisition;" but may it not be that we have here a carefully veiled allusion — and if so, one of our earliest — to a "cypher key" of the "secret work?" The classification of the various "virtues" and the use of "Friendship" where we now have "Relief" are interesting. Hall evidently had trouble in reading the handwriting of Moody, who doubtless wrote, "Perseverence Lodge, held at the Fleece, New Palace Yard, Westmins.," and probably "Britishers' Lodge." Gould tells us (History, Am.ed., iii., 235) that the Prince of Wales was initiated "at a special Lodge at the Star and Garter, Pall Mall, February 6th, 1787."
This Lodge is mentioned on the Lists, 1781-1791, as No. "29 Britannic Lodge, Star and Garter, Pall Mall." Perseverence Lodge is given on the same Lists as No. "398 L. of Perseverence, Golden Fleece, Palace Yard," dating from 1776, and is evidently the Lodge formed May 7th, 1776, styled on the 1778 List, No. "492 King's Arms L. Krew, Surrey."

75

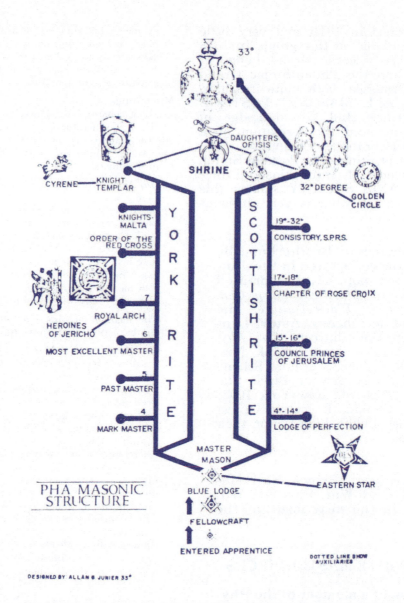

THE PHYLAXIS SOCIETY SUBSCRIPTION CARD

Subscription rate: $5.00/Yr.

Mail to: James E. Herndon, MPS
Executive Secretary
1574 Ivanhoe Street
Denver, Colo. 80220

Gentlemen:

    Enclosed is my subscription the the Phylaxis Magazine.

_____ Check Enclosed _____ amount payable to Phylaxis Magazine

Name: _____

Address: _____

City: _____ State: _____ Zip Code: _____

A SOCIETY FOR PRINCE HALL FREEMASONS WHO SEEK MORE LIGHT AND WHO HAVE LIGHT TO IMPART

THE PHYLAXIS

SEPTEMBER 1975

Volume II   Number 3

THE PHYLAXIS
Published at Jefferson City, Mo., by
THE PHYLAXIS SOCIETY

Arthur H. Frederick M.P.S. .... Editor
Box 43, Roxbury, Massachusetts 02119

OFFICERS

Joseph A. Walkes, Jr, M.P.S. .... President
P. O. Box 3151, Ft. Leavenworth, Kansas 66027

Herbert Dailey, M.P.S. .... First Vice President
1616 South Cedar, Tacoma, Washington 98405

Zellus Bailey, M.P.S. .... Second Vice President
7039 Dover Court, St. Louis, Missouri 63130

James E. Herndon, M.P.S. .... Executive Secretary
1574 Ivanhoe Street, Denver, Colorado 80220

Alonzo D. Foote, Sr., M.P.S .... Treasurer
P.O. Box 99601, Tacoma, Washington 98499

SUBSCRIPTION RATE: FOR ONE YEAR, $5.00

The Phylaxis Magazine is the official publication of the Phylaxis Society. Any article appearing in this publication expresses only the opinion of the writer, and does not become the official pronouncement of the Phylaxis Society. No advertising of any form is solicited or accepted. All communication relative to the magazine should be addressed to the Editor. Inquiries relative to membership must be addressed to the Executive Secretary. Membership is by invitation and recommendation only. The joining fee is $3.00. Dues are $5.00 per year in advance, which amount includes a subscription to the "Phylaxis" magazine for one year.

All rights reserved. No part of this work may be reproduced or transmitted in any form or by any means, electrical or mechanical, or retrival system, without written permission from the publisher.

**1975 DUES
ALL 1974 MEMBERS ARE REQUESTED TO FORWARD THEIR 1975 DUES ($5.00) TO THE EXECUTIVE SECRETARY.**

INDEX

A Word from the President	78
Prince Hall Masonry and the Civil War	79
Prince Hall's Letter Book	83
References	84
The Masonic Addresses and Writings of Ira S. Holder, Sr., M.P.S.	86
The Holy Saints John & Lodge of St. John at Jerusalem	86
John Pine noted Masonic Engraver was Black	88
The Phylaxis, Philaoetyes and M.P.S.	90
Prince Hall Bi-Centennial	90
The Membership Committees goal	93
The Table Lodge	94
The Ceremony of the Seven Toasts	95
A Bright Mason	99

A WORD FROM THE PRESIDENT

"My aim, is to perserve the memory of the things I love, to be truthful to them and therefore to write as well about them as I can."

The response to our Special March issue in commemoration of the 200th Anniversary of the initiation of Prince Hall has been beyond our expectations, and we plan to continue issuing Special Editions in March each year, in tribute to *"The Master"* Prince Hall.

At the 109th Annual Communication of the Prince Hall Grand Lodge of Missouri, your President received a plaque on behalf of the Conference of Prince Hall Grand Masters and the Grand Lodge of Missouri for the Phylaxis Society. The award was presented by M. W. T. Roosevelt Butler, Grand Master of Kansas, and M. W. William Reynolds, Grand Master of Missouri.

The Society thanks the Conference of Prince Hall Grand Masters.

Bro. Ira S. Holder, Sr., M.P.S. (New York) has been named *"Fellow"* of the Phylaxis Society (F.P.S.) in recognition of his service to the Society, humanity, and Prince Hall Masonry. Bro. Holder is also to receive the distinguished *"Certificate of Literature for 1975."* This will mark a milestone for the Society, as this will be the first time either of these awards have been given. The awards will be presented in New York.

(Continued on Page 93)

PRINCE HALL MASONRY AND THE CIVIL WAR

PART III
PHOENIX LODGE NO. 1

by
JOSEPH A. WALKES, JR., M.P.S. (KANSAS)

A MASTERPIECE

It has been shown, that the first Prince Hall Military Masonic Lodge was attached to the 54th Massachusetts Regiment, and that the Lodge was probably named after Bro. Lewis Hayden, Grand Master of Prince Hall Masons for Massachusetts.

The second Prince Hall Military Masonic Lodge to serve during the Civil War was Phoenix Lodge No. 1, and its existence was well known throughout Masonic research literature.

Other than African Lodge 459, there is no other Prince Hall Lodge that has had its charter or warrant reproduced in so many Masonic history books.

And like its forebear, African Lodge 459, those Masonic "scholars" and "historians" who attempted to show there "knowledge" of Prince Hall Masonic history merely showed their ignorance.

Statements such as, "The charter states that it was granted by the '29th U. S. Colored Troops' in New York. There was no 29th U. S. Colored Troops," but it is possible and probable the printer reversed the "9" and it should have been the "26th Colored Regiment" sponsored by the Union League Club of New York,"[1] written by those who claim to be students of Masonry, shows the abuse and mistreatment that Prince Hall Masonry has had to suffer at the hands of those who have no business in attempting to write about Prince Hall Masonry, and it may very well be more desirable if they left the subject alone, and allowed the Prince Hall Mason himself to write about his Masonry, for often these "errors" have been all to deliberate.

While on the other hand, those Prince Hall Masons who write their history must carefully verify there facts before they pass it on to the Prince Hall Craft. Harry E. Davis, in his Freemasonry Among Negroes, stated that the 29th Regiment Connecticut Colored Troops was organized in New Haven in February 1864, and that it was a State Volunteer Organization but was frequently called a Federal regiment, hence its identity is often confused.[2]

The earliest recruit for the 29th Regiment, Connecticut Colored Infantry, was enlisted August 11, 1863, but most of the men came to the regiment at its rendezvous in "Fair Haven" during the last three months of the year. The full number was attained in January 1864. For lack of officers it was not mustered into the United States service until March 8, 1864.[3]

Warrant granted by "Compact Grand Lodge" of New York for a Negro Military Lodge during Civil War

PHOTO OF WARRANT

79

The warrant was issued under the authority of the Grand Lodge of New York (National Grand Lodge) and was signed by David Gordon as Grand Master, and attested by Samuel J. Scottron, Grand Secretary, Pro. Tem.[4]

The warrant appointed Alexander (the warrant reads Alex) Heritage Newton as Worshipful Master. Bro. Newton was a Commissary Sergeant in Company E, and his date of enlistment was December 18, 1863.

PHOTO OF NEWTON IN UNIFORM

His life was very impressive and inspiring. A life that was dedicated to the upbringing of his race, devotion to his religion and his love of Prince Hall Masonry. Though his parents had been slaves, he was "free" born in Newbern, (on Craven Street), Craven County, North Carolina. A self educated man with high intelligence, who would author a autobiography of his life to include a sketch of the 29th Regiment.[5]

As Bro. Newton would write, "I have named the book, "Out of the Briars," because the figure is a befitting one in my own life. Although free born, I was born under the curse of slavery, surrounded by the thorns and briars of prejudice, hatred, persecution, and the suffering incident to this fearful regime. I, indeed, came out of the briars torn and bleeding. I came out of poverty and ignorance. I did not have any of the advantages of the schools. I learned what little I know by listening to the educated white people talk. I picked up a great deal in this way."[6]

In this autobiography one can see the workings of Prince Hall Masonry and the African Methodist Episcopal Church both having played a major role in sustaining Black America during the dark days of slavery, as page after page we are introduced to such Prince Hall Masons as Paul Drayton[7], Dr. Peter W. Ray[8], John Milton Turner[9], William Paul Quinn[10], and many other Craftsman.

His military records states that he joined the 29th on March 8, 1864, ten days before the warrant was issued, but in his autobiography, he quotes this date, as the date the regiment broke camp and left New Haven for Annapolis, Maryland.

The regiment spent eight to ten days in Maryland, then departed for Hilton Head, South Carolina. Therefore, if the warrant was issued on the 18th of March, it must have arrived to Bro. Newton in South Carolina, and would be the second warrant dispatched to a Prince Hall Worshipful Master while on duty in this Southern State.

Bro. Newton was appointed a Sergeant, October 31, 1864 and was mustered out, October 24, 1865.

The Senior Warden, was Bro. John A. Andrews, a Private in Company D. Bro. Andrews was a resident of Fairfield. He enlisted December 16, 1863. He joined the 29th, March 8, 1864, and was mustered out October 24, 1865.

The Junior Warden was Bro. Richard Giles, a Corporal of Company H. His residence was New Haven. Date of enlistment was December 31, 1863. He joined the 29th also on the 8th of March 1864, and likewise was mustered out October 24, 1865.

The warrant of Phoenix Lodge made it clear that it was restricted in its jurisdiction to the 29th Regiment only, and it was further commanded to "in no manner whatever to interfere with the rights of any established Lodge or Grand Lodge!

The right to work as a Lodge was limited to "so long as the above Regiment shall remain together, as such, and not longer," and it further enjoined that when the Regiment was mustered out, the warrant be deposited with the Grand Master of New York. Samuel J. Scottron, who signed the warrant as Grand Secretary (Pro Tem) became Grand Master of this same National Grand Lodge.[11]

80

The warrant is the only known charter of its kind in existence.[12]

Harry E. Davis, the Prince Hall Historian, states that the Regiment was disbanded in the latter part of 1865, after its final service on the Mexican border. It arrived at Brazos De Santiago, Texas, July 3, 1865. From there it went to Brownsville, Texas.

The Regiment arrived back in Hartford, November 24, (Bro. Newton states October the 24th), and the next day the unit was paid and discharged. The 29th fought at Petersburg, Virginia, August 12th to September 24th, 1864, Chapins Farm, Virginia, September 29th, 1864; Richmond, Virginia, September 29th to October 1st, 1864; Darby Town Road, Virginia, October 13th, 1864 and Kell House, Virginia, October 27th and 28th, 1864. The Regiment suffered 470 casualties.[13]

The Worshipful Master, Bro. Newton, in his autobiography, does not mention the Lodge, nor does the name of Bro. Andrews, the Senior Warden or Bro. Giles, the Junior Warden appear in his book.

As a Commisary Sergeant, he would normally store his supplies in a house or under some shelter, so these areas are probably where the Lodge was meeting.

Under the title *"Religious and Civic Pioneering Among the Craftsmen"* from P.G.M. Aldrage B. Cooper's book, *"Footprints of Prince Hall Masonry in New Jersey,"*[14] a section is set aside for Bro. Newton, and it is herwith printed in its entirety. Though incorrect in many details, it is

ALEXANDER HERITAGE NEWTON was born in New Bern, North Carolina in 1837. His father was a slave, but his mother was a free women. Young Newton accompanied his family when they moved North and settled in New Haven, Connecticut, where Newton volunteered for service in the 29th Regiment of United States Colored Troops. He served as Commissary Sergeant on the Non-Commissioned Staff of that Connecticut Volunteer Infantry, and won a promotion from a Sergeancy of Company E on October 24, 1865. This record is to be found in the office of the Adjutant General at Hartford, Connecticut.

While he was in that Regiment, Newton and his military associates were granted a warrant by the Compact Grand Lodge in New York, under the date of March 18, 1864, to open and hold a Lodge under the title of Phonex Lodge, Number 1. Alexander Newton was named first Master of that Military Lodge, the only Lodge of its kind known to have existed during the Civil War. In view of the date of dissolution of that Lodge, it is quite probable that Newton was the only Master of that Lodge. The Regiment in which he soldiered served on the Mexican Border, and when it was disbanded in the latter part of 1865, the warrant was surrendered to the parent body in accordance with the terms under which it had been issued.

The Williamson Collection on Negro Masonry at the 136th Street Branch of the New York Public Library houses the original charter issued to Phoenix Lodge, and the author has had the pleasure of examining the document in the presence of the founder of the Collection. A full page photograph of the document appears in the Voorhis volume on Negro Masonry.[15]

Where Newton received the degrees of Symbolic Masonry is not definitely known. He may have received them in a New York City Lodge affilitated with the Compact Grand Lodge in New York previous to his selection as Master of the Regimental Lodge, or in the Military Lodge, or even in Connecticut in a previously established Lodge, although the Grand Lodge of Connecticut was not formed until 1873.[16]

After he had received his schooling in New York City, Pennington Seminary in New Jersey, and Lincoln University in Pennsylvania, Newton was admitted into the Ministry of the African Methodist Episcopal Church. In 1870 he was taken into the Philadelphia Conference of the Church. Later he was assigned to a Pulaski, Tennessee charge. He was ordained a Deacon at Nashville in 1873, and, as an Elder in the Church, he was transferred to Pine Bluff, Arkansas. In turn, Newton was transferred to the Louisiana Conference, then to the North Carolina Conference, where he was stationed at Raleigh. In 1880, the well-traveled pastor finally came into the New Jersey Conference, where he was to remain, this first assignment being at Morristown. After Morristown Newton moved to Trenton and Camden in succession. The edifice presently occupied by the Macedonia congregation was completed during Newton's pastorate.

Although it is probable and possible that Newton may have been associated with the Craft in Morristown and Trenton, the oldest record extent with his name on the roll of Rising Sun Lodge, Number 1, Camden. At that time that Lodge had six Past Grand Masters of Masons in New Jersey on its register.

Early in the 1900's Newton was named Grand Chaplain, which office he held until his demise. As a member of Grand Lodge, R. W. Alexander H. Newton was the Representative of Grand Lodge of Colorado Near New

81

Jersey, and for several years officiated as Chairman of the Committee on Charity and the Committee on Memorials. In 1911 Newton introduced a resolution before the Grand Lodge which suggested a simple method of participation by every craftsman in the acquisition of a home for indigent Masons. But the proposition, after due consideration, was turned down.

Alexander Newton was a Royal Arch Mason and a Knight Templar, and in the latter body he held a position in the Grand Commandery. With another New Jersey Mason of reknown, Newton was one of the incorporators of the Supreme Council, Ancient and Accepted Scottish Rite, N.J.; the date of the incorporation of the body being September 21, 1898, and the place of incorporation, Camden, New Jersey.

Brother Newton was an Active for New Jersey and a member of DeHugo Consistory, Number 2, in Camden. He held the office of Treasurer-General, H.E., from 1908 to 1917, and in the latter years he was named Grand Prior of the Supreme Council, serving the office until his death.

R. W. Alexander

Herritage Newton, D.D.

The middle name of Alexander Heritage Newton was selected for the name of the Military Lodge that was instituted at Camp Kilmer, New Brunswick, on March 8, 1949.

Newton is described as a Christian man possessing eloquent dignity, and he was admired as a man of culture, and orator and a powerful preacher. After a fruitful sojourn on this earth, and at the age of eight-four Newton retired on May 4, 1921, mourned and missed by his hosts of friends, his family and fellow-craftsmen.

A late Grand Master of New York, M. W. David W. Parker, in his address to his Grand Lodge on June 1, 1921, referred to the fact that Alexander Newton, in March of that year, had been present in Brooklyn attending the Easter Service of King David Consistory. Continuing, the speaker described Newton as a "splendid character and a Christian gentleman."

The following is taken from the resolution adopted by the New Jersey Grand Lodge, on December 27, 1921, at its Annual Communication:

"... we meet at this hour to pay tribute of love and respect to his memory.... His counsels were wise because his knowledge was thorough. His friendship was sincere because his nature was free from guile and hyprocrisy. His labors were unremitting becuase his love for the Institution and its craftsmen was earnest and steadfast. His speech was direct because his heart was sincere and true. He loved life and his fellows. He ornamented and adorned the spheres in which he moved. He reaps in our abundant tears our boundless regret. He sowed in brotherhood and fellowship. The dew of love and sympathy moistens the eyes of his brethren and enriches their hearts with blessed understanding of his virtues and good qualities. His record as Grand Chaplain is that of a life well-spent in the service of his fellowmen. All who knew him loved him and honored him for this strength of character, his broad sympathies and for the earnestness with which he labored for the betterment of humanity. He was a loving and faithful husband and patriotic citizen."

As stated above, after the regiment was disbanded, the warrant was returned in accordance with the injuction. Bro. Newton then returned to his wife's home in Brooklyn, New York, where he registered as a citizen of the United States, he could have returned the charter at this time.

Cont. Next Page

PRINCE HALL'S LETTER BOOK

BY
William H. Upton, P.G.M.

**Continued from Page 75
March Issue**

Warrant arrives.
(12) Hall, in the "Columbian Centinal," newspaper, of Boston, of May 2nd, 1787.
"By Captain Scott, from London, came the charter" etc.

The article is printed in full in the "Critical Examination," and elsewhere. African Lodge was organized under the Warrant, May 6th, 1787.

(13) Hall to William White, Esq., Grand Secretary, London. May 17th, 1787.
Acknowledges with thanks receipt of "the constitution, together with your receipt for payments for it;" explains why White did not receive the money sent two years before, "and we have lost the whole of it;" promises to "send a copy of our by-laws and a list of the Lodge" to the Grand Master; "and by the grace of God I shall endeavour to fulfil all that is required of me in the charter, and as I shall make the constitution my guide, I hope we shall adorn our profession as Masons."

(14) Hall to "Rowland Holt, Esqr., De. G. M. of the Grand Lodge of England." May 17th, 1787.
Similar to No. 13. "I have sent you a copy of our by laws, together with list of the members of the Lodge. We shall always be willing to contribute so far as in us lies to that laudable custom among . . . Masons from the foundation thereof."

This last apparently refers to the Grand Charity fund, **Grand Charity.**
This last apparently refers to the Grand Charity fund, to which African Lodge sent contributions received in Nov., 1787; Nov. 1789; April, 1792; Nov., 1793; and Nov., 1797, besides others apparently not received. I am not aware that any other New England Lodge ever contributed to it at all. See No. 30 below.

(15) Hall to Moody. May 18th, 1787.
Acknowledges receipt of letter, "together with the constitution and calendar for the Lodge, and the book you sent me," which last he found "very instructive." "Dear Brother, nothing could give me and the Lodge more pleasure than when we open'd the constitution to find so grand a piece of true workmanship thereon, which we have shown to some Masters of other Lodges here, which all agree with us in giving praise to the workman thereof. But the contents thereof and the precepts therein contained shall be our chief study and guide."

A very manly and grateful letter of thanks for Moody's great kindnesses to the writer, "though a stranger." "All the account I can give for it is that you are a sincere and true brother Mason." The book mentioned was doubtless Noorthouck's edition of the "Constitutions," published in 1784.

(16) Petition to the Senate and House of Representatives of Massachusetts. October, 17th, 1787.
Asks them to provide means for the education of coloured children.

(17) Hall to Moody. May [sic,? *recte* November] 17th, 1787. Unsigned.
Sends regards ect. "I sent you a letter and a small trifle in [care] Capt. Scott, but don't know whether you received them or no, for it is hard trusting when one hath once bit. Then Mr. Hartfield told me that he delivered to you yourself." Intends to "keep the feast" on St. John's Day next and to send money to the Grand Charity "by the first safe hands."

This is but a fragment of a letter. From No. 19, November would appear to be the true date.

(18) Hall to [Capt.] James Scott. August 2nd, 1788.
Sends him $10 and certain letters, to be delivered to "Mr. White."

(19) Hall to Moody. August 23rd, 1788.
Similar to No. 17. "I sent you a letter November last . . . and also acquainted you that I sent you a small present."

(Continued on Page 85)

PHOENIX LODGE NO. 1, cont'd.

In 1877, the two Grand Lodges of New York (National and Independent) consolidated and the warrant became the property of the present Prince Hall Grand Lodge of New York.

Not much is known of the subsequent career of this Army Lodge. It's minutes and paraphernalia were presumably lost with the records of the Grand Lodge which disappeared after the consolidation.

This has been a brief look at Prince Hall Masonry and the Civil War. The mere fact that Prince Hall Mason's were indeed holding Lodge within the lines of the Union Army is remarkable, but what is even more remarkable is the fact that Prince Hall Masons have indeed held Lodge in every war from that time to Vietnam, within the United States Armed Forces "lines."

Cont. on Next Page

REFERENCES:

1. John Black Vrooman and Allen E. Roberts, *Sword and Trowel — The Story of Traveling and Military Lodges* (Missouri: Missouri Lodge of Research, 1964) P. 101.

2. Harry E. Davis, *A History of Freemasonry Among Negroes in America* (United Supreme Council, A.A.S.R. Northern Jurisdiction, U.S.A., Prince Hall Affiliation Inc., 1946) P. 185.

3. Record of Service of Connecticut Men in the Army and Navy of the United States During the War of the Rebellion by the Adjutant General, P. 859.

4. In the *Complete History of Widow's Son Lodge No. 11, F & A.M. of Brooklyn, New York,* by Ira S. Holder Sr., and Courtenay L. Weltshire (page 20), appears a notice or summons dated November 19, 1866, notifying the Lodge that the Annual Grand Communication would be held on December 26, 1866, and was signed by the same Samuel J. Scottron as Grand Master. The signatures on the warrant of the Phonix Lodge and the summons on Widow's son Lodge are the same.

5. Alexander Heritage Newton, D.D., *Out Of The Briars* (Florida: Mnemosyne Publishing Co., Inc., 1969).

6. *Ibid,* Preface, p. viii.

7. *Ibid.,* p. 28. William H. Grimshaw, *Official History of Freemasonry Among The Colored People in North America* (New York: Books for Libraries Press, 1971) P. 244, states that in 1859, Paul Drayton, Grand Master of New York granted a warrant to nine Master Masons, residing in Hartford, Conn., to organize a new Lodge of Master Masons, under the title of Widow's Son Lodge, F. & A.M. which was duly established and chartered by the Grand Lodge of New York. Though this date does not agree with the *Prince Hall Masonic Yearbook* (Grand Master's Conference of Prince Hall Masons, 1968) P. 46, which gives a date of 1849. Bro. Newton may have been raised in one of the lodges set up in that state by New York.

8. *Ibid.,* P. 28, also, Davis *op cit.,* P. 244, states that "In 1864 the Supreme Council of the United States (Prince Hall Affiliation) was organized in New York City with Ill. Peter W. Ray as its Grand Commander."

9. *Ibid.,* P. 112. James Milton Turner, outstanding Prince Hall Mason from the M. W. Prince Hall Grand Lodge F & A.M., of Missouri was a Negro Leader and Minister to Liberia. Helped to raise funds and served as trustee to Lincoln University in Jefferson City, Missouri. He secured $75,000 from Congress to the Cherokee Nation for its Negro tribesmen. There is a Lodge from this Jurisdiction named after him.

10. *Ibid.,* P. 27. William Paul Quinn was a member of the National Compact.

11. See reference No. 4.

12. Harold Van Buren Voorhis, *Negro Masonry in the United States,* (New York: Henry Emmerson, 1949) P. 42.

13. Black Historian, George W. Williams in his *"History of Negro Troops in the War of the Rebellion"* states that this regiment made a splendid reputation, losing 19 Enlisted Men killed, 2 Officers wounded, 120 Enlisted Men wounded, 1 Enlisted Man missing, making the total casualties of 143, page 135. The figures do not agree with the Adjutant General's report yet Williams work was based on "military records."

14. Aldrage B. Cooper, *Footprints of Prince Hall Masonry in New Jersey* (New York: Press of Henry Emmerson, 1957) P. 193.

15. Voorhis, *op cit.,* P. 44-45.

16. Prince Hall Grand Lodge F. & A.M. of Connecticut was organized November 3, 1873. Grimshaw, *op cit.,* states January 7th, 1874. Both dates are right. The establishment of this Grand Lodge was completed at Hartiford, Jan 7th. In the Masonic Convention held at New Haven, Nov. 1873, the representatives issued the following: *"Resolved,* That in the withdrawing from the Grand Lodge of the State of New York, that we do it with the kindest of feelings toward them in the past; and it is hoped that the establishment of a Grand Lodge in the State of Connecticut will be the means of cementing the ties of affection and brotherly love in the future." They had five subordinate Lodges with a membership of 212. (Taken from the Proceedings of the Prince Hall Grand Lodge F & A.M., of Missouri of 1875.)

1975 DUES
ALL 1974 MEMBERS ARE
REQUESTED TO FORWARD THEIR
1975 DUES ($5.00) TO THE
EXECUTIVE SECRETARY.

PRINCE HALL'S LETTER BOOK Continued

St. John's Day.

(20) Hall to "The Honourable, the Select men of the Town of Boston." June 2nd, 1789.

"A number of free blacks of the town of Boston," "as we have not any place of worship, and as we do celebrate the 24th day of the month in as serious a manner as we can," and "as Almighty God in his goodness hath sent a preacher among us, and he is willing to preach to us a sermon on that day," ask the use of "the Hall to preach in on that day, for this time only, as we shall not request if of your Honours again."

"The Hall" was probably Faueuil Hall; the preacher, Bro. Marrant mentioned below.

(21) Hall to Holt, Dep. G.M. June 4th, 1789. Not signed.

Reports "received into the Lodge since August two members, namely John Bean and John Marrant, a black minister from home but last from Brachtown, Nova Scotia." Will contribute to Grand Charity on St. John's Day.

Hall's use of the word "home" is interesting.

(22) Hall to White. June 4th, 1789. Not signed.

Has received no acknowledgment of the $10 sent the Grand Charity by Capt. Scott.

(23) A Sermon by John Marrant.

Undated, but doubtless preached before the Lodge June 24th, 1789. It was revised by Hall, before being copied. The ink is so faded as to render the sermon practically illegible; but it seems to contain nothing of special histrocial interest.

(24) "Some Remarks on Mr. John Edwards complete History or Summary of all the Dispensations and Methods of Religion from the Beginning of the World to the Consummation of All Things."

Edwards' work was in two volumes. Hall's abstract fills some 35 pages.

(25) "The Lives of Some of the Fathers and Learned and Famous Divines in the Christian Church from our Lord and Saviour Jesus Christ."

Tertulian, Cyprian, Origen, Augustine, Chrysostom, Gregory and others are mentioned. Marrant's sermon was evidently greatly indebted to these Lives.

(26) Hall to White. November 9th, 1789. A fragment, unsigned.

Complains that he has no acknowledgment of letters sent, or of $10 sent to the Grand Charity in August, 1788.

Printed in full, from a copy furnished by the Grand Secretary of England, in the Proceedings of the (white) Grand Lodge of Massachusetts for 1869. From that version it appears that he had sent copies of the sermon, "preached on St. John's Day by our Brother John Marrant." Only the first part of the letter appears in the letter book, and it differs slightly from the printed ersion.

(27) Hall to Lady Huntingdon. Not dated.

Conveys her his "humble thanks" for the labours of John Marrant, "whom you, under God, hath raised up to be a faithful labourer" etc.; praises Marrant's zeal "since he hath been amongst us, which hath been one year." "We, the members of African Lodge, have made him a member of that honourable society, and chaplain of the same, which will be a great help to him in his travels, and may do a great deal of good to society."

Mentions that Marrant is about to "return to you."

Selina, Countess of Huntingdon, born 1707, died 1791, was head of a sect of Calvinistic Methodists who became known as "The Countess of Huntingdon's Connection." I I have an impression that she was related to William Shirley, mentioned in No. 34.

Certificate.

(28) Masonic Certificate.

"And the light shineth in darkness and the darkness comprehendeth not." Bro. John Dodd having requested a "certificate," "We . . . recommend him, as we found him, a true and lawful brother Master Mason, and his behaviour with us was orderly [and] decent." Dated "at the sign of the Golden [Fleece] in Water Street, Boston." Signed, "Prince Hall, G.M.," "Cyrus Forbes, S.G.W.," "George Middleton, J.G.W."

Hall, "Grand Master."

Appears to be in a form in common use — except as to the titles of the officers — at that day. The use of those titles is suggestive, — especially as this was some months before the organization of the present (white) Grand Lodge of Massachusetts, with whose alleged "exclusive territorial jurisdiction" — asserted, for the first time, long subsequently — the existence of "Negro Masonry" is said to conflict; — thereby rendering itself, it is said, "clandestine." Compare Hall's mention of "the Grand Lodge" in No. 35, below.

(29) A Charge to African Lodge.

Undated: but in No. 31 Hall indicates that he delivered it at Charlestown, June 25th, 1792, probably in connection with a St. John's Day outing. From the number of copies which he distributed, we might almost infer that it was printed.

(30) White to Hall. August 20th, 1792.

Sends printed Proceedings of the Grand Lodge and calendar for the year; acknowledges receipt of sermon and of the Lodge's contributions to the Grand Charity, 24 Nov., 1787, and 18 April, 1792; and asks if certain Lodges are still "in being, as we have never heard from them since the commencement of the late war in America, or indeed, long before: and in case they have ceased to meet, which I rather apprehend, they ought to be erased from our list of lodges."

Printed in full in the "Critical Examination," and elsewhere.

ON BEHALF OF THE EXECUTIVE COMMITTEE, I WANT TO THANK THE MEMBERS OF THE NORTHWEST CHAPTER OF THE PHYLAXIS SOCIETY FOR THE FINANCIAL CONTRIBUTION TO THE *PHYLAXIS MAGAZINE.*

JOSEPH A. WALKES, JR. M.P.S.
PRESIDENT

THE MASONIC ADDRESSES AND WRITINGS OF Ira S. Holder Sr., M.P.S. (New York)

"Whence came You!" and Whither Are You Travelling? Cont. From P. 73 March Issue

One of the first requirements expected of a candidate seeking entrance within the protals of all Masonic Lodges, is that he not only believe in God, the Divine Creator of all things, but also in the teachings and precepts of the Book of Sacred Law. This Great Light has been the guide to many symbolic interpretations of Freemasonry through the ages. It is interesting to note that some of its passages are so similar to some found in our present Ritual, that one can readily see the relationship between its teachings and Freemasonry.

I would at this point like to direct your attention to a Biblical story found in the book of Judges, Chapter 19, of a certain Levite of the tribe of Israel, who lived on the side of Mt. Ephraim. This man, a stranger and wayfarer, was on an important mission. He had gone to bring his concubine (who had left and gone to live with her father in Bethlehem-Judah) back home. After several days delay, he finally started his trip home with his male servant who had accompanied him on his long journey. After travelling all day, the sun began to sink into the West and the shadows of night began to enshroud the country-side, their thoughts, quite naturally turned toward finding lodging for the night; so they halted their journey in Gibeah. After many unsuccessful attempts to obtain lodging; tired, weary and no doubt disgusted, they sat down beside the road to rest and ponder their predictment. Suddenly the Levite looked up and saw coming toward him an old man. Somehow, the old man seemed to sense the plight of the stranger, for as he drew near he addressed the tired and neglected man in the following manner:

"Whither Goest Thou? and From Whence Comest Thou?"

The stranger replied in the following manner: "We are passing from Bethlehem-Judah toward the side of Mt. Ephraim, from thence am I: and I went to Bethlehem-Judah, but I am now going to the house of the Lord; and there is no man that receiveth me to house."

This Biblical quotation found in Judges, Chapter 19, verse 17, as compared with our Masonic question and subject —

"Whence Com You? and Whither are you Travelling?" is adequate proof of the aforementioned statement. In evaluating these two questions, it is easy to see that they are identical in structure and implication; they both show that we must possess three (3) requisites so vital and necessary to advancement.
1. A mission to perform.
2. Determination to perform that mission.
3. A constant travel towards our objective.

"Whence Come You? And Whither Are You Travelling?"

From the Lodge of the Holy Saints John at Jerusalem. This answer is another eminating from the Great Light as previously outlined. There have been many opinions expressed as to the Saints John referred to in our Masonic Ritual. For a fuller and further clarification, I would like to read a portion from Coil's Masonic Encyclopedia, page 592 (quote).

"St. John or Saints John has always been a popular and much used name among Freemasons and has come to be employed so frequently and in so many different ways as to cause some confusion. There are St. John the Baptist, The Holy Saints John, St. John Lodges, St. John Masons, St. John Masonry, and St. John Days, to which, of course are added the many lodges with St. John as their proper name.

The Holy Saints John & Lodge of St. John at Jerusalem

The Gothic legends related to the building of King Solomon's Temple, approximately 1000 years before there was a Saint John but, nevertheless, the first legendary lodge was said to be that of St. John, presumably meaning a lodge at Jerusalem dedicated to St. John the Baptist. That St. John was the energetic forerunner of Christ and the one who baptized Him in the River Jordan. In some places St. John the Evangelist, also called the Mystic, was deemed more to be revered and was substituted. In other places or most places, it was not known

Cont. Next Page

HOLDER, Cont'd.

which was right and it was not questioned why there should be any necessity for a choice, so that both were adopted as the Patron Saints and lodges came to be dedicated to the Holy Saints John and were supposed to be replicas of some Lodge of the Holy Saints John at Jerusalem." (End of quote) Coil further expresses the opinion that St. John the Baptist was the first Patron Saint (of Masons) St. John the Evangelist being somewhat later . . .

This is true as far as England is concerned. In one of the old minute books in existance, that of the Lodge of Edinburgh (Mary's Chapel #1) of the sixteenth century by the great Scottish Historian, David Murray Lyon, there is a memorandum of an order eminating from the Warden General fixing the particular day for each year to be observed by lodges in their election of "Wardens" (as the Worshipful Master at that time was called.) The following is the memorandum: (quote).

"27th, November 1599. First it is ordained that all Wardens shall be chosen each year precisely on St. John's Day, to wit, the 27th, day of December etc." (End of Quote) "Lyon's History of the Lodge of Edinburgh," page 40.

From the minute book of the Lodge of Edinburgh is also found the following: (quote)

"27th, December, 1599. On which day the Deacon and Masters of the Lodge of Edinburgh elected and chose John Broun as their Warden by the majority of votes for one year to come." (End of quote) Lyon's "History of the Lodge of Edinburg," page 41.

Robert F. Gould one of the world's outstanding Historians, comments as follows: (quote)

"The custom of meeting annually upon the day of St. John the Evangelist in conformity with the order of the Warden General with the exception of Mother Kilwinning (December 20) appears to have been observed with commendable fidelity by each of the early Lodges whose minutes have come down to us." (End of Quote)

This practice can be verified in Edinburgh 1599, Aberdeen 1670, Melrose 1674, Dumblane 1696 "Yorston Edition of Freemasonry."

The Scottish Masons from time immemorial duty kept St. John's the Evangelist Day, and in later times the feast of their Patron St. Andrew.

***The custom of holding Lodge assemblies on St. John the Baptist's Day was never a custom of the Scottish Fraternity until after the erection of *Grand Lodge in 1736.*
***The raising of the 24th, of June to the rank of a red-letter day in Scottish Masonic Calendar is more likely to have come after the example of the English Grand Lodge in 1717.

It therefore becomes evident from the historical record that as far as the two Saints John are concerned, only one of them was originally the Patron of the Masons — the Baptist in England, and the Evangelist in Scotland, instead of the two together, as we have them now. How these two became joint Patrons of the Masonic Fraternity thus becomes an interesting and historical question. One very reasonable assumption for the joining of the Saints John is that it was done by *Later Times Masons.* Earlier they (the Masons) had One Meeting Date, June 24th, as in England and/or December 27th, as in Scotland.

Originally, one installation a year was the customary proceedure: one in summer and the other in winter — and one Patron Saint was all they had, and sufficient. Later, they found it expedient to install twice a year as is found in the early record, it seemed natural to make these installations twice, and six months apart. Since one of these installations already seen on one of these St. John's Days, what more natural than the other St. John be similarly taken into the fold as a co-patron? and so it would appear the Masonic co-patronage of the two Saints John historically came about.

"Whence Come You? And Whither Are You Travelling?"

The Biblical story depicts the Stranger as one who was leaving all of the many inducements, everything and everyone behind him; despite his many hinderances, his determination was to reach home, his objective. Spiritually, we too have an objective, we must put behind us all of the corruptive elements that would become hinderances, even those close to us who are not condusive to spiritual growth and strive to reach our objective — that spiritual perfection which can be found only in a dedicated and consecrated life.

Masonically — the profane comes from ignorance and darkness of the outer world of sin and corruption, destitute, impoverished and penniless; seeking entrance by knocking on the door of a Masonic Lodge. In this pathetic state he is admitted within its portals; his entrance is but the first progressive step in the beginning of his travel in search of the true Masonic Light which is given him by symbols and precepts. Progress on the part of the brother can only be assured or measured by his eagerness and desire to absorb its teachings. Just as a child grows from day to day under proper care and guidance into maturity and manhood, so must the Freemason show steady signs of progress and advancement, by constantly seeking for the Moral, Spiritual and

(Continued on Next Page)

87

Intellectual Light which comes from the primal source of all things — the Grand Architect of the Universe, the Creator of the earth and all that it illuminates: travelling toward that Symbolic Truth to that undiscovered country from whose bourne no traveller ever returns. Thus, man's career is ended and the influences of his life, the harvest of his deeds — all are now taken from his control. Man goest to his eternal home.

JOHN PINE

NOTED MASONIC ENGRAVER WAS BLACK

BY

KEITH ARRINGTON
Assistant Librarian
Iowa Masonic Library
Guest Writer

PINE'S LIST OF LODGES

John Pine, (1690-1756), engraver and close friend of the painter, Hogarth, achieved his most lasting fame as a member of the Masonic fraternity by engraving the frontis-piece to Dr. James Anderson's Constitutions of 1723. This same engraving was used again in the 1738 edition of Anderson's Constitutions. Of particular interest to the readers of PHYLAXIS MAGAZINE is the fact that Brother Pine was black.

Pine, a member in 1725 of the lodge at Globe Tavern, Moorgate, (where his name is spelled 'Pyne'), also engraved the quaint Lists of Lodges from about 1725 to 1741. One person, who saw one of the original lists, reported that they were in the form of a packet of loose cards, unnumbered, rather than being bound into a book. These lists showed, (a) the sign of the tavern or inn where the lodge met, (b) the street or location of the inn, and (c) information as to meeting nights.

The first page of the 1725 List of Lodges pictured the engraved signs of The Goose and Grid Iron, Queen's Head at two locations, Horn, King's Head, Griffin, Three Compasses, and Fountain Tavern.

The Book of Constitutions came about when the Grand Lodge, organized in London in 1717, ordered Rev. James Anderson, D.D., in 1721, to "digest the old Gothic Constitutions in a new and better method." A committee of fourteen learned brethren examined the results of his work and after a few changes, it was printed for the benefit of the lodges in 1723. The Iowa Masonic Library has two copies of the original 1723 edition as well as copies of the 1738 second edition. The frontispiece shown with this article was copied from one of the 1738 copies.

One writer says: "The earliest example of the engraver's art that brings the insignia of the Garter into connection with Freemasonry is Pine's famous frontispiece to the "Book of Constitutions,'" 1723, which was reproduced in the corresponding Irish Book of Constitutions, Dublin, 1730. In the foreground of the frontispiece, the Duke of Montagu, apparelled in the full robes of a Knight of the Garter, hands the Book to his successor, the Duke of Wharton, who is clad in Ducal Robes. Notwithstanding the limitations of black and white, the engraver has successfully indicated the light tint of the Duke's Garter."

88

Pine's Famous Frontispiece

Bro. John Pine by Hogarth

Brother Pine served as Marshal of the Processions on January 29, 1730, when Lord Kingston, G.M., escorted the Duke of Norfolk, G. M. Elect, from the Duke's House in St. James Square (London) To Merchant Taylor's Hall. "The Marshall, Mr. Pyne, is to bear a Truncheon painted blew and tipt with gold."

Hogarth painted his friend Pine twice. The portrait with this article was painted by Hogarth in 1755, in the style of Rembrandt. Hogarth also included Pine in a satirical painting called "The Gate of Calais," in which he depicted Pine as a monk. From this, Pine acquired the nickname of "Friar Pine." Hogarth's satire was especially evident in his famous Masonic painting, "Night." But, that is another story.

John Pine was described as fat and jovial, was born in London and spent his entire life there. Other than his Masonic engravings, he roduced an unbelievable quantity of art, chiefly in the form of book illustrations. His first important work was a series of large and impressive engravings, which he published in 1730. Entitled "The Procession and Ceremonies observed at the Time of the Installation of the Knights Companions of the Most Honourable Military Order of the Bath upon Thursday, June 17, 1725," these plates contain portraits of the Knights and their esquires. The Iowa Masonic Library owns a 1730 first edition of this large 15 by 20 inch book, bound in leather.

In "The English Print," Basil Gray wrote: "The only good English engraver between 1730 and his death in 1756 was John Pine, who was, like Hogarth, trained as a silversmith's engraver and who surpassed Hogarth in heraldic and decorative engraving." Probably because of Pine's superb heraldic work, he was made Bluemantle Pursuivant in the College of Heralds in 1743 and took up residence there.

A monumental work was an exquisite edition of "Horace" in which the whole text was engraved and illustrated with ancient bas-reliefs and representations of gems. Known as "Pine's Horace," this was published in two volumes in 1733 and 1737 and is now a collector's item of considerable value.

The "Dictionary of National Biography," whose approximately 70 volumes list the most important British personages through the years, devotes about two full columns to John Pine and almost as much space to his son, Robert Edge Pine, who was also an artist. Robert Edge Pine migrated to America after the signing of the Declaration of Independence,

89

with intention of painting the important persons involved in the Revolution as well as scenes of interest. He spent three weeks at Mt. Vernon, painting George Washington and his family.

THE PHYLAXIS, PHILALETHES AND M.P.S.

It has come to our attention that our Caucasian Counter-part, the Philalethes Society is quite upset because we utilize the initials M.P.S. (Member, Phylaxis Society) which they also use to designate "Member, Philalethes Society."

They have stated that since they have been using these initials since 1928 that we should reverse ours to "P.S.M." so as not to create "confusion." The use of the initials by us is to designate *our* members, and it is used within *our* organization, for our *own* purpose.

The use of initials to designate a member of a particular organization is not new. In 1883, there was in New York a Black self-improvement organization, named the *Pheonix Society*, Bro. Peter Vogelsang, featured in the article, *Prince Hall Masonry and the Civil War*, which has been published in the *Phylaxis Magazine*, was a member. This organization like-wise used the same initials to designate their members.

England use's the initials M.P. to designate a member of Parliment, and so do several other countries that have a Parlimentary type government. Should one cease using these initials merely because another has a simular usage?

The United States Army uses the initials M.P. to designate Military Police, should it demand that other countries stop using the initials M.P.

The Phylaxis Society also uses the initials F.P.S. to designate Fellow of the Phylaxis Society, so does the Philalethes Society, should we therefore do away with the word "Fellow" also. The American Lodge of Research (New York) also uses the term Fellow, should not they also drop its usage. Of course this has not bothered the Philalethes Society as this is a Caucasian body.

The Phylaxis Society will not allow any outsiders to dictate policies to us, nor interfer in the workings of our organization. Especially a non-Prince Hall Masonic group.

The Phylaxis Society has attempted to maintain friendly relationship with this Caucasian Masonic research society, as we agree with its purposes and goals, i.e., *More Light*.

Some of their members we can count as friends, while on the other hand, we note that a few of its members are quite Anti-Prince Hall, and have attacked our fraternity in words, and that one of its members is directly interfering with our members by soliciting their membership in a organization that we have deemed to be "non-conducive" to Prince Hall Masonry.

The Phylaxis Society wants to make it unmistakenly clear, so that there will be no misunderstandings by any organization or groups. We do not interfer in the affairs of any organization and we will not tolerate any interference, in the internal affairs of ours.

Prince Hall Bi-Centennial

By
E. H. Corbett M.P.S. (NY)

Two hundred years ago, Prince Hall and fourteen other colored brethren were entered, passed and raised in an Irish Military Lodge outside of Boston, Mass. He came as a candidate freeborn, of lawful age and well recommended. This is the legal action that introduced masonry among men of color in the United States of America. When this Military lodge left Boston on March 17, 1776 the Master of the Lodge W.M. J. B. Batt left a permit for Prince Hall and the others to meet as a lodge. They met for 8 years and in 1784 Prince Hall wrote the Grand Lodge of England for a charter, after several delays he finally received it in 1787. The Lodge was recorded in the records of the Grand Lodge of England as African Lodge No. 459. This Lodge formed itself into a Grand Lodge in 1791, and called itself African Grand Lodge of North America. Many other Lodges throughout the world established themselves into a Grand Lodge the same way at that time. Among them are Scotland, Holland and several Grand Lodges in Germany were established at the same time. The argument against Prince Hall Masonry in the United States is based on prejudice and racial hatred, and not facts. The fact is that PH Grand Lodge was established in the State of Massachusetts 1 year before the Grand

Lodge of Massachusetts which is white. The colored brethren started their Grand Lodge in 1791 and the white brethren started theirs in 1792. Several Grand Lodges were established in England at the same time Prince Hall received his charter. The facts are that with this charter still in our possession we have a legal and valid document 188 years old, and this is black history because that piece of paper is original. (We don't have to beg, we don't have to borrow, and we don't have to steal: We possess.) Now that we have what we need to practice Freemasonry we should persue our labors diligently with all deliberate speed. Arguing over who is right and who is wrong, and who is legitmate and who is illegitimate is a waste of time for Prince Hall Masons. We are correct, period; not let us develope ourselves as masons should.

We should be about the business right now of building Prince Hall Hospitals and Prince Hall Universities of higher education. Prince Hall Grand Lodges should come together and make substantial contributions to such a Hospital and University. Those rich Grand Jurisdictions in the South should lead the way because they have been blessed with more members and more money, which are two necessary ingredients for making this project a success. The public and the communities in which we live must know the good effects of Freemasonry. There is no better way to make our presents felt then to satisfy a public need. No better way to create public trust and respect than to build those facilities to serve their needs. We as Masons should be the greatest contributors to the happiness of mankind, Masons should be known not by what they say and not by what they preach, but by what they do. Action will always prove more beneficial rhetoric. We as masons must provoke our Grand Lodges to action if our fraternity is to survive, and no one will question our legitimacy, no one will question our intergrity if they see us produce. A Builder must build as a teacher must teach and a preacher must preach. Would any of us want to use a surgeon who has never operated or to fly with a pilot who has never flown a plane. By the same token, we shouldn't call ourselves masons if we are not practicing masons.

This year many Grand Lodges of PH origin will be celebrating the Bi-centennial anniversary of Prince Halls initiation into the lights, rites and benefits of the Fraternal Order. It is with regret that more unity and more prosperity does not exist among the Lodge of the world at this celebration. The PGM of Washington State, William Upton (white) now deceased, said that he wished no monument be erected upon his grave until such time as Masons, both black and white could stand over his hollow spot and shake hands as brothers under one faith, one hope, and one fraternity. It hasn't been done yet and the way things are going two hundred years from today it still might not be accomplished. The book of Revelation which is our masonic trestle board stands supreme. The time has come when we all must re-dedicate and re-obligate our lives to the principles of our Masonic Fraternity. The Public also must re-dedicate theirs to their particular religious conviction. We all need that sweet hour of prayer in the mist of this economic mess we find ourselves in today. For when the body could not be raised, the question was ask, What shall we do? and all of masonry knows the answer. The strong grip from the black hand of Solomon raised both black and white masons. Read, (Song of Solomon, Chapter 1, 5 & 6 verses Holy Bible). Many white writers have made an attempt to exclude it, discredit and belittle it. They were all unsuccessful, and what kind of masonry would we have without the legend of Solomon. It is a good thing that it is a landmark, and can never be removed.

In conclusion I would love to leave you with a question that can be discussed in your lodge. What would Prince Hall think of Masonry and its membership if he were alive today?

BRO. KIVIE KAPLAN PASSES

Bro. Kivie Kaplan of the Caucasian Grand Lodge of Massachusetts A.F. & A.M. and the National President of the N.A.A.C.P. recently died in New York City.

The 71 year old philanthropist and retired industrialist succumbed to a heart attack at La Guardia Airport in New York.

Bro. Kaplan was one of 20 signers of *"An Open Letter To Members of the Grand Lodge of Massachusetts A.F. & A.M.,"* dated October 31, 1969.

The letter attacked the segregationist attitudes of Caucasian Masonic bodies and compared it to the Ku Klux Klans, and requested the reaffirmation by that body of the regularity and legitimacy of the Prince Hall Grand Lodge of Massachusetts A. F. & A.M.

91

Welcome to New Members

Horice R. Rice, 1484 Union St., Brooklyn, NY 11213.

James W. Davis, M.W. Grand Master, 540 33rd Avenue South Seattle, Washington 98144.

Edward H. Corbett, 220 Schenectady Ave., Brooklyn, NY 11213.

Randall Palmer, 408 Osage, Leavenworth, Kansas 66048.

Robert Williams, 316 31st Street, Seattle, Washington 98122.

Dr. William E. Allen, M.D., 720 North Sarah St., St. Louis, Missouri 63108.

Robert T. Herbert, 552 Mitchell St., Uniondale, NY 11553.

Ira S. Holder, Jr., 768 Nostrand Ave., Uniondale, NY 11553.

James F. Collington, 8715 Hayshed Lane, Apt No. 32, Columbia, Maryland 21045.

Albert E. Carter, 811 East Boulevard, Baton Rouge, Louisiana 70802.

Charles E. Johnson, 4907 W. Paine, Apt. 415, St. Louis, Mo. 63108.

Clyde F. Payne, 67 Hawthorne St., Brooklyn, NY 11225.

James C. Faircloth, 6770 Madrona Ave., Fort Lewis, Washington 98433.

Isaac Gaiters, 2533 Kitchemer St., Vancover, B.C. Canada V5K3C7.

Levi Towsent, 2202 29th Avenue, So. Seattle, Washington 98114.

James Brown Ellison, 2588 Seventh Ave., New York, NY 10039

George A. Shannon, P.O. Box 127, Pleasant Hill, La. 71065.

Randolph S. Flourney, E Co., 709th Maint Bn, Ft. Lewis, Washington 98433.

Raymond Showers, 1305 N. 55th St., Philadelphia, Pa. 19131.

Marvin D. Boozer, 750 Georgia Ave., Brooklyn, NY 11207.

Lincoln Davis, 660 St. Nicholas Ave., NY., NY. 10030.

Thomas A. Edwards, 507 Ralph Ave., Brooklyn, NY 11233.

Ruben S. Nutter, 115 Kickapoo St., Leavenworth, KS. 66048.

Early A. Douglas, 2114 E. Columbia St., Seattle, Washington 98122.

Daniel L. Lunsford, 10705 101st. Ct., S.W. Tacoma, Washington 98433.

Jalester Linton, 417 Kickapoo, Leavenworth, Ks. 66048.

John Billings, Jr. 119-18 196th St., St. Albans, NY 11412.

Elwood R. Clough, 735 Gates Ave., Apt. No. 4F, Brooklyn, NY 11221.

Booker T. McFarland, P.O. Box 343, Many, La. 71449.

Arthur W. Harris, 145-15 130th Ave., So. Ozone Park, NY 11436.

Harry Stephens, Jr., 626 Riverside Dr., NY, NY 10031.

Leo D. Johnson, 333 Lafayette Ave., Apt 18A, B'klyh, NY 11238.

John G. Dunn, 253 N. Broadway, Yonkers, NY 10701.

Rev. Norris Poyner, 33 State St., N. Babylon, L.I., NY 07631.

Dr. John W. Davis, Prince Hall Ambassador or Good Will, 112 Reade St., Englewood, New Jersey 07631.

Louis Carter, Grand Master, 35 St. Nicholas Place, NY, NY 10027.

James A. Mingo, P.O. Box 2959, Washington, D.C.

PHYLAXIS PROFILE
Dr. William M. Freeman, M.P.S.

SU PROFESSOR NAMED IN WHO'S WHO IN SOUTH

Dr. William M. Freeman, professor of education at Southern University has been selected for the "Who's Who in the South and Southwest" publication.

The Selma, Alabama native joined the SU faculty in September 1957. He has authored two books and has published more than a dozen scholarly papers and articles in educational, scientific and research journals. He has done extensive traveling in this country and abroad.

In 1959 he was sent to 32 foreign countries by the U.S. State Department as a good will ambassador. His other honors include a listing in "Who's Who in American Education," a 33rd degree Prince Hall Mason, High Priest of the Royal Arch Chapter and Worshipful Master of Twilight Lodge No. 66 and he holds office in the Grand Lodge of Louisiana.

Dr. Freeman holds membership in the Mt. Zion First Baptist Church; is a life Member in the SU Alumni Federation; L.F.A.; N.E.A., the

NAACP and the Omega Psi Phi Fraternity, Inc.

His advanced education was acquired at the University of Denver (B.S., M.Ed., Ph.D.), the Denver School of Religion (M.R.Ed.) and the University of Southern California where he has done two years of post-doctoral study.

A WORD FROM THE PRESIDENT, cont'd.

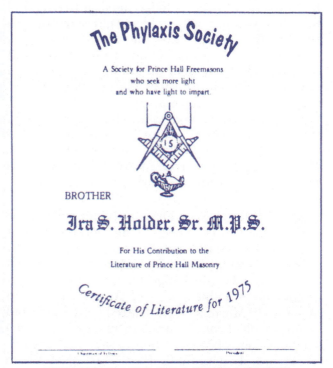

CERTIFICATE OF F.P.S.

CERTIFICATE OF LITERATURE

The Executive Committee is scheduled to hold its first annual meeting in Denver, Colorado in September. At which time a complete review of the Society, its programs and goals will be made.

Congratulations are in order to the members of the Gateway Chapter of the Phylaxis Society in St. Louis for the great assistance they rendered the Grand Lodge in the building of the Masonic library there.

A special thanks to all of the members of the Membership Committee who are actively seeking new members. We are asking all of our active members to bring in a member. We need the help of all.

The Society has a six panel exhibition of Prince Hall and Caucasian Masonic magazines and newspapers. The display appeared in Jefferson City, Missouri and Leavenworth, Kansas. It will be on loan to the Gateway Chapter in St. Louis and the Northwest Chapter in Seattle/Tacoma, Washington. This will be the first of a number of traveling Masonic exhibitions from the Society.

JOSEPH A. WALKES, JR., M.P.S.
President

THE MEMBERSHIP COMMITTEE'S GOAL

Any well run or governed organization whose source of income is derived entirely from the members on its rolls through the payment of Joining Fees, Dues etc., whether its operation is Local or National in scope, such as the Phylaxis Society, must have, as a part of its operational structure a standing Membership Committee. It is the duty and the responsibility of this Committee to recruit and encourage individuals or groups to join its organization and work for its best interest. The Phylaxis Society being a comparatively new Organization, is steadily making progress, not at the rate we would like at present, but gradually we are adding new members to our ranks. The Membership Committee is now compromised of three (3) Members: Ira S. Holder, Sr., Chairman representing the East Coast Area, Bro. Robert L. Hughes the West Coast Area, Bro. William M. Freeman the South-South-West Area. Despite the fact that we are operating with a limited number of Committee Members, I must say: the Committee is doing a good job and should be commended.

In order to adequately cover such an extensive area as the United States effectively, this Committee should be increased by at least three (3) additional Members, and the entire area divided into six (6) equal parts. I fully realize that they are quite a number of Members at present who belong and are a part of the Military establishment; for the purpose of gaining and encouraging new members from this source, and continuing this contact, I suggest that a member of the Military be added to the Membership Committee, in addition to the three (3) previously proposed; and that he be directly responsible for all Military Members both here and over-seas. This new Member, like all of the other Committee Members will render a periodical Progress Report to the Chairman on his activities and accomplishments ect. The full strength of the Committee will be seven (7) for full coverage of the entire United States and the Military both here and abroad.

At such time as the Organization's strength is increased to a sizable number, and it id desirable to have representation in other parts of the globe, additional Members should be added accordingly.

With such a strong Membership Committee, I am confident that we can achieve our goal of 500 Members by the end of 1975.

Should Prince Hall Masonry Explore the Table Lodge?

(PHYLAXIS NOTE: While the ceremonies of a Table Lodge are unfamiliar to many Prince Hall Masons generally, they may be traced back two centuries in English Masonry, and detailed records exist of their observance in France at an even earlier period. According to custom, Table Lodges were always held in the Entered Apprentice's Degree. The Ceremony is impressive. Should Prince Hall Masonry explore the Table Lodge? Only you can answer the question.)

THE TABLE LODGE

Civilized people the world over cherish the family feasts; Christmas, and New Year, Harvest Home and, in this country, Thanksgiving Day. Such gatherings are more than mere opportunities to eat; they are spiritual solidifications of family ties, opportunities for mutual rejoicing, a means by which the family becomes more closely knit.

Most American lodges know "the fourth degree" in which lodge members mingle in an anteroom or dining room for the after-meeting coffee and sandwich or more pretentious meal.

The Masonic banquet, in which an elaborate menu is served, followed by the introduction of one or more speakers by a toastmaster, the whole in commemoration of some anniversary, such as St. John's Day observance, or as a commencement of a new year, is common.

Famous Masonic authority H. L. Haywood in *"More About Masonry"* says: "In the Eighteenth Century Lodges the Feast bulked so large in the life of the lodge that in many of them the members were seated at the table when the lodges were opened and remained at it throughout the Communication, even when the degrees were conferred. The result was that Masonic fellowship was good fellowship in it, as in a warm and fruitful soil, acquaintanceship, friendship, and affection could flourish — there was no grim and silent sitting on a bench, staring across at a wall. Out of this festal spirit flowered the love which Masons had for their lodge. They brought gifts to it, and only by reading of old inventories can any present day Mason measure the extent of that love; there were gifts of chairs, tables, altars, pedestals, tapestries, draperies, silver, candle-sticks, oil paintings, libraries, Bibles, mementos, curios, regalias, and portraits. The lodge was a home, warm, cofortable, luxurious, full of memories, and tokens, and affection, and even if a member died his presence was never wholly absent; to such a lodge no member went grudgingly, nor had to be coaxed, nor was moved by that ghastly, cold thing called a sense of duty, but went as if drawn by a magnet, and counted the days until he could go.

"What business has any lodge to be nothing but a machine for grinding out the work! It was not called into existence in order to have the minutes read! Even a mystic tie will snap under the strain of cheerlessness, repetition, monotony, dullness. A lodge needs a fire lighted in it, and the only way to have that warmth is to restore the lodge Feast, because when it is restored good fellowship and brotherly love will follow, and where good fellowship is, members will fill up an empty room not only with themselves but also with their gifts."

In a few Grand Lodges in the United States the ancient custom of the Table Lodge is still preserved; some Masonic authorities believe that it might be revived in all Grand Lodges to the enlightenment and pleasure of the brethren.

The Table Lodge is no mere banquet with entertainment; it is a special lodge ceremony in itself, with a ritual, formalities and a special terminology which is of some interest.

The Iowa Grand Lodge Library possesses "A Ritual for a Table Lodge of Ancient Free and Accepted Masons," translated and adapted from an old French ritual in possession of the Grand Lodge of Masons in Massachusetts, by R. W. Frank B. Crandall, Past Master of Caleb Butler Lodge, A. F. and A.M., of Ayer,

94

Massachusetts. Somewhat abbreviated, it is as follows:

ARRANGEMENTS FOR A TABLE LODGE: As a Table Lodge is part of the mysteries of the Order, the lodge should be held in a place as securely tyled as the lodge-room. The table is set up in the shape of a horseshoe and is large enough, if the place will allow, to permit all to be seated on the outer side of the table. The Worshipful Master is always placed at the East, facing the middle of the table, with the Chaplain at his right and the Wardens at the two ends of the table in the West. The Master Masons occupy the South, taking care to yield the places nearer the East to guests, if any be present. The Entered Apprentices should be on the North near the Chaplain and the Fellowcrafts occupy the rest of this part of the table.

All that constitutes the table service should be set in three parallel lines, that is to say, the plates form the first line, the bottles and glasses, the second, and the food and lights, the third.

Everything that is used at the banquet changes its name: glasses are called *cannons*; bottles, *casks*; red wine, *red powder*; white wine, *strong powder*; bread, *rough asblar*; food, *materials*; lights, *stars*; plates, *tiles*; knives, *swords*; and salt, *sand*.

OPENING: Invocation. *(When everything has been arranged, the Worshipful Master rises, raps three times on the table, and the Wardens reply in like manner.)* WM. — Brothers Senior and Junior Wardens, invite our Brethren on the Columns of the North and South to assist us in opening a Lodge of Entered Apprentices and one of Table Instruction.

(Senior and Junior Wardens repeat.)

W.M. — Brother Senior Warden, are your a Mason?

S.W. — All my Brethren know me to be such.

W.M. — What is the first care of a Mason?

S.W. — To see if the Lodge is tyled.

W.M. — Satisfy yourself.

S.W. — It is Worshipful.

W.M. — What is the second?

W.W. — To see if all the Brethren are in order. *(After looking about.)* They are, Worshipful.

W.M. — Why are we met together?

S.W. — To erect Temples to virtue and dig dungeons for vices.

W.M. — How long must we work?

S.W. — From midday to midnight.

W.M. — How long a time is required to make an Entered Apprentice?

S.W. — Three years.

W.M. — What is your age?

S.W. — Three years.

W.M. — What is the hour?

S.W. — Almost midday.

W.M. — In consideration of the hour and age, inform our Brethren that a Lodge of Entered Apprentices and one of Table Instruction are open and that we are about to begin our works in the usual manner.

(Senior and Junior Warden so inform. The Brethren show the signs of an Entered Apprentice, then give the Battery, three times three, and cry "VIVAT.")

THE CEREMONY OF THE SEVEN TOASTS

FIRST TOAST: (The W.M. raps once and the S.W. and J.W. do the same.)

W.M. — Brothers Senior and Junior Wardens, cause the arms to be charged and aligned for the first Toast.

Senior and Junior Wardens so do. The cannons are charged.)

W.M. — Brothers Senior and Junior Wardens, are the cannons charged and aligned?

S.W. and J.W. — Yes, Worshipful.

(All rise.)

W.M. — Brothers Senior and Junior Wardens, announce to our Brethren that the toast that I have the pleasure to propose is that to the President of the U.S.

(Senior and Junior Wardens so do.)

W.M. — Right hand to arms. *(The right hand touches the glass.* Ready. *(The glass is raised, the arm extended to the height of the breast.)* Aim. *(The glass is brought to the lips.)* Fire. Good Fire. Fire all! *(All drink.)* Present arms. *(The glass is brought to the second position, all imitating the W.M. Then the glass is carried to the left breast, then to the right breast, and then again to the second position, so that the motion makes a triangle. When this has been done thrice, the glass is brought to the table in three movements, that is to say, at the first it is carried horizontally a little to the left, then to the right, and then forcibly to the table. The battery, three times three, is then given and the acclaimation "VIVAT" is given thrice. The foregoing should be done with exactness and evenness so that the whole company may execute the same movements at the same time and that the lgasses shall strike the table with one blow.)* Advance swords. *(The knife is raised, the arm ex-*

95

*tended to the height of the breast.) *Poise swords. *(The knife is elevated slightly.)* Salute with swords. *(Done.)* Swords at rest. *(The handles strike the table at the same time. Battery.)*

SECOND TOAST: *(The W.M. raps once and the S.W. and J.W. do the same.)*

W.M. — Brothers Senior and Junior Wardens, cause the arms to be charged and aligned for the second toast.

S.W. and J.W. — Brethren on my Column, in all your grades and stations, charge and align your arms for the second toast of obligation which the Worshipful Master is about to propose. *(The cannons are charged.)*

W.M. — Brothers Senior and Junior Wardens, are the cannons charged and aligned?

S.W. and J.W. — Yes, Worshipful.

(All rise.)

W.M. — Brothers Senior and Junior Wardens, announce to our Brethren that the toast that I have the pleasure to propose is that to the Most Worshipful Grand Master and the Most Worshipful Grand Lodge.

(S.W. and J.W. so do.)

W.M. — Right hand to arms.

The ceremonies attending these commands are the same as in first toast.)

(Continued on Page 22)

NOTES, QUERIES AND INFORMATION ON ITEMS OF MASONIC RESEARCH

By

THE PHYLAXIS SOCIETY
P.O. Box 3151
Ft. Leavenworth, Ks.
66027

THIS SECTION IS PRESENTED TO OUR READERS, and relates to matters pertaining to Prince Hall Masonic history, biography and tradition.

We invite our readers and members to send such material that is appropriate for use in this column. It must be stressed that this page is for EXCHANGE of information and opinion concerning Prince Hall Masonry and does not pretend to provide the final answers to any query.

Each query is numbered to identify the subject matter.

4. GRIMSHAW: From Alphonse Cerza, Past President of the Philalethes Society comes information on P.G.M. William Henry Grimshaw *"Official History of Freemasonry Among The Colored People in North America,"* that several years ago the Negro Universities Press, 51 Riverside Avenue, Westport, Ct. 06880, published a fasimile of this volume. It is not known if the book is still available or if they sold them all.

2. BI-CENTENNIAL: *Prince Hall Medallion:* An exquisite medallion of Prince Hall commemorating our 200 years of Freemasonry has been provided by the Prince Hall Bicentennial Commission, and is available for only $6.00 plus $1.00 for shipping and handling. You will treasure this commemorative medallion for years to come. Send check or money order to: Prince Hall Bicentennial Commission, c/o Prince Hall Grand Lodge, 454 West 155th Street, New York, New York, 10032.

13. PAST MASTER'S DEGREE: From Grand Master Jno G. Lewis, Jr., M.P.S. (Louisiana) comes an interesting statement. "I have been alarmed at the erosion of respect and regard for Symbolic Masonry in favor of the so-called higher degrees. I think this had its inception in going beyond the third degree to confer upon the Mater-elect a so-called "Past Master's degree."

I think it would be a very excellent thing for the Conference of Grand Masters to endorse a "ceremony of investitute" for Masters elect. There can be no controversy over the fact the highest degree in Ancient Craft Masonry as it has been practiced the last two hundred years is the third degree.

It is improper and does violence to the masonic etiquette and protocol to go outside of its accepted sphere in our concept of the structure of the masonic institution in search for a means for qualifying a Master-elect for presiding over his lodge.

14. 100 MOST INFLUENTIAL BLACK AMERICANS: We note with much pride in the May 1975 issue of *Ebony Magazine*, the many Prince Hall Masons who made the list.

Bro. Thomas J. Bradley, Mayor, Los Angeles, Calif.; Bro. John H. Johnson, Editor, Ebony, Jet Magazine, etc; John G. Lewis M.P.S., Sovereign Grand Commander, Southern Jurisdiction, Grand Master of Prince Hall Grand Lodge of Louisiana; Bro. Thurgood Marshall, Associate Justice, Supreme Court, Bro. Charles B. Rangel, U. S. Representative of New York; P.G.M. Hobson B. Reynolds, Grand Exalted Ruler, I.B.P.O.E.W. (Elks); Frank M. Summers, Sovereign Grand Commander, Northern Jurisdiction and Bro. Percy E. Sutton, President, Borough of Manhattan, New York, to name but a few. We also note, for the first time the absence of Non-Prince Hall "Masonic" leaders. We do continue to regret that the name of our Imperial Potentate continues to remain off of the list.

15. NON-PRINCE HALL GRAND MASTERS: The following list of so called "Grand Masters" was taken from Vol. XIX No. 4, Dec. 74 issue of the *York Rite Bulletin* the official Organ of the so called National Grand Lodge, Free and Accepted Ancient York Masons, National Compact, Prince Hall Origin, Inc.

Matthew Brock of Columbus, Ohio, National Grand Master from 1963 remains in this office. J. B. Lett, Route 1, Box 253, Peterman, Ala. 36471; B. J. Slater, 4031 So. Elati St., Denver, Colo. 80200; Carl A. Hendricks, 332 W. 118th St., Los Angeles, Ca. 90061; Saml. E. McCants, 400 West 26th St., Wilmington, Dela. 19802; W. C. Johnson, 502 N.W. 4th St., Gainesville, Fla. 32601; Benjamin Barton, 2306 Blvd., Granada, S.W. Atlanta, Ga. 30311; Isaiah Daniels, 9528 S. Avalon Ave., Chicago, Ill. 60628; Wiley Williams, 1036 Ivanhoe Ct., Gary, Ind. 46404; Waldo Monroe, 400 Wisconsin Ave., Lawrence, Kansas 66044; Lance Leonard, RFD No. 1, Box 58A, Independence, La. 70443; Carlin R. Woodhouse, 2110 N. Pulaski, Baltimore, Md. 21217; Robert Vaughn, 4170 Russel St., Detroit, Mich. 48207; Alphonso L. Greer Jr., 1201 12th St. Ave., Minneapolis, Mn. Bethune Park, Apt. 410, 55411; Pink Colvin, P.O. Box 573, Moss Point, Miss. 39563; James Keller, 5547 Frieling St., St. Louis, Mo. 63140; Christopher Carter, 32N. 7th St., Newark, NJ 07107; James Brown, 1941 3rd Ave., Apt. 16D, NY, NY Franklin Plaza 10029; Ted Williams, 813 W. Virginia Ave., Bessemer City, NC 28016; Jefferson Tufts, 3585 E. 1st St., Cleveland, Ohio 44120; M. M. Beatty, 1555 North Quaker, Tula, Okla. 74106; Cleveland Young, 4365 Concord Dr., Trevosa, Pa. 19047; Freddie Footman, Route No. 3, Box 216, St. Matthews, S.C. 29135; Theo Waters, 819 Riddle St., Knoxville, Tenn. 37914; M. J. Anderson, P.O. Box 1296, 1017 E. 11th St., Austin, Texas 78700; J. W. Pritchett, 1203 Maxine Rd., Martinsville, Va. 24112; Geo. C. Lindsey, 1710 E. St., SE, Washington D.C. 10003; James R. Harrston, Drawer EE, Northfork, W. Va. 24868; Willie Franklin, 3342 North 15th St., Milwaukee, Wis. 53206.

The National Grand Lodge (or Compact) was disbanded in 1877, but yet from this hybrid has spewed a horde of Non-Prince Hall lodges.

16. NEGRO MASONRY IN THE UNITED STATES. It has been noted that Bro. Arthur H. Frederick of Mount Zion Lodge No. 15 of the Prince Hall Grand Lodge of Massachusetts is making his *Negro Masonry in the United States* available at $2.95 (Prince Hall Craftsman, Vol. XIII, No. 3, Second Qtr. 1975) Bro. Frederick M.P.S., is the Editor of the *Phylaxis Magazine* and his address is P.O. Box 43, Roxbury, Massachusetts 02119.

17. UNIVERSAL LEAGUE OF FREEMASONS (U.L.F.). is said to have been created in 1905, or about this time, and has headquarters in Geneva, Switzerland. The American headquarters is said to be in El Paso, Texas under LTC (R) Harvey Newton Brown.

The Foreign Correspondent of the Grand Lodge of Georgia (Caucasian) states, "Apparently the U.L.F. gathers its members from all types of Masonic bodies regular, or irregular, without discrimination or care as to source. It obviously hopes to become some day a sort of super type "one world" Masonic government."

"The Secretary of the U.S. group in an unsolicited and unacknowledge letter to the Foreign Correspondent of the Grand Lodge of Georgia, stated on August 2, 1968, "I do not feel that Masonry has brought me closer to God, for frankly I do not know what "God" is (quote marks are his) nor does anybody else; and the term "closer to God" baffles me. Just another cliche which "sounds good."

The letter from which this is quoted was in-regard to his comments about a Lodge of Research Paper which he happened to see and to comment on.

Several Grand Lodges have banned their members from membership or participation in this U.L.F., the latest being the edict of the Grand Master of the Grand Lodge of Pennsylvania (Caucasian), Brother John K. Young, issued an Edict prohibiting Pennsylvania Freemasons from any form of activity with this league; that any Pennsylvania member now belonging must renounce his membership in the U.L.F. or face Masonic charges. The Grand Master cited a previous action by the United Grand Lodge of England with reference to the U.L.F.

97

The U. S. Group Secretary and representative, as said above, is a resident of El Paso, Texas, and by all accepted theories of Masonic law he is subject to the Masonic law of the Grand Lodge of Texas while he resides within that Grand Jurisdiction. After several altercations with the Grand Lodge of Texas and a flat refusal to acknowledge the Masonic Jurisdiction of that Grand Lodge over him, he was cited and tried by the Grand Lodge of Texas Committee and was sentenced to five years suspension from all rights and privileges of Freemasonry.

The PHYLAXIS SOCIETY stated its official position in the Phylaxis Magazine (Volume 1, Number 1, January 1974), that the Universal League of Freemasons is "Non-conducive" to Prince Hall Masonry. History has clearly showed us our mistakes in forming the National Grand Lodge or Compact, and it has cost us dearly as this disbanded body invades our jurisdictions with their clandestine Lodges.

It had come to our attention that a Past Grand Master from the Most Worshipful Prince Hall Grand Lodge of Michigan had been appointed as National Deputy of the U.L.F. replacing a "Deputy" who was forced to withdraw his membership by the Grand Master of California.

We cannot understand, why this P.G.M., would accept such a position, nor why he would join an organization that has been judged by American Masonic bodies, as Clandestine.

The Phylaxis Society will not brand this organization as such, but we maintain that it is non-conducive to Prince Hall Masonry. The U.L.F. has shown by its newsletters to have an understanding attitude towards Prince Hall Masonry, and it has defended P.H.A. against racially motivated attacks from Caucasian Masonic bodies, but, the mere fact that it accepts, "regular, irregular and clandestine" "Masons" into its ranks is cause for the Phylaxis Society to take the stand that it does.

8. P.G.M. Alexander G. Clark, Sr., (Missouri and Iowa). From the Federal Register, Tuesday, June 3, 1975, Volume 40, Number 107, Page 23907:

The following properties have been determined to be eligible for inclusion in the National Register.

* * *

IOWA
Muscatine County

Muscatine, Clark, Alexander, Property 125-123 W. 3rd and 307-309 Chestnut.

98

TABLE LODGE, cont'd. from Page 96

THIRD TOAST: (The Senior Warden raps once. The J.W. does the same. The the W.M. responds in like manner.)

W.M. — Brothers Senior and Junior Wardens, what do you desire?

S.W. — Worshipful Master, the Junior Warden and I beg to allow the arms to be charged and aligned for a toast that we wish to propose.

W.M. — Brethren, in all your grades and stations charge and align your arms for a toast that our Brothers, the Wardens, wish to propose.

(The cannons are charged.)

W.M. — Brothers Senior and Junior Wardens, are all the cannons charged and aligned?

S.W. and J.W. — Yes, Worshipful.

(All rise.)

W.M. — The East yields to your desires. What is the toast that you wish to propose?

S.W. — It is to you, Worshipful. Brethren on my Column, in all your grades and stations, the toast which the Junior Warden and I have the pleasure to propose is that to our Worshipful Master.

J.W. — *(Repeats.)*

S.W. — Right hand to arms. *(Repeat procedure.)*

(The ceremonies accompanying the foregoing commands are repeated. The W.M. does not drink. The W.M. responds with the same ceremonies.)

FOURTH TOAST: (The W.M. Raps once and the S.W. and J.W. do the same.)

W.M. — Brothers Senior and Junior Wardens, cause the arms to be charged and aligned for the fourth toast.

S.W. and J.W. — *(So do.)*

W.M. — Brothers Senior and Junior Wardens, are the cannons charged and aligned?

S.W. and J.W. — Yes, Worshipful.

(All rise.)

W.M. — Brothers Senior and Junior Wardens, announce to our Brethren that the toast that I have the pleasure to propose is that to the Wardens.

S.W. and J.W. — *(So do.)*

(Follow ceremony with all but the Wardens drinking.)

FIFTH TOAST: (Same ceremony of having cannons charged, etc.)

W.M. — Brothers Senior and Junior Wardens,

announce to our Brethren that the toast that I have the pleasure to propose is that to our Brethren in the armed forces of the United States.

(Same procedure.)

SIXTH TOAST: (Same ceremony of having cannons charged, etc.)

W.M. — Brothers Senior and Junior Wardens, announce to our Brethren that the toast that I have the pleasure to propose is that to the other officers, new initiates and visiting brethren.

(Same procedure.)

SEVENTH TOAST: (Same ceremony of having cannons charged, etc.)

W.M. — Brothers Senior and Junior Wardens, announce to our Brethren that the toast that I have the pleasure to propose is that to all Masons wheresoever spread over the face of the globe.

(At swords rest, the W.M. and all present cross their arms, joining the right and left hands, and form a chain. The serving Brethren also join in the chain, swinging the arms back and forth, they sing.)

Sould 'auld acquaintance be forgot,
An' never be brought to mind?
Should auld acquaintance be forgot.
An' days o' auld lang syne?

CHORUS:

For auld lang syne, my dear,
For auld lang syne.
We'll take a cup o' kindness yet
For auld lang syne.

CLOSING:

W.M. — Brothers Senior and Junior Wardens, are all the Brethren in order?
S.W. and J.W. — They are, Worshipful.
W.M. — What is the hour?
S.W. — Midnight.
W.M. — What is your age?
S.W. — Three Years.
W.M. — In consideration of hour and age, inform all our Brethren both on the Column of the North and South, that we are about to close this Lodge, ending our work in the usual manner.
S.W. — Brethren on my Column, I inform you, on behalf of the Worshipful Master, that we are about to close this Lodge, ending our work in the usual manner.
J.W. — (Repeats.)
(All show signs of Entered Apprentice, give battery, cry "VIVAT" thrice.)
W.M. — My Brothers, the Lodge is closed.
S.W. and J.W. — (Repeat.)

A Bright Mason

A Western subscriber asks us to tell what a bright Mason is. The phrase, "he is a bright Mason," is usually applied to one who is well posted in the lectures of the various degrees, and can communicate them without hesitation and correctly. This requires, of course, a retentive memory and a readiness to learn. But it must be remembered that Masonry does not wholly consist of ceremonies and ritual.

We have seen men who could confer degrees, give the lectures complete without missing the smallest word, but who could hardly be regarded as bright Masons.

The brightness of Masonry lies beneath the veil of allegory and the surface of symbolism, and takes hold of the heart with its tenderest sympathies and affections. The brightness of Masonry is not confined to the lodge-room, but shines from the soul in the life and actions of the man. It is seen in the cheerful countenance, in the kind words and good deeds, in the journeyings on errands of mercy, even barefoot if necessary, in the shielding of a brother's good name, in manifestation of good-fellowship that makes association pleasant.

Parrots jabber away, but their gibberish is meaningless. A Masonic parrot may recite the words of the ritual, be familiar with every step to be taken in the ceremonies, and to the casual observer appear "bright," but like the thin wash of gold upon a brass foundation, the tarnish will soon appear and the brightness be destroyed. There must be the true, pure metal in order to secure the proper and permanent brilliancy.

The work of the bright Mason is soulful and earnest. He feels that he has something important and good to communicate and he does it with a feeling that carries conviction to the listener. We remember when a boy frequently hearing a good old lady, nearly seventy years of age, speak in church prayer-meeting and the whole burden of her few words of exhortation was for whole-heartedness in devotion and work. "I tell you, brothers and sisters," she would say, "there is no blessing or success attending half-hearted service. The whole heart, not a part of it, must be in whatever we do," Precisely is it so in all Masonic work. The whole heart must be in it, and he who thus lives and acts will be a bright Mason, even though he may stumble over big words in the ritual. — *Masonic Advocate*.

99

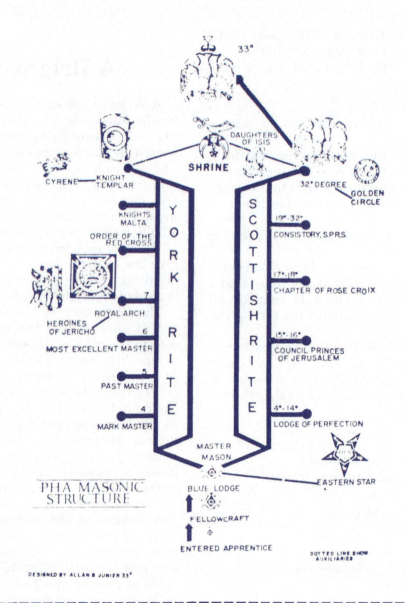

THE PHYLAXIS SOCIETY SUBSCRIPTION CARD

Subscription rate: $5.00/Yr.

Mail to: James E. Herndon, MPS
Executive Secretary
1574 Ivanhoe Street
Denver, Colo. 80220

Gentlemen:

Enclosed is my subscription the the Phylaxis Magazine.

_____ Check Enclosed _____ amount payable to Phylaxis Magazine

Name: _____

Address: _____

City: _____ State: _____ Zip Code: _____

A SOCIETY FOR PRINCE HALL FREEMASONS WHO SEEK MORE LIGHT AND WHO HAVE LIGHT TO IMPART

THE PHYLAXIS

DECEMBER 1975

Volume II   Number 4

A SOCIETY FOR PRINCE HALL
FREEMASONS WHO SEEK MORE
LIGHT AND WHO HAVE LIGHT TO
IMPART.

THE PHYLAXIS
Published at Boston, Mass. by
THE PHYLAXIS SOCIETY

Arthur H. Frederick M.P.S..................................Editor
Box 43, Roxbury, Massachusetts 02119

OFFICERS

Joseph A. Walkes, Jr., M.P.S..............................President
P.O. Box 3151, Ft. Leavonworth, Kansas 66027

Herbert Dailey, M.P.S...................First Vice President
1616 South Cedar, Tacoma, Washington 98405

Zellus Bailey, M.P.S.......................Second Vice President
7039 Dover Court, St. Louis, Missouri 63130

James E. Herndon, M.P.S................Executive Secretary
1574 Ivanhoe Street, Denver, Colorado 80220

Alonzo D. Foote, Sr., M.P.S.................................Treasurer
P.O. Box 99601, Tacoma, Washington 98499

SUBSCRIPTION RATE: FOR ONE YEAR, $5.00

The Phylaxis Magazine is the official publication of the Phylaxis Society. Any article appearing in this publication expresses only the opinion of the writer, and does not become the official pronouncement of the Phylaxis Society. No advertising of any form is solicited or accepted. All communication relative to the magazine should be addressed to the Editor. Inquiries relative to membership must be addressed to the Executive Secretary. Membership is by invitation and recommendation only. The joining fee is $3.00. Dues are $5.00 per year in advance, which amount includes a subscription to the "Phylaxis" magazine for one year.

All rights reserved. No part of this work may be reproduced or transmitted in any form or by any means, electrical or mechanical, or retrival system, with out written permission from the publisher.

**1976 DUES
ALL 1975 MEMBERS ARE
REQUESTED TO FORWARD THEIR
1976 DUES [$5.00] TO THE
EXECUTIVE SECRETARY.**

INDEX

A Word from the President	102
Those Magnificent Masonic Buffalo Soldiers	103
The Masonic Address and Writings of Ira S. Holder, Sr., M.P.S.	106
Welcome to New Members	111
The Phylacis Society and the Missouri Masonic Library	111
The Masonic Service Association of the United States	112
The Masonic Address and Writings of Ira S. Holder, Sr., M.P.S.	113

A WORD FROM THE PRESIDENT

The Executive Committee held its first meeting September 6-7th at the Holiday Inn Downtown, in the Mile High City of Denver, Colorado.

The members were greeted by Most Worshipful David L. Holliman, Grand Master of the Prince Hall Grand Lodge of Colorado.

At this important first meeting a complete review of the structure, programs and the goals of the Society was made, with many recommendations adopted.

Your President was awarded **"Fellow of the Phylaxis Society"** (F.P.S.) for his **"Masterpiece" Prince Hall Masonry and the Civil War**, which appeared in three parts in the **Phylaxis Magazine**.

Summary of the business handled was:

1. Welcome by the Executive Secretary, James E. Herndon M.P.S. (Colorado), host of the meeting.
2. Welcome by Grand Master Holliman
3. Report of the President
   (a) Report of the Membership Committee
4. Report of the First Vice President
   (a) Report of the Northwest Chapter
5. Report of the Second Vice President
   (a) Report of the Gateway Chapter
   (b) Report of the Non-Prince Hall Committee
6. Report of the Executive Secretary
7. Report of the Treasurer presented by Bro. Herbert Daily M.P.S. (Washington)
8. Incorporation of the Society
9. Adoption of the By-Laws of the Northwest Chapter
10. Changes to the By-Laws of the Phylaxis Society
11. Membership Committee
12. LTC Harvey N. Brown, Secretary of the Universal League of Freemasons (U.L.F.) and relationship with this organization.
13. Mr. Alphonzo Cerza, Past President of the Philalethes Society and relationship with this organization.
14. The Phylaxis Magazine
15. Exhibit, **The Documents of Grand Master Prince Hall**, presented by the President.

The next Executive Committee meeting is scheduled to be held in March 1976 in Seattle/Tacoma, Washington.

It is a honor to announce that two more members have been nominated as Fellows of the Phylaxis Society. Bro. Arthur H. Frederick (Massachusetts) and Bro. Charles H. Wesley (Washington, D.C.). The

Continued on page 110

THOSE MAGNIFICENT MASONIC BUFFALO SOLDIERS

PART I

BY

JOSEPH A. WALKES, JR., F.P.S. [KANSAS]

The annals of Military Freemasonry maybe described as a veritable romance of "goodwill upon earth," this is not to deny the civil records of the Craft the possession of an abundant fund of varied interest on the same excellent lines both in their archeological and historical aspects.

But, after all, the warrior members of the Brotherhood are those who have always carried its influence into what are still the most strenuous paths of romance—those of military adventure.

Fighting Freemasons, the Influence
of the Brotherhood in War by
J.H. Manners Howe, Dec. 11, 1909

Prince Hall Masonry from its inception has always played a major role in sustaining Black America. Nowhere is this more evident than in the wars fought by Blacks for America.

As has been seen in **Prince Hall Masonry and the Civil War,**[1] the Black soldier brought with him his religion, his love of life and freedom, and his Masonry.

First, was the Lewis Hayden Military Lodge attached to the 54th Massachusetts Regiment and Pheonix Lodge No. 1 of the 29th Regiment Connecticut Colored Infantry during the Civil War, which set the precedent for Prince Hall Masonry.

To better understand the concept of these Lodges and their tradition, it must be made clear that they had long existed in the British Army. The earliest warrant creating a traveling or moveable Lodge was issued in 1732 by the Grand Lodge of Ireland[2] and by 1813, the time of the union of the two Grand Lodges in England, there would be approximately 352 military Lodges between the Grand Lodges of Ireland, Scotland and England.[3]

Though all military Lodges supported the traditions of the fraternity in the upholding of Masonic obligations, and ritualistic work, their failure to maintain minutes of their communications or submit reports to their Grand Lodges, is the reason that there is little known of their existance within the Prince Hall family. Some military Lodges ceased to work owing to the loss of their warrants, often due to leaving their property behind, when moving from one station to another, and also the sheer inability to continue their labors due to an insufficient amount of members, are some of the reasons that they fell from favor with most Grand Lodges.

Yet Prince Hall Masonry continued the tradition, and after the Civil War issued the following guidelines to govern such Lodges:

REGULATIONS OF MILITARY LODGES

It being essential to the interests of the Craft, that all military Lodges should be strictly confined to the purpose for which their warrants were originally obtained, and as very great abuse may arise from the improper initiations of Masons by such Lodges, every warrant, therefore, which is held by a military Lodge, shall be forfeited, unless the following laws be complied with, in addition to those specified under the rule regulating subordinate Lodges.

1st. No warrant shall be granted for the establishment of a military lodge, without the consent of the Commanding Officer of the regiment, battalion or company, to which it is to be attached, having been first obtained.

2nd. No military Lodge shall, on any pretence, initiate into Masonry, any inhabitant or sojourner at any town or place at which its members may be stationed, or through which they may be marching, or any person who does not, at the time, belong to the military profession, nor any military person below the rank of corporal, except as serving brethren or by dispensation from the Grand Master.

3rd. When any military Lodge under the Constitution of a M.W.G. Lodge, under the jurisdiction of this M.W.N.G. Lodge, shall be in foreign parts, it shall conduct itself so as not to give offence to the Masonic authority of the country or place in which it may sojourn, never losing sight of the duties it owes to the Grand Lodge, to which communication is ever to be made, and all fees and dues regularly transmitted.

4th. If the regiment, battalion, or military company to which a military Lodge is attached, be disbanded or reduced, the brethren shall take care that the warrant be carefully transmitted to the Grand Lodge, that it may not fall into improper hands, but if a competent number of the brethren remain together, they may apply for another warrant, of the same number, to be holden as a civil Lodge, at such place as may be

103

OFFICERS JOPPA MILITARY LODGE No. 150.
FRANK D. CLINTON, Master.
Ft. D. A. Russell, Wyo.

convenient, and which may be approved by the Grand Master. Such warrant to be granted without any additional expense. [4]

The statement, **"that the terms Corporal and serving brothers"** was stricken out and replaced with **"proper and acceptable material only to be the standard."**

The history of military Lodges have always had its ups and downs, most fading out with occasional restorations after more or less prolonged life, this, however regretable was the inevitable outcome of the military life, the constant traveling from station to station, war, and the death or retirement of members.

After the Civil War, they would ride into the Indian Territory of the West, the greatest military Cavalry unit America ever assembled. These were **"The Buffalo Soldiers"**, so named by the Indians they fought. Magnificant Black men, who would ride across the frontiers of the early west and into the pages of the history of an often ungrateful nation.

Much has been written about these Troopers, but very little is known of the Prince Hall Masonic Lodges that sustained them. Harry A. Williamson, Harry E. Davis, Harold V.B. Voorhis, John Black Vrooman and Allen E. Roberts are the exceptions, having briefly

104

mentioned the existance of such Lodges in their books. [5]

The famous 9th and 10th Cavalry Regiments was organized in 1866. [6] The duties of the Ninth were to protect the stagecoach lines, to establish law and order along the Mexican border, and to keep the Indians on reservations. The Tenth some would say, would become better known than the Ninth for their frequent encounters with hostile Indians, this may or may not be true, but what is true, together, they became a legend, in their own time.

BALDWIN LODGE NO. 16

The first Masonic Lodge attached to either units, was with the Tenth Cav. Dispensation for a Lodge was granted in 1883 by the Prince Hall Grand Lodge of Texas, under title of Baldwin Lodge at Camp Rice, Texas. [7] The Lodge was probably named after T.A. Baldwin, a Caucasian Captain, Commanding Officer of A Troop. Baldwin was born in New Jersey and would become a Brigadier-General and Commander Officer of the Tenth Cav. It was under his command, that the 10th Cav., led by Black Noncommissioned Officers, that saved Col. Teddy Roosevelt, a Mason, and his Rough Riders from being massacred at the famous charge up San Juan Hill.

Camp Rice was initially a railroad construction camp, but was selected as a site for a camp of one company of Cavalry in 1882. It would become the homeof A Troop, 10th Cav. for a time. [8] The base camp for the regiment was actually Fort Davis, Texas, and it is here where Baldwin Lodge would first be situated.

In the Spring of 1885, the Regiment with the Lodge now numbered 16 by its Mother Grand Lodge of Texas[9] moved into the military department of Arizona and the land of the Apache, where Geronimo, The Kid, Mangus, Cochise, and other Chieftains held sway. [10]

By 1887 the Lodge would be located at Fort Verde, Arizona Territory with 13 members on its roll, and by 1888 it would have 16 members with for Past Masters. One, Bro. Benj. F. Potts being commissioned District Deputy Grand Master,[11] and Arizona becoming the Sixth Masonic District of the Texas Jurisdiction. [12]

In 1889, the Lodge would move to Fort Apache and it would be here that it would find another Prince Hall Lodge from a sister Jurisdiction attached to another Troop within this Cavalry unit and also the 24th Infantry Regiment. This Lodge, Eureka Military #135 was one of two military Lodges chartered by the Prince Hall Grand Lodge of Missouri. [13]

It would be between these two Lodges from two different Prince Hall Jurisdictions, sharing the same Fort within the same military units, that the first demit would be recorded. The member having this distinction was Bro. Charles H. Chinn, recorded as

Senior Warden of Eureka #135 in 1885[14] and later Secretary of Baldwin #16, having demitted to the Texas Lodge, Nov. 5, 1891.

In 1895, Bro. James A. Brown, Treasurer and long time member of Baldwin #16 is recorded in the proceedings of that Grand Lodge as having died Feb. 5, 5895.[15]

His death, the first for the Lodge, needs more than just a passing mention, as it reveals the hardships that these units faced.

Orders 2, Troop I, Feb. 11

It becomes the sad duty of the Commanding Officer, Troop I to add to its record the tragic death, by freezing of 1st. Sergt. James Brown. His life was sacrificed in the frightful storm of the 5th inst., while attempting to return from an authorized absence of a few hours to the town of Havre. His riderless horse, returning to the post, announced the melancholy news of his death. Sergt. Brown joined the regiment as a recruit in July, 1867, and was assigned to Troop I on its organization, Aug. 15, 1867. He was appointed corporal Jan. 1, 1868, promoted to sergeant Jan. 1, 1869, appointed first sergeant Aug. 1, 1872, in which position he served until his death, when he was, in date of warrant, probably, the senior first sergeant on the active list of the Army. He took part in every campaign and in all of the numerous engagements against hostile Indians in which the Troop has participated since its organization, and was severely wounded by an arrow in battle with overwhelming numbers of Cheyennes on Beaver Creek, Kansas, Oct. 18, 1868. For his conspicuous gallantry on this occasion he was recommended for a medal for honor by Gen. Eugene A. Carr, who was a witness of his bravery. He was in every sense a gallant and efficient soldier. He knew no fear, and there were no difficulties too great for him to attempt to surmount. His untimely death has deprived the regiment and the Army of a model soldier.

S.L. Woodward
Captain 10th Cav., Commanding Troop I [16]

Concerning the Beaver Creek incident, Troop I was escorting Brevet-Major-General Carr, of the Fifth Cavalry, to his command at Beaver Creek. On the march the Troop was attacked by a force of about 500 Indians. After proceeding, regardless of the enemy's firing and yelling, far enough to gain a suitable position, the command was halted, and the wagons were corralled close together, and the troop was rushed inside at a gallop.

The Troop was then dismounted, tied their horses to the wagons and formed outside the corral of wagons. There followed a volley which drove the Indians back as though they were thrown from a cannon.

A number of warriors, showing more bravery than the others, undertook to stand their ground. Nearly all of these, together with their ponies were killed. Three dead warriors lay within fifty yards of the wagons. The Indians were demoralized by these results, they did not renew the attack.[17]

NEXT MISSOURI TAKES THE LEAD

REFERENCES

1. Joseph A. Walkes, Jr., **Prince Hall Masonry in the Civil War,** Phylaxis Magazine, Vol. 1, Number 3, P. 29, Vol. II, Number 1, P. 47, Vol. II, Number 3, P. 79.
2. Albert G. Mackey, Encyclopedia of Freemasonry (New York, Macoy Publishing and Masonic Supply Company, Inc.) 1966, P. 667.
3. Frederic Adams, MA., D. Litt, Traveling (or Ambulatory) Military Lodges, Transactions, The American Lodge of Research F. & A.M., Vol. VII, No. 2, P. 199, January 29, 1958 to December 29, 1958.
4. Proceedings of the Sixth Triennial Session of the Most Worshipful National Grand Lodge of Free and Accepted Ancient York Masons of the U.S.A., held in the City of Baltimore, October A.D. 1865, P. 25.
5. A Chronological History of Prince Hall Masonry 1784-1932 by Harry A. Williamson, P. 85; Harold Van Buren Voorhis **Negro Masonry in the United States,** (New York, Henry Emmerson Press, 1949) P. 42; Harry E. Davis, **A History of Freemasonry Among Negroes in America** (United Supreme Council, A.A.S.R. Northern Jurisdiction, U.S.A. Prince Hall Affiliation Inc., 1946) P. 185.
6. 28th day of July 1866, U.S. Congress and General Orders No. 92, A.G.O., Nov. 23, 1866.
7. Proceedings of the Prince Hall Grand Lodge of Texas 1883, Page 51, henceforth called Proceedings of Texas.
8. John M. Carroll, **The Black Military Experience in the American West** (New York, Liveright Publishing Co., 1971) P. 113, 114.
9. Proceedings of Texas 1885, P. 47
10. Carroll, **op. cit.,** P. 137
11. Proceedings of Texas, 1888, P. 30.
12. Ibid
13. Proceedings of Prince Hall Grand Lodge of Missouri 1888, P. 109, henceforth called Proceedings of Missouri.
14. Proceedings of Missouri, 1885, P. 109.
15. Proceedings of Texas, 1895, P. 105.
16. Army & Navy Register, The U.S. Military Gazette, Washington, D.C., Vol. XVII, No. 8, Feb. 23, 1895, P. 120.
17. Carroll, **op. cit.,** P. 83.

105

THE MASONIC ADDRESSES AND WRITINGS OF
Ira S. Holder, Sr., M.P.S.
[New York]

STORMY IS THE ROAD

A MASTERPIECE

The above topic is chosen to depict the writer's own evaluation and conclusion of a Historic Masonic Event which transpired in 1897 (78 years ago) followed by the outpouring of hateful venom and ridicule from some of those who were considered as leaders of the Masonic Fraternity—holding high places in Masonic Councils throughout the United States and elsewhere.

Before going into the subject matter, however, I think it is not only proper, but imperative, that I begin by asking the following questions, so that you too will be able, after reading the full story, to render your own evaluation and conclusion:

1. What is Freemasonry?
2. What is its purpose and objective?

The answers to these importnat questions are best described or defined in the German Handbook or Masonic Encyclopedia published in 1900 as follows:

"Masonry is the activity of closely united men who, employing symbolic forms borrowed principally from the Mason's trade and from Architecture, work to enoble themselves, and others, and thereby to bring about a Universal League of mankind, which they aspire to exhibit even now on a small scale.

It would be well that we also get the thinking of another Masonic Scholar, Joseph Fort Newton, author of a number of Masonic books, qouting from "The Builders:"

"Masonry is more than an institution, more than a tradition, more than a society, Masonry is one of the forms of the Divine Life upon earth. No one can hope to define a spirit so gracious, an Order so benign, an influence so prophetic of the present and future upbuilding of the race."

It is on such a premise which clearly answers and defines the questions listed above, that the pillar and very foundation of Freemasonry is established. All persons seeking admittance within the portals of Freemasonry make known their belief in One Supreme Being who is the Father and Creator of all mankind. They also support their claim by kneeling before its sacred altar on which rests the Holy Bible, confirming their willingness to obey its laws and edicts. How, then, can such persons repudiate all of the many things they swore to uphold? By resorting to all kind of immoral and unMasonic conduct while proclaiming to be advocates of thier belief in the Fatherhood of God and the Brotherhood of man? Freemasonry was intended to be a universal organization embracing all races of mankind, the rich, the poor, the small and the great, into a bond of Fraternal Brotherhood, among whom no animosity should ever exist. Dedication to serve should be the main attribute. "Let him who is the greatest of all be the servant of all." This should be their motto.

In looking around and about us today, one can readily see that the members of this great Fraternity have a long and "Stormy Road" to travel towards its ultimate objective—an Organization embracing all races of mankind working together for the good and welfare of each other in bond of true Fraternal Brotherhood.

"Stormy is the Road" is chosen as an example, to depict the plight of two Prince Hall Masons who petitioned Freemason's Grand Lodge (white) of the State of Washington, asking for permission to obtain the privilege of Masonic Fellowship with Masons in the area, Gideon S. Bailey and Con A. Rideout. Now let us look at the qualifications of these two distinguished Brothers, both of whom were of irreproachable character and standing in the community, men whose overall qualifications would grace any Masonic Lodge.

GIDEON S. BAILEY served at one time as a Justice of the Peace. He received his Degrees in Masonry in a Lodge Chartered by the Grand Lodge of Pennsylvania (Prince Hall) in 1815.

CON A. RIDEOUT was a practicing attorney. He received his Masonic Degrees in a Lodge also Chartered by the Grand Lodge of Pennsylvania. (Prince Hall)

The Annual Sessions of Freemason's Grand Lodge (white) of the State of Washington began on Wednesday, June 9, 1897, with M.W. Yancy Blacock, Grand Master, presiding, when the Petitions from Bros. Gideon S. Bailey and Con A. Rideout were brought before the Body for their consideration. The

106

Grand Master accepted the Petitions of the two distinguished Prince Hall Brothers and immediately appointed a "Special Committee" of three Grand Lodge Officers, instructing them to return a recommendation to the next Grand Lodge Session the following year. The members of this history-making "Special Committee" are as follows:
1. R.W. THOMAS M. REED
2. R.W. JAMES E. EDMINSON
3. R.W. WILLIAM H. UPTON

Before proceeding further, I think it is important that you be given a brief outline on the background and qualifications of this important "Special Committee."

THOMAS M. REED was born in Kentucky and made a Mason there. He moved to the Pacific Coast in his early manhood and was prominent in its history, especially in California, Idaho and Washington. He held several public offices and was the last Territorial and the first State Auditor of Washington. He was chiefly instrumental in organizing the Grand Lodge of Washington in 1858, and had been its Grand Secretary since its organization, except during three years in which he was Grand Master and one year in which he was absent in Idaho. He was a Republican.

JAMES E. EDMINSON was born in Arkansas and was made a Mason there after having in his youth served in the Confederate Army. He received a college education, becoming a practicing attorney, filled many positions of honor and trust and had been a Democratic Candidate for Superior Judge. He became Grand Master in 1890, and at the time of his death had been for eight consecutive years Chairman of the Committee on Jurisprudence. In that position he established a high reputation for the breadth and accuracy of his knowledge of Masonic Jurispurdence, cogency and reasoning, conservation and unvaring candor and frankness.

WILLIAM H. UPTON was at that time a Grand Warden and was installed Grand Master in 1898. He was born in California and educated in New England. After residing some years in the South, he returned to the Pacific Coast in 1880. He was a Republican, a lawyer by profession, and when appointed to the Committee had completed his second term as Judge to the Superior Court of the State. He compiled and edited the Masonic Code of Washington, published by his Grand Lodge in 1897.

During the intervening months following the Committee's appointment, no time was lost in gathering, examining and evaluating every piece of information, wherever found, that would shed any light in establishing the origin, status and legitimacy of Prince Hall Masonry, overlooking nothing that would support their efforts and contribute in some measure to its findings. After exhausting every available source in their search for supporting facts pertinent to their inquiry, the Committee arrived at the following conclusions:
1. That the origin, status and legitimacy of Prince Hall Masonry was authentic in every respect.
2. That its Grand Lodge Jurisdiction was undisputed and in accordance with the customs of that time and period.

With such concrete facts, the "Special Committee" completed its work and submitted its Report to the presiding Grand Master, Most Worshipful Archibald W. Frater, on Wednesday, June 15, 1898, as Freemason's Grand Lodge began its Session. The "Special Committee" was asked to report on its findings; the Chairman rose and gave the following Report of the Committee:

RECOMMENDATION:

Having thus set forth our views upon the import subject submitted to us, your Committee now submit to this M.W. Grand Lodge four (4) Resolutions, and recommend that they be adopted, to wit,

RESOLVED, that in the opinion of this Grand Lodge, Masonry is universal, and without doubt; neither race or color is among the proper tests to be applied to determine the fitness of a candidate for the Degrees of Masonry.

RESOLVED, that in view of the recognized laws of the Masonic Institution and the facts of history apparently well-authenticated and worthy of full credence, this Grand Lodge does not see its way clear to deny or question the right of its constituent Lodges, or of the members thereof, to recognize as Brother Masons, Blacks who have been initiated in Lodges which can trace their origin to Prince Hall Lodge #459, organized under the Warrant of our R.W. Thomas Howard, Earl of Effingham, acting Grand Master under the authority of H.R.H. Henry Frederick, Duke of Cumberland, etc. Grand Master of the Most Ancient and Honorable Society of F. & A.M. Masons in England, bearing date September 29. A.L. 5784 or to our R.W. Bro. Prince Hall, Master of said Lodge; and in the opinion of this Grand Lodge, for the purpose of tracing each origin, the African Grand Lodge of Boston organized in 1808, subsequently known as Prince Hall Grand Lodge of Massachusetts, the first Grand Lodge (African of North America in the **Commonwealth of Pennsylvania organized in 1815 and the Hiram Grand Lodge of Pennsylvania may justly be** regarded as legitimate Masonic Grand Lodges.)

RESOLVED, that while this Grand Lodge recognizes no difference between Brethren based upon race or color, yet it is not unmindful of the fact that the white and colored races in the United States have in many ways shown a preference to remain in purely social matters, separate and apart. In view of this inclination of the two races, Masonry being

107

pre-eminently a social institution, this Grand Lodge deems it to be the best interest of Masonry to declare that if regular Masons of African decent desire to establish, within the State of Washington, Lodges confined wholly or chiefly to Brethren of their race, and shall establish such Lodges strictly in accordance with the Landmarks of Freemasonry and in accordance with Masonic Law as heretofore interpeted by Masonic Law as heretofore interpeted by Masonic tribunals of their own race, and if such Lodges shall in due time see fit in like manner to erect a Grand Lodge for the administration of their affairs, this Grand Lodge, having more regard for the good of Masonry than for any mere technicality, will not regard the establishment of such Lodges or Grand Lodge as an invasion of its jurisdiction, but as evincting a disposition to conform to its own ideas as to the best interests of the Craft under peculiar circumstances; and will ever extend to our colored Brethren its sincere sympathy in every effort to promote the welfare of the Craft or inculcate the pure principles of our Art.

RESOLVED, that the Grand Secretary be so instructed to acknowledge receipt of the Communication from Gideon S. Bailey and Con A. Rideout, and forward to them a copy of the Printed Proceedings of this Annual Communication of the Grand Lodge, as a response to said Communication.

Fraternally submitted,
Thomas M. Reed
William H. Upton
James E. Edminson

THE STORM ERUPTS

Needless to say, the stunning effect of the "Special Committee's" Report—recognizing the origin and legitimacy of the Prince Hall Grand Lodge of Massachusetts, not only shocked, but rocked the very foundation of many Grand Masonic Jurisidctions throughout the entire United States and elsewhere, to the extent that many of them severed all Masonic fraternal connection with the Grand Lodge of the State of Washington within a year's time. To add to all of this, the Members of the Committee were subjected to scurrilous abuses both at home and aborad, for the stand they took in their Report. These abuses so incensed one of the members of the "Special Committee", R.W. William H. Upton, that he expressed himself in the following manner:

"I have not been particularly intimidated by the knowledge which had come to me, not merely by what had appeared in print, but by abusive letters, that the undertaking would subject me to scurilous abuse and cowardly vituperation; for since I have learned how thin the veneer of Masonry and of civilization is upon some men who have held high places in Masonic Councils; and that as one eminent Brother has expressed it, men whom I have been wont to look up to as leaders, are fifty years behind the times and a thousand years behind the principles they profess, I have become indifferent to their abuse. As Lawrence Dermott expressed, "I do not find that the calumny of a few modern Masons has done me any real injury."

William H. Upton, one of the members of the "Special Committee" became Grand Master in 1898. In order to justify his actions and in support of his thinking, he forwarded copies of the Report to Masonic Grand Lodges throughout the world, seeking and asking for their impressions and opinions, whether for or against the findings of the Committee.

In order that you too may be able to evaluate and draw your own conclusion, I think it is imperative that I bring you a few excerpts from some of the many letters received concerning the action taken by the Grand Lodge of the State of Washington. The following are some of the many comments both pro and con:

> "The Grand Lodge of England knows no distinction of race, color or creed, so long as the fundamental principles of Ancient Freemasonry are faithfully observed, and it would not be likely to cease intercourse with a Grand Lodge which pursued a similar policy."

—O—

> "The Constitution and By-Laws of our Grand Lodge founded on the "Old Charges", according to which: position, nationality or color, religion or political opinion are no objection to election of Freemasons. Thence it results, that we are bound to recognize Negro Lodges—provided they are established strictly in accordance with the Landmarks of Masonry quite as much as Mohamedan or Indian ones."

—O—

> "You know how I have always insisted that the Lodge is my family, and I have a right to bar the entrance of any many whom I do not want to meet, simply because such is my desire and because I shall not be comfortable in his society. Therefore, you are again fully justified in permitting, but refraining from forcing, the Lodges to admit colored visitors.
>
> I know the matter bristles with difficulties, owing to social considerations in your country, and it seems to me that you have come to a wise and workable compromise, on which I congratulate all concerned."

—O—

> "I think there is no middle ground between rigid exclusions of Negroes or recognition and affiliation with the whole mess.

108

If they are not Masons, how protect them as such or at all? If they are Masons, how deny them affiliation or have two supreme powers in one Jurisdiction.

I am not inclined to meddle in the matter. I took my obligations to white men, not to Negroes. When I have to accept Negroes as Brothers, or leave Masonry, I shall leave it."

— O —

"My opinion is that Negroes can make as good a show for the legality of their Grand Lodges as the whites can. It is only a matter of taste, and not of laws. I am satisfied that all the world outside the United States will ere long recognize them, and I think we had much better acknowledge them, than to blend them into our organization."

— O —

"If the Lodge of Negroes are regular, place them on the Register of the Grand Lodge of Washington as equals, but as rivals, never. I do not say that any Landmark would be violated, for there are two or more Grand Lodges at work in some of the States last century, and even at the present time, two or more Grand Lodges often claim Jurisdiction in the same District or Territory, or country. But when one Grand Lodge becomes wholly Sovereign, as respects to its recognized Jurisdiction, and has absorbed all Subordinate Lodges therein, experience has proved that thereafter it would not be for the true interests of the Craft to permit another Grand Lodge ever entering into its Territory, and such invasion should be objected to by all its peers.

In this view of the matter, it seems to me that some other course should be adopted than that followed by the Grand Lodge of Washington."

— O —

In all fairness, I think it only proper that you know something of the personal feelings and opinions of this Masonic Pillar of Strength, who as a Member of the "Special Committee" was abused and subjected to many uncomplimentary remarks for his stand.

The following remarks will give you an insight of the feelings of this Pillar of Strength, R.W. William H. Upton:

"It is not true that Masonry compels me to recognize every Mason as my social equal, or to take him into my family or Lodge. For though all Masons are as Brethren upon the same level, yet Masonry takes no honor from a man that he had before; nay, rather, it adds to his Honor, especially if he has deserved well of the Brotherhood, and avoid ill manners. If the law of Freemasonry excludes Blacks, you do well to object to their presence. If it does not, and you are willing to submit to its Laws, Freemasonry can do without you—is better off without you—though you represent a dozen Grand Lodges and carry half a million so called "Masons" with you. Masonry does not exist to vindicate the social supremacy of the "Caucasian race," and the man who is particularly fearful of losin his social standing, is usually the man whose Social Standing rests on a very unsubstantial foundation.

"Let us be honest. If there is any man in America—Black or White—who is wholly free from race prejudice, he may thank God that he is exceptionally favored."

"I cannot claim to be free from race feelings; but, it seems to me that if there are two places where it ought to be held in check, they are in the Church and in the Masonic Lodge. Not that men need worship or lodge together—that is a different thing."

Masonry gives every Mason in the Universe an absolute veto on any other man's entering his Lodge as a Visitor or candidate; but it does not seem that when we are called upon to pass upon the question whether a certain man is a Mason, we ought to be able to put race prejudice beneath our feet. Whether we can do so or not, the fact remains that the color of Prince Hall's shin did not vitiate his initiation.

"We are taught to regard the whole human species as one family, the high and low, the rich and poor; who, as children of the same parent, and inhabitants of the same planet, should support and protect each other."

OUR RESPONSIBILITY
— O —

My Brothers, I have endeavored to bring you a story which I am sure should be of interest to all of us as Prince Hall Masons. It is not fiction, neither is it a fairy tale concocted for one's amusement; it is a bona fide actual happening which took place many years ago; the stunning effect disrupted Freemasonry the world over. As Prince Hall Masons, we too were involved—every member of the Prince Hall Family was the innocent victim of the disciples of hate, who unleashed their poisonous venom in furious anger and disregard.

Since it is a matter of vital importance and concern to all of us, where ever disbursed, to know the true facts as they are revealed, in like manner it is also fitting that you evaluate the recorded facts as outlined, and arrive at your own conclusion based on what transpired. Before doing so, however, it is well that you remember the purpose and objective of Freemasonry as previously outlined:

"It is to create Universal League of united men, working to enoble themselves and others."

It is on the basis of this expressed outline, that I have sought to show by the selected title: "Stormy is the Road" the many hinderances and obstacles which are at present strewn along the Masonic Path of Freemasonry, especially for Blacks. These hinder-

109

ances must be surmounted before the fulfillment of the purpose and objective of Freemasonry is attained. One may ask, how can this be done? This can be done, and it will be done through strength and Masonic Solidarity. We must combine our forces, and maintain that degree of unity among ourselves which is so vital and important to the success of any undertaking before the achievement of the goal we are striving for is assured. This must be considered the first step in achieving our ultimate objective—United Solidarity. The next step is equally important to the success of our objective. It also presents a direct challenge to the entire Prince Hall Fraternity. This challenge calls for the implimentation of a combined Public Enlightenment Program embracing every Grand Jurisdiction and all Subordinate Lodges of the Prince Hall Fraternity. In this our Bi-centennial year, the time is ripe, and long overdue for informing the public at large of all of the pertinent facts pertaining to Prince Hall—Our Patron Saint—his life, his efforts on behalf of those less fortunate than himself. And above all, how he, along with 14 other Blacks were initiated into the Masonic Fraternity on March 6, 1775, Military Lodge #441 which was attached to an Irish Regiment under the command of General Gage during the Revolutionary War; while their Regiment was stationed in Boston, Mass. how he applied to the Grand Lodge of England for a Charter which was issued on September 29, 1784. How that Charter was given to Capt. James Scott, a brother-in-law of John Hancock (one of the signers of the Declaration of Independence) for presentation to Prince Hall on his return home to America. How after 3 years of waiting, the Charter was delivered to Prince Hall on April 29, 1787. How this Charter is now held for safe keeping, in a vault of one of the banks in Boston, Mass. There is a lot to tell, and it is our duty and also our responsibility to tell the full story, so that the youngest child will know everything about this immortal—Prince Hall; so that when this youngster of today becomes the young man of tomorrow, he will know where to go to obtain membership in a bona fide Masonic Lodge. In this manner, if such a program is insitutited, within a short time we will see the enlargement of our Membership Rolls, thus decreasing the strength of the many non-Prince Hall and clandestine groups, who are at present sapping the strength and life blood of our Fraternity by literally taking, before our very eyes many young and unsuspecting victims into their ranks. These innocent victims, after finding out the error of their ways, seldom, if ever, try again to reconstruct their lives by seeking membership in regular Masonic Lodges. Instead, they become disillusioned and in many cases lose all interest in the Masonic Fraternity. This tragic situation, for such it is, is the direct cause of thousands of brilliant, enthusiastic young men being lost annually to the Prince Hall Fraternity, through our negligence, our lack of concern, and above all our complacency. Wake up, my Brothers! Now is the time for action; there is much to be done. We have been literally sleeping too long. It is time that the entire Prince Hall Fraternity awake from its slumber and begin a combined massive Public Enlightenment and Awareness Program to eradicate once and for all, this Masonic Cancer which is steadily sapping our strength and vitality.

It is safe to say, that after the start of such a Program, on an extensive scale, within a year's time, I guarantee the results will be astounding. Our membership Rolls will be increased and above all we will be a much stronger Organization both financially and in every respect; and in a position to meet all adverse circumstances that may arise.

Yes, my Brothers, we have much to do to improve the image of Prince Hall Masonry. Let us from this day on Re-dedicate and Re-Obligate ourselves anew and thereby practice the exemplification of the true principles of Freemasonry as we travel "The Stormy Road." Let us show through actions, through our conduct and through our daily lives in our dealings with others that, although at times hinderances of various kinds may be placed in our Masonic Path to impede our travel toward our goal, in spite of this, we will continue on our journey with renewed determination, striving and looking ahead toward a brighter and better tommorrow.

A WORD FROM THE PRESIDENT
Continued from page 102

complete list of Fellows follows: Ira S. Holder, Sr. (New York) '75; Joseph A. Walkes, Jr., (Kansas) '76; Arthur H. Frederick (Massachusetts) '76; Charles H. Wesley (Wash., D.C.) '76.

The Society is only authorized 15 Fellows, representing Prince Hall and the fourteen "Fellows" raised with him.

The Society has embarked on a program to have a number of the documents of Prince Hall placed on display at the Prince Hall Elementary School in Philadelphia, Pennsylvania. Bro. Raymond Showers M.P.S. (Pennsylvania) is the Society's representative to the school.

Our Membership Committee is doing an outstanding service for the Society by seeking out interested Prince Hall Masons who seek more light and have light to impart.

We are asking each member to bring in a member, so we can double our membership, and thereby better able to achieve the goals and aims of this Research Society which is to serve Prince Hall Masonry.

Joseph A. Walkes, Jr., F.P.S.
President

Welcome to New Members

Harold L. Hood, 441 Clinton Ave., Albany, New York 12206

William L. Turner, HHC BKK Det., APO S.F. 96346

John Davis, 140-6 Bellamy Loop, Bronx, NY 10475

Wendell P. Henderson, 2953 Gunther Ave., Bronx, NY 10469

John B. Lopos, Post Office Box 397, Homer, La 71040

Alexander Jones, 474 Ronkonkoma Ave., West Hempstead, LI, NY 11552

Samuel P. Jenkins, Editor, Plumb Line, 1630 Curtis St., Baton Rouge, Louisiana 70807

Flave K. Green, 116-47 228th Street, Cambraia Heights, NY 11411

Asa Bernard Sampson, Sr., 4247 South 2nd Ave., Minneapolis, Minnesota 55409

Richard R. Taylor, 132-36 155th St., Jamaica, NY 11434

M.W. William Reynolds, Post Office Box 91, Kansas City, Missouri 64141

Lawrence A. Jones, Jr., 1800 E. Linwood Blvd., Kansas City, Missouri 64109

Clarence W. Hugh III, 6 North White Plains, Ny 10601

Eual Davis, 1320 South 54th St., Tacoma, Washington 98408

Columbus Black, 3002 South 14th St., Tacoma, Washington 98405

Robert H. Dabman, Jr., 414 East 63rd St., Tacoma, Washington 98404

Robert M. Ferrell, 201 Woodland Hills, White Plains, NY 10603

John W. Sturdivant, PSC #3 Box 13344, APO S.F., Ca 96311

Leon Kelly, 1110 South 17th St., Tacoma, Washington 98408

Robert L. Branch, 8309 Milwaukee St., Ft. Lewis, Wash. 98499

Marvin Blythers, 10405 Montrose Avenue, S.W., Tacoma, Washington 98499

William R. Clark, HHC 2/47th Inf. 9 Inf. Div., Ft. Lewis, Washington 98433

Leslie C. Norris, Jr., 928 East 223rd St., Bronx, NY 10466

Walter J. Grange, 43 Rutland Rd., Brooklyn, NY 11225

Landron Jackson, Jr., 522 Dakota St., Leavenworth, Ks. 66048 Recommended by Joseph A. Walkes, Jr., F.P.S.

Jack Louis, 117-23 140th St., Jamaica NY 11436 Recommended by Ira S. Holder, Sr., F.P.S.

David G. Lewis, SS 080-24-3660, Box R 34, APO NY 09696

Alfred A. Clarke, 132 East 39th St., Brooklyn, NY 11203 Recommended by Ira S. Holder, Sr., F.P.S.

David J. Davenport, 49 Crown St., Apt. 19E, Brooklyn, NY 11225 Recommended by Ira S. Holder, Sr., F.P.S.

Victor O. Morris, 16 Harrison St., Poughkeepsie, NY 12601 Recommended by Ira S. Holder, Sr., F.P.S.

Richard M. Palmer, 230 Heaney Ave., Lawnside, New Jersey 08045 Recommended by Bro. William M. Freeman M.P.S.

Alfred L. Fileds, 710 Riverside Drive, New York, New York 10031 Recommended by Bro. Ira S. Holder, Sr. F.P.S.

Edmond M. Coleman, 3435 E. 27th Ave., Apt. #4, Denver, Colorado 80205 Recommended by Bro. James E. Herndon M.P.S.

Will McCoy, Jr., 2522 S "J" Street, Tacoma, Washington 98405 Recommended by Herbert Dailey M.P.S.

THE PHYLAXIS SOCIETY AND THE MISSOURI MASONIC LIBRARY

The Most Worshipful Prince Hall Grand Lodge of Missouri has taken steps towards the creation of a Masonic library within its Grand Masonic Temple in St. Louis.

The Chairman and driving force behind this important contribution to Masonic education is Bro. (Dr.) William E. Allen, Jr., M.D., M.P.S.

The Phylaxis Society realizing the significance of this undertaking has been lending a hand, so to speak, through our Second Vice President Zellus Bailey M.P.S., together with several members of the Society across the country. Many have donated their time and Masonic books to launch this worthwhile project.

The Phylaxis Society is also pleased to learn that two of our Caucasian Masonic friends, both from the Grand Lodge A.F. & A.M. of Iowa have also donated a sizable number of books. Which merely goes to show that friendly and fraternal intercourse between our fraternities can and should take place at all levels.

We are happily reminded that Iowa maintains the world's largest Masonic library and it was began with a $5.00 contribution (see Vol. 1 Nr. 1, **Phylaxis Magazine**).

The Phylaxis Society is asking its members across the country, and non-members who may read this page to donate items of Masonic interest to this library dedicated to Prince Hall Masonry. Items can be sent to:

Dr. Wm. E. Allen, Jr., M.D., M.P.S.
720 North Sarah Street
St. Louis, Missouri 63108

Guest Writer
CONRAD HAHN

PRINCE HALL MASONIC POSTAGE STAMP
(See page 113 — No. 5)

THE MASONIC SERVICE ASSOCIATION OF THE UNITED STATES

BY

CONRAD HAHN
EXECUTIVE SECRETARY MSA

GUEST WRITER

The Masonic Service Association of the United States is a voluntary association of American Grand Lodges. Membership is limited to recognized Grand Lodges of the United States and its possessions. At the present time forty-four Grand Lodges are members, including those in Puerto Rico and the Philippines. The latter voted to join the Association in January, 1946, when that country was still a territory of the United States.

There are no memberships for individuals. The Constitution of the Association declares that it "shall be composed of the Grand Lodges of the United States which have heretofore voted, or may hereafter vote, to become members." Grand Lodges become and remain members "of their own free will and accord."

The founding of The Masonic Service Association in 1919 is one of the inspiring stories of American Freemasonry's capacity to respond to a great national challenge and a global opportunity. When Masons in uniform in World War I requested Masonic service and assistance, in cantonments and behind the lines in France, their brethren at home hurried to respond to their needs.

Continued on page 114

NOTES, QUERIES AND INFORMATION ON ITEMS OF MASONIC RESEARCH
By The Phylaxis Society, P.O. Box 3151, Ft. Leavenworth, Ks. 66027

THIS SECTION IS PRESENTED TO OUR READERS, and relates to matters pertaining to Prince Hall Masonic History, biography, tradition and interest.

We invite our readers and members to send such material that is appropriate for use in this column. It must be stressed that this page is for EXCHANGE of information and opinion concerning Prince Hall Masonry and does not pertend to provide the final answers to any query.

Each query is numbered to identify the subject matter.

11. PRINCE HALL MILITARY OFFICERS. 4 Star General "Chappie" James was made "a Mason on sight" by M.W. James Black, Grand Master of the Prince Hall Masons of Illinois and placed on the rolls of a military Lodge within that jurisdiction.

18. CONFERENCE OF PRINCE HALL GRAND MASTERS will meet in Colorado Springs in 1976, and in the Bahamas in 1980 instead of Bston, Massachusetts which has been the practice every ten years. There are presently 24 Masonic Lodges and 16 O.E.S. Chapters in the Bahamas which is one of the younger Prince Hall Jurisdictions.

8. P.G.M. ALEXANDER CLARK. From the Alexander Clark Historical Society, Muscatine, Iowa comes the following: The Alexander Clark House in Muscatine, Iowa was included in the NBC Today Show Bi-Centennial "salute" to the state of Iowa. The program was aired the morning of October 10, 1975.

Alexander Clark (1826-1891) was a Black leader of Iowa during the post Civil War period. Mr. Clark was a prominent spokesman for Black rights and served as United States Consul General and Minister to Monrovia, Liberia, from 1890 until his death.

Clark's accomplishments include among many others:

1. Spokesman in support of the Iowa constitutional amendment assuring all people the right to vote;
2. Grand Master of the Prince Hall Grand Lodge of Missouri Free and Accepted Masons, with jurisdiction over Missouri, Iowa, Minnesota, Tennessee, Arkansas, and Mississippi; and later Colorado.
3. Through lawsuits registered in the name of his daughter, Susan V. Clark, Clark sought to end policies excluding Black children from public schools. As a result, the Iowa Supreme Court ruled in 1868 that no pupil could be excluded from any common school because of race, nationality, religion, dress, or any other distinction which would deny equality of educational opportunity.
4. As Editor-owner of Chicago **Conservator** in the 1880's, his writings were ranked among the political literature of the day, especially his scathing review of the Supreme Court decision on civil rights and his indignant views of President Hayes' policies.

The Alexander Clark House, owned by the Alexander Clark Historical Society, was relocated in the spring of this year when the structure was threatened with demolition. The house has been placed on the National Register of Historic places.

For additional information contact, Mrs. Ried Motley, 1920 Fifth Ave., S.E., Cedar Rapids, Iowa 52403.

18. RECOGNITION. A special committee of the Caucasian Grand Lodge of Wisconsin headed by Bro. George R. Currie, former Chief Justice of the Supreme Court of Wisconsin set up to study Prince Hall Masonry in Wisconsin, having completed its two year investigation, submitted a favorable report to its Grand Lodge. The committee found that the Prince Hall Grand Lodge of Wisconsin and its constituent Lodges requires observances of and conformity to established and accepted Masonic ritual and doctrine, particularly the obligation of secrecy, with only minor variations that should not be used to hold back recognition of Prince Hall Masons of Wisconsin. The PHYLAXIS SOCIETY plans to publish the entire report in a future issue of the Phylaxis Magazine.

5. PRINCE HALL MASONIC POSTAGE STAMP. Sheets of 100 stamps with the likeness of Prince Hall may be purchased through Bro.Samuel P. Jenkins, M.P.S., Box 2974, Baton Rouge, Louisiana 70821.

The United States Government issued Masonic postage stamps in commemoration of the 100th Anniversary of two Prince Hall Lodges in New York City.

These were the first Masonic postage stamps ever permitted to go through the United States Mail. The two Lodges were Celestial No. 3 and Hiram No. 4, which were warranted in the spring of 1826 by the Prince Hall Grand Lodge of Massachusetts.

The stamps could not be sold to any individual and only used between 1-31 March 1926 only. 10,000 of the stamps were printed, and the die had been destroyed. From the Masonic Tidings, 1926.

THE MASONIC SERVICE ASSOCIATION OF THE UNITED STATES

Continued from page 112

To their dismay, Masons learn that they were denied the opportunity to serve their sons and brothers in uniform because the national government refused to work with fifty or more Masonic groups who wanted to do their bit. "Give us one Masonic agency to deal with," said governmental officials.

Far-sighted and responsible Masonic leaders recognized the need and the opportunity for Masonic service. They went to work to create such an agency. But progress was painfully slow. Fears about jurisdictional sovereignty had to be overcome. The ancient specter of a General Grand Lodge had to be banished.

By the time the representatives of twenty-two Grand Lodges assembled in Cedar Rapids, Iowa, in November, 1918, the first World War had ended. But the dedicated Masons who attended that meeting recognized a continuing responsibility to our servicemen. Demobilization would not be a short-term achievement. They also envisioned the future usefulness of a national Masonic agency, in peace time as well as in war. They hammered out the structure of The Masonic Service Association to take home for the approval of their Grand Lodges, and went to work to make it a reality.

On November 11, 1919, the first meeting of The Masonic Service Association of the United States took place at Cedar Rapids, Iowa. Thirty-four Grand Lodges were represented. The dream had come true.

"The object of this Association shall be the Service of Mankind, through education and enlightenment, financial relief and Masonic visitation, and ministering to, comforting and relieving the members of the Fraternity and their dependents, particularly in times of disaster and distress, whether caused by war, pestilence, famine, fire, flood, earthquake or other calamity."

Freemasons had seen the need for "a united voice, a united front, some agency which would enable American Masonry to negotiate, whether it be with the government or otherwise...a new opportunity for service..." Out of that opportunity grew the well-known literature and information service of the Association, its program of "Education and Enlightenment".

The eduational program was initiated in 1920 with the publication of Speakers' Bulletins, the first a description of the work of the Association, and the second a discussion of "The Fatherhood of God", by Melvin M. Johnson of Massachusetts. These pamphlets ran a considerable length, sometimes as much a sixty pages.

In 1923 they were modified to the present Short Talk Bulletin, which appears monthly for use in lodges of the member Jurisdictions. The first of these was "Paul Revere, a Champion of Religious Liberty". Ever since, Short Talks have been published regularly to provide supplementary educational materials for lodges and interested individuals. There are now more than 630 separate titles, all of them kept in stock at the Association's headquarters in Silver Spring, Md. Back issues are sold for twenty cents each.

They have been written by outstanding Masonic authors and scholars like Joseph Fort Newton. In 1924-25 a new contributor appeared, who was destined to become the Association's Executive Secretary in 1929, Carl H. Claudy. For almost thirty years, from 1929 to 1958, The Short Talk Bulletins were the work of his inspired pen.

Under his leadership the Association broadened its educational service by publishing more extensive studies of Masonic history, symbolism, practices, philosophy, and statistics,—generally known as Digests. These are made available to Grand Lodge officers and leaders of the Craft. In addition, the Association makes special studies at the request of Grand Lodge officers and committees. It carries on a considerable "information bureau" by correspondence with inquiring brothers. It makes available for consultation by Grand Lodge committees on education all its resources of personnel and materials, including the extensive Masonic library maintained at its headquarters. As the "servant of American Freemasonry", the Association exists to help the Grand Lodges in gathering and exchanging information, ideas, and tools for Masonic education.

The great tenet of Relief, which called the Association into being in 1919, has not been neglected. Repeatedly the Association has been called upon to investigate the needs of Masons and their families in times of wide-spread catastrophe, to make these needs known to all Grand Lodges in the United States, and to serve as the clearing house for funds contributed for the relief of distressed Master Masons who are victims of such disaster.

As early as 1923 the Association acted for American Grand Lodges in sending money to Japan to relieve the suffering caused by the Japanese Earthquake. In 1927 it performed brilliantly in the investigation of needs and in the coordination of relief activities for the victims of the great Mississippi Valley Flood. More than $600,00.00 was contributed by Grand Lodges to that humanitarian effort. From 1923 to 1975 the Association has appealed for such relief funds twenty-five times.

When World War II broke out, American Freemasonry was ready to serve its sons and brothers in the armed forces. It now had a single agency to carry on a program of friendly counsel and wholesome relaxation for lonesome boys in training camps and even abroad. Between 1941 and 1946 the Association established more than seventy Masonic Service Centers near training camps and military bases, where servicemen could go for entertainment in a clean and wholesome atmosphere. It was able to staff them with trained and dedicated leaders, members of the Craft, who loved and admired the boys they served. With a unified agency to deal with government officials, to establish consistent Masonic policies in the administration of those "homes away from home", and to economize by "centralized" purchases of supplies and equipment for the program, American Freemasons got a dollar's worth of value for every one of the million and a half dollars which they contributed to that remarkable service. Through their Masonic Service Association during World War II American Grand Lodges proved that the denial of their "bit" in 1917-18 had been a serious mistake.

So respected and admired was the work of Field Agents in this welfare work for our sons and brothers in uniform that military leaders and government officials requested its extension into Service and Veterans Hospitals, when the mounting number of casualties filled these institutions as the was was drawing to a close.

Since July 1, 1946, The Masonic Service Association has been carrying on, in behalf of United States Grand Lodges, an extensive program of hospital visitation. to bring to our hospitalized sons and brothers the warm greetings and handclasp of a Brother Mason, a morale-building gift of some simple creature comfort, or the patient and willing performance of some little service that a bed-ridden patient cannot do for himself.

The Veterans Adminsistration is still expanding its hospital facilities. Service incurred disabilities have a way of developing many years later. Our government is naturally concerned to care for those who have borne the battle, no matter when their disabilities occur. Freemasons, likewise, continue their service of brotherly love for the lonely patients in V.A. Hospitals.

At present there are more than 100 regular and volunteer Field Agents of the Masonic Service Association, specially trained, visiting in Service or V.A. Hospitals. Their performance is one of the finest public relations programs that American Freemasonry enjoys today.

The Hospital Visitation Program is supported entirely by voluntary contributions. Not a cent is taken from the Association's income from dues paid by member Grand Lodges. That must be allocated to the administrative and educational activities of the Association. Contributions are received largely from Grand Lodges which vote special funds or assessments, or which make special appeals to the Craft.

The administrative and educational services of the Association, which include its publications, are maintained by the annual dues paid by member Grand Lodges. These dues are based on a per capita of a few cents per member in each Jurisdiction.

The management and direction of the Association's affairs are vested in an Executive Commission, which consists of a Chairman and one member from each of five geographical divisions, all elected annually.

The Executive Commission elects and appoints the Executive Secretary, who also acts as Treasurer of the Association. It also appoints such other officers, committees, or employees it considers necessary. The Executive Commission is responsible for doing whatever is necessary to carry out the purposes of the Association, in accordance with the policies determined or approved by the delegates, usually the Grand Masters, who represent the member Grand Lodges at the Association's annual meeting.

The annual meeting must be presided over by one of the delegates elected from the floor. All acts of the Commission and its appointed officers must be approved by a vote of the representatives of member Grand Lodges. Complete reports are made and published. the Chairman and members of the Executive Commission must be elected annually. Each member Grand Lodge has one vote. Control of the Association therefore rests in the Grand Lodges which compose the Association through the franchise of their delegates.

The usefulness of American Freemasonry's agency for service has been fully demonstrated. It has truly been a servant, not only for the Grand Lodges in its membership, but for individual Masons and Constituent lodges who seek its help and counsel. The Masonic Service Association has been able to "speak as one voice" for the Fraternity; it has demonstrated to mankind that Masons are devoted to Brotherly Love, Relief, and Truth.

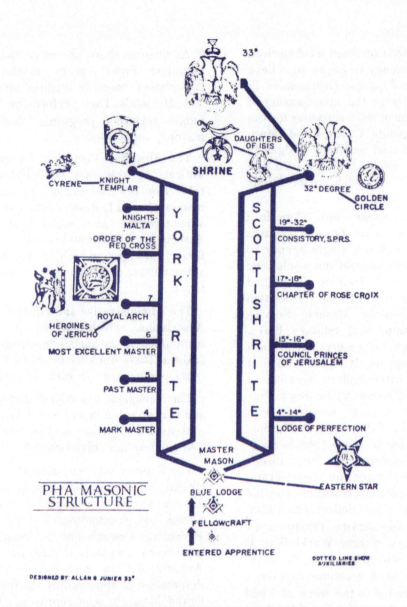

THE PHYLAXIS SOCIETY SUBSCRIPTION CARD

Subscription rate: $5.00/Yr.

Mail to: James E. Herndon, MPS
Executive Secretary
1574 Ivanhoe Street
Denver, Colo. 80220

Gentlemen:

Enclosed is my subscription the the Phylaxis Magazine.

_____ Check Enclosed _____ amount payable to Phylaxis Magazine

Name: _____

Address: _____

City: _____ State: _____ Zip Code: _____

A SOCIETY FOR PRINCE HALL FREEMASONS WHO SEEK MORE LIGHT AND WHO HAVE LIGHT TO IMPART

THE PHYLAXIS

MARCH, 1976

Volume II   Number 5

"SPECIAL ISSUE" COMMEMORATION OF THE 201st ANNIVERSARY OF THE INITIATION OF PRINCE HALL MARCH 6th, 1775

A SOCIETY FOR PRINCE HALL FREEMASONS WHO SEEK MORE LIGHT AND WHO HAVE LIGHT TO IMPART.

THE PHYLAXIS
Published at Boston, Mass. by
THE PHYLAXIS SOCIETY

Arthur H. Frederick, M.P.S. .... Editor
Box 43, Roxbury, Massachusetts 02119

OFFICERS

Joseph A. Walkes, Jr., M.P.S. .... President
P.O. Box 3151, Ft. Leavenworth, Kansas 66027

Herbert Dailey, M.P.S. .... First Vice President
1616 South Cedar, Tacoma, Washington 98405

Zellus Bailey, M.P.S. .... Second Vice President
7039 Dover Court, St. Louis, Missouri 63130

James E. Herndon, M.P.S. .... Executive Secretary
1574 Ivanhoe Street, Denver, Colorado 80220

Alonzo D. Foote, Sr., M.P.S. .... Treasurer
P.O. Box 99601, Tacoma, Washington 98499

SUBSCRIPTION RATE: FOR ONE YEAR, $5.00

The Phylaxis Magazine is the official publication of the Phylaxis Society. Any article appearing in this publication expresses only the opinion of the writer, and does not become the official pronouncement of the Phylaxis Society. No advertising of any form is solicited or accepted. All communication relative to the magazine should be addressed to the Editor. Inquiries relative to membership must be addressed to the Executive Secretary. Membership is by invitation and recommendation only. The joining fee is $3.00. Dues are $5.00 per year in advance, which amount includes a subscription to the "Phylaxis" magazine for one year.

All rights reserved. No part of this work may be reproduced or transmitted in any form or by any means, electrical or mechanical, or retrival system, without written permission from the publisher.

1976 DUES
ALL 1975 MEMBERS ARE REQUESTED TO FORWARD THEIR 1976 DUES [$5.00] TO THE EXECUTIVE SECRETARY

INDEX

Should Prince Hall Masons Celebrate The Bi-Centennial — Yes	120
Should Prince Hall Masons Celebrate The Bi-Centennial — No	121
The Masonic Addresses and Writings of Ira S. Holder, Sr., F.P.S.	122
Joseph G. Findel, Honorary Prince Hall Grand Master	126
Prince Hall: A Great Negro American	131
A Charge Delivered to African Lodge, June 24, 1792	132
The Master's Sign	134
A Prince Hall Masonic Classic	135
Welcome New Members	138
Notes, Queries and Information on Items of Masonic Research	139
Report from Wisconsin	140
Masonic Duty	140
The Phylaxis Society and the Prince Hall Confession of Masonic Faith	141
Phylaxis Profile	142
The Lady Freemason	143

A WORD FROM THE PRESIDENT

With this issue of the **Phylaxis Magazine**, the Phylaxis Society once again pays homage to **"The Master"** Prince Hall. Out of esteem we sometime refer to him as **"The Master"** or **"Grand Master"** or simply as **"Our Patron"**. For he is all of these to us, and the Society takes time out every March to publish a special issue dedicated to his memory.

As this is the Bi-Centennial year for our country, we have some things that must be said. We have seen those from Massachusetts who perch like vultures in Masonic institutions in that State, who would attempt to distort the truth to discredit Prince Hall and the fraternity that he founded; and those from North Carolina, who as a so called Past Grand Master from that State, would journey to Washington, D.C. to publish an un-Masonic pamphlet attacking Prince Hall, who was a thousand times more of a Freemason than this individual from the Tar Heel State.

We have seen those, now deceased from New York who like some profane would attempt to hide his identity by publishing attacks on our fraternity while claiming the printing was from a "research club" in Alaska. And even those from New Jersey who once we considered a friend, now in his dotage, and under the benign bias and influence of those from Massachusetts, became a "turncoat", while proclaiming his so called honorary membership in a Black so called "regular" Lodge, chartered by the Caucasian Grand Lodge of that State, a Lodge which has no justification for being in existence. And of course there are those of our "hue", but not of our kind, who would degrade the very name of Prince Hall, by falsely claiming some sort of "Masonic blood-line" to him!

But yet in all, the Phylaxis Society feels sorry for those who carry such hatred in their hearts, for a Freemason, they will never be, and we, as a Society composed of Prince Hall Freemasons will stand proudly before the entire Masonic world and acknowledge our debt to **"our Patron"**, our **"Master"**, to Prince Hall, our "Grand Master"!

As an organization we have been said to be "young", often "brash". Some have said we are "bitter", or even "militant". Some like our "friend" in El Paso, Texas, has even called us "racist". To say we have made a number of enemies is to put it mildly. And we wonder why? How can an organization whose only interest is to preserve and protect our fraternity stir such feelings. Could it be because we question the motives of those who would harm our fraternity, or is it because we would expose those who would change their white Masonic aprons for a white hood.

But it really does not bother us, what people outside

Continued on page 138

AMERICA'S BI-CENTENNIAL

BY
EDWARD H. CORBETT, M.P.S. [NEW YORK]

"Masons employ themselves diligently in their usual vocations, live creditable, and conform with cheerfulness to the government of the country in which they reside."

In 1775, America was at war with England. The fighting was for independence from a repressive government. England had raised taxes on the colonists beyond their ability to pay, she had also levied fines on them for their failing to pay. The colonists grew angry at the presence of British war ships off its shores and soldiers on the soil, so war was inevitable. During the war the battle of Bunker Hill was fought on the 17th day of June. Grand Master Joseph Warren lost his life while defending the liberties of his country. He had received his commission to act as Grand Master for the continent of North America from the Grand Lodge of Scotland, March 3, 1772. Prince Hall had petitioned Grand Master Warren for recognition as a Masonic Lodge under his jurisdiction but before any action was taken Warren was killed. Boston, Mass. had become a garrison for the British Army and regular meetings of all Masonic lodges were terminated in that city. After the war the brethren found themselves dispersed throughout the country. In 1777, enough Masons came together to hold a meeting and elected Joseph Webb as their Grand Master. A committee was formed to consider the conduct of those who assume the powers and prerogatives of a Grand Lodge within the group. They were to examine the extent of their authority and jurisdiction in acting as a Masonic body after the death of their appointed Grand Master by legal authority. After having fought a war with the Mother country and won independence, all political, economical, cultural, as well as fraternal ties had been broken. There were two Grand Jurisdictions in Boston before the war. St. John's Grand Lodge and St. Andrews Grand Lodge formerly called Massachusetts Grand Lodge. One was set up by the Grand Lodge of England and the other by the Grand Lodge of Scotland. The committee reported back that since the political head of this country having destroyed all connection and correspondence between the subjects of these states and the country from which the Grand Lodge originally derived its commissioned authority. And since we must be beholden under the civil authority to the country in which we reside in, the brethren did assume elective supremacy, and choose a Grand Master, with independent powers and prerogatives, to be exercised on principles consistent with the regulations and constitutions pointed out in ancient Masonry. The committee went on to say "That in the history of our craft we find that in England there are two Grand Lodges independent of each other, in Scotland, the same. In Ireland another, independent of either England or Scotland. It is clear that the authority of some of their Grand Lodges originated in assumption, or otherwise they would acknowledge the head from whence they derived. Your committee is therefore of the opinion that the doings of the present Grand Lodge were dictated by principles of the most approved authority".

These were the arguments used to re-establish white Grand Lodges in America after the Revolutionary War. If they were good enough to establish white Grand Lodges in this country they ought to be good enough to establish Black Prince Hall Grand Lodges in this country. However Prince Hall Masonry is not a discriminating body. We have accepted some white applicants, and they've become worthy brothers among us. But here we are in the year 1976, less than a quarter of a century from the year 2000, and men of the same persuasion can't see fit to have an intelligent dialogue between them.

African Grand Lodge of North America was established in Boston, Mass., June 24, 1791. Its Grand Officers were Prince Hall, Grand Master; Nero Prince, Deputy Grand Master; Cyrus Forbes, Senior Grand Warden; George Middleton, Junior Grand Warden; Peter Best, Grand Treasurer; Prince Taylor, Grand Secretary. This Grand Lodge consisting of men of color was established the same as any other in those days. When Prince died in 1807 the Grand Lodge changed its name to Prince Hall Grand Lodge, F. & A.M. The undeniable fact that Hall functioned as a Grand Master and that a full list of Grand Lodge officers was elected at that assembly indicates strongly that this was the first Grand Lodge in America for men of color.

Regardless of what the social conditions are in this great United States of America, we as Prince Hall Masons must remain head and shoulders above the crowd. We must be dignified in all our deliberations, remembering the lessons we learn in our travels. A house divided against itself cannot stand. If America's Bi-Centennial doesn't light the way and show its citizens how to make crooked things straight, how to change ignorance into knowledge, and how to make darkness into light then we will have missed the opportunity to improve our great society. With the way things are going today, after another two hundred years there might not be trace, track or rememberance, to recall our existence anywhere in the universe. We must live as builders today so that death and destruction will be despised and regretted everywhere in the world. America must listen.

SHOULD PRINCE HALL MASONS CELEBRATE THE BI-CENTENNIAL

PHYLAXIS NOTE: Jerry Marsengill is a well known Masonic writer, a member of Home Lodge No. 370 A.F. & A.M. of Des Moines, Iowa; Secretary of Research Lodge No. 2 A.F. & A.M. of Des Moines; Grand Master, Grand Council of Royal and Select Masters of the State of Iowa, A Fellow of the Philalethes Society and Associate Editor of the Philalethes Magazine. Author of a number of Masonic articles, and the book **"Negro Masonry in Iowa"**. Joseph A. Walkes is a member of King Solomon Lodge No. 15 F. & A.M. of Fort Leonard Wood, Missouri and Honorary Member of Canal Zone Military Lodge, Fort Clayton, Canal Zone; Prince Hall Military Consistory #304 Frankfurt, German, and Allah Temple, Kansas City, Missouri. The President and Fellow of the Phylaxis Society. Author of a number of Masonic articles, and the book "Documentary History of King Solomon Lodge No. 15 F. & A.M."

The opinions expressed are not necessarily those of the the Phylaxis Society.

A RESOUNDING YES!

By
JERRY MARSENGILL, F.P.S.
Grand Master, Grand Council
R & SM [Cau.] Iowa

Guest Writer

This article should probably be entitled "Fools Rush In Where Angels Fear to Tread". Why should a Caucasian be arrogant enough to tell Black Masons what they should and should not celebrate?

I am not one who believes that a minor matter of skin pigmentation, and regardless of the ravings of racists on both sides of the issue, that is all that separates us, should make a difference in any citizens of our country or should make any one group of our citizens stand aloof from the historical celebrations of that country.

This country is far from perfect, we all know that. What we need, rather than any particular group trying to disassociate itself from the general level of life in the country is participation in all endeavors by every citizen.

Segregation does not work! It didn't work in the armed forces, it doesn't work in public life. The duplicate school systems of our southern states should prove that segregation is not feasible. Not only was the "separate but equal" educational system not equal, both black and white students suffered from the effort of trying to maintain two separate systems.

The entire idea of black separatism is just as wrong as the idea of segregation. It plays into the hands of white racists.

If the black man will stand aside and keep himself out of the mainstream of life in this country, the segregationist will obtain what he wants without putting forth any effort. This country is not set up to handle two separate civilizations; not black and white, not Christian and Jewish, not Catholic and Protestant. The entire idea of our Declaration of Independence is that all men are created free and equal and are endowed with certain unalienable rights by their Creator.

Yes, some of the authors of these fine sounding phrases did not practice them, but that makes them none the less pertinent for our present day. The fact that Jefferson and Washington owned slaves is well known. They were as much the victims of their time as the architects of those times. It is a peculiar trait among human beings that they can condemn entire groups of people while treating individuals with dignity or that they can brutalize individuals while insisting on the rights of the group. This is the trait which allowed Jefferson to fulminate against the institution of slavery while personally reaping the benefits of owning slaves. It is also the peculiar refuge of the racist. We all know the stock tag which begins "I am not a racist. Some of my best friends are, Jews, Negroes, Catholics, (pick one) but......."

But regardless of the pecularities and hypocricies of the men who wrote our Constitution and our Declaration of Independence, the documents are relevant for all of us black and white. All men are created equal. This is the fundamental truth of our country. And with all its faults, it is still our country. We have enough enemies in various parts of the world without one segment of our population excluding themselves from life in the country.

There are still vast gaps between the words of our historic documents and the practices in our modern world. But Blacks have gained over the past 50 years. Segregation has, to a great extent, been abolished. Blacks have made gains in jobs, in society, and in education. None of these gains were made by those who would exclude themselves from society. They were made by those who have fought for their rights under American constitutional law. Historically black men have much stake in America's past, and in its future, as do any white men. That the contribution of black men has not been recognized until lately is not the fault of history. It is the fault of racists who have written our histories solely from a Caucasian point of view. The answer to this is not a separate black history, it is a history in which the contribution of all men, white, black, red, and yellow can be objectively assessed. This won't occur tomorrow, it won't occur in the near future, it won't occur at all unless the black men who want to be a part of the mainstream of life will be willing to work and to fight for what they believe in.

Continued on page 124

SHOULD PRINCE HALL MASONS CELEBRATE THE BI-CENTENNIAL

AN ADAMANT "NO"

By
JOSEPH A. WALKES, JR., F.P.S. [Kansas]
President, Phylaxis Society

The two hundredth birthday—the Bi-Centennial of the United States will soon take place, whether or not Black America will celebrate it or not, remains a mystery.

A warning was sounded in of all places, the **National Geographic** (Vo. 146, No. 1, **"Firebrands of the Revolution"** by Eric F. Goldman, P. 8), "As for the Negro, generally he seems little interested in, if not downright hostile to, what he considers a celebration of the Black's degradation as a slave."

The subject was further explored in the August Special Issue of **Ebony** Magazine. Whether or not the Blackman will participate is academic as the choice is left to him, but as a fraternity, which accepts the date of our beginning as March 6, 1775, we may want to consider, that we, **"Masonically"** may want to participate.

In this I say No! An Adamant No! Prince Hall Masonry should not participate in a farce. Let our Caucasian Masonic counterparts toot their horns, beat their breast, and tell of their heros, who were Masonic, and signers of the Declaration of Independence and leaders of the country two hundred years ago. It is a fine and noble and glorious history that they boast, but what they don't say is the fact that these so called Masonic heroes were not the noble gentlemen they would have you to believe, but men who played the game of Masonry and slavery as well. How can an individual bow at the altar of Masonry and declare an oath of the Brotherhood of Man, under the Fatherhood of God, and then return home to profane his Black slave and prostitute his Black woman. A desecration of the concept of Masonry, a charade, a lie, a hypocrisy. And we are asked to celebrate!

Prince Hall Masonry as an organization has been attacked and abused for these many hundreds of years at the hands of our Caucasian Masonic brethren.

In 1795, Dr. Jeremy Belknap recorded from a letter from Rev. John Elliot, one of the founders of the Historical Society of Massachusetts, and pastor of the New North Church, "And, what is still more remarkable, **white and black Masons** do not sit together in their Lodges. The African Lodge in Boston, though possessing a charter from England, signed by the Earl of Effingham, and countersigned by the Duke of Cumberland, meet by themselves; and white Masons, not more skilled in geometry than their Black brethren, will not acknowledge them. The reason given is that the Blacks were made clandestinely in the first place, which being known, would have prevented them from receiving a charter. But this inquiry would not have been made about **white lodges**, many of which have not conformed to the rules of Masonry. The truth is, they are ashamed of being on an **equality with Blacks**. Even the fraternal kiss of France, given to **merit**, without the distinction of colour, doth not influence Massachusetts Masons to give an embrace less emphatical, or tender and affectionate to their **Black brethren**. These, on the other hand, valuing themselves upon their knowledge of the craft think themselves better Masons in other respects than the **whites**, because Masonry considers all men **equal who are free**; and Massachusetts law admit of no kind of slavery. It is evident from this that neither **"avowedly nor tacitly"** do the Blacks admit the preheminence of the **whites**; but as evident that the preheminence is claimed by the **whites**."

And as late as 1948, Thomas J. Harkins, P.G.M. of the Caucasian Grand Lodge of North Carolina would be assailing Prince Hall Masonry as to how "ridiculous and how false and fallacious that these Negroes received any Masonic light what-so-ever!" (Thomas J. Harkins, **Symbolic Freemasonry Among the Negroes of America** (Asheville, N.C.) P. 11)

But the historian Dr. Belknap would record in 1795, "Having once and again mentioned this person (Prince Hall), I must inform you that he is Grand Master of a lodge of free Negroes, composed wholly of Blacks, and distinguished by the name of the **"African Lodge"**. It was begun in 1775, while this whole town was garrisoned by British troops, some of whom held a lodge, and initiated a number of Negroes."

Of the above passages, one was written in 1795 the other in 1948, and clearly shows that audacity of those who play the game of Masonry. And we are asked to celebrate? We can clearly see the abuse that Prince Hall Masonry has had to endure for 200 years, and we are asked to celebrate?

Are we to celebrate the schizophrenia of American Masonry, and the games they play? They profess to believe in the existence of God; and say, "by the exercise of brotherly love we are taught to regard the whole human species as one family; the high and the low, the rich and the poor, who, as created by one Almighty Parent, and inhabitants of the same planet, are to aid, support, and protect each other. On this principal, Masonry unites men of every country, sect,

Continued on page 125

THE MASONIC ADDRESSES AND WRITINGS OF
Ira S. Holder, Sr., F.P.S.
[New York]

HOW LONG IS YOUR CABLE-TOW?

Tuesday, May 4, 1965

WORSHIPFUL MASTER,
GRAND LODGE OFFICERS, (Past & Present)
PAST MASTERS,
GUEST VISITOR W.M.: HALLEY MARVILLE
SENIOR & JUNIOR WARDENS,
VISITING BRETHREN OF THE CRAFT,
MEMBERS OF CARTHAGINIAN LODGE #47,

GOOD EVENING:

Allow me if you will the pleasure of complimenting you for the unique and distinguished manner in which you have, not only conducted but maintained your lodge since its early inception on October 18, 1904. The many outstanding accomplishments along with the numerous persons who have served this Lodge and the Grand lodge with distinction are many. Time will not permit me to elaborate at this time, but for the sake of brevity allow me to name one, the late Harry A. Williamson whose outstanding Historical Masonic Knowledge and Ability was world wide. His demise is not only a tragic loss to this Lodge, but to the entire Masonic fraternity whereever found. It was my pleasure and an honor to meet and know this brilliant Masonic Scholar during his declining years. These, my brothers and many other contributing factors are most gratifying. Truly the accomplishments of your Lodge just didn't happen, they were achieved through hard work, diligent planning and the ingenious foresight of its many Masters and Past Masters, whose destiny it was and still is to chart the course of this progressive and outstanding Lodge. Many of these stalwarts, for such they are, have been called from their labors, many others are here in our midst.

Tonight we do them honor, by paying them a well deserved tribute. It is their night — "PAST MASTERS NIGHT." Past Masters, I salute you. My message to you is devoid of any flowery or emotional terms; but rather calls for a self appraisal and an examination of one's self, to see if you as leaders have measured up to that which is expected of you, by "going the length of your Cable-Tow." My subject therefore is:

HOW LONG IS YOUR CABLE-TOW?

All of us are quite familiar with the term "Cable-Tow" as exemplified in the three (3) symbolic degrees, but for a better clarification, let us scrutinize its origin, meaning and other pertinent aspects, so that we may be able to draw a true perspective. The word "Cable-Tow" as used in the three (3) symbolic degrees are two separate and distinct words combined as one, each of which can be used independently of the other. In separating them, we find that the word, "Cable" is of Dutch origin, meaning a great rope, or hawser which when fastened to the anchor of a ship holds it fast. "Tow" is of Anglo Saxon origin, meaning to lead or draw along the water.

Albert Mackey renowned Masonic Scholar, Historian and Ritualist tells us that the combined word as we know it, is derived from the German word "Kabeltau" (spelled "KABELTAU") having the same meaning as previously outlined. (quote) "A rope or line for drawing or leading." (End of Quote)

Albert Pike also a noted Masonic Scholar, tells us that the word is derived from the Hebrew word "KHABELTO" (spelled "KHABELTO") meaning his anchor rope or the rope by which one is bound."

Whether our "Cable-Tow" came from the German "KABELTAU" or the Hebrew "KHABELTO" is unimportant, the important thing is that the meanings are similar and the use of the Cable or Cable-Tow in ancient times furnishes a clue to its symbolism in Masonry. We are exhorted to "go the length of our Cable-Tow," which carries with it a great deal of Masonic significance and implications; but we must first determine its length, in order to know the distance we must travel.

"HOW LONG IS YOUR CABLE-TOW?"

The Cable's length is said to be equivalent to "three (3) English nautical miles." Rev. F. De P. Castello has this to say in his "Geometry of Freemasonry" (Author's Transactions) Vol. 1 page 286: (quote) "The Cable's length has always been understood to be 720 feet, which is twice 360, the measure of the Circle; making one circle to stand for the spiritual in Man and the other for the material. He believes that the "length of my Cable-Tow" to mean, that, "I will go as far in

122

assisting my brethren as my moral principles and my material condition will permit." (end of quote) Your Cable-Tow is as long as the arm of brotherly kindness that reaches out to aid a distressed or fallen Brother. It stretches forth a helping hand to cheer and comfort those who are bereaved and sorrowful. It goes as far as is humanly possible for any charitable act to be extended to those who are in want. It will also travel as far as your good will will allow it to travel.

The "CABLE-TOW" is a nautical term for a hawser and is used in tying up a vessel to a wharf. And from this simple expression we derive the truth that, as the nautical cable-tow binds a vessel to its wharf so that it cannot advance or make progress, so the Masonic "CABLE-TOW" symbolically binds the candidates life to darkness and ignorance of the most vital things to him, keeping him chained to failure and preventing his growth and unfoldment to higher states of knowing, feeling and thinking.

But, whereas in the case of a vessel, an external power removes the cable-tow, in the case of Man, he himself must through effort, struggle and application release himself from those things which bind him to failure symbolically represented by the "CABLE-TOW".

The average man of today, like the candidate, who comes to us, is in darkness as to a proper understanding of himself. He knows not God, he knows not his own mind, he knows nothing about his own soul, he knows nothing about the wonderful body of his, his temple wherein his soul dwells, he knows nothing about the requirements for obtaining health, happiness, wisdom, love and success. He may know something of eternal things — a little Botany, Chemistry, Physics, Etc., Etc., — but about himself he knows absolutely nothing. He truly dwells in a house of darkness. And yet Man's most important knowledge is about himself.

The average man of today, like the candidate, desires "light" and to be released from darkness or ignorance. What light does he seek? Light on the fundamental and most vital things that concern Man. What are they? His knowledge of God and his relationship to Him; understanding of himself; of the laws of health, of success in laudible undertakings; understanding of what constitutes happiness and how to obtain same. There is not a man today who, having sought happiness outside of himself in material possessions or in fame or glory, is satisfied and happy within himself. True wisdom is to be gained within ourselves, by releasing ourselves from the things which bind us to ignorance and darkness and by cultivating the good, the pure, the beautiful and the true within ourselves.

From what must we release ourselves? From slavery and adverse and undesirable conditions, circumstances, habits, thoughts and environments. How? By removing the "Cable-Tow."

And what does the "Cable-Tow" stand for? Every strand of the "Cable-Tow" stands for some vice, weakness, habit or shortcoming, thus laziness, anger, passion, hate, jealousy, lust, selfishness, self-indulgence, lack of energy, pride, prejudice, physical debility, worry, pessimism etc. All these are like so many strand which make up the symbolic "Cable-Tow", which must be removed by our own efforts, strand after strand, before we can hope to obtain the most vital things which we all seek.

Freemasonry teaches no impractical lessons. Its formula consisting of rules and tenets for the guidance of the living of a successful life, has been tried and tested and lived by those who have gone before us, and it is for us to try them out in our lives and find them equally beneficial.

In days gone by Masonry was mystical and practical, in the sense that the candidate had to live a practical life as outlines by our tenets and precepts, and his progress depended not as today upon how fast he committed to memory the Ritual, but upon how well he put our teachings into practise.

Thus, release yourself from the strand of laziness. It binds you to ignorance, failure and stagnation. Do not be lazy with yourself, mental laziness is one of our worst enemies. We find it trouble to think for ourselves. We are too lazy to use our minds. Yet thought precedes action, and moulds our lives for failure or success. Dare to think for yourself, don't let others do it for you. Think only constructive, upbuilding, cheerful, optimistic thoughts.

Release yourself from anger and passion. Nothing is accomplished through anger. It weans away from you friends who otherwise would help you. It makes you and others miserable. Passion results in consuming your vitality which otherwise should go into productive channels. Passion wastes your energies, leaving you limp, weak and useless. We speak of the conservation of our natural resources. Let us apply conservation with ourselves. Let us conserve our forces, energies, potencies, and capabilities for worthy and noble work.

Release yourself from pride. More men remain in darkness and ignorance through false pride than through any other reason. Most men are too proud to own up they don't know or that they are ignorant. And this pride prevents them from seeking the assistance of good men who could help them in knowledge and understanding. A wise man is meek and lowly and humble, while only fools are filled with pride. some men prefer to remain in darkness rather than admit they are ignorant. Put pride aside, seek the company of good men who can help you.

Continued on page 125

CELEBRATE BI-CENTENNIAL?
YES — Cont. from page 120

How many white Americans know that the first man to spot the American continent was a black lookout on one of Columbus' ships, Martin Pinzion? How many white Americans know that the first man to fall in the cause of liberty was the Negro, Crispus Attucks?

In each of this country's wars, from the Revolution to Vietnam, black men have shed their blood alongside white men, sometimes far out of proportion to their percentage of the general population. Can any man stand and say that these sacrifices were in vain or that the country for which these men died is not relevant to him? I would say no! The contributions of black men to this country can not be overlooked.

When I was a high school freshman my favorite author was a Frenchman named Alexander Dumas. Some twenty years after (to steal a phrase from one of his titles) I found he was a black man. I could care less what color he was. He was, and is, my favorite author. One of the authors of many best selling novels in my youth was Frank Yerby. I had read most of his output before I learned he was black. His writing was interesting and vivid.

Who is our greatest constitutional lawyer? A 33° P.H.A. Mason, Thurgood Marshall.

Who was the man who rebuilt the economy of our southern states nearly single handed? One of our own Iowans, Dr. George Washington Carver.

This line of thought could be carried through all fields of human endeavor. Black men have too much of a stake in our history for anyone to try to exclude them from any of our national ceremonies. This country is far from perfect but it will never be made perfect without all people participating to try to develop perfection.

Freemasonry today has the same kind of divided thinking which the rest of the American life has.

P.H.A. lodges are not recognized. I won't endeavor to add to the voluminous literature on the subject except to say that I feel that the non-recognition of P.H.A. Freemasonry is a social problem rather than a Masonic problem. When we change the thinking of the general population of this country we can probably change the thinking of many Freemasons. When I have spoken on Negro Freemasonry or Symbolic Freemasonry among Negroes in the United States which is a more accurate title, I have answered most of the questions about what one does when black and white Masons meet with a question of my own: "What do you do when you hear the Grand Hailing Sign, stop and check the dues card of the brother giving it?" Most of the time it works.

I strongly feel that Black Masons will not be given any recognition without asking for it, asking for it, and asking for it again.

Nevertheless, I cannot feel that black Masons can take themselves out of a bi-centennial celebration any more than other black men can and should. When Frederick Douglass was asked to speak at the centennial celebration he castigated the United States for not living up to the promises expressed in the freedom documents, but he spoke. He did not let the racists and the prejudiced win by default. I would not be one of the more peaceable black men were I black. If I experienced some of the discrimination which many people do, I would be one of the more militant blacks.

I would hope, however, that I would not stand aside from anything which affects the entire country but would be present adding my voice to the general tumult trying to secure the rights which are mine merely by the fact of my birth.

Jerry Marsengill

Black Masons, together with white Masons, should celebrate our bi-centennial. They don't have to dress up in ridiculous costumes, pretending to be the minute-men of 1776, they don't have to pretend that the past 200 years have been years of progress for all men. We know they have not. Yet, under no other system of government, have all men had more rights than are secured to us by our form of government. If they have not been equally applied in the past, that is not the fault of the documents, it is the fault of the men administering them.

Continued on page 141

CELEBRATE BI-CENTENNIAL?
NO — Cont. from page 121

and conciliates true friendship among those who might otherwise have remained at a perpetual distance." But how many Caucasian Grand Lodges like Illinois, in the year 1851 pass in their Grand Lodges, "Resolved, that all subordinate Lodges under this jurisdiction be instructed to admit no Negro or mulatto, as visitors or otherwise, under any circumstances whatever." Or have imposed on every Master Mason under their jurisdiction an obligation not to be present at the making of a Negro a Mason.

You may ask, what has this to do with the celebration of the Bi-Centennial. It is this. As a Masonic organization whose Credo reads that our doors are opened wide to men of good report, whether Aryan or Hottentot, history has clearly shown that we have allowed men of all races, colors, and hues into our Altars. To participate **"Masonically"** in an occasion, when we **"Masonically"** are not yet "free", we do no more than play into the hands of those **"Masonic"** hypocrites who, play the game of Masonry.

History has shown that the Prince Hall fraternity had chartered Caucasian Jewish Lodges, all Spanish speaking Lodges, intergrated Lodges as well as all Black Lodges, and our minutes clearly reflect that we have allowed Caucasian "regular" Freemasons to visit at their will, and of these facts we can **"Masonically"** celebrate with pride.

But, if we **"Masoncially"** participate in a **"Masonic"** farce, would we not do a **"Masonic"** injustice, to those brave Prince Hall Masons, White, Black, Brown and Red, who have stood before their altars as brothers under the banners of Prince Hall Masonry as true Masons, while being stoned, and abused by those who played the game of Masonry. And they have played that game for 200 years, and nothing has changed, are we to celebrate? No!

HOW LONG IS YOUR CABLE-TOW?
Cont. from page 123

Release yourself from worry. Worry never solved your problems. In fact, by worrying you weaken your mental powers so that you have less chance of solving your problems. Some say, "How can I stop worrying when adversity faces me?" Well, you have will power. Use it. Change your thought. Think of success. Think that you will come out on top. If you don't you will at least come out better than by worrying about your troubles.

These are some of the things you must release yourself from. As you study yourself you will find, oh, so many things from which you can become free.

Happiness and advancement in life go hand in hand; and if we are to possess them we must look within ourselves, in our make-up and discover the causes that hold us back. For, in most cases, the causes can be discover within ourselves. Don't be an ostrich and hide your head in the sand and say there is nothing the matter with you. Don't be blind to your faults. Seek them out and eliminate them from your being.

We, brethren who have taken our degrees, have we really released ourselves from the "Cable-Tow"? Or have we simply gone through a pantomime, a mock performance? Have we really made an attempt to remove the "CABLE-TOW?" Have we really tried to understand its real meaning? Brethren let the Symbolic Cable-Tow be a lesson to you.

I would in closing, further crave your attention and indulgence, as I bring you the following poem, entitled:

"HOW LONG IS YOUR CABLE-TOW, BROTHER?"
by Bro. W.A. Spalding of Los Angeles

"How long is your Cable-Tow, brother?
Does it span across the street?
Can it stretch the length of a hand-throw,
Or perhaps a thousand feet?

"Is there any definite measure
That cold mathematics may teach
To give the scope of your cable,
And limit its ultimate reach?

"For who shall count in units
Of foot, or yard or mile,
The length of a hearty handshake,
The breadth of a cheery smile;

"Or estimate the distance
A human heart may go,
When a brother reaches a brother
With the length of his Cable-Tow?

"Every one has his troubles;
Reverses and sorrows must come;
And the hour of sorest trial
Is when they are striking home;

"And sickness and death are the portion
That fate allots to all —
Our brother is sitting in sackcloth,
And his face is to the wall.

"Ah, then is the time propitious —
Occasion waits sublime
For the cable reaches farther
Than at any other time.

"For the pull is very little,
And it giveth strength to the strong.
How long is your Cable-Tow, brother?
How long — how long?"

THANK YOU.

125

JOSEPH G. FINDEL HONORARY PRINCE HALL GRAND MASTER

BY

JOSEPH A. WALKES, JR., F.P.S. [KANSAS]

Within the pages of Prince Hall Masonic history, there is no more interesting figure than the famed German Masonic writer and scholar, Gottfried Joseph G. Findel (1828-1905).

As a writer he was mainly noted for his **General History of Freemasonry,** which was published in 1861 and translated into English in 1865 and 1866.[1] This work was the forerunner of Robert Freke Gould's great **History of Freemasonry,** published in three volumes from 1882 to 1887.[2]

Bro. Findel was initiated in Lodge Eleusis Zur Vershwiegenheit at Bayreuth on Oct. 19th, 1856. He founded the Union of German Freemasons in 1860 and was the editor of an interesting Masonic journal at Leipzig in 1858, entitled **Craft Lodge.** In 1874 he published **Genius and Form of Freemasonry.**

It would be Bro. Findel's History of Freemasonry,[3] that would come to the attention of the Grand Master of Prince Hall Masons in Massachusetts, the fire-brand and very remarkable Lewis Hayden who would note in the appendix of his pamphlet, War of Races,[4] that "speaking of the Lodges of Colored people which worked separately", Bro. Findel says, "it was long doubted whether these were legally constituted, until Brother Dr. R. Barthelmess, of Brooklyn, demonstrated, that such was the case, so that their recognition can no longer with any show of reason, be withheld."[5]

During this period, it was evident to the Prince Hall Masonic Grand Lodges in the country, that the Caucasian Grand Lodges in the United States would neither recognize them or acknowledge them as Masons, even though they had in their possession a Charter from the Mother Grand Lodge of England.

Realizing that they could only expect racism from their American counterparts, who devised as a convenient weapon against Prince Hall Masonry the so called doctrine of exclusive Grand Lodge jurisdiction, which even the racist Masonic hypocrite General Albert Pike declared as a false Masonic law,[6] the Prince Hall Grand Lodges led by Bro. Justin Holland of Ohio,[7] and the Grand Lodges of Missouri, New York and Massachusetts, began to seek Masonic recognition abroad, and within a short time, fraternal recognition was accorded them from six foreign Masonic powers, The German Grand Lodge League representing eight Grand bodies, France, Italy, Hungary, Peru and the Dominican Republic.[8]

While the debate concerning Prince Hall Masonry was ranging in European Masonic circles, American Caucasian Jurisdictions protested vigorously against any recognition of their Black countrymen, but found themselves often in a rather precarious position when distinguished French and German Masons, Caubet, Grimaux, Dr. Barthelmess and Bro. Findel began to test their Grand Lodge regularity, and found them not as regular as they had claimed.[9]

In 1870, Grand Master Lewis Hayden and the Prince Hall Grand Lodge of Massachusetts would issue the following resolution in a form of a certificate.

WHEREAS, from the beginning of our Masonic existance, we knew of no Historian, in Europe or America, who has made mention of our being an organized body of Masons, execpt in a disparaging manner, until **Bro. J. G. Findel** published his inestimable "History of Freemasonry", in which we find a different spirit toward us, that of "Truth, characterized by **"Brotherly Love"**, expressed in the following words, "It was long doubted whether these were legally constituted, until Brother Doctor R. Barthelmess, of Brooklyn, demonstrated from the history of their first beginning, that such was the case, so that their recognition can no longer, with any show of reason, be withheld;"

AND WHEREAS, true to the above expressions, he stands to day vindicating our cause in his own glorious and triumphing **Fatherland**, the champion of truth and justice in the endeavor to establish our disputed Masonic claim before the civilized nations of the earth:

NOW THEREFORE, BE IT RESOLVED, that he be, and is hereby, elected a Life Member of the M.W. Prince Hall G.L. of the State of Massachusetts, with the rank and title of **"Honorary Grand Master"**

RESOLVED, FURTHER, that the proper documents be forwarded to him, under the Seal of this Grand Lodge and that the Grand Secretary transmit to his address copies of these resolutions and proceedings.

Done in Boston, Massachusetts, this 25th day of August, A.D. 1870, A.L. 5870, and in the 86th year of our Masonic Existence.

LEWIS HAYDEN, Grand Master

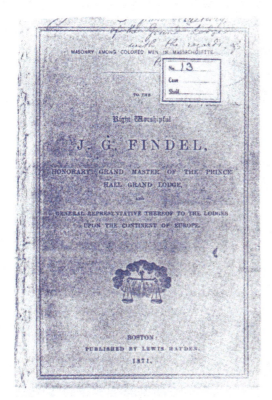

Frontispiece of Hayden's book

The Collar, Apron, Jewels, and Gauntlets of a Honorary Grand Master was sent to Bro. Findel, and Grand Master Lewis Hayden, an author of a number of pamphlets, would dedicate his famous **Masonry Among Colored Men in Massachusetts**[10] to this dedicated German Masonic scholar and Mason, and would begin with the famous lines:

My Dear Sir and Brother: As we read of the struggle of our fathers against the oppressions brought to bear upon them, previous to and since the commencement of our government, to dispossess them of what manhood they possessed, we find that they had to struggle to maintain even the smallest claim to humanity, so that none need be surprised that, after having refused them the means of education, of which Prince Hall complained in an address delivered before our lodge in 1792, nay, more, in parts of the country the education of our people was absolutely forbidden, by laws the spirit of which can be seen by reference to the action of the house of delegates of Virginia, and which expressed the American sentiment of that day—they sought to extract, by a system of laws, even the power of reason, as the following shows: "We have, as far as possible, closed every avenue by which light might enter their (the slave's) minds. If we could extinguish the capacity to see the light, our work would be complete and we would be safe."

No one will question the fact that the Masonic fraternity was represented by the men who passed such laws as those alluded to, the baneful effects of which we are contending against to this day. For the old adage is literally true, "that those we wrong, we hate." They have wronged us and our fathers; hence they hate us. And were they the same men in their lodges they have shown themselves to be in their several legislative halls, I repeat that none need be surprised to find that in the organization of their lodges and Grand Lodges have they persistently rejected the colored Masons, regardless of their claim as men and Masons. And to do so, they have resorted to all kinds of subterfuges, ignoring truth, landmark, and usage; all have been thrown to the wind."[11]

Bro. Findel proved himself a dedicated fighter for the recognition of Prince Hall Masonry on the shores of Europe, and his eloquence was equal to Grand Master Hayden.

"After I had already demanded, ten years ago, the

Bro. J. G. Findel, Honorary Grand Master of the Prince Hall Grand Lodge of Massachusetts and General Representative thereof to the Lodges Upon the Continent of Europe.

127

recognition of the Colored Grand Lodge as a matter of justice and fraternity, and a Masonic duty, by order of the Just and Perfect Prince Hall Grand Lodge, in Boston, I addressed some time ago the request to the German Grand Lodge to be recognized and eventually get into closer brotherly connection with them. Now, the Grand Lodge of the Eclectic Union, Frankfort, on the Maine, which, in the so-called Jew's question, was ahead of all in decidedly maintaining the correct Masonic ground, was also the first to officially congratulate me upon my appointment as an Honorary Grand Master, and to unreservedly declare in favor of recognizing my consistituents. From the nine German Grand Lodges, the Grand Lodge of Hungary approved of getting into closer connection by mutual representation. The Grand Lodge "Zur Sonne", in Bayreuth, had actually recognized the colored Grand Lodges of America before allowing its filial lodge in Karlsruhe to issue circulars to them, and by receiving from them and receipting contributions for Strasburg and Kehl. It would be an outrage at once revolting and demoralizing to assess on Colored Lodges contributions for Masonic purposes, and afterwards deprive these colored brethren and Lodges of their charter as Masons, and shut them out from the Lodge. He, who knows the delicacy of sentiment and the noblesse of our Bro. Von Cornburg, will not doubt for a moment that he and with him his Lodge mean to resolutely come forward in the defense of the colored brethren. But by this very acceptance of money contributions, and the thanks tendered to the colored brethren, especially those of Ohio, for their brotherly advances, have not only the brethren in Karlsruhe, Kehl and Strasburg, not only the Grand Lodge "Zur Sonne", but all German Masons have taken upon themselves a debt of honor from which they can never withdraw. The Grand Lodge of Hamburg being, as a matter of course, in the very beginning, in favor of recognition, did not want to take the lead in this affair, exposed, as it already is, to the hatred of the American Grand Lodges. The Grand Lodge Royal York in Friendship, at Berlin, in declining to enter into closer connection, has expressly recognized the Prince Hall Grand Lodge as being **just** and **perfect**. In the Grand Lodge of Saxony further inquiries were to be made before definitely adopting a resolution."[12]

After a bitter attack against Prince Hall Masonry by European Representative of the Caucasian Grand Lodge of New York, Bro. Findel was quick to come to the defense of his Black brethren.

"Bro. Von Mensch did not go to the trouble of inquiring into and getting acquainted with the circumstances, materials and facts of the case, else he could have never made such awkward and untenable statements.

Grand Master Lewis Hayden

There is nothing easier than to refute him point by point.

First, it is quite an unworthy imposition to the union of the German Grand Lodges if Bro. Von Mensch refers to the benefit of being able to attend American Lodges, and to solicit the council and support of American brethren, thereby putting down purely external advantages and enjoyments as a motive for the Grand Master's verdict. Such feeble arguments will hardly have any weight with us, for our German brethren as a rule are little edified by the American Grand Lodges and can, if most of the Grand Lodges had their ban upon us, attend the three Hamburg (German) and the colored Lodges.[13]

Not much better is his referring to the exclusive right of territorial jurisdiction asserted by the American Grand Lodges which is founded on the Monroe Doctrine, but not on the general right of Masons, and is partly a prejudice and partly an injustice. In Berlin there are three Grand Lodges working side by side, in Paris two, and in former times there were two in London and two in New York. How can the American Grand Lodges claim the exclusive right of jurisdiction in view of the Colored Grand Lodges, which not accepted by them, but suppressed, were by force of inexorable necesssity compelled to start Lodges and Grand Lodges of their own, that with some exceptions have been longer in existence there than most of the white Lodges. Here is not an acknowledge absolute theory to be upheld, but facts and historical rights are to be considered. We Free Masons recognize no difference of color or race and we hold the Grand Lodges of the white and Colored men equally entitled to recognition. Still more, there is a duty of humanity which we have to fulfill to the Colored men, to recognize them; means to elevate them intellectually and morally, to benefit them and to eminently act like a Mason. To recognize them and to enter into intellectual communication and brotherly intercourse with them, is not only our, but principally the American Mason's duty, and if they from a hatred and prejudice against the race, rid themselves of this duty, then, surely it would not incumbent upon the union of German Grand Lodges to act alike." 14

Resolution Certificate presented to Bro. Findel.

All of the Masonic regalia presented to Bro. Findel by Grand Master Lewis Hayden and the Prince Hall Grand Lodge of Massachusetts was placed on exhibition in the Masonic Museum of the Grand Lodge Zur Sonne (The Sun) in Bayreuth, in Baveria.

But when Adolph Hitler came to power he destroyed or descrated every Masonic edifice in Germany. The Museum of the Grand Lodge Zur Sonne did not escape his wrath. The only items remaining today is the Grand Master Jewels which was presented to Bro. Findel.

In a recent letter to the Phylaxis Society, the curator of the German Masonic Museum in Bayreuth wrote the Phylaxis Society:

Bayreuth, Dec. 10, 1975

Dear Brother Walkes:

We acknowledge the arrival of your brotherly letter dated Nov. 29, 1975.

The Honorary (Grand Master's) Jewels which Brother Grand Master R.W. Findel has received from the Prince Hall Grand Lodge of Massachusetts, and of which you have pictures, is exhibited at the "Deutsches Freimaurer Museum" in Bayreuth.

On July 12, 1970 (Prince Hall) Military Lodge #140 with 107 people and on August 27, 1972, Lodge #144 with 25 members have visited our musuem.

From the first Lodge we received a large engraved plaque and from Lodge #144 an engraved dipper. Both pieces are exhibited and a beautiful memory for us.

With Brotherly Greetings:
Henrich Wilhelm Lorenz, 33°

EUROPEAN LODGE TOURS GERMAN MASONIC MUSEUM

Prince Hall Military Lodge #140 visiting German Masonic Museum with Bro. Lorenz, curator.

And so, a small portion of Prince Hall Masonry is preserved, thousands of miles from the country of Prince Hall, and symbolically within the glass case that holds the jewels of a Grand Master, is the story of the legendary Lewis Hayden and the early history of the Prince Hall Grand Lodge of Massachusetts. It, symbolically is the story of European Freemasons, Bro. Findel, and others, who was true and just to the spirit of Freemasonry. It is the story of the struggle of Prince Hall Masonry to be accorded its rightful place in the Masonic community. It symbolically is the story of the fight against American racism as practiced by the Caucasian Grand Lodges then, as they practice it today, and the fascism of Hilterism against

129

Jewels presented to Joseph Gabriel Findel

Freemasonry in Europe, both being no more or no less the same, partners of hate. And it is symbolic that in this decade that Prince Hall Military Lodges stationed in Germany, would pay its respects to this Museum that holds so many memories of our Prince Hall Masonic past.

REFERENCES

1. William R. Denslow, **10,000 Famous Freemasons**, reprinted in the Transactions of the Missouri Lodge of Research (Trenton, Mo., 1958) P. 49
2. Robert Freke Gould (1836-1915) was a founder of the famous Quatour Coronati Lodge No. 2076 of London, in 1884. He wrote **The Four Old Lodges** in 1879 and in 1899 **Military Lodges**. His greatest work was his **History of Freemasonry**, published in three volumes from 1882 to 1887. Denslow, op. cit., P. 132-133.
3. Translated from German by Asher & Co., 13 Bedford Street, London, 1866.
4. Lewis Hayden, **Grand Lodge Jurisdiction Claim or War of Races** an address before the Prince Hall Grand Lodge of Massachusetts, Festival of St. John the Baptist, June 24, 1868, by Lewis Hayden, Grand Master, P. 92.
5. Ibid, P. 92
6. Charles H. Wesley, **The History of the Prince Hall Grand Lodge of the State of Ohio 1849-1960** (Wilberforce, Ohio, Central State College Press, 1961) P. 72, states "In this connection, General Albert Pike on February 7, 1877, sent a letter to the Supreme Council of Peru with the following statement, quoted in **Ohio Masonry**, 1925: "The doctrine of exclusive Grand Lodge jurisdiction had grown up in the United States, and has been accepted here as politic and in the interest of harmony. It does not prevail in Europe, and is not a part of Masonic organic law, and its zealots here have not been content to stop when they pushed it to the verge of absurdity."
7. Wesley, op.cit., P. 73 "Since foreign lodges had no such views as American Lodges, correspondence and contacts were kept up with these Lodges. The one Prince Hall Mason most interested was Justin Holland who conducted this work in a most effective manner."
8. Harry E. Davis, **A History of Freemasonry Among Negroes in America** (United Supreme Council, A.A.S.R. Northern Jurisdiction, U.S.A., Prince Hall Affiliation) Inc., P.112-113, states "These recognitions were accorded not only by formal decree of these jurisdictions but by the interchange of representatives between them and Ohio, the reciprocal elections of honorary members, and the conferring of jewels and other Masonic honors upon these representatives." Wesley, **op. cit.**, P. 80, states "These recognitions were important not only to the Grand Lodge of Ohio but also to Prince Hall Masons generally, for they gave evidences of approval and of brotherhood at a period in history when such sanctions were needed. Prince Hall Masons had been rebuffed as well and were unrecognized by American Masons. While these recognitions had little influence on American attitudes toward Prince Hall Masons, they were of inestimable value in strengthening the morale and giving assurance to Prince Hall Masons that they were upon sound foundations and that segregation and denial of fellowship could not invalidate their foundations in Masonic history and tradition.
9. Davis, op. cit. P. 114
10. Lewis Hayden, **Masonry Among Colored Men in Massachusetts**, Masonic Journal, Vol. 1, No. 1, 2, & 3, (Moline, Illinois, June 1879)
11. Lewis Hayden would publish, **Caste Among Masons** in 1866; **Grand Lodge Jurisdictional Claim or War of Races** in 1868; and **Masonry Among Colored Men in Massachusetts**, in 1871. All of the pamphlets deal with the question of legitimacy, but they contain valuable historical material.
12. Proceedings of the Prince Hall Grand Lodge of Ohio, 22nd Annual Communication, August 21, 1872, P. 71.
13. Refers to the German Lodges in New York, and the clash between the Grand Lodge of Hamburgh and the Caucasian Grand Lodge of New York, one of the most shameful incidents in Masonic history. The Committee on Foreign Correspondence of the Caucasian Grand Lodge of New York reported concerning the German Lodges in New York under the jurisdiction of the Grand Lodge of Hamburgh "It has not withdrawn or offered to withdraw the Charters of its illegitimate subordinates. Though apprised of the universal sentiment which prevails among the Grand Lodges of United States in condemnation of its acts, it persists in keeping up the Lodges in the Jurisdiction of New York, in violation of our laws and in defiance of our authority. This is not all. It is indeed, but a tithe of her offending. It is a venial, and excusable offence in comparison to a much greater **which she is seeking now** to perpetuate. **Because we have declared** her two subordinates irregular, **and suspended intercourse with her** till their Charters are recalled, she has invented a means of reprisal, a mode of retaliation, which for deliberate revenge has no parallel in the history of Masonry. ***** She (The Grand Lodge of Hamburgh) is not only to recognize these bodies (Prince Hall) herself as regular and legitimate Lodges and Grand Lodges, but she is trying to persuade the other Grand Lodges of Europe to do the same thing." Lewis Hayden, **Grand Lodge Jurisdictional Claim or War of Races** (Boston, Edward S. Coombs, 1868) P. 63-64.
14. Ohio Proceedings, op. cit., P. 72.

(NOTE: ALL ITEMS FOR THIS ARTICLE WERE TAKEN FROM THE PRIVATE COLLECTION OF JOSEPH A. WALKES, JR. HOUSED IN LEAVENWORTH, KANSAS.)

Congressional Record

PROCEEDINGS AND DEBATES OF THE 91st CONGRESS, FIRST SESSION

Vol. 115   WASHINGTON, WEDNESDAY, MAY 7, 1969   *No. 74*

House of Representatives

PRINCE HALL: A GREAT NEGRO AMERICAN

HON. PHILIP J. PHILBIN
OF MASSACHUSETTS
IN THE HOUSE OF REPRESENTATIVES
Wednesday, May 7, 1969

Mr. Philbin. Mr. Speaker, I wish unanimous consent to revise and extend my remarks in the Record about America's first Negro Mason an outstanding, loyal citizen and patriot, Prince Hall, of colonial Boston.

Thanks to the alertness and kindness of our very dear friend and great Negro leader, Mr. Ernest Petinaud, whom we of the House so highly esteem for his peerless character, dedicated service, and inspiring loyalty, not to speak of his outstanding contributions to our activities, my attention has been drawn to the most extraordinary historic part played by the illustrious Prince Hall, outstanding Boston leader of the colonial period, who served with the advice and assistance of the famous John Hancock, and with great distinction, under the then Gen. George Washington in the Revolutionary War.

It should be noted that this able, farsighted, distinguished Negro leader, a Boston landowner and voter, most vigorously demanded that his State free its slaves, and his city educate its Negro children. He established a school in his own home to educate the people.

He was a man of ability, forthrightness, patriotism, and courage, endowed with commonsense, balance, and good judgement, determined to do his part to end the loathesome discrimination which Negroes faced. He furnished the sagacious leadership by which the laws against his people were changed and their cause was meaningfully advanced.

His eloquent voice spoke out boldly and loudly for justice, and for righting the cruel wrongs from which his people suffered.

His wise, gallant leadership had broad ramifications and produced enduring, effective results.

The deep, sweeping influence of the words and deeds of Prince Hall, which gave his people the courage to cry out boldly against discrimination and prejudice, and strive for recognition as free men and women, was a clear, stirring, clarion call that has come down through the years, and still animates people of every race, class, and creed to persist indomitably in the struggle, not yet won, to liberate the spirit, the body, and the mind of man from discrimination, persecution, and injustice.

Prince Hall was, in truth, an apostle of enlightenment and tolerance for the whole human race of his time, and a fearless leader who inspired his people to achieve ever higher levels of acceptance, dignity, and justice in the American society. His battle was historic and heaven sent. His cause must continue today until every vestige of racialism, hatred, prejudice, and discrimination has been driven from our beloved land—until the majesty of the rule of law is assured for all and true human brotherhood is enthroned in our Nation and the world.

While Prince Hall made lasting patriotic contributions to the Nation, to the Negro Masons he served so well, and to the country he loved with all his heart and soul, like a great symphony of constitutional justice, his words, noble deeds, and his holy cause are indelibly and ineradicably woven into the fabric of our American system of freedom, justice, and equality under law for all.

Prince Hall stood in his great day and spoke out militantly for truth, humanity, and freedom. Let this Nation continue his fight for tolerance and equal treatment under the law for everyone, regardless of race, creed, or class, in our society, so that the full glory and completeness of our marvelous American dream of liberty and justice for all will be totally realized, and everyone in America can be placed, as true justice demands, on a "footing with kings."

131

A CHARGE
DELIVERED TO THE BRETHREN
OF THE
AFRICAN LODGE
ON THE 25TH OF JUNE 1792

At the Hall of Brother William
Smith in Charlestown by the
Right Worshipful Prince Hall
And published at the request of the Lodge

"Dear and well beloved Brethren of the African Lodge, as through the goodness and mercy of God, we are once more met together, in order to celebrate the Festival of St. John the Baptist, it is requisite that we should on these public days, and when we appear in form, give some reason as a foundation for our so doing, but as this has been already done, in a discourse delivered in substance by our Late Reverend Brother John Marrant, and now in print.

I shall at this time endeavour to raise part of the superstructure, for howsoever good the foundation may be, yet without this it will only prove a Babel. I shall therefore endeavour to show the duty of a Mason; and the first thing is, that he believes in one Supreme Being, that he is the great Architect of this visible world, and that he governs all things here below by his almighty power, and his watchful eye is over all our works. Again we must be good subjects to the laws of the land in which we dwell; giving honour to our lawful Governors and Magistrates, giving honour to whom honour is due, and that we have no hand in any plots or conspiracies or rebellion, or side or assist in thim: for when we consider the bloodshed, the devastation of towns and cities that hath been done by them, what heart can be so hard as not pity those different brethren, and keep at the greatest distasnce from them. However just it may be on the side of the oppressed, yet it doth not in the least, or rather ought not abate that love and fellow-feeling which we ought to have for our brother fellow men.

The next thing is love and benevolence to all the whole family of mankind, as God's make and creation, therefore we ought to love them all, for love or hatred is of the whole kind, for if I love a man for the sake of the image of God which is on him, I must love all, for he made all, and upholds all, and we are dependant upon him for all we do enjoy and expect to enjoy in this world and that which is to come. Therefore he will help and assist all his fellow-men in distress, let them be of what colour or nation they may, yea even our very enemies, much more a brother Mason. I shall therefore give you a few instances of this from Holy Writ, and first, how did Abraham prevent the storm, or rebellion that was rising between Lot's servants and his ? Saith Abraham to Lot, let there be no strife I pray thee between me and thee, for the land is before us, if you will go to the left, then I will go to the right, and if you will go to the right, then I will go to the left.

They divided and peace was restored. I will mention the compassion of a blackman to a Prophet of the Lord, Ebedmelech, when he heard that Jeremiah was cast into the dungeon, he made intersession for him to the King, and got liberty to take him out from the jaws of death. See. Jer. xxxviii 7-13.

Also the prophet Elisha after he had led the army of the Framites blindfold into Samaria, when the King in a deriding manner said, my Father (not considering that he was as much their Father as his) shall I smite, or rather kill them out of the way, as not worthy to live on the same earth, or draw the same air with himself; so eager was he to shed his brethren's blood, that he repeats his bloodthirsty demand, but the Prophet after reproaching him therefore, answers him no, but set bread and water before them; or in other words, give them a feast and let them go home in peace. See 2 Kings, vi. 22.23.

I shall just mention the good deeds of the Samarian, though at that time they were looked upon as unworthy to eat, drink or trade with their fellow-men, at least by the Jews; see the pity and compassion he had on a poor distressed and half dead stranger. See Luke x. from 30 to 37. See that you endeavour to do so likewise. But when we consider the amazing condescending love and pity our blessed Lord had on such poor worms as we are, as not only to call us his friends but his brothers, we are lost and can go no further, in holy writ for examples to extend as to the love of our fellow men. But I am aware of any objection that may arise (for some men will catch at any thing) that is that they were not all Masons, we allow it, and I say that they were not all Christians, and their benevolence to strangers ought to shame us both, that there is so little, so very little of it to be seen in these enlightened days.

Another thing which is the duty of a Mason is, that he pays a strict regard to the stated meetings of the Lodge for Masonry is a progressive nature, and must be attended to if ever he intends to be a good Mason; for the man that thinks that because he hath been made a Mason; and is called so, and at the same time will wilfully neglect to attend his Lodge, he may be assured he will never make a good Mason, nor ought he to be looked upon as a good member of the craft. For if his example was followed, where would be the Lodge, and besides what a disgrace is it, when we

132

are at our set meetings, to hear that one of our members is at a drinking house, or a card table, or in some worse company, this brings disgrace on the Craft. Again there are some that attend the Lodge in such a manner that sometimes their absence would be better than their Company (I would not here be understood a brother in disguise, for such and one hath no business on a level floor) for if he hath been displeased abroad or at home, the least thing that is spoken that he thinks not right, or in the least offends hime, he will raise his temper to such a height as to destroy the harmony of the whole Lodge; but we have a remedy and every officer ought to see it put in execution.

Another thing a Mason ought to observe, is that he should lend his helping hand to a brother in distress, and relieve him, this we may do various ways; for we may sometimes help him to a cup of cold water, and it may be better to him than a cup of wine. Good advice may be sometimes better than feeding his body, helping him to some lawful employment, better than giving him money; so defending his case and standing by him when wrongfully accused, may be better than cloathing him, better to save a brother's house when on fire, then to give him one. Thus much may suffice.

I shall now cite some of our fore-fathers, for our imitation: and the first shall be Tertullian, who defended the Christians against their heathen false accusations, whom they charged with treason against the empore and the Emperor, because of their silent meetings; he proved that to be false for this reason, for in their meetings, they were wont to pray for the prosperity of the Empire, of Rome, and him also; and they were accused of being enemies to mankind, how can that be, said he, when their office is to love and pray for all mankind. When they were charged with worshiping the Sun, because they looked towards the East when they prayed; he defended them against this slander also, and proved that they were slandered, slighted and ill treated, not for any desert of theirs, but only out of hatred of them and their profession.

This friend of the distrest was born in Carthage in Africa, and died Anno Christi, 202.

But I have not time to city but one more (out of hundreds that I could count of our Fathers, who were not only examples to us, but to many of their nobles and learned.) that is Augustine, who had engraven on his table these words:

He that doth love an absent Friend to jeer,
May hence depart, no room is for him here.

His saying was that sincere and upright prayer pierceth heaven, and returns not empty. That it was a shelter to the soul. A sacrifice to God and a scourge to the Devil. There is nothing, said he, more abareth pride and sin that the frequent meditation on death, he cannoth die ill, that lives well, and seldom doth he die well, that lives ill: Again, if men want wealth, it is not to be unjustly gotten, if they have it they ought by good works to lay it up in heaven: And again, he that hath tasted the sweetness of divine love, will not care for temporal sweetness. The reasonable soul made in the likeness of God, may here find much distraction, but no full satisfaction; not to be without afflictions, but to overcome them in blessedness. Love is as strong as death; as death kills the body, so love of eternal life kills worldly desires and affections. He called Ingratitude the Devil's squorge, wherewith he wipes out all the favours of the Almighty. His prayer was — Lord give first what thou requireth, and then reqire of me what thou wilt, — this good man died anno Christi. 430.

The next is Fulgentius, his speech was, why Travel in the world which can yield me no future, not durable reward, answerable to any pains. Thought it better to weep well, then to rejoice ill, yet if joy be our desire, how much more excellent is their joy, who have a good conscience before God, who dread nothing but sin, study's to do nothing but to accomplish the precepts of Christ. Now therefore let me change my course, and as before I endeavoured amongst my noble friends to prove more noble, so now let my care and employment be among the humble and poor servants of Christ, and become more humble that I may help and instruct my poor and distressed brethren.

Thus my brethren, I have quoted a few of your reverend fathers, for your imitation, which I hope you will endeavour to follow, so far as your abilities will permit in your present situation and the disadvantages you labour under on account of your being deprived of the means of education in your younger days, as you see it is at this day with our children, for we see not withstanding we are rated for that, and other town charges, we are deprived of that blessing. But be not discouraged, have patience, and look forward to a better day. Hear what the great Architect of the Universal world saith, AEthiopa **stretch** forth her hands unto me. Hear also the strange, but bold and confident language of **T. Hulk**, who just before the Executioner gave the last stroke, said I challenge you to meet me a hundred years hence. But in the meantime let us lay by our recreations, and all superfluities, so that we may have that to educate our young generation, which was spent in those follies. Make you the beginning, and who knows but God may raise up some friend or body of friends, as he did in Philadelphia, to open a school for the Black here, as that friendly city has done there.

I shall now show you what progress Masonry hath made since the siege and taking of Jersulam in the year 70 by Titus Vespasian, after a long and bloody siege, a million of souls having been slain, or had perished in the city, it was taken by storm and the city

133

set on fire. There was an order of men called the order of St. John besides their other engagements, subscribed to another by which they bound themselves to keep up the war against the Turks, these men defended the temple when on fire, in order to save it, so long, that Titus was amazed and went to see the reason of it, but when he came so near as to behold the **Sanctum Santorum**, he was amazed, and shed tears, and said, no wonder these men fought so long to save it. He honored them with many honors, and large contributions were made to that order from many kingdoms; and were also knighted. They continued 88 years in Jerusalem, till that city was again retaken by the Turks, after which they resided 104 years in the Cyrean City of Ptolemy, till the remains of the Holy Conquest were lost.

Whereupon they settled on the Island of Cyprus, where they continued 18 years, till they found an opportunity to take the Island Rhoes, being masters of that they maintained it for 213 years, and from thence they were called Knights of Rhodes, till in the year 1530, they took their residence in the Island of Malta, where they have continued to this day, and are distinguished by the name of the Knights of Malta. Their first Master was Villaret in the year 1099. Fulco Villaret in the year 1322, took the Island of Rhoes, and was after that distinguished by the title of Grand Master, which hat devolved to his successors to this day.

Query, Whether at that day, when there was an African church, and perhaps the largest Christian church on earth, whether there was no African of that order; or whether, if they were all whites, they would refuse to accept them as their fellow Christians and brother Masons, or whether there were any so weak or rather so foolish, as to say, because they were Blacks, that would make their lodge or army too common or too cheap? Sure this was not our conduct in the late war; for then they marched shoulder to shoulder, brother soldier and brother soldier, to the field of battle; let who will answer he that despises a black man for the sake of his colour, reproacheth his Maker, and he hath resented it, in the case of Aaron and Miriam. See for this Numbers xii.

But to return. In the year 1787 (the year in which we received our charter) there were 489 lodges under charge of his late Royal Highness the Duke of Cumberland; whole memory will always be esteemed by every good Mason.

And now, my African brethren, you see what a noble order you are members of. My charge to you is, that you make it your duty to live up to the precepts of it, as you know, that they are all good; and let it be known this day to the spectators, that you have not been to a feast of Bacchus, but to a refreshment with Masons; and see to it that you behave as such, as well at home as abroad; always to keep in your minds the obligations you are under both to God and your fellow men. And more so, you my dear brethren of Providence, who are at a distance from, and cannot attend the Lodge here but seldom, yet I hope you will endeavor to communicate to us by letters of your welfare, and remember your obligations to each other, and live in peace and love as brethren.

We thank you for your attendance with us this day, and wish you a safe return.

If this we by the grace of God, live up to this our profession; we may cheerfully go the rounds of the compass of this life. Having lived according to the plumb line of uprightness, the Square of justice, the level of truth and sincerity. And when we are come to the end of time, we may then bid farewell to that delightful sun and Moon, and the other planets, that move to beautifully round her in their orbits, and all things here below, and ascend to that new Jerusalem, which we shall not want these tapers, for God is the Light thereof; where the Wicked cease from troubling, and where the weary are at rest.

> Then shall we hear and see and know
> All we desired and wish'd below,
> And every power find sweet employ,
> In that eternal world of joy.
> Our flesh shall slumber in the ground,
> Till the last trumpet's joyful sound,
> Then burst the chains with sweet surprise,
> And in our Saviour's image rise.

THE MASTER'S SIGN

BY

JAMES C. FAIRCLOTH, M.P.S.

[Washington]

The velvet darkness of midnight wraps me in an inky cloak, as I walk restlessly along the murmuring shoreline of Puget Sound. Unable to sleep, I had tangled my mind with ponderous thoughts; Who am I, where am I bound, is man alone in the universe? So without a goal or direction, I had wandered along the rocky salt shore where the tide ebbs and flows around me. In the errie reflections of far off lights, I suddenly see a shadowy figure approaching me along the beach. The lonely place, the late hour and man's natural caution combines to make the hackles raise on my neck and prickling sensations play along my spine. Was this person male or female, friend or enemy, evil or good; I have no way of knowing.

Continued on page 137

A PRINCE HALL MASONIC CLASSIC

THE PHYLAXIS SOCIETY takes pride in reproducing this Masonic Classic, and by so doing, we hope it will find its way into Masonic libraries around the world. Prince Hall Masonry has over the years produced masterpieces of Masonic literature, and this work must be classed as one.

ADDRESS OF
ALEXANDER CLARK, P.G.M. OF IOWA
Past Grand Master of the Grand Lodge of Missouri, and R.W.N.D.G.M., before the National Grand Lodge of North America, March 13, 1873, In Bethel Church, Philadelphia, Pa.

The Congress of Seventeen Seventy-four (1774) germinating in the Revolution of Seventeen Seventy-six (1776) the Convention of Seventeen Eighty-seven (1787), forming the Federal Constitution, presents no grander theme for the future historian, or will be more prolific of comment, or the causes of more earnest thought and study than our present convention. The three first were significant of great events, followed by good results — so will the latter. The importance of our convention is one of great magnitude. The sacredness of the ground on which the city is founded and in which our present communication is held, made more sacred by the memories of the past as well as by the name of the city — Brotherly Love, — combining in itself the four cardinal virtues, viz: temperance, fortitude, patience and justice; if these be with us we are not barren, but will be fruitful. It has long been the custom of our Order to commemorate the important events which gave birth to Masonic art, and angel of mercy to the scattered tribes of apostate men. When this heavenly messenger came forth from the regions of mind, and by his powers of attraction had gathered a portion of the scattered energies of spirits, immortal, he brought them to his own temple for a sanctuary from the stormy hurricane, the dew, the rain and the sunbeam. This temple is based upon truth, and support by the firm pillars of liberal art and science. Ascending by the golden steps of "faith, hope and charity," as we plant our feet within its courts, and turn to look forth upon that vast theatre of matter over which storms of misfortune brood, and around which burning fires throw their radiant glare, one gleam of light from the throne of the Invisible reveals the army of Jehovah stretched out over the trembling broken fragment of a ruined world, while passion, the tyrant of that realm, rides upon the merciless storm; the wildest fury reigns, until earth, which was once without form and void again becomes one dreary uncultivate waste. Man who was made by his Creator for the social intercourse with his fellow man, now becomes a wandering exile, isolated in his enjoyments with no heart to beat responsive with his own. Thus he treads the dark and dreary path of life alone. Amid the beating storms and burning suns, he rushes with the velocity of time, downward to the grave. Thus generation after generation pass away, leaving no trace behind them; no sculpured columns rise to point out their resting place. But lifting our eyes to the trestle board of science, we see a hand which draws the design for the transformation of this heterogeneous mass into the dwelling places for man's conveniences. This proud task has been reserved for the combined powers of art and science, whose faithful votaries have floated timber from the mountains, hewn rocks from the quarries, and thrown them into piles of surpassing grandeaur, whose marble base, granite walls and brilliant domes have beautified the lawns of the Euphrates and the Nile, and have gilded the hill-tops of Judea with the richest golden hue. For that operative and speculative, Masonry, single or combined, have lived for ages — centuries — none will deny. For that sacred canon which teaches us that Solomon's Temple existed, confirms us in the great truth that the operative craftsman smoothed the rough ashler, squared the cedar timbers in Lebanon's forests, and gave form and finish to that grand and imposing edifice which was the signal triumph of art and science. Reflecting the rich and costly material of Lebanon and Tyre, combined to beautify and adorn and outer chambers of that temple dedicated to the worship of the ever living God. Thus the disciples of religion and reason, have in all ages, gone hand in hand.

The moral and divine precepts of the sacred scriptures, have from time immemorial, been introduced under symbolic expressions of Masonic art; yet we do not hold that Freemasonry is religion, but we know it to be its legitimate offspring, and the world's benefactor in uniting in the strongest ties, people of every nation, color, and religious creed. Its language is universal throughout the entire globe, and when spoken, its voice of supplication will never be disregarded. It ever has been and ever will be heeded, whether upon the bloody field of battle or in the merry parlor circle. It has often unnerved the strong arm, suspended the fatal blow, raised a fallen brother, broke the prison fetters, succored the distressed carried consolation and joy to the widow's heart, supported the helpless orphan, and brought peace and gladness to the bereaved.

Our beloved Order excludes from its walls the Atheist, and irreligious libertine. To me grand and most glorious thought, that he who knocks at the door of Masonry and gains admittance, must be a believer

135

in God, acknowledging Jehovah to be the Supreme Ruler of the Universe, be he Jew or Gentile, Greek or Barbarian, Catholic or Protestant, white or black, rich or poor — all alike must recognize and acknowledge this great fundamental principle in Masonry, enabling all alike to meet upon the level of the Masonic pavement of life and light.

Woman, fair woman, the idol of man's affection, she is the exception — she is not permitted to pass through our mystic Order, nor bask in the sunlight of its secrets — not that we as men or Masons, distrust her great virtues, confidence or genius, but simply because Masonry in the primitive age was more operative than speculative. Our ancient fathers, no doubt, believed that her sex and physical weakness unfitted her for a hewer of wood, a quarrier of stone and a carrier of mortas as an operative Mason. Now, though Masonry be more specultaive than operative, it is natural that all the ancient rules and regulations would be strictly adhered to. This in my opinion, is the cause of women's exclusion from our honorable Order. But brethren, when we consider that the great end and object of Masonry is to promote the great principle of love to God, peace on earth and good will and kindness to all mankind it is clear to the mind of every thinking Mason, that God himself has made woman Masons; so far as their great virtues are concerned, for women's inborn nature is charity, and we as men or Masons at best, are far behind them in this christian charities and deeds of mercy. Then let us ever cherish them in their order of courts, that they may entwine about us as the tender vines entwines the sturdy oak.

I now see brethren before me who have passed the higher degrees of Masonry, and partaken at the festive board of banquets and awards that await the true Templar. Brethren to us who have passed that Order where none are admitted but those who believe in the blessed Redeemer, to such let me say, brethren be of good cheer; look forward, the future is full of hope for the true Knight Templar; though our be dark, or the cruel prejudice of caste and the withering curse of slavery has stamped itself upon us as a people, the experience of the past years fill the present with freedom. Beauties that fill our fond hopes for the future, grand beyond conception.

The learned Dr. Johnson once said of Homer: "that nation after nation and century after century had been able to do little more than transpose his incidents; new-mane his acts, and paraphrase his sentiments. The sweetness of his numbers and grandeur of his sentiments could not be impaired by the lapse of time." The same thing may be said, and is characteristically true of Masonry. The divinity of its principles, the purity of its sentiments, and the exalted character of its aims, are more enduring than the Egyptian pyramids; more valuable than fine gold or the pearls of princesses, and more enduring than inscriptions on lead, incased in granite. The inherent life, the vital energy of Masonry, its power to fashion and elevate the sentiments and aspirations of the soul in the generations yet to come, with a vigor not less fruitful than in the centuries of the past, is not a matter of question at least to those who have felt the touch of its inspiration, and whose hearts have been warmed by its mystic fires. Masonic principles and sentiments lose nothing by time; they will be as fresh, distinct and pure in the next generation as in this; and as well calculated to define, direct and quicken human sympathy and emotion, centuries hence, as they were in ages past. The problems of Euclid will be as clear to the last generation of mathematicians as they were to his countrymen; nor will they have lost any of their freshness and importance, when the last human mind shall contemplate the wonderful clearness and acumen of the ancient Greeks. so when the last apprentice shall receive that solemn and impressive charge to inculcate his three-fold duty to God, his neighbor and himself, he will not have less reason for a sense of the great responsibility, than he who was first made conscious of the nature of Masonic obligation, or he who shall be last raised to the sublime degree of a Master, and be admitted to the enjoyment of privileges less extensive and refined, or a brotherly regard and friendship, less sincere, than he who besides being a man, was first endowed with the attributes of a Mason.

All these considerations, in connection with the purity of the principles which it embodies, the noble sentiments which it encourages and fosters are mainly the advantages and inducements which Masonry holds out for good men to connect themselves with its interests, and to avail themselves of its benefits both for moral and social improvement and happiness. Having now obtained a view in the distance of a temple worthy of our admiration, and caught some glimpses of its beautiful form and magnificent proportions, let us not vainly suppose that we have reached thelimits of our observation, nor forget that we are but proselytes of the gate; that the glories of the inner temple, its golden pillars, its candle sticks, its altars, and more than all its mysterious Holy of Holies are yet beyond us, and, therefore, let it be remembered that upon all who stand within this temple gate there rests the great obligation to encourage science, genius and intellectual culture, and strive for moral development, and cultivate and practice every social virtue and christian grace; for whatever its calculated to refine and expand the intellect, whatever tends to elevate and ennoble the soul, whatever clothes human character with grace and meekness, should be sought and improved by every man and especially by every Mason: for, brethren, we may extol the beauties of Masonry, we may say as it often has been said, and wisely too, that Masonry is an empore upon whos dominion the sun never rises or sets; taking its rise in the eastern hemisphere and is daily planting its glories upon the western continents, on every sea, in every isle, wherever a human being is found bearing the image of his Maker, there is a Mason's badge to be found. Kings and monarchs of the earth have been proud to wear it in every age and every land, much less us. Oh! then, in God's name, let us wear it worthy of all the virtues herein mentioned. The Roman Emperor Constantine, when marching at the head of an army to meet Maxentius, his rival, in a deadly conflict on the fate of which hung the future destiny of the Roman Empire, being oppressed with fear in his own strength, prayed in a loud voice that some god would assist him in his hour of great peril, and the result of this prayer was, that there appeared in the heavens above their heads a resplendent cross emblazoned in golden letters with this inscription: "**In Hoc Signo Vinces.**" Depending upon this, he went into the battle and came out victorious, and ever afterwards the cross was displayed in the van of the Roman Legions as the banner of the Caesars. Can we learn in this moral faith in God, and go forward squaring out lives by the square of virtue, ever remembering that our greatest danger is from the household of faith.

The example of fallen Rome and divided Greece is ever before us; the voice which comes from among the ruins of those once mighty powers constantly urge us to shun the rock of division upon which they fell, and to stand firm as a rock, and united by a band which cannot be broken in the history of nations. Masons my learn many important lessons. Our blessed Lord hath said "that a man's foes shall be those of his own household." National affairs have too often verified this great truth. The worst foes of Greece and Rome, were Grecian and Romans. The worst enemies of our beloved nation have not been the kings and rulers of other governments, but the children of our own land. Our dear lamented and martyred President, Abraham Lincoln, fell not by the hand of a foreigner, but in sight of his own home—the Nation's house—he perished by the hand of the assassin, one who was born under the same flag that has waved in triumph over us for near a century. Masonry has nothing to fear from open enemies. How many nations, empires, and kingdoms have risen - paraded their brief stay upon the earth - have fallen, crumbled in pieces, and are numbered among the things in the eternal past; but Masonry as if by divinity, it stands firmer than ever before. Then, brethren, let us be faithful and true to Masonry and its interests; let us guard zealously the portals of our beloved Order, and see that the unworthy enter not our door; for the sun as he rises in the east or stands in the south at high meridian, or sets in the west at dawn of eve, finds in all of his rounds no brighter star nor sheds his rays on a purer altar.

(PHYLAXIS NOTE: The Alexander Clark House, owned by the Alexander Clark Historical Society has been placed on the National Register of Historical Places in the United States. His house is located in Muscatine, Iowa and was shown on the NBC Today show in its Bicentennial salute to the State of Iowa. The Phylaxis Society will continue to publish the Masonic speeches of Past Grand Master Alexander Clark and will donate the issues of the Phylaxis Magazine to be placed in this historic site, which honors this great dedicated Prince Hall Freemason.)

Grand Master Clark

MASTER'S SIGN — Cont. from page 134

Sensing me standing quietly for his approach, the figure hesitates momentarily. Are the same thoughts and sensations flickering through his mind? Then with only a single "Hello" of greeting the stranger steps up to me and extends his hand, which I hesitatingly take.

As our right hands meet, all apprehension and caution leave my mind with unexpected relief, for an ancient and honorable sign is exchanged and both of us know here is a brother: Now with no qualms each of us may with confidence turn our backs to each other, continue our separate paths and fear no evil. We know full well that a tried and true brother is within shouting distance if assistance should be needed.

The stranger who is my brother continues his way and I, with all my questions answered, my faith reaffirmed in the wisdom of The Supreme Architect of our Universe, return to the comfort of my home for rest and refreshment.

137

Welcome to New Members

Orien B. Jeans, 1824 25th Ave., Seattle, Washington 98122. Recommended by Irvin Hawkins, M.P.S.

George W. Derritt, Sr., 916-5th Avenue, Leavenworth, Kansas 66048. Recommended by Joseph A. Walkes, Jr., F.P.S.

Thomas F. Bragg, 1020 Miami, Leavenworth, Kansas 66048. Recommended by Joseph A. Walkes, Jr., F.P.S.

John Thomas Minter, 729 Metropolitan, Leavenworth, Kansas 66048. Recommended by Joseph A. Walkes, Jr., F.P.S.

Joseph Lee Hardy, 2021-B Hibiscus LN C/H APO 96334. Recommended by Herbert Dailey, M.P.S.

Henry A. Smith, 1772-17th Ave., So. Seattle, Washington 98144. Recommended by Irvin Hawkins, M.P.S.

Herman W. Richards, Co A 2/1st Inf., Ft. Lewis, Washington 98433. Recommended by Daniel Lunsford, M.P.S.

Kenneth Swanigan, 599 Union Ave., N.E. Renton, Washington 98055. Recommended by Marvin Blythers

Ralph H. Benjamin, P.O. Box 148, New York, New York 10037. Recommended by Ira S. Holder, Sr., F.P.S.

Edward Lewis, Sr., 145-57 Lakewood Ave., Jamaica, N.Y. 11435. Recommended by Ira S. Holder, Sr., F.P.S.

Bertrand W. Racker, 104-16 193rd St., Hollis, New York 11412. Recommended by Ira S. Holder, Sr., F.P.S.

James A. Davenport, 2112 Seaview Ave., W. Tacoma, Washington 98466. Recommended by Herbert Dailey, M.P.S.

Vullie Johnson, 2210 S. 15th St., Tacoma, Washington 98405. Recommended by William D. Green, M.P.S.

Billy V. Morris, West 709 Woodway Ave., Spokane, Washington 99218. Recommended by Herbert Dailey, M.P.S.

Walter C. Harris, 811 Choctans, Hartshorne, Oklahoma 74547. Recommended by William M. Freeman, M.P.S.

Daniel L. Lawray, 6520 Thurgood Circle, Jox, Florida 32209. Recommended by William M. Freeman, M.P.S.

Matthews Deloch, Jr., 5033 Cates, St. Louis, Missouri 63108. Recommended by James Walker, M.P.S.

John Raye Smith, 3601 S. W. Graham St., Seattle, Washington 98126. Recommended by William D. Green, M.P.S.

Eli J. Allen, III, RD #3 Laurel Park, Wappingers Falls, New York 12590. Recommended by Ira S. Holder, Sr., F.P.S.

Leonard R. Carey, P.O. Box 272, Box Elder, South Dakota 57719. Recommended by James E. Herndon, M.P.S.

James A. McNair, 276 Lawrence St., Uniondale, New York 11553. Recommended by Ira S. Holder, Sr., F.P.S.

David P. Thomas, 7110 Woodrow St., St. Louis, Mo. 63121. Recommended by James Walker, M.P.S.

Jack Strong, 1440 Griffin Lane, Bossier City, Louisiana 71010. Recommended by William M. Freeman, M.P.S.

Louis Roberts, 2512 B. Stila Coom Woods Dr., Stila Coom, Washington 98388. Recommended by Herbert Dailey, M.P.S.

William Gardner, 4141 39th Ave., Renton, Washington 98188. Recommended by Levi Townsent, M.P.S.

Jessie Thompson, 716 Mandana Blvd., Oakland, California 94610. Recommended by Herbert Dailey, M.P.S.

James E. Adams, 33 Washington Ave., Wyandanch, New York 11576. Recommended by Ira S. Holder, Sr., F.P.S.

Harold Stanley Banner, 1013 Kingston Drive, Cherry Hill, New Jersey 08034. Recommended by the Executive Committee

Hollies W. Jones, 2600 Niagara Street, Denver, Colorado 80207. Recommended by James E. Herndon, M.P.S.

Will Joe Davis, 13301 South Park Ave., Tacoma, Washington 98444. Recommended by Herbert Dailey

Marshall E. LaNier, Jr., 606 Highway 303, Apt. B, Grand Prairie, Tex. 75050. Recommended by I.H. Clayborn, M.P.S.

Lonnie McCoy Bright, 149E 23rd St., New York, New York 10010. Recommended by Ira S. Holder, Sr.

Freddie L. Stripling, 3680 Ivanhoe St., Denver, Colorado 80207. Recommended by James E. Herndon, M.P.S.

Lionel A. Estwick, 2395 Tiebout Avenue, Bronx, New York 10458. Recommended by Ira S. Holder, Sr., F.P.S.

Tommy R. Kennedy, 2430 Oneida Street, Denver, Colorado 80207. Recommended by James E. Herndon, M.P.S.

Donnel Kinnison, 2821 Hudson St., Denver, Colorado 80207. Recommended by James E. Herndon, M.P.S.

Harry Edwards, 2540 Leyden Street, Denver, Colorado 80207. Recommended by James E. Herndon, M.P.S.

Benjamin Newman, Sr., 6113 N. 24th St., Tacoma, Washington 98406. Recommended by Herbert Dailey, M.P.S.

A WORD FROM THE PRESIDENT
Continued from page 118

of the Prince Hall family feel about us, for it is this family, this fraternity, this Prince Hall solidarity that we are dedicated to serve, and it is only to our "peers" that we must satisfy.

So we walk with pride, and we will proclaim from the high valley's for the entire Masonic world to hear and understand, that we are Prince Hall Freemasons "for a' that and a' that!"

We proudly dedicate this issue to Prince Hall, and to all Freemasons, who carry his name, where so ever dispersed around the globe.

JOSEPH A. WALKES, JR., F.P.S.
President

NOTES, QUERIES AND INFORMATION ON ITEMS OF MASONIC RESEARCH
By The Phylaxis Society, P.O. Box 3151, Ft. Leavenworth, Ks. 66027

THIS SECTION IS PRESENTED TO OUR READERS, and relates to matters pertaining to Prince Hall Masonic history, biography and tradition.

We invite our readers and members to send such material that is appropriate for use in this column. It must be stressed that this page is for EXCHANGE of information and opinion concerning Prince Hall Masonry and does not pretend to provide the final answers to any query.

PINES FAMOUS FRONTISPIECE of Anderson's Constitutions of 1723 which appeared on page 89 of the **Phylaxis Magazine** has brought in a number of questions, which we will try to answer. The frontispiece was also used without alterations in 1738, it shows a classical arcade in the foreground of which stand two noble personage, each attended by three others of whom one of those on the left carries cloaks and pairs of gloves. The principal personages are Montagu and Wharton. Montagu is wearing the robes of the Garter, and is handing his successor a roll of the Constitution, not a book. This may be intended for Anderson's as yet unprinted manuscript, or, more likely it indicates that a version of the Old Constitution was regarded at the time as part of the Grand Master's equipment. Behind each Grand Master stand their Officers, Beal, Villeneau, and Morris on one side, and on the other Desaguliers, Timson, and Hawkins, Deseguliers as a clergyman and the other two in ordinary dress—as Grand Wardens.

DR. CHARLES H. WESLEY, "Fellow of the Phylaxis Society" is noted by Alphonse Cerza, Past President and Fellow of the Philalethes Society in the December issue of its publication, The **Philalethes Magazine** to the fact "that it is reported that Dr. Charles H. Wesley, an outstanding scholar affiliated with the Prince Hall organization, is researching the subject of Prince Hall and is planning on writing a biography based on available records and correcting the erroneous information presented years ago by Grimshaw. I have in my library a copy of Dr. Wesley's "The History of Prince Hall Grand Lodge of the State of Ohio, 1849-1960," published in 1961, and it is an outstanding book.

JOHN W. DAVIS, "Member of the Phylaxis Society" and "The Prince Hall Ambassador of Good Will", seems to be everywhere. His picture appeared recently in **JET** magazine, Jan. 15, 1976 issue, page 11, which noted that "former president of West Virginia State College, **John W. Davis**, now 83, is expected to be one of the guests at the January inauguration of Liberian President William Tolbert (a Prince Hall Mason). The first and last Black AID director to the country, Davis has been invited as a guest to every Liberian inauguration and lives in Tolbert mansion. He is given credit for developing Liberia's education system and being the father of their fishing industry."

While in the recent issue of the **Phyramid** (A.E.A.O.N.M.S., 1st Qtr., Vol. 34, Number 135), photo's of Bro. Davis, a Past Imperial Potentate receiving the Prince Hall Shrine education and humanitarian award of the year are shown. There is also a photo of Bro. Davis at the Prince Hall Shrine Archives at the Moorland-Spingarn Research Center at Howard University, Washington, D.C., where he addressed the Nobles on the significance of the depositing of the Prince Hall Shrine Archives there. There are approximately 350 Prince Hall Shrine Temples and Courts located in 39 states in the U.S.A. and overseas, with Shrine Clubs located in the Bahama Islands, Belgium, Canada, England, France and Japan.

NON-PRINCE HALL ORGANIZATIONS: In the recent issue of the respected Caucasian publication, **Royal Arch Mason** magazine, space was given concerning the William Banks organization, known as the "International Free and Accepted Modern Masons" of Detroit, Michigan, and their purchase of a local TV station.

The **Royal Arch Mason** magazine, which is edited by P.G.M. William R. Denslow, son of the famous scholar and writer P.G.M. Ray V. Denslow, author **"Regular, Ir-regular and Clandestine Lodges"** and host of important well-known books on Masonry, stated, **"Thinking first that it was of Prince Hall affiliation"**. The **Phylaxis Society** takes strong exception to this statement. Does the **Royal Arch Mason** magazine think that the Prince Hall Fraternity involves itself with such commercial enterprises as selling insurance and buying TV stations? It would the **Royal Arch Mason** magazine better if they would use the pages of their magazine for Masonic pursuits and not propaganda for the William Banks organization. And we would suggest some of our Caucasian Masonic friends that they pick up a copy of P.G.M. Denslow's book on Ir-regular and Clandestine Lodges and pick up the listing of the non-Prince Hall bodies listed.

MORE LIGHT IN MASONRY: The self-teaching audio Masonic Leadership Course, produced for the Masonic Service Association in 1974 by Imagination Unlimited is still available at a cost of $36.

You receive a durable white album containing five standard cassettes on which are recorded ten lessons, a Workbook with questions, answers, Guides for

139

Action, cartoons and practical suggestions for "growing" leaders. A certificate of completion is awarded by the Masonic Service Association to individuals who complete the self-teaching course. Write Imagination Unlimited, Box 70, Highland Springs, Virginia 23075.

PRINCE HALL MASONIC POSTAGE STAMP (seals). Sheets of 100 stamps with the likeness of Prince Hall may be purchased from the Executive Secretary, James E. Herndon, M.P.S., 1574 Ivanhoe Street, Denver, Colorado 80220. Lodge secretaries and individual brethren who may do some Masonic communicating should consider placing these seals on each of their Masonic letters in this the 201st year of the raising of Prince Hall. Cost is $2.00 per sheet.

THE MASONIC SQUARE — A magazine for Freemasons Everywhere; is a new Masonic magazine published quarterly in England. Published in mid-March, June, September and December by A. Lewis, Ltd., Terminal House, Shepperton, Middlesex TW17 8AS, England. Subscription cost is $4.00.

The Phylaxis Society has also received a catalogue from the same source with many fine Masonic books, rituals, Masonic music, Bibles, regalia and other items that is of interest to the Craft. Any of our readers interested in receiving a copy of this publication's subscription form, let us know, as the Phylaxis Society has a number of them on hand.

AN EVENING OF MASONIC MUSIC: A 12 inch stereo record, plus a 12 page booklet. Side one has The Lodge; Processional March; Opening Hymn; Lead Kindly Light (hymn); The Fellowcraft's Journey by Mozart; Die Maurerische Trauermusik by Mozart which is the Masonic Funeral Music; Closing Hymn; Hands Across the Sea (poem); The Level and the Square (Song); and side two has Brotherhood; Banquet Night by Kipling (poem); The Worshipful Master's Song; Charity (quotation); the E.A. Song, and a number of others that would be of interest to Lodges. The cost is $12, from A. Lewis Ltd., Terminal House, Shepperton, TW 17 8AS, Middlesex, England.

THE PHYLAXIS SOCIETY AND THE REPORT FROM WISCONSIN

The recent report coming from the so called "Committee on Non-Recognized Grand Lodges" of the Caucasian Grand Lodge F. & A.M. of Wisconsin, dealing with its two year study of Prince Hall Masonry and of the Most Worshipful Prince Hall Grand Lodge F. & A.M. of Wisconsin is like a breath of fresh air, though a little late. The old saying of better late than never may apply, but the Society doubts it, for a number of reasons.

This distinguished Committee headed by George R. Currie, State Supreme Court Judge recommended that the Prince Hall Grand Lodge be recognized, which is all well and good.

But the fact remains and the Phylaxis Society maintains that Prince Hall Masonry has always been as regular and legitimate a Masonic body as any that lies in these United States of America.

The Phylaxis Society can show, without a shadow of a doubt, that most, if not all Caucasian Grand Lodges in this country, has had a "cloudy" beginning, or at one time or the other was dormant. There is even one Caucasian Grand Lodge who at one time was debating with another Caucasian Grand Lodge as to which was the oldest between the two.

It is rather amusing, as the truth of the matter is one claims 1733 as its date of birth, when in reality it was not organized until 1792, and the other was began clandestinely, without any authority what so ever!

The Phylaxis Society received copies of the report directly from the Caucasian Grand Lodge of Wisconsin, and though the report had been widely distributed within Caucasian Masonic circles, the Phylaxis Society was refused permission to reprint it in the **Phylaxis Magazine.** And we wonder why?

Prince Hall Masonry has been around for 200 years, if we accept the date of the raising of Prince Hall, and for 200 years, we have proclaimed that we were a regular and legitimate Masonic body!

If this report is adopted by that Grand Lodge, it would be something to behold, and especially the reaction from its other Sister jurisdictions in view of the storm that P.G.M. Upton and the Caucasian Grand Lodge of Washington created in 1899 when they attempted also to recognize Prince Hall Masonry. It would indeed be interesting to see if our Caucasian counterparts have grown up!

MASONIC DUTY

A well-read Mason is a rare thing, much rarer than it should be. Masonic literature is available at very reasonable prices and many excellent works on the history, traditions, symbolism, jurisprudence, etc. of our Institution have seen the light in the last two decades. There are Masonic libraries, too; many a Lodge and Grand Lodge have one. But—are they doing any good? Are the books being circulated or are they catching dust and gathering mildew on some forgotten shelf or in a locked bookcase?

Every Mason should read up on Masonry and should know enough of it to prevent his having to confine himself to a few commonplaces, or making a fool of himself, when he is called upon to address the Lodge.

THE PHYLAXIS SOCIETY AND THE PRINCE HALL CONFESSION OF MASONIC FAITH

In this declaration of the principles of the **Phylaxis Society**, we call upon the words of Bro. George W. Crawford, from his book **Prince Hall and His Followers** (1914).

So far from lamenting the absolute disassociation of Negro Masonry from the white Masonry of this country, our attitude towards that fact should be that of serene indifference. Because of what it is meant to imply, and because of its usual accompaniment of degradation, the Negro people frequently find themselves compelled to oppose the separation of the races. This fact is often seized upon by detractors, both within and without the ranks, as evidence of our lack of proper racial self-esteem. More is the reason, therefore, that on those occasions when it does not hurt to be by ourselves, we ought to be conspicuous in our contentment to have it so.

THE FOLLOWERS OF PRINCE HALL ARE REGULAR MASONS. Why should they crave "recognition" from those whose Masonic divestment have left them still clothed in all the pettiness and prejudice of the profane; and to whom the word brother is a designation of a social status rather than of the universal kinship of men?

THE FOLLOWERS OF PRINCE HALL BELIEVE IN THE UNIVERSALITY OF MASONRY. Shall they feel aggrieved at being denied affiliation with those whose Masonry is of such sort that they halt the worthy candidate at the porch of the Temple to inquire if he be Aryan, or Finn or Hottentot?

THE FOLLOWERS OF PRINCE HALL ARE PROUD OF THEIR MASONRY. Shall they therefore aspire to assume Masonic offices for those who would deem it a condescension to accept the same? Or shall they desire to take their distress to those who would consider any proffered relief not the charity of a Mason but the alms of a profane?

The only recognition which Negro Masons could ever accept without self-stultification would be recognition coupled with union with them under the wide baldachin of universal Masonry, from which the white brethren have drawn themselves apart. As to recognition on any other basis - a fig!

**** CREDO ****

I BELIEVE IN GOD, GRAND ARCHITECT OF THE UNIVERSE, THE ALPHA OF THE UNRECKONED YESTERDAYS, THE OMEGA OF THE IMPENETRABLE TOMORROWS, THE BEGINNING AND THE ENDING.

I BELIEVE IN MAN, POTENTIALLY GOD'S OTHER SELF, OFTEN FALTERING ON HIS WAY UPWARD BUT IRREPRESSIBLE IN THE URGE TO SCALE THE SPIRITUAL ANNAPURNAS.

I BELIEVE IN FREEMASONRY - THAT CORPORATE ADVENTURE IN UNIVERSAL BROTHERHOOD, DESPISING KINSHIP WITH NO CHILD OF THE ALL-FATHER.

I BELIEVE IN PRINCE HALL MASONRY, A DOOR OF BENEVOLENCE, SECURELY TILED AGAINST THE UNWORTHY, BUT OPENED WIDE TO MEN OF GOOD REPORT, WHETHER ARYAN OR HOTTENTOT.

I BELIEVE IN MASONIC VOWS — THE TRUTHS OF TRUE MEN PLIGHTED IN THEIR BETTER SELVES.

The **Phylaxis Society** stands behind these words, and declares it before the entire Masonic world, where-so-ever-a-Freemason be dispatched. And to those who are the enemies of Prince Hall Freemasonry

TAKE DUE TIME AND TIMELY NOTICE, and govern yourself accordingly.

CELEBRATE BI-CENTENNIAL? YES — Cont. from page 124

If one wishes the racists and the prejudiced among us to have a completely lily white bi-centennial celebration, then, by all means, he should refuse to participate. If voices are not raised telling others what is wrong, not only in the country, but in the Masonic institution at this time, then the racists will win.

If the Prince Hall Masons refuse to lend their voices to the bi-centennial celebration whether in gratitude for the gains which have been made (and many have been made) or in protest for the restrictions which still exist, they have no one but themselves to blame for their exclusion.

If all Negroes in this country will passively stand aside as the 200th birthday of our country is celebrated, they will probably get a left handed compliment from the Ku-Klux-Klan and other such groups of white hooded morons. By keeping quiet and ignoring the celebration, they will be known as "good nigras who know their place".

I can't feature this attitude. Whether in gratitude for gains, or in protest for goals not yet attained, I believe P.H.A. Masons have a definite stake in our country and a definite place in the bi-centennial celebration.

141

PHYLAXIS PROFILE

DR. WILLIAM E. ALLEN, JR., M.P.S.

William E. Allen, Jr., M.D., St. Louis, has been selected as the first Black Radiologist in the world to receive a Gold Medal from the American College of Radiology.

Dr. Allen was honored for distinguished achievements in radiology and in the medical field when the A.C.R. held its annual meeting and convocation in New Orleans.

The late J. Frank Walker, M.D., of Atlanta, Ga., and Albert Jutras, M.D., of Amost, Quebec, Canada, also were cited for their contributions. Dr. Walker, a former president of the American College of Radiology and a former speaker of the House of Delegates of the American Medical Association, was awarded the medal posthumously.

Previous Medal recipients include Mme. Marie Curie (1931); Dr. Alber Soiland (1933), a founder of the College; Dr. Antoine Lacassagne (1963), of France; and those physicians and scientists who have been outstanding leaders in their fields of medicine.

Only 58 Gold Medals have been awarded by the College since 1927, when the first was presented to William D. Coolidge, Ph.D., a pioneer in the development of X-ray tubes and radiologic equipment.

Dr. Jutras is only the second Canadian to be singled out for this highest award by the College, which is the professional medical association for physicians who specialize in the use of X-rays and radioactive substances for diagnostic and therapeutic purposes.

Dr. Allen was elected to Fellowship in the A.C.R. in 1945. After receiving an M.D. degree from Howard University in 1930, he served his radiology residency in St. Louis at City Hospital No. 2 and Homer Philips Hospital.

Dr. Allen has been active in organized medicine on all levels. He is a member of the St. Louis Society of Radiologists and the Missouri chapter of the A.C.R., where he serves on the board of directors. He holds membership in the National Medical Association where he has served with distinction as Vice-President and as Chairman of the Council on Scientific Exhibits, the Radiological Society of North America, the Society of Nuclear Medicine, and the American Society of Therapeutic Radiologists.

He was director of the department of radiology and director of the radioisotope laboratory of Homer G. Phillips Hospital. He was also director of the department of radiology at St. Mary's Infirmary and People's Hospital. He is at present retired from these posts and is serving as radiotherapist to the St. Louis University Hospitals, consultant in radiology to the Missouri State Crippled Children's Service, associate clinical professor of radiology at St. Louis University School of Medicine, and assistant clinical professor of radiology at the Washington University School of Medicine.

In 1933, he organized one of the first approved American training schools for Black X-ray technologists at St. Mary's Infirmary.

To advance the study of radiology, he has provided scholarships for students from Haiti, Nigeria, Liberia, and South Africa. He is presently engaged in a project to install a Cobalt 60 unit for cancer management in the John F. Kennedy Memorial Hospital, Monrovia, Liberia. This unit will become the first single supervoltage therapy machine in Western Africa.

Dr. Allen's wife, Para Lee Bates, formerly of Waco, Tex., is a former head nurse at Homer Phillips Hospital.

In 1949, Dr. Allen and eight other radiologists established the section on radiology of the National Medical Association, and he served as the section's first chairman.

In the course of his long career, he has received numerous awards including the Special Silver Plaque Award of the St. Louis Branch of the N.A.A.C.P., the Distinguished Service Award of the N.M.A. and the Howard University Distinguished Alumni Award.

Dr. Allen is a member of the Most Worshipful Prince Hall Grand Lodge F & A.M. of Missouri serving in the office of Grand Medical Examiner. He is also Chairman of the newly established Grand Lodge Library Committee for that Jurisdiction. He is a member of Square Deal Lodge F. & A.M. of St. Louis, Missouri and a member of the Phylaxis Society.

THE LADY FREEMASON
How She Came to be Initiated

The initiation of the Hon. Miss Elizabeth St. Leger, afterwards the wife of Richard Aldworth, Esq., has long been a recognized fact in the history of Freemasonry in Ireland.

The Lodge Doneraile, No. 44 of Ireland (now dormant), where she was initiated, was what may be called an aristocratic, or at least a highly respected Lodge, including the elite of that very populous and delightful country around Doneraile. The Lodge meetings were generally held in the town, but sometimes under the presidency of Lord Doneraile at his residence, Doneraile House, County Cork, as in the instance about to be related.

Miss St. Leger was the youngest child and only daughter of the Rt. Honourable Arthur St. Leger, created first Viscount Doneraile, by Queen Anne, 23re June, 1703, and Elizabeth, daughter and heiress of John Hayes, Esq., of Winchelsea. His Lordship died in July, 1727, and was succeeded by his eldest son; the brother of the subject of our sketch.

Miss St. Leger had been reading at the library window, and the light of the afternoon having failed, she fell asleep. She knew that the Lodge meetings were sometimes held at the house, but she had no idea, on that evening, when she entered the library, that a meeting was about to be held in the next room. It happened on this particular occasion that the house was undergoing certain internal alterations. The Lodge was held in a large room on the ground floor, separated from another. The alterations having required the removal of some of the panelling from the larger room, a portion of this had been taken down and the bricks loosely replaced, without mortar, in the position they were ultimately to occupy. Against these loose bricks the oak panelling had been temporarily reared. The sound of voices in the next room restored her to consciousness, and from her position behind the loosely placed bricks of the dividing wall she easily realized that something unusual was taking place in the next room. The light shining through the unfilled spaces of the temporary wall also attracted her attention. Prompted by a not unnatural curiosity, Miss Leger determined to gratify her curiosity, removed one or more of the loose bricks, and thus was easily enabled to watch the proceedings of the Lodge for that night. For some time her interest in what was transpiring was sufficiently powerful to hold her spellbound, the quietness of her mind remained undisturbed for a considerable period, and it was not until she realized the solemnity of the responsibilities undertaken by the candidate that she understood the terrible consequences of her action. Becoming aware from what she heard that the Brethren were about to separate, she for the first time felt tremblingly alive to the awkwardness and danger of her situation and the wish to hide her secret by making good her escape without observation took possession of her thoughts. Her passage into the hall was easy, but it happened that the doors of the two rooms were close together. Outside in the hall the Tyler was on guard and from this point her retreat was cut off. Miss St. Leger realizing that the Tyler, Lord Doneraile's butler, well knowing the condition of the temporary wall, would at once, from her frightened appearance grasp the situation, became nervous and agitated, and, being in the dark, she stumbled and overthrew something, said to be a chair or some ornamental piece of furniture. The crash was loud and the Tyler who was in the lobby burst open the door, and with a light in one hand and a drawn sword in the other appeared to the now terrified and fainting lady. The old and trusted family servant, divided between his affection for his young mistress and the duties he owed to the Lodge, hesitated whether he should call for aid from the household or alarm the Lodge. Fearing however to leave the door of the Lodge unguarded he decided to summon his master. This of course brought Miss St. Leger's brothers into the hall.

They were soon joined by the members of the Lodge present, and, but for the prompt attitude of her brother and other promenent members, her life would have fallen a sacrifice to what was then considered a crime. The first care of his Lordship was to resuscitate the unfortunate lady without alarming the house, and endeavor to learn from her an explanation of what had occured. The young lady having been carried back into the library, and restored to consciousness, they learned what had occured. On hearing this many of the members became furious. She was placed under guard of the Tyler and another brother, in the same room in which she was found. The brothers reassembled and deliberated as to what, under the circumstances, was to be done, and for two long hours she could hear the angry discussion, and her death proposed and seconded in calming in some measure, the angry and irritated feelings of the rest of the members, and after

Cont. Next Edition

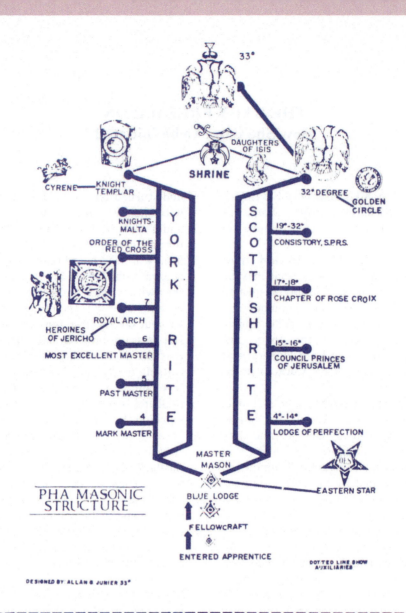

THE PHYLAXIS SOCIETY SUBSCRIPTION CARD

Subscription rate: $5.00/Yr.

Mail to: James E. Herndon, MPS
Executive Secretary
1574 Ivanhoe Street
Denver, Colo. 80220

Gentlemen:

Enclosed is my subscription the the Phylaxis Magazine.

_____ Check Enclosed _____ amount payable to Phylaxis Magazine

Name: _____

Address: _____

City: _____ State: _____ Zip Code: _____

A SOCIETY FOR PRINCE HALL FREEMASONS WHO SEEK MORE LIGHT AND WHO HAVE LIGHT TO IMPART

THE PHYLAXIS

JULY, 1976

Volume II   Number 6

A SOCIETY FOR PRINCE HALL
FREEMASONS WHO SEEK MORE
LIGHT AND WHO HAVE LIGHT TO
IMPART.

THE PHYLAXIS
Published at Boston, Mass. by
THE PHYLAXIS SOCIETY

Arthur H. Frederick, M.P.S...Editor
Box 43, Roxbury, Massachusetts 02119

OFFICERS

Joseph A. Walkes, Jr., M.P.S...President
P.O. Box 3151, Ft. Leavenworth, Kansas 66027

Herbert Dailey, M.P.S......................................First Vice President
1616 South Cedar, Tacoma, Washington 98405

Zellus Bailey, M.P.S....................................Second Vice President
7039 Dover Court, St. Louis, Missouri 63130

James E. Herndon, M.P.S..............................Executive Secretary
1574 Ivanhoe Street, Denver, Colorado 80220

Alonzo D. Foote, Sr., M.P.S...Treasurer
P.O. Box 99601, Tacoma, Washington 98499

SUBSCRIPTION RATE: FOR ONE YEAR, $5.00

The Phylaxis Magazine is the official publication of the Phylaxis Society. Any article appearing in this publication expresses only the opinion of the writer, and does not become the official pronouncement of the Phylaxis Society. No advertising of any form is solicited or accepted. All communication relative to the magazine should be addressed to the Editor. Inquiries relative to membership must be addressed to the Executive Secretary. Membership is by invitation and recommendation only. The joining fee is $3.00. Dues are $5.00 per year in advance, which amount includes a subscription to the "Phylaxis" magazine for one year.

All rights reserved. No part of this work may be reproduced or transmitted in any form or by any means, electrical or mechanical, or retrival system, without written permission from the publisher.

1976 DUES
ALL 1975 MEMBERS ARE REQUESTED TO FORWARD THEIR 1976 DUES [$5.00]

INDEX

A Word from the President	146
The Masonic Address and Writings of Ira S. Holder, Sr., F.P.S.	147
Notes, Queries and Information on Items of Masonic Research	149
Militant Master Mason	150
Executive Metting Held	154
Planning for Spiritual Growth	155
L. Sherman Brooks, Masonic Calligrapher	158
The Lady Freemason	158
Welcome New Members	159
The Origin and Objects of Ancient Freemasonry	160

146

A WORD FROM THE PRESIDENT

The **Phylaxis Society** is an international Masonic research society, with members around the globe, and in order for it to operate properly it must rely on the fraternal good will and fellowship of Freemasons, Prince Hall and "Regular," across the entire Masonic community.

The Society would like to take time out to give thanks to several of these outstanding Brethren, and also a silent thanks to those whom because of the Masonic status quo in this country, we can not acknowledge in print.

To all who wrote, praising our special March issue, which each year is dedicated to our founder, and esteem **"Master,"** Prince Hall, to whose memory this Society cherishes.

To the Most ∴ Worshipful ∴ Prince Hall Grand Lodge F. & A.M. of Washington and to Grand Master James W. Davis, M.P.S., for allowing the **Phylaxis Society** to hold our annual Executive meeting in the Grand Masonic Temple in Seattle, and allowing us to participate in its formal dance in the Grand Ballroom of the Olympic Hotel.

To Bro. Herbert Dailey, M.P.S., First Vice President, and his lovely wife, our host, while in the "Great Northwest!"

To the President and members of the **Northwest Chapter of the Phylaxis Society.**

To the Most ∴ Worshipful ∴ Prince Hall Grand Lodge of the Most Ancient and Honorable Fraternity of F. & A.M., state of New York for allowing the **Phylaxis Society** to make its "Fellow of the Society" and "Certificate of Literature" awards to Bro. Ira S. Holder, Sr., F.P.S., at its Mid-Season Grand Lodge Session at the Park Sheraton Hotel, and to Bro. Arthur H. Frederick, F.P.S., Editor of the **Phylaxis Magazine**, who made the presentation.

To Grand Master Jno G. Lewis, Jr., M.P.S. of the Most ∴ Worshipful ∴ Prince Hall Grand Lodge F. & A.M. of Louisiana and Soverign Grand Commander, SMJ, for his constant support and encouragement to the Society.

To Grand Master Charles Jenkins of the Most ∴ Worshipful ∴ Prince Hall Grand Lodge F. & A.M. of Iowa, who as a courtesy will make the presentation of **"Honorable Fellow of the Society"** to two worthy Freemasons and supporters from the Most ∴ Worshipful ∴ Grand Lodge A.F. & A.M. of Iowa.

To the Deutsches Freimaurermuseum in Bayreuth, German Federal Republic and its curator, Bro. Henrich Wilhelm Lorenz who has taken an interest in the Society.

To the Schomburg Center for Research in Black Culture, New York Public Library, West 135th Street

Continued on page 163

THE MASONIC ADDRESSES AND WRITINGS OF IRA S. HOLDER, SR., F.P.S. [NEW YORK[

THE POWER OF TOGETHERNESS

BY
IRA S. HOLDER, SR.

Thursday, October 4, 1973

W.M. William B. Armstrong,
R.W. Jessie Short, D.D.G.M.,
Grand Lodge Officers (Past and Present)
Past Masters,
Senior and Junior Wardens,
Visiting Brethren of the Craft,
Member of African Lodge 459-63,

GOOD EVENING:

In looking around, I note the presence of many new faces who were not present seven (7) years ago when I was invited to address the Lodge by P.M. William J. Davis who was then your Worshipful Master. On that occasion I prefaced my remarks with a brief bit of your Lodge's History — African 459 — 63. Therefore, in all fairness to those who were not present on that occasion, I will endeavor to highlight some of the History of this illustrious Lodge for their benefit.

I think you will agree with me that every member of all Prince Hall Masonic Lodges should know something about the History of their individual Lodge. So many times we run across members of some of our Lodges, who, strange as it may seem, know absolutely nothing of their Lodge's History. With this in mind, it becomes incumbent upon the various Masters of all Lodges to see that their Lodge's History is not only made known to its members, but is written and documented for posterity.

African Lodge 459 — 63 is not only historic by virtue of its name, which is that of our Mother Lodge of which our Patron Saint — Prince Hall was its first Worshipful Master — African Lodge 459 in Boston, Mass; it can also trace with pride since its early beginning, many capable and outstanding leaders who contributed much to the Fraternity.

The first temporary name of the organized group in Club form, was the Ionic Fraternal Club. Those present at the Club's first meeting were: Bro. Francis F. Giles, at that time a member of Widow's Son Lodge #11, Mr. A.P. Portias, J. Francis Mickens, W.R. Lee, William Odell, Cornelius Moore and Samuel W. Green. The meeting was presided over by R.W. Walter A. Marable the D.D. Grand Master of that time.

The group was Dispensated as a Lodge on November 19, 1921. Warranted July 21, 1922 at Ionic Temple, 165 Cleremont Ave., Brooklyn, N.Y.

Truly the many accomplishments of this distinguished Lodge just didn't happen; they were achieved through the diligent planning and constructive foresight of its Worshipful Masters, whose responsibility it was and still is to this day. Down through the years this Lodge has served the Fraternity with distinction, producing 1 Grand Master, M.W. Francis F. Giles, a Deputy Grand Master and many others to this day, including R.W. William J. Davis, Past D.D. Grand Master and R.W. Jesse Short presently serving in the same capacity. I could go on and on elaborating on the accomplishments of this Lodge, time however will not permit me to do so.

The topic I have chosen for this occasion is: THE POWER OF TOGETHERNESS.

While doing research, preparatory to writing the History of my Lodge — Widow's Son #11, my interest was aroused by reading in one of the old Minute Books, of the constant visitation (at every stated Communication of our Lodge) by members of one of our sister Lodges here in Brooklyn during the year 1900. (73 years ago.)

I bring you this bit of historic information for two reasons:
1. To give you an insight of Masonry in action during that early period, when the attendance at Masonic Communications was a regular function, eagerly looked forward to with great anticipation; when Masons travelled long distances to fellowship and fraternize with their Brothers.
2. To point out to those who are responsible for writing the minutes of the Lodge, the importance of writing all of the transactions as they occur. Remember.....you are recording History, and as such, all details must be clearly stated for posterity.

"THE POWER OF TOGETHERNESS"

Many of the customs as practiced in Freemasonry today can be traced back to the medieval period of the 11th to the 13th centuries when Operative Masons

147

plied their trade, by travelling all over Europe, building great cathedrals and magnificent gothic structures. They protected themselves and their craft from intruders and outsiders by uniting into guilds or what we would term today unions or fraternities.

Before the Operative Mason could work as a "Master of the Craft" or master workman, he had to serve an apprenticeship for seven (7) long years, doing many menial jobs and being subservient to all other Master Workmen with whom he came in contact. At the exiration of his apprenticeship, he had to prove himself, by doing some piece of intricate work requiring all of the knowledge and skill taught him during those seven (7) long and trying years. This piece had to meet all of the specifications of the exacting Master Workman. Then, and only then, was he deemed eligible to be termed "A Master of the Craft," with the freedom to travel to foreign countries pursuing his trade.

The Operative Mason was the first to show the world and exemplify "THE POWER OF TOGETHERNESS" or unity by banning themselves together into guilds for their own protection and strength.

With the amalgamation of four (4) Lodges to form the Premier Grand Lodge of England in the year 1717, M.W. Antony Sayer was elected as the first Grand Master of a Grand Lodge, under whose guidance and leadership came the standardization of Freemasonry throughout the civilized world. This achievement came about after much thought, careful planning and most of all by Masons working together as a team, for the ultimate good of all.

This was the second great instance of "THE POWER OF TOGETHERNESS" in action.

In my opening remarks, I mentioned the visitation of eight (8) members of one of our sister Lodges whose constant attendance at the regular monthly Communication of Widow's Son Lodge #11, in the year 1900 is a matter of record. We must commend them highly for this fine exemplification of "THE POWER OF TOGETHERNESS" and Brotherly Love, by travelling together in unison to visit a sister Lodge, to share and enjoy the fellowship of each other. Remember....The right of every Mason to visit and sit in every Lodge is an inherent right. It is the 14th of Albert Mackey's twenty one (21) "LANDMARKS."

This is the third (3rd) instance of "THE POWER OF TOGETHERNESS" in action.

How can we forget that memorable day — August 28, 1963, when thousands upon thousands of Civic Leaders and dedicated individuals journeyed to Washington, D.C. by every conceivable means of transportation possible, to take part in that epoc making and historic "FREEDOM MARCH", the like of which has never been seen before nor since. Never before in the history of our civilization has one man influenced, impressed and inspried so many individuals to follow his call for a general assembly of persons dedicated to the cause Freedom fro enslavement, and to show the world the power of Civ Disobedience through Non-violence.

For those who journeyed to Washington, it was day, long to be remembered. A day when they literal "WENT TO THE MOUNTAIN TOP AND VIEWE THE PROMISE LAND." A day when they heard th man of the hour — Dr. Martin Luther King's no famous message to his people — "I HAVE DREAM." Never before had a black man evoked suc enthusiasm and promise through his oratory as on th occasion. Truly it can be said, all persons of color an the world at large has lost the greatest mobilizin influence in our time; surely his good deeds will follo him.

This, my Brothers, is the fourth (4th) instance which "THE POWER OF TOGETHERNESS" wa really in evidence. We are proud of the fact that Prin Hall Masons were active participants in what ha become the most history making event of all time

In view of all that has been said and shown of "TH POWER OF TOGETHERNESS," one is prone to asl Where is the spirit of "TOGETHERNESS" Freemasonry that was so evident among the membe of the Craft seventy three (73) years ago? Where that dedication to the principles of Freemasonry tha was always manifested by Masons, showing the concern for each other? Where is that love and trus for each other that is definitely an important part Freemasonry? Where is that active participation the affairs of the Lodge, without which no Master program can be a success? I am afraid that spirit concern for each other is no longer in evidence, it woefully lacking in our daily contacts with each othe Something is definitely wrong. We have strayed fro the old paths, both as individuals and as a Lodge. Wh is it that no sooner a newly made Brother is Raised, w seldom if ever see anything of him? He seldom if eve attends the Regular Communication of his Lodge, an in fact, he rarely participates in its program activities. The answer is — he did not see in us, Masons, what he was looking for and expected to fin — an unfolding of the true spirit of Brotherhood an concern for each other.

Brothers, let us seek the old paths of those eight (8 members previously referred to, manefested so nobel in the year 1900. Let us examine ourselves anew, th fault definitely lies with us; as Masons we have not ye learned and put into practice "THE POWER O TOGETHERNESS." We have allowed ourselves t become stumbling blocks in the way of other hindering their progress by allowing petty jealousie bickerings, envy, and the formation of cliques an many other forms of non-Masonic conduct to mar ou character and hinder the progress of our Lodge. W have allowed ourselves to become so obsessed wit

Continued on page 15

148

NOTES, QUERIES AND INFORMATION OF ITEMS OF MASONIC INTEREST
By The Phylaxis Society, P.O. Box 3151, Ft. Leavenworth, Ks. 66027

THIS SECTION IS PRESENTED TO OUR READERS, and relates to matters pertaining to Prince Hall Masonic history, biography and tradition.

We invite our readers and members to send such material that is appropriate for use in this column. It must be stressed that this page is for EXCHANGE of information and opinions concerning Prince Hall Masonry and does not pretend to provide the final answers to any query.

DR. WILLIAM E. ALLEN, JR., M.P.S. The Phylaxis Profile for our March issue (page 142) Masonic history was overlooked. He was initiated into John F. Cook Lodge #10 F & A.M., Washington, D.C. May 26, 1926, over forty years a Shriner, over twenty years a 33rd, and a Past Master of Square Deal Lodge #159 F & A.M. of the Missouri Jurisdiction.

PRINCE HALL MASONIC POSTAGE STAMP. In our December issue, we gave the impression that the photograph appearing on page 112, was an actual postage stamp. They are not. They are "**seals**" which was developed by the Prince Hall Grand Lodge of Maryland and the Grand Lodges of Texas, Louisiana and Mississippi.

ALPHONSE CERZA, Past President of the Philalethes Society sent us news of interest, that on March 7th, 1976 on Chicago TV Station WGN, on the program known as Issues Unlimited, Prince Hall Grand Master James Black appeared and explained about the Prince Hall organization. It was a panel type program and the Grand Master was asked questions by those on the panel. He made a fine impression and answered all questions fairly and completely. Some were a bit ticklish such as those about the penalties but he did a fine job even with these. He is to be congratulated on his fine public relations effort.

PHILLY STREET NAMED FOR PRINCE HALL MASON: A section of Sixth Street in Philadelphia from Vine Street to Washington Avenue was recently renamed Richard Allen Avenue in honor of the founder of the African Methodist Episcopal Church. Bro. Allen together with Absolom Jones, the first ordained Black Episcopal priest in America and the first Master of the African Lodge of Pennsylvania approx. 1797, and later first Grand Master, founded Prince Hall Masonry in the State of Pennsylvania. An interesting book "**Richard Allen — Apostle of Freedom**" by our Charles H. Wesley, F.P.S. (Washington, D.C., The Associated Publishers, Inc. 1935 & 1969) recalls the life and times of this historic Prince Hall Mason.

THE UNITED SUPREME COUNCIL 33°, Ancient & Accepted Rite of Freemasonry, Southern Jurisdiction, U.S.A., Prince Hall Affiliation will meet in Washington, D.C. beginning October 30th through November 2nd, 1976.

THE SCHOMBURG CENTER FOR RESEARCH IN BLACK CULTURE: Which houses not only the collection of Bro. Arthur Schomburg, who was Grand Secretary of the Prince Hall Grand Lodge of New York, but also the world's largest collection on Prince Hall Masonry, the Harry A. Williamson Masonic collection, at the 135th Street Branch of the New York Public Library, according to the April 8th issue of **JET** magazine is having financial problems, and Ruth (Mrs. Ralph) Bunch, the widow of Black America's greatest diplomat, co-chairs an effort to raise funds to save it. Many of the material that appears within the pages of the **Phylaxis Magazine** has often come from this library. It is hoped that all of the members of the Society and all of Prince Hall Masonry will support the effort to raise funds for this shrine to Prince Hall Masonry.

TRANSACTIONS OF THE PHYLAXIS SOCIETY: Copies of the Transactions of the Phylaxis Society can be purchased from Bro. Herbert Dailey, M.P.S., 1st Vice President, 1616 South Cedar, Tacoma, Washington 98405 for $2.00. It includes the History of Phylaxis Society; John Pine — Noted Masonic Engraver was Black by Keith Arrington; Caucasian Prince Hall Lodge by Joseph A. Walkes, F.P.S.; and the Iowa Masonic Library by Jerry Marsengill. Each of these articles appeared in earlier issues of the Phylaxis Magazine.

DR. JOHN W. DAVIS, M.P.S. The Prince Hall Ambassador of Good Will requested the names of Prince Hall Masonic Brethren who during the last 200 years have added significantly to Prince Hall Freemasonry. The names submitted by the Phylaxis Society were: Prince Hall; John Morant; Prince Saunders; Richard Allen; Absolom Jones; James Forten; Dr. Martin R. Delany; Lewis Hayden; John T. Hilton; Richard H. Gleaves; Thomas Stringer; Paul Drayton; Arthur Schomburg; Harry Albro Williamson; Harry E. Davis; Samuel W. Clark; Justin Holland; William H. Parham and Jeremiah A. Brown; Dr. Charles H. Wesley; Aldrage B. Cooper; George W. Crawford; Peter W. Ray; Moses Dickson; Alexander Clark, Sr.; Hiram Rhoades Revels; James Milton Turner; Oscar J. Dunn; Oscar De Priest; John Wesley Dobbs; John G. Lewis, Sr.; and Amos T. Hall. Can you identify these historic Prince Hall Masons?

BACK COVER OF THIS ISSUE: Was done by L. Sherman Brooks, a member of the Philalethes Society. His address is Rural Box 321, R.F.D. (Rt. 380), Jamestown, New York 14701. Bro. Brooks is presently doing the Prince Hall Credo for the Phylaxis Society.

Cont. on Page 153

MARTIN R. DELANY MILITANT MASTER MASON

BY

JOSEPH A. WALKES, JR., F.P.S. [KANSAS]

"I rise, your Royal Highness, to thank his lordship, the unflinching friend of the negro, for the remarks he has made in reference to myself, and to assure your royal highness and his lordship that **I AM A MAN!**"

Remarks of Martin R. Delany upon being introduced to His Royal Highness Lord Brougham at the International Statistical Congress, London, July 1860.

When one attempts to write a article about Martin Robinson Delany, the writer must approach this subject with caution and discreet, with awe and appall, with irony and contradiction.

Martin R. Delany was a goliath among men, a man who lived so many different experiences, that it is often difficult to separate the several phases of this extraordinary, incredible Prince Hall Mason, who was a man of contradictions, ambitions, inconsistency, pessimism, sensibility, irony and greatness.

Born in Charlestown, Virginia in 1812, the son of free Negroes, Samuel and Pati Delany. His paternal grandfather was a prince of the Mandingo tribe who had been captured in the Niger Valley, sold in slavery, and subsequently brought to America. He received something of an education in Pennsylvania, became active in social and educational projects in the Pittsburg area, studied medicine but settled into dentistry, traveled in the south, started a newspaper, **The Mystery** in Pittsburg, and was associated with Frederick Douglass in bringing out the famed newspaper **The North Star**, of whom Douglass said, "I thank God for making me a man simply; but Delany always thanks Him for making him a Black Man!"[1] Returned to the study of medicine, became involved in an emigration scheme in Central America, put his ideas into print in **"The Condition, Elevation, Emigration, and Destiny of the Colored People of the United States Politically Considered"** (Philadelphia 1852) all by the time he was forty,[2] and though these many activities would seem to paint a picture of this extraordinary individual, in reality it barely touches the surface of the complexity and make-up of this Mason of contradictions.

Delany became a fiery spokesman for Black manhood in the years before, during, and after the Civil War. This short, stocky, Black militant attended Harvard Medical School until prejudice forced him out. His hatred of racism led him to consider the use of force and Negro resettlement in Africa as solutions to the problems of slavery and discrimination.

He awoke every morning, thankful, he said, that God had made him a Black Man, and he advocated violence to halt slave catchers, and in his 1852 history of Black Americans he insisted, "We must make an issue, create an event, and establish a national position for ourselves."[3]

He not only proposed a Black exodus to Africa, but in 1860 explored the continent for a suitable site.[4]

Major Martin R. Delany, Past Master, Past District Deputy Grand Master.

150

Delany is recorded in American military history as the first Black Major in the United States Army, appointed to this rank directly from civilian life by President Lincoln, who called Delany a "most extraordinary and intelligent Black man." [5]

Delany had eleven children, seven having lived. In keeping with his personality, he named his offsprings after Black heroes. The eldest, he named Toussaint L'Ouverture, after the first military hero and liberator of Haiti, who drove the powerful armies of Napoleon into the sea; the second Charles Lennox Remond, after the Black abolitionist and fellow Prince Hall Mason, who with Delany recruited for the 54th Massachusetts Infantry, the first Black regiment from a Northern State during the Civil War with the added distinction of having the first Prince Hall Military Lodge attached to it, the third, Alexander Dumas, from the brilliant author of **The Three Musketeers** and **The Count of Monte-Cristo**, the fourth, Saint Cyprian from one of the greatest of the primitive Bishops of the Christian Church and the name of his Masonic Lodge, the fifth, Faustin Soulouque, after the late Emperor of Haiti, the sixth, Rameses Placido, from the good King of Egypt, "The ever-living Rameses II," and the poet and martyr of freedom to his race on the Island of Cuba, the seventh, the daughter Ethiopia Halle Amelia, the country of his race, to which is given the unequalled promise that "she should soon stretch forth her hands unto God." [7]

In 1850, the Federal Fugitive Slave Law was signed into law. It allowed any claimants of a runaway slave to take possession of a Black upon establishing proof of ownership before a Federal Commissioner. No safeguards, such as a jury trial or judicial hearing for the captive, were included. The act provided fines of $1,000 and imprisonment for six months of citizens or officials who failed to aid in the capture of fugitives. Southerners thought that this tough measure would be sufficient to halt the escape of their slaves.

Grand Master Lewis Hayden of the Prince Hall Grand Lodge of Massachusetts, who had escaped slavery himself and hid many fugitives in his house, placed two kegs of explosives in his cellar and announced he would blow up his house, rather than let slave catchers enter. [8]

While in Kentucky, Reverend Bird Parker, pastor of Quinn Chapel A.M.E. Church, Jessie Merriweather and others met to organize a Prince Hall Lodge in Louisville. Because of the climate made possible by the Fugitive Slave Act, the members decided to establish their lodge over the river in New Albany, Indiana for safety sake. Crossing the Ohio River, in skiffs at midnight, sometimes amid high waters and heavy drifts, at the risk of their lives, and then walking five miles to the city to attend lodge. [9]

Bro. Delany responded to this atrocious law in a speech at Alleghany City, Pennsylvania, in which he proclaimed:

"Honorable mayor, whatever ideas of liberty I may have, have been received from reading the lives of your revolutionary fathers. I have therein learned that a man has a right to defend his castle with his life, even unto taking of life. Sir, my house is my castle; in that **castle are none but my wife and my children**, as free as the angels of heaven, and whose liberty is as sacred as the pillars of God. If any man approaches that house in search of a slave, I care not who he may be, whether constable or sheriff, magistrate or even judge of the Supreme Court — nay, let it be he who sanctioned this act to become a law, surrounded by his cabinet as his body guard, with the Declaration of Independence waving above his head as his banner, and the constitution of his country upon his breasts as his shield, — if he crosses the threshold of my door, and I do not lay him a lifeless corpse at my feet, I hope the grave may refuse my body a resting place, and righteous Heaven my spirit a home. O, No! He cannot enter that house and we both live." [10]

Of the Masonic life of Bro. Delany there is only brief glimpses recorded in all too brief snatches in printed masonic historical books, phamplets, papers and proceedings of various Prince Hall Grand Lodges.

Of his early Masonic beginnings we are indebted to his son, himself a Prince Hall Mason, Alexander Dumas Delany, who reprinted his father's famous Treatise in 1904, [11] and recorded in the biographical sketch that "early in mature life he joined the masonic fraternity, taking thirty degrees in his home Lodge in Pittsburg and the "three side degrees" in London, England [12] a few years subsequent to the publication of this book (Treatise) (My Italics) which shows the recognition of our order in foreign lands."

Masonically, Bro. Delany is better known for his Treatise, **The Origin and Objects of Ancient Freemasonry, Its Introduction into the United States and Legitimacy Among Colored Man,** which he delivered before St. Cyprian Lodge No. 13, June 24th, 1853 in Pittsburg, and is the earliest printed work on Prince Hall Masonry.

Silas H. Shepherd in his **"Notes on the Literature dealing with Prince Hall Masonry,"** wrote of Delany's work that "The first part of his treatise shows that he followed the traditions of such writers as Anderson, Preston and Oliver, in addition to bringing in traditions of Africa, with which he has something in common with Albert Churchward's **"Signs and Symbols of Primordial Man,"** in that he credits Africa with being the place where Freemasonry originated."

151

"The main feature of the treatise is, however, to show the legitimate origin of Freemasonry among colored men and the subject is handled with skill and ability."

"Robert F. Gould warns against reading books that are inclined to stress tradition and treat the traditions as history; but if we can read theories that are far short of historical accuracy to get former conceptions with some degree of satisfaction, it should not be dangerous to read the theories of this talented colored Mason on Moses deriving his wisdom from the Ethiopians. The Mason who has the opportunity to read this treatise will find keen enjoyment and many profitable suggestions, for it is written in true Masonic spirit.[13]

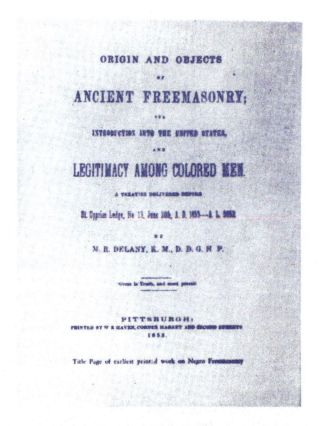

Title page of Delany's Treatise

Another brief reference is provided by Charles H. Wesley's well known **"History of the Prince Hall Grand Lodge of Ohio,"** in that Bro. Delany, then Master of St. Cyprian Lodge in 1847 played a significant role in initiating seven Masons from Cincinnati, who later were chartered as Corinthian Lodge No. 17 by the Grand Lodge of Pennsylvania, which became the corner stone of the "Mother of Masonic Lodges", the Prince Hall Grand Lodge of Ohio, as Corinthian Lodge No. 1.[15]

It is also known that Bro. Delany was appointed District Deputy of the Western District at the organization of the National Grand Lodge (or National Compact) in 1847.[16]

Little else is known of the active participation in Masonry of Bro. Delany, other than the fact that twenty seven years later at the Semi-Annual Communication of the Prince Hall Grand Lodge of Pennsylvania, June 24, 1874 it is sadly recorded that "The Committee on Appeals reported that in the case of Bro. Martin R. Delany that had inquired and received a letter from St. Cyprian Lodge No. 13, stating that he had been suspended for non-payment of dues some 14 years back. That he had been written to with no response on his part."

"Further, that before leaving Pittsburg, over fifteen years since he borrowed $50.00 from the Lodge, which he never repaid."

"That, not withstanding, had the Brother applied for reinstatement, they, no doubt, would have done so."

"The committee therefore report that from the evidence of the records he is a suspended member."

"On motion, it was:

Resolved, that the Report of the Committee be approved."

"Moved that the appeal of M. R. Delany be returned to him with our disapproval. Moved that the statement just read from the W. Master of St. Cyprian Lodge No. 13 be forwarded to the M.W. National Grand Master, with the request that it may be read in the Grand Lodge of South Carolina. Carried!"[17]

This writer is not certain if this was the end of his brilliant active Masonic life, further inquiry would have to be made, but of Bro. Delany it must be said that he served Prince Hall Masonry, the Craft and his people well.

REFERENCES

1. Peter M. Bergman, **The Chronological History of the Negro in America** (New York, Evanston and London, Harpers & Row. Publishers, 1969) P. 97.
2. Frank A. Rollins, **Life and Public Services of Martin R. Delany** (New York, Armo Press and the New York Times, 1969) P. ii.
3. William Loren Katz, **Eyewitness: The Negro in American History** (New York, Toronto, London, Pitman Publishing Corporation, 1967) P. 142-143.
4. Martin R. Delany and Robert Campbell, **Search For A Place, Black Separatism and Africa, 1860,** (The University of Michigan, Ann Arbor Paper-back, 1971.) It is interesting to note that while in the Republic of Liberia Bro. Delany was in the company of Past President Joseph J. Roberts, Charles B. Dunbar, both who would serve as Grand Masters of this African Prince Hall Lodge. President Roberts serving three years and Dunbar two.
5. Rollins, op cit, P. 171.
6. Joseph A. Walkes, Jr., **Prince Hall Masonry in the Civil War,** "Phylaxis Magazine" Vol. 1, Number 3, P. 29; Vol. II, Number 1, P. 47 and Vol. II, Number 3, P. 79.
7. Rollins, op cit, P.29.
8. Katz, op cit, P. 189.
9. **Prince Hall Masonic Yearbook,** 1968, (Published under the auspices of the Grand Master's Conference of Prince Hall Masons of America.) P. 91

152

10. Rollins, **op cit**, P. 76.
11. Martin R. Delany. **The Origin and Objects of Ancient Freemasonry; its Introduction into the United States and Legitimacy among Colored Men** — A Treatisie Delivered Before St. Cyprian Lodge No. 13, June 24th, A.D. 1853 A.L. 5853 (Pittsburg, W. S. Haven, Corner Market and Second Streets, 1853) (Re-published by A. D. Delany, Xenia, Ohio, 1904).
12. While in England, Bro. Delany was associated with Henry Peter Brougham (Lord Brougham and Vaux called by Delany, the unflinching friend of the Negro) (1778-1868) Lord High Chancellor of England from 1830. B. Sept. 19, 1778 at Edinburgh, Scotland. With Sydney Smith and Jeffrey, founded the **Edinburg Review** in 1802. Practiced at the English bar in 1808 and member of parliament in 1810. He carried the measure making slave trade a felony and defended Queen Caroline as her attorney general in trial (1820). He was a founder of London Univ. in 1828 and by a famous speech in 1831 helped pass the Reform Bill. He was the original "learned friend" in Peacock's **Crochet Castle**. The brougham (carriage) is named for him. He was initiated, passed and raised in Fortrose Lodge, Stornoway, Scotland on Aug. 20, 21, 1799 and on June 24, 1800 affiliated with Canongate Kilwinning Lodge in Edinburgh. D. May 7, 1868. William R. Denslow, **10,000 Famous Freemasons** (Missouri; Lodge of Research, 1957) P. 136.
    Bro. Delany very well may have received his "three side degrees" while attending the Congress of the National Association for the Promotion of Social Science at Glasgow, Scotland, in September 1860.
13. Silas H. Shepherd, **An Invaluable Bibliography** (The National Trestle Board, March 1922) P. 29. Brother Shepherd was Chairman on Masonic Research of the Caucasian Grand Lodge of Wisconsin.
14. Charles H. Wesley, **The History of the Prince Hall** Grand Lodge of the State of Ohio 1849 — 1960 — An Epoch In American Fraternalism (Wilberforce, Ohio, Central State College Press, 1961) P. 57 SEE NOTE:
15. **Ibid**, P. 31.
16. Harry E. Davis, **A History of Freemasonry Among Negroes in America** (United Supreme Council, A.A.S.R. Northern Jurisdiction, U.S.A. (Prince Hall Affiliation) Inc., 1946) P. 272.
17. Proceedings of the Most Worshipful Prince Hall Grand Lodge F. & A.M. of Pennsylvania, 1874. P. 96.
    NOTE: In a letter dated July 18, 1963, written by Harold V. B. Voorhis, author of **Negro Masonry in the United States** (1940), then a advocate of the regularity of Prince Hall Masonry, having twenty three years later made a complete about face, became quite anti-Prince Hall, the letter, addressed to Jerry Marsengill, author of **Negro Masonry in Iowa**, who at the time was collecting data for his book wrote "... if you are going to try and show the derivation of the Ohio Grand Lodge... you have a problem! This rather pointed observation by Voorhis is in conflict with the official history as written by Bro. Wesley. Voorhis, at one time a careful masonic researcher, historian and writer, in his attempt to discredit Prince Hall Masonry, made the same mistakes that most Caucasian Masonic historians make in researching the Black experience. As a Caucasian they simply have no knowledge of this Black experience, and not having any personal experience with the Black community, can not understand that Blacks for the most part did not leave the kind of records which allow a traditional historical approach to research. This is not to necessarily condemn the writings of all Caucasians who have attempted to scientifically inquire into the Masonic history of the Black man, but for the large part most can be dismissed, because of their lack of not fully understanding the race. There research can not be complete without exploring the full range of the Black experience.
    This is why most Caucasians can not understand that **"The History of the Black Man in the United States is the History of Prince Hall Masonry!"**

NOTES, QUERIES AND INFORMATION ON ITEMS OF MASONIC INTEREST
Cont. from Page 149

ASA B. SAMPSON, JR., M.P.S. of Minneapolis writes that he came across an interesting book. "**Middle Class Blacks in a White Society — Prince Hall Freemasonry in America**" by William Alan Murashin (University of Calif. Press, Berkley, Los Angles, Calif.) We have not seen it, but we are very interested.

PRINCE HALL MASONIC YEARBOOK: The long awaited Prince Hall Masonic Yearbook which lists all of the Prince Hall Masonic Lodges around the globe is finally off the press. Copies can be received from Thomas G. Waldon, P.G.M., Executive Secretary-Treas., 2322 Tippecanoe, Terre Haute, Indiana 47807. Copies of the year book is $2.00. Copies of the **Prince Hall Counsellor** can also be received from the Executive Secretary-Treasurer of the Conference of Grand Masters Prince Hall Masons of America.

PRINCE HALL 1735-1807, Life and Legacy in the Era of the American Revolution. A Bicentennial Study, by Charles H. Wesley, M.P.S. is being published by the Afro-American Historical and Cultural Museum. 1316 Arch Street, Suite 900, Philadelphia, Pa. 19107. Contents:

   Preface
I The True Prince Hall
II In the War Years
III The Approaches to British Masonry
IV Antislavery and Education
V Prince Hall in the Community
VI The First Master of African Lodge
VII Motivation and Expansion
VIII The Heritage of Prince Hall
IX They Faced Segregation in their Brotherhood
X Epilogue
   Appendices
   Bibliography
   Index

WE FORGOT TO ADD THE BY-LINE

On page 143 of the March issue of the Phylaxis magazine, we failed to give the proper By-Line for the article — The Lady Freemason — How She Came To Be Initiated, which was writted by Bro. Arthur H. Frederick, M.P.S. [Mass.]. We are sorry for this omission. This fine article is continued in this issue.

153

EXECUTIVE MEETING HELD HERNDON NAMED "FELLOW"; MARSENGILL, ARRINGTON HONORED

Members of the Executive Committee of the **Phylaxis Society** held their annual meeting in the **"Great Northwest"** of Seattle, at the Grand Masonic Temple of the Most Worshipful Prince Hall Grand Lodge F & A.M. of Washington.

Host of the yearly event, was Bro. Herbert Dailey, M.P.S., First Vice President and the Northwest Chapter of the Phylaxis Society.

All aspects of the Society was reviewed with the President giving the annual State of the Society review, and all officers giving their yearly report.

TRANSACTIONS

Bro. Herbert Dailey, presented courtesy copies of the first issue of the long awaited Transactions of the Phylaxis Society, which was begun as a trial project, and enthusiasticly received by those in attendance. It is hoped that it will be greatly expanded in the future, and become a worthy program of the Society.

AWARDS

James E. Herndon, M.P.S., Executive Secretary was named a "Fellow of the Society". He is a member of Centennill Lodge #4 in Denver, Colorado, where he was recently honored as Master Mason of the Year.

Jerry Marsengill, a well known Masonic writer and Bro. Keith Arrington, Assistant Librarian of the Iowa Masonic Library, both members of the Grand Lodge of Iowa A.F. & A.M. were named as "Honorary Fellows of the Phylaxis Society."

Highlights of the meeting was a trip to Cassia Lodge #5 of Tacoma, Washington, and tours of Fort Lewis, a military base that brought back many memories, and of Seattle.

The next meeting of the Phylaxis Society will be held in historic Leavenworth, Kansas, headquarters of the Society.

THE POWER OF TOGETHERNESS
Cont. from Page 148

this form of conduct that it has become a part of us. It has also attracted the attention of others, and is stifling the very existence and weakening the foundation of our Lodge and the Fraternity as a whole.

My Brothers, I am asking each and every one here assembled to re-examine themselves once again, to see if in any way, as individuals or collectively, we are responsible for impeding the progress of our Lodge by engaging in any form of conduct un-becoming to members of our Fraternity. Let us, like the disciples of old, begin by saying: Lord, is it I? We can and must improve the image of Freemasonry by endeavoring to make full use of "THE POWER OF TOGETHERNESS" for the good of our Lodge and the Fraternity at Large.

In closing, allow me the pleasure of sharing the following poem with you, entitled:

Keith Arrington

Jerry Marsengill

"THE REAL MASON"

My Brother, Masonry means more than just to wear a pin
Or carry a Dues Card so the Lodge will let you in.

You wear an emblem on your coat, and on your hand a ring,
But if you're not sincere at heart that doesn't mean a thing.

It's just an outward sign to show the world that you belong
To this Fraternal Brotherhood, that teaches Right from Wrong.

What really counts lies buried deep within the human breast;
Masonic Teachings brings it out and puts it to the test.

If you can do outside the Lodge the things you learn within;
Be just and upright to yourself, and your fellowmen.

Console a Brother when he's sick, or help him when in need,
Without a thought of reward for any act or deed.

Conduct yourself in such a way the world without can see,
None but the best can meet the test laid down by Masonry.

Respect and live up to your trust, and do the best you can.
Then, then you can tell the world you are a Mason and a Man.

Thank You.

IRA S. HOLDER, SR.

PLANNING FOR SPIRITUAL GROWTH

Copyright, 1974, by the Masonic Service Association of the United States. Reprinted by special permission.

This is the keynote address given by the Executive Secretary of the Masonic Service Association, M.W. Brother Conrad Hahn, at a Warden's Seminar held at the time of the 148th Annual Communication of the Grand Lodge of Michigan in Detroit on May 29, 1974.

The word "spiritual" in the title was chosen because I want to impress upon your minds that **Freemasonry is nothing** if it is not concerned with spiritual values, the moral and spiritual growth of individuals, and thereby, the spiritual impact it makes, or **should** make, on the community in which it exists.

When we talk about **planning**, we must, of course, become involved in some very practical matters of organizing, recruiting, selecting and establishing goals, handling people, choosing materials, providing financial resources, etc.

But over all, there must be a dominant purpose and philosophy at which all planning is aimed. In Masonry that guiding principle is a spiritual one: "to make good men better in the Brotherhood of Man under the Fatherhood of God";—express it how you will.

So, Brother Wardens, in all the planning for your Lodge's activities next year, remember this guiding principle: "Masonry is a spiritual force, and everything the Lodge may do, should enrich the spiritual experiences of its members, their family and their friends."

One of the first questions a Warden approaching the East should ask himself is: "How well do I know my Lodge, i.e., the members of the Lodge?" Not only the active members (usually too few), but all of them, the inactive, the non-resident as well as the local residents.

Lucky is the Warden approaching the East whose Lodge maintains a card catalog of its individual members. These cards are prepared at the time a man joins the lodge, such as his full name, date of birth, residence, family, dates he received the degrees, and subsequently, any offices he may hold or committees he may serve on.

In addition, such information as his job or profession, his educational achievement, his church affiliation (active or passive?), his memberships in other social, community, or professional groups, the hobbies he enjoys—all can be meaningful knowledge for the officers who want to know their members. To be effective leaders, they must know the human material from which they choose the workers in their quarry.

Making progress is the Lodge which, lacking such valuable storehouse of biographical information, undertakes the job of compiling such a catalog.

Some of you are already saying to yourselves, "Good Lord, no! I can hear our Secretary growling, 'Impossible! I've got more than enough to do already!'"

I'm inclined to agree with your Brother Secretary. Making such a catalog is **not** one of his official responsibilities. Let it be done by a special membership committee. One reason why Masonry has attendance problems is that we don't enlist enough members to do some service for the Lodge. When all they can do is sit on the side-lines to watch the degree work, they soon get bored by the repetition and stay away from the lodge. Such a membership committee, I believe, could keep three or four Brothers performing a valuable service for the Lodge, and **if** intelligently selected, properly instructed, **praised** and **appreciated** (note the spiritual techniques suggested here), would increase the number of real builders in the lodge.

I can also hear someone saying, "That's an awful lot of work; no one's going to take on such a load." Of course it requires some real labors; but I don't believe **no one** will do it. This is where the effective leader will use the spirit of Masonry to secure the workers he needs, if he himself is convinced of the usefulness of the project.

If he will choose a man to head the committee, who has had some clerical experience, one who had done record keeping, or who has an interest in research activities, I believe he can make a willing worker by emphasizing the importance of such work for the lodge's future, as well as for the present officers, by appealing to his pride in doing volunteer work, by treating him always with the real spirit of Masonry, i.e., appreciation and praise—without any expression of disappointment, disapproval or blame, should he be reluctant, or stubborn in his willingness to serve. A Brother always deserves your affectionate respect for what he is.

What has been said so far, about one project for improving the Lodge's resources, is obviously applicable to any activity which you may plan for your year in the East, be it an educational program, a ritual rendition, a table lodge, a family night, a celebration, —yes, even a business meeting.

Now, a few words about ritual exemplifications. Masonry, without its ritual, would no longer be Masonry and would quickly wither and die. It's the ritual that holds men to Masonry, whether they are active or inactive.

Some years ago, when I was principal of a country day school in Connecticut, I became aware that many of the fathers who sent their children to the school were Masons, but most of them **never** attended lodge.

I made a quiet verbal survey of their attitude to Masonry by asking the question, "Why do you keep on paying annual dues to an organization whose meeting you never attend?" A large number replied in a

155

sentence which I can generalize as follows: "Because the degrees made me feel that I had come in contact with something inspiring, something noble, and I don't want to let go of it!"

After 15 years of visiting with Masons in Jurisdictions all over the United States I am **positive** that it's the spiritual appeal of Freemasonry that gives it its strength. So I repeat, "Masonry is a spiritual force, and everything a Lodge may do, should enrich the spiritual experiences of its members, their families, and their friends."

If the ritual is truly the "heart" of Freemasonry, which keeps the spiritual interest of its members pulsating Masonically, the ritual work of a lodge should always be done **well**. It should be a matter of pride to the officers especially. It should be zealously performed as one of the lodge's most important functions. It should always be done **for** the initiate, with the deep conviction that on this particular exemplification depend the Masonic commitment, the Masonic enthusiasm, and the Masonic devotion of this particular initiate.

Each part of each degree should be done seriously, solemnly—as a necessary step to the climax of Symbolic Masonry's initiatory process—to that high moment when a Brother is raised from a dead level to a living perpendicular,—a symbolic expression for the deeply spiritual and mystic transformation which every new Mason should have undergone if the ritual work was seriously and meaningfully performed.

But it happens only when he has been the beneficiary of serious, solemn degree work in every step of his initiation, beginning with his reception in the first degree, and proceeding through every impressive direction, explanation, and obligation, every lecture, charge, and investiture,—to that proud moment when he is informed that he is now a Master Mason, entitled to all the rights, lights, and benefits of this Worshipful Lodge.

Unfortunately, it doesn't happen with every candidate, because it happens only when the ritualists of a lodge do good work, i.e., ritual work which is thoroughly learned and memorized, which is interpreted spiritually and meaningfully, and which is deliberately aconsciously aimed at the initiate,—**not** to amuse him or merely to pass him through a routine, but to inspire him, to stimulate his noblest hopes and aspirations.

No Brother should be elected or appointed to a lodge office if he is unwilling or unable to memorize the ritual of the three degrees. Exceedingly few men are really unable to memorize. That's usually an excuse, a poor one, for unwillingness to make the effort. Anyone of normal intellectual ability can **memorize, if he sets his mind to do it.**

Furthermore, it's a very useful personal discipline, not only for the officers, but for every Brother who wants Symbolic Masonry to make its spiritual impact on the candidates. While memorizing is not an easy discipline for most of us, Brethren should be required to develop that skill as a natural development of their Masonic growth. That is one of the distinctions which mark a man as a Mason. Those who would do away with the candidates' requirement to "pass a proficiency test", because "busy men no longer have time to do a little memorizing", seem largely unaware of what makes Masonry so spiritually appealing. Self-discipline is one of the most important techniques in developing spiritual awareness. Memorizing the lectures and obligations is such a discipline, without which a good man is not led to improve himself in Masonry. A short handbook on how to acquire this discipline can be found in a **Short Talk Bulletin** published by the Masonic Service Association in October, 1962, "The Learning and Delivery of Ritual."

While letter perfect renditions of the ritual are highly desirable, they should never be regarded as the goal of memorization. Nothing is harder to listen to than a perfect memorization of a passage of ritual which is delivered in a monotonous or sing-song tone of voice without variation of emphases, without change of pitch or stress, without obvious understanding of the words being delivered. Masonic ritual contains archaic and unusual words—a heritage from the past. Those who would be good ritualists must not merely memorize those words; they must know what each one means, what each phrase is intended to express, what its modern version would be if translated literally into current language or idiom. A good ritualist finds that perfect memorization is a powerful aid to this kind of interpretation, for it enables him to speak readily with **understanding**, with **sincerity**, with **conviction**.

Such words and phrases as "curiously trace nature, through her various windings, to her most concealed recesses" suggest a reverence for man's curiosity and the development of our modern scientific methods. A good rendition of that ritual instruction requires much more than a perfect memorization of the words; it requires a broad understanding of modern man's accomplishments and a sincere reverence for the Great Artificer—spiritual effects which shine through a Master's pronunciations, his tone, his emphases, and his obvious understanding of the words he is speaking. That is the most important quality we should aim for in a good ritual performance.

In reviewing the publication, **Planning for the East**, one soon becomes aware that the Service and Education Committee is primarily concerned with the necessity for good and wholesome instruction **about Masonry** within the constituent lodges. It has done a tremendous job in providing a plan for Masonic education, in the detailing the steps to be taken in recruiting the manpower, digging out source materials, and defining the activities and duties of the Brethren who will be involved in such a program, specifically, the Lodge Education Officer and the Intenders, on whom Masonic education for candidates and new members will depend **absolutely**.

Study it well, Brother Wardens, for there is your trestleboard for Masonic enlightenment, for good and wholesome instruction for the Craft, if you intend conscientiously to discharge **that** responsibility as Worshipful Master of your lodge.

Like all good things in Masonry and in life, it's not an easy accomplishment. It's a program that calls for hard work, for zeal and determination, no matter how many discouragements and disappointments your efforts may suffer, and it will require a steady, smiling confidence which must energize your labors 365 days in the coming year!

As merely one "for instance", think of the job of recruiting, enlisting, and supervising the Intenders who are to train, instruct, inspire, and accompany the candidates and new Master Masons of your lodge next year. It will test your knowledge of the membership to find the right men for those positions; it will test your powers of leadership (particularly, persuasion and fraternal loyalty) to get those Brethren to say Yes; it will test your planning and your patience to check on their labors, to see that they faithfully perform all the duties of their office; it will test your powers of diplomacy and tact to stimulate them to greater effort or to improve their performance; and it will test your appreciation and brotherly love to give them the praise and the spiritual approval which all voluntary effort deserves. Rembember, however, that every test is also an opportunity—for the Worshipful Master with skill and wisdom,—to enrich the labors of his Lodge.

A program of good Masonic education should be set up and put to work, first of all, for initiates and new members, but once that labor is being effectively carried out, a program for the older members should also be set in motion by some competent Masonic instructors in the Lodge. In my opinion, the lack of such educational work in the average Lodge is the principal reason for the loss of interst and the consequent poor attendance in Masonry, over which spokesmen have been wringing their hands for at least a century.

One of the weaknesses of Masonic education is the speed with which the average candidate is rushed from one degree to another, so that the ritual becomes the only Masonic education he receives. He has barely time enough to do a little memorizing in order to "pass a proficiency", before he is rushed through another perplexing, incompletely understood degree, just so he can be made a member of the Lodge in time for the next class in one of the appendant bodies.

Why this unseemly haste? A Lodge of Master Masons does not exist for the purpose of furnishing members for another organization. Its purpose is to make **Master** Masons. Then why not take enough time to do just **that** by educating men in the history, philosophy, ideas, and **activities** of Masonry? If Grand Lodge has legislated a **maximum** waiting period, why not take advantage of it?

Unfortunately, the rapid progress of the individual from one degree to another continues, with an appalling dearth of Masonic education and enlightenment **between** the degrees. No wonder the ritual work is regarded less and less as a mystic experience to inspire a man and to improve his heart and mind for the art of living. "Look, Man, let's tell it like it is! This ritual stuff is just a formality to make him a member. Let's not get so serious about it. Take it easy. If it's gotta be done, just read it from a book."

No wonder Grand Lodge leaders become alarmed about the shoddy products of that kind of Masonic education, and propose legislation to enforce waiting periods before a newly made Mason can become a member of an appendant body! A waiting period for what? Well, we're told, a waiting period in which he can ripen and become a better-informed Master Mason!

That's nonsense, of course. It's putting the horse behind the cart. If a lodge has no time to ripen a candidate, to give him good and wholesome instruction, **before** it raises him to the sublime degree of Master Mason, it won't find the time to do it after he signs the bylaws and is told that he's a Master Mason, "entitled to all the rights, lights, and benefits . . . etc." And do you think you can get the average new member to come back to lodge for such educational experiences, when you didn't require them **between** the degrees? Of course not!

Between the degrees. There are the appropriate waiting periods in which Symbolic Lodges should educate, instruct, ripen, develop and **grow** the Master Masons which the Craft sorely needs. Before you raise a man to the sublime degree, make sure he's worthy of that title. That way, you may help to restore some of the pretige and significance of the words, **a Master Mason.**

Remember, Freemasonry is nothing if it's not a spiritual force, exerted by men who are really Master Masons!

157

L. SHERMAN BROOKS
Masonic Calligrapher

The Post Journal, Jamestown, N.Y., March 6, 1976

Finishing Touch
L. Sherman Brooks adds decorative colored capital letters to his latest work. A professional scribe, his work recently appeared in three different publications.
Post-Journal Staffoto by Richard W. Hallberg

Most people stare at L. Sherman Brooks' checks . . .and almost every thing else he writes.

That's because his penmanship usually flows in Gothic, Roman, italic or some other exotic style.

Mr. Brooks is a skilled calligrapher, a professional scribe. His work is known as far away as Geneva, Switzerland. Sample of his work have recently appeared in circulating Masonic publications as "The Empire State Mason," for which he authored and lettered a poem, and "The Oregon Freemason." And last month's issue of the Mason's historical magazine "Philalethes," contained a poem which took him approximately 60 hours to letter and decorate with detail.

Mr. Brooks is a native of West Ellicott and a senior draftsman at Blackstone Corp. In his spare time he works on his lettering hobby, which is now a small business. Besides the poetry he lettered for the Masons, he has lettered a eulogy which was presented to a widow and a poem for a bridegroom to give his new bride. Among other projects, he has lettered a plaque for the Lakewood American Legion and is currently developing and alphabet for a book publishing firm. "I've been working on the alphabet for four months and I'm only up to the letter 'J'," he said.

Mr. Brooks frequently display his art work at local shows. For the bicentennial, he lettered the Declaration of Independence in an orange circle using a 1,000-year-old Carolinguian script. It will be overlaid with Thomas Jefferson's quotation: "The whole art of government consists of the art of being honest." He plans to enter his work in an art show in New York City sponsored by the Society of Scribes, of which he is a member.

Mr. Brooks, who by his own admission had "terrible" handwriting in elementary school, learned the skill for the art of calligraphy while attending Celoron High School. His skill improved while he was in the Navy, he said. He was sent to train with a Roman Catholic nun in New York City for 16 to 18 weeks. "She was a perfectionist and it was from her that I learned the rudiments of calligraphy," he said.

Mr. Brooks works on his art approximately 20 hours a week, usually getting up at 5 a.m. and lettering for two hours before going to work. He is a firm believer that hard work and practice are the only ways to success. "If you are undertaking something complex, study and analyze it and then go forth and achieve your goal," he said.

PHYLAXIS NOTE: Bro. L. Sherman Brooks, who did the back cover of this issue, address can be found in the Notes, Queries and Information section on page 149.

THE LADY FREEMASON
How She Came to be Initiated
by Arthur Frederick, F.P.S. [Mass.]
Cont. from Last Edition

They were soon joined by the members of the Lodge present, and, but for the prompt attitude of her brother and other promenent members, her life would have fallen a sacrifice to what was then considered a crime. The first care of his Lordship was to resuscitate the unfortunate lady without alarming the house, and endeavor to learn from her an explanation of what had occured. The young lady having been carried back into the library, and restored to consciousness, they learned what had occured. On hearing this many of the members became furious. She was placed under guard of the Tyler and another brother, in the same room in which she was found. The brothers reassembled and deliberated as to what, under the circumstances, was to be done, and for two long hours she could hear the angry discussion, and her death proposed and seconded in calming in some measure, the angry and irritated feelings of the rest of the members, and after much had been said and many thing proposed, it was resolved to give her the option of submitting to the Masonic ordeal up to the point in the ceremonial of which she had been a witness (F.C.), and if she refused the brethren were again to consult. Being asked to decide, the fair culprot, endowed with a high sense of honour, and exhausted and terrified by the heated feelings of the debate, which she could not avoid hearing, and yet notwithstanding all, with a secret pleasure, and unhesitatingly accepted the offer. She was recorded and took place at a time when Miss St. Leger, was a young girl and unmarried, and was probably about the year 1710. It may be mentioned that the inmates of the house apart from those referred to, were in perfect ignorance of the transaction. The Honourable Elizabeth St. Leger was afterwards married to Richard Aldworth Esq., of Newmarket, County Cork, who was the son of Sir Richard Aldworth, Provost Marschal of Munster.

Thus vanishes the story of the clock case, with all its romantic details; Cork and Newmarket are deprived of the honour of her introduction into Freemasonry, and although the latter town, indeed, may almost claim her as its own, as it was the scene of many of her Masonic acts and benevolence. She also attended all the Masonic assemblies and processions, and generally added lustre to the Craft, which had so reluctantly adopted her as its first and only daughter. Placed as she was, by her marriage with Mr. Aldworth, at the head of a very large fortune, the poor in general, and the Masonic poor in particular, had good reason to record her numerous and bountiful acts of kindness. Nor were these marked by ostentation—far from it. It has been remarked of her that her custom was to seek out bashful, misery, and retiring poverty, and with a well directed liberality to soothe many a bleeding heart. She was the best and kindest of women. She did not neglect altogether the other duties of the Craft, and was, as far as she went, a most exemplary Freemason, and frequently on the occasion of the Masonic procession, it was her custom, to precede the Lodge in an open pheaton. A single glance at her portrait will show a woman of strong mind, inflexibility of purpose, and rectitude of life, and it is recorded that she possessed, most fully, all those tender sensibilities of heart which it has pleaded the Architect to implant in woman. She was strictly religious, as well as punctual and scrupulous in her Masonic duties, and in all the relations of life, whether as wife, mother, relative, friend, she stood pre-eminent. One circumstance, before, concluding, is worthy of notice, and should serve as a lesson to those who boast the superiority of manly descretion and understanding. Mrs. Aldworth had such a veneration for Freemasonry that she would never suffer it to be spoken of lightly in her hearing, nor would she touch on the subject but with the greatest caustion, even when in company with her most intimate friends, whom she knew were not Freemasons, and when she did it was under evident embarassment and with a trembling apprehension lest she might in a hasty moment comit a breach of Masonic duty. The Hon. Mrs. Aldworth lived until she was 80 years of age. She died in 1773, and was buried in the Davies Vault in the Old St. Finnbarr Cathedral, Cork. In the Parish Church of Doneraile a table is erected in her memory.

WELCOME TO NEW MEMBERS

It has been brought to our attention, that some unscrupulous individual in El Paso, Texas, has been using the addresses of our members, published in this section to send unsolicited applications for membership in a non-Prince Hall organization. For this reason, we shall no longer publish the full addresses of our members. For those members who have received applications for membership in this organization, we recommend that you destroy it!

David L. Holliman, Denver, Colorado 80231, recommended by James E. Herndon, F.P.S.

Courtenay L. Wiltshire, Brooklyn, New York 11213, recommended by Ira S. Holder, Sr., F.P.S.

William H. Whitley, Brooklyn, New York 11213, recommended by Ira S. Holder, Sr., F.P.S.

Paul J. Cooper, Brooklyn, New York 11213, recommended by Ira. S. Holder, Sr., F.P.S.

William E. Spencer, Tacoma, Washington 98404, recommended by Herbert Dailey, M.P.S.

Carlton B. Tucker, Tacoma, Washington 98444, recommended by Herbert Dailey, M.P.S.

Joe E. Benton, Seattle, Washington 98122, recommended by Herbert Dailey, M.P.S.

Julis A. Headen, Tacoma, Washington 98404, recommended by Herbert Dailey, M.P.S.

Alexander Reed, Tacoma, Washington 98444, recommended by Herbert Dailey, M.P.S.

Jimmy Simmons, Brenerton, Washington 98310, recommended by Herbert Dailey, M.P.S.

Baldwin Leonard, Tacoma, WAshington 98405, recommended by Herbert Dailey, M.P.S.

William Michael, Tacoma, Washington 98465, recommended by Herbert Dailey, M.P.S.

Marshall S. Johnson, Pittsburg, Pennsylvania 15206, recommended by Ira S. Holder, Sr., F.P.S.

Joseph I. Cloyd, Denver, Colorado 80207, recommended by James E. Herndon, F.P.S.

Alfred Bowler, Allison Park, Pennsylvania 15101, recommended by Ira S. Holder, Sr., F.P.S.

Reprinted by permission from the
Schomburg Center for Research in Black culture
The New York Public Library
Astor, Lenox and Tilden Foundations

THE
ORIGIN AND OBJECTS
OF
ANCIENT FREEMASONRY;
ITS
INTRODUCTION INTO THE UNITED STATES,
AND
LEGITIMACY AMONG COLORED MEN
A TREATISE DELIVERED BEFORE
ST. CYPRIAN LODGE, NO. 13, JUNE 24, A.D. 1853
A.L. 5853
BY
M.R. DELANY, K.M., D.D.G.H.P.
Re-published by A.D. Delany, Xenia, Ohio, 1904

"Great is Truth, and must prevail."

PITTSBURG:
Printed by W.S. Haven
Corner Market and Second Streets
1853

Entered according to Act of Congress, in the year 1853
By
M.R. DELANY
In the clerk's Office of the District Court
of the Western District of
Pennsylvania

DEDICATION.
[Second Edition]

To the memory of my sainted Father and Mother, whose manifest interest in the amelioration of the deplorable condition of their benighted race was exceeded only by their earnest anxiety and untiring endeavors to rear their children to a proper manhood and womanhood, I most affectionately dedicate the second edition of this little volume.

PREFACE TO THE PRESENT EDITION

My prime object in re-publishing this sketch of freemasonry written by *Martin R. Delany, M.D., a half century ago, (prior to my birth) is not a mercenary one. Though, as I have attempted it, (at the suggestion of an old family acquaintance, the owner of an original copy, which, for the first time in my life, I saw, last fall, while on a visit at my old home in Ohio,) I hope to realize some pecuniary compensation therefrom. The friend referred to, with others, heartily endorsed the undertaking, believing it will be beneficial an inspiring to those who may read it.

Although I am a charter member of Mt. Nebo Roya Arch Chapter, No. 12, F. and A.M. and am at this tim scribe of the same, having been initiated in Richmon Lodge, F. and A.M., Little Rock, Ark., as recently a July, 1901, and "raised" the following December, I ar as "green as Jonah's gourd" in the work of the orde

But since my perusal of this small treatise I hav been impelled to study freemasonry more intently an thereby to be a mason in fact. Though the little work the product of the mind of my lamented father, I trus that I shall not be regarded vain-glorious when I stat that I commend it to the brethren of the fraternity a worthy the careful consideration of any one c whatever race or station in life.

His duty to man may become more evident, hi obligations to his order more binding, his relation t God closer.

Finally, Brethren, whether or not it seem irrevelan to my preface, let me call your attention to th impressive lines quoted in the work from a poem c that scholar, teacher, prince of preachers, an patriach, the late Rt. Rev. Daniel Alexander Payne sixth Bishop of the African Methodist Episcopa Church.

How applicable are these lines in these days of th venomous vituperation of our despised and onc dejected, but now hopeful race. May they inspire, ye spur us, to think and act correctly, and to insist upo the same on the part of all those whith whom we com in contact; and by this course "give the lie" to th slanderous utterances of our pretentious friends an avowed enemies; for, as is well said, "One is no always responsible for what is said derogatory to hi reputation, but he is responsible for its truthfulness.
Yours fraternally
A.D. DELANY

A BRIEF BIOGRAPHICAL SKETCH
OF THE AUTHOR

Major Martin R. Delany born May 6, 1812, was native of Charlestown, Va., and boasted of being pur African blood. He was said to have descended partiall from African kings and chieftians, his materna ancestry being Mandingo, his paternal, Golah.

At first, a medical student under the late Dr LeMoyne, of Pennsylvania, father of Dr. LeMoyne inventor of the world-famous crematory for th incineration of the dead, he subsequently took medical course in lectures and surgery in Harvar University. It is claimed that he was the first colore student to matriculate in that renowned school. At th age of thirty-one he married Miss Catherine A.

160

youngest child of Mr. Charles Richards, a man of means, of Pittsburg, Pa., the father of whom is said to have owned the first brick house built in Pittsburg. Their union was blessed with eleven children[1], the writer of this sketch being the seventh.

Early in mature life he joined the masonic fraternity, taking thirty degrees in his home lodge in Pittsburg, and the three "side degrees" in London, England, a few years subsequent to the publication of this book, which shows the recognition of our order in foreign lands. While in the latter country, where he spent the half of eighteen months, the other nine months having been spent in his ancestral land, Africa. as a member of an exploring expedition party, he was elected to membership of the International Statistical Congress, the late Lord Henry Brougham, President, and was made a F.R.S. (Fellow of the Royal Society.)

Immediately preceding the close of the late civil war he was commissioned, by the late President Abraham Lincoln, Major of the 104th Regiment of South Carolina, and was continued in service on the staff of Gen. Dan E. Sickles. He was a nominee for Lieutenant Governor of South Carolina on the same ticket with the late Judge Green as Governor. It was proved subsequently that the nominees were elected by ten thousand and some hundred majority, but were counted out. Therefore, Major Delany was virtually Lieut. Governor of South Carolina for six months and ex-officio Governor eighteen months, Judge Green dying six months after the election. He held several government and state offices, one of which was a member of the staff of Gov. Scott, with the rank of Lieutenant Colonel, and one, inspector of customs.

At the close of a useful and eventful career he quietly passed away in the bosom of his family, Jan. 24, 1885.

Yours fraternally,
A.D. DELANY

**THIS LITTLE TREATISE
IS MOST RESPECTFULLY DEDICATED
TO THE
MASONIC FRATERNITY
THROUGHOUT THE WORLD
BY THE AUTHOR**

PREFACE

CORRESPONDENCE

PITTSBURGH, June 27, A.D. 1853, A.L. 5853

Brother Martin R. Delany:

SIR—The undersigned have been appointed a Committee from St. Cyprian Lodge, No. 13 of A.Y. Masons, to solicit the Treatise delivered by you on the 24th of June, A.D. 1853, A.L. 5853, for publication in pamphlet form, hoping thereby to subserve the cause of the Craft generally, and that of the colored Masons in the United States in particular.

Such a dissertation on Masonry has long been needed, to set the public mind, and that of the unskilled in the Craft, right on several important and essential points in Masonic jurisprudence, and we are fully assured that in your Treatise, this has been accomplished.

With high regard, fraternally yours,
ELIAS EDMONDS
THOMAS NORRIS
W.J. TRUSTY

PITTSBURGH, June 30, A.D. 1853, A.L. 5853

Companion and Sir Knight:

The undersigned, by a resolution of a Grand Lodge Communication, were appointed a Committee to solicit, in conjunction with a Committee from St. Cyprian Lodge, No. 13, a copy of the able Treatise delivered by you on the occasion of the last Annual Festival of St. John the Baptist. We take pleasure in uniting our own with the sentiments contained in the above note, and hope ever to remain

Yours, in the ties of Fraternal esteem,
WM. B. AUSTIN, D.D.G.M.
ALFRED H. JOHNS
JAMES GRIGG
FRANCIS J. HALL
JONATHAN GREEN

PITTSBURGH, June 30, A.D. 1853, A.L. 5853

Gentlemen, Brethren, Companions, and Sir Knights:

I have received a note jointly from a Committee appointed by St. Cyprian Lodge, No. 13, and a Communication held by the District Deputy Grand Master, desiring that the Treatise delivered by me before the public, on the 24th day of June inst. (the Annual Festival of our Patron, St. John the Baptist) be published in pamphlet form. With this request I readily and cheerfully comply.

Permit me to say, in this connection, that whatever undue and unwarrantable obstructions may be thrown in our way by American Masons, and they are many — though there are some honorable exceptions — it is within the power of the Grand Lodge of England to decide in the matter, and at once establish our validity. For this purpose, I now suggest, through you, that all of our Subordinate Lodges throughout the United States, at once petition their respective Grand Lodges, and the Grand Lodges respectively agree, and together with the National Grand Lodge, meet by

161

delegated representatives of Past Masters—not to exceed three from each Grand Lodge, and the same number from each District over which there may be a District Deputy Grand Master, the National Grand Lodge sending one for each State Grand Lodge—in a National Grand Masonic Convention, for the single purpose of petitioning the Grand Lodge of England for a settlement of the question of the legality of Colored Masons in the United States, claiming to have originated from the warrant granted to Prince Hall, of Boston. This should at once be done, to settle the controversy, as it would to us be a great point gained, because it would be the acknowledgement and establishment of a right among us as a people, which is now disputed, but which legitimately belongs to us.

We have for years been fraternally outraged, simply for the want of a proper and judicious course being pursued on the part of our Masonic authorities, and the present loudly calls upon us for action in this matter. We are either Masons or not Masons, legitimate or illegitimate; if the affirmative, then we must be so acknowledged and accepted—if the negative, we should be rejected. We never will relinquish a claim to an everlasting inheritance, but by the force of stern necessity; and there is not that Masonic power in existence, with the exception of the Grand Lodge of England, to which we will yield in a decision on this point. Our rights are equal to those of other American Masons, if not better than some; and it comes not with the best grace for them to deny us.

The suggested Convention should be held in some central place, during the ensuing three years of the National Grand Lodge administration, and in not less than one year from this date, so that full time may be given, for reflection and action, on the part of the various Subordinate and Grand Lodges.

Let not the hopes of our brethren languish, through calumny and slander may have done their work.

> O, Slander! foulest imp of hell!
>   Thy tongue is like the scorpion's sting!
> Nor peace nor hope can near thee dwell;
>   Thy breath can blast the fairest thing!
> O, could I grasp the thunderbolt!
>   I'd crush thee, limping fiend of hell!
> From earth I'd chase thy serpent soul,
>   And chain thee where the furies dwell!
>   BISHOP PAYNE

Fraternally Yours,
In the bonds of Union and Fellowship,
M.R. DELANY
To Elias Edmonds, Wm. B. Austin, &c. Committees

A TREATISE

"Great is Truth, and must prevail."

To introduce the subject of Ancient Freemasonry at this period, with a design to adduce anything new, at least to the enlightened, would be a work of supererogation, having the semblance of assumption, more than an effort to impart information.

Summoned by your invitation to deliver a Treatise, I have chosen for my subject, THE ORIGIN, OBJECTS, AND INTRODUCTION OF FREEMASONRY INTO THE UNITED STATES—and also its introduction among colored men in this country. I shall, therefore, proceed at once to the discharge of my duty, doing the best I can according to the opportunity and means at hand for the accomplishment of this end.

Masonry was originally intended for the better government of man—for the purpose of restraining him from a breach of the established ordinances. The first law given to man was by God himself—that given in the Garden of Eden, forbidding the eating of the reserved fruit. (Gen. 2:17) The first institution was that of marriage. (Gen. 2:21, 24) The first breach of the law was committed by eating the forbidden fruit. (Gen. 3:6) The first punishment inflicted on man was by God himself, for a breach of the law. (Gen. 3:16-19) The first city was built by Cain, and named after his first-born son, Enoch.

MAN FROM ADAM TO NOAH

During the period from Adam to Noah, the life of man was of long duration, each individual living through several hundred years of time. His habits, customs and manner of living were simple; residing in thinly peopled localities, for there were then no densely populated cities, and relying mainly on husbandry as a means of support.

MAN FROM NOAH TO SOLOMON

From Noah to Solomon, the character of man underwent an entire and important change. Noah's three sons, scattering abroad over the earth, built great cities, and established many and various policies, habits, manners and customs, for the government of their people. At this period, it will be remembered, a general separation in interests and sympathies took place among these brethren, (the children of one household parentage,) which continued to manifest itself in hostile array until the building of the temple by Solomon, king of Israel. I do not intend to assert that hostilities then entirely ceased, but that mankind were better governed after that period, will not be denied.

In the earliest period of the Egyptian and Ethiopian dynasties, the institution of Masonry was first established. Discovering a defect in the government of man, first suggested an inquiry into his true state and condition. Being a people of a high order of intellect, and subject to erudite and profound thought, the Egyptians and Ethiopians were the first who came to the conclusion that man was created in the similitude of God. This, it will be remembered, was anterior to the Bible record, because Moses was the recorder of the Bible, subsequent to his exodus from Egypt, all his wisdom and ability having been acquired there; as a proof of which, the greatest recommendation to his fitness for so high and holy an office, and the best encomium which that book can possibly bestow upon him in testimony of his qualifications as its scriptor, the Bible itself tells us that "Moses was learned in all the wisdom of the Egyptians."

The Ethiopians early adduced the doctrine and believed in a trinity of the Godhead. Though heathens their mythology was of a high and pure order, agreeing in regard to the attributes of the Diety with the Doctrine of Christians in after ages, as is beautifully illustrated in the person of Jupiter Ammon, the great god of Egypt and Ethiopia, who was assigned a power over heaven, earth and hell, as well as over all the other gods, thereby acknowledging his omnipotence—all other gods possessing but one divine attribute or function, which could only be exercised in his particular department of divinity.[2]

What is God that man should be his image, and what knowledge should man obtain in order to be like God? This wisdom was possessed in the remotest period by the wise men of Egypt and Ethiopia, and handed down only through the priesthood to the recipients of their favors, the mass of mankind being ignorant of their own nature, and consequently prone to rebel against their greatest and best interests.

God is a being possessing various attributes: and all Masons, whether Unitarian, Trinitarian, Greek, Jew or Mohammedan, agree upon this point, at least without controversy. Where there are various functions, there must be an organ for the exercise of each function,—and this conclusion most naturally led man to inquire into his own nature, to discover the similitude between himself and his Creator.

golden streets,"—holding in his left hand a sceptre, figurative of his earthly power; his right hand grasping a thunder-bolt, the ancient idea of the power and terrors of hell.

(Continued in next edition)

A WORD FROM THE PRESIDENT
Continued from page 146

Branch, who has been so kind to us over the years in our search for items of Prince Hall Masonic historical interest.

To the Iowa Masonic Library of the Most ∴ Worshipful ∴ Grand Lodge A.F. & A.M. of Iowa, who has likewise aided us in our quest for Masonic material.

And to the countless others, who have helped us pursue **"More Light!"**, thanks!.

This issue is dedicated to a great and noble Prince Hall Freemason, **Dr. Martin Robinson Delany** and to **St. Cyprian** (now St. Cyprian-Alpha) Lodge No. 13, of Pittsburg, Pennsylvania.

The Society is quite honored to be able to reproduce the first printed work on the subject of Masonry among the Black man in the United States.

This work is historic, and is as much a part of Prince Hall Masonry as the charter of African Lodge #459, granted by the Mother Grand Lodge of England to Prince Hall and the members of African Lodge No. 1.

The **Phylaxis Society** is dedicated to the masonic education of the Prince Hall fraternity, to the preservation of our Masonic heritage and the safe guarding of our solidarity from its enemies. Masonic education is an adventure which we want to share with you, it is a fascinating journey into our "profession," it is above all a learning experience that makes us proud of the fact, that we are Prince Hall Freemasons.

A Special thanks to M.W. Samuel T. Danials, Grand Master Most Worshipful Prince Hall Grand Lodge F. & A.M. of Maryland and Chairman of the Steering Committee; M.W. John G. Lewis, Jr., Grand Master of the Most Worshipful Prince Hall Grand Lodge F. & A.M. of Louisiana; M.W. I. H. Clayborn, Grand Master Most Worshipful Prince Hall Grand Lodge F. & A.M. of Texas, and Dr. James W. Davis, Prince Hall Ambassador of Good Will, for their kind invitation to me to be in attendance at the 57th Session of the Conference of Grand Masters Prince Hall Masons of America, held May 5-6-7th in Colorado Springs, Colorado. And a special thanks to all the Grand Masters in attendance, for their kind reception to me.

JOSEPH A. WALKES, JR., F.P.S.
President

FOOTNOTES

1. Names of children in order of their birth: Genefred L'Ouverture, Toussaint L'Ouverture, Catherine Matilda, Martha Priscilla, Chas. Lenox Remond, Martin R. Boling, Alexandre Dumas, St. Cyprian, Fonston Sonlouque, Placido Remeses, Hallie Amelia E. (Toussaint L'Ouverture was born after the death of Genefred L'Ouverture.)

2. Jupiter was represented as seated on a throne of gold and ivory—figurative of heaven, as the "pearly gates and

THE PHYLAXIS

SEPTEMBER, 1976

Volume II   Number 7

A SOCIETY FOR PRINCE HALL
FREEMASONS WHO SEEK MORE
LIGHT AND WHO HAVE LIGHT TO
IMPART.

THE PHYLAXIS
Published at Boston, Mass. by
THE PHYLAXIS SOCIETY

Arthur H. Frederick, M.P.S.................................Editor
Box 43, Roxbury, Massachusetts 02119

OFFICERS

Joseph A. Walkes, Jr., M.P.S.........................President
P.O. Box 3151, Ft. Leavenworth, Kansas 66027

Herbert Dailey, M.P.S..........................First Vice President
1616 South Cedar, Tacoma, Washington 98405

Zellus Bailey, M.P.S.........................Second Vice President
7039 Dover Court, St. Louis, Missouri 63130

James E. Herndon, M.P.S.................Executive Secretary
1574 Ivanhoe Street, Denver, Colorado 80220

Alonzo D. Foote, Sr., M.P.S..........................Treasurer
P.O. Box 99601, Tacoma, Washington 98499

SUBSCRIPTION RATE: FOR ONE YEAR, $5.00

The Phylaxis Magazine is the official publication of the Phylaxis Society. Any article appearing in this publication expresses only the opinion of the writer, and does not become the official pronouncement of the Phylaxis Society. No advertising of any form is solicited or accepted. All communication relative to the magazine should be addressed to the Editor. Inquiries relative to membership must be addressed to the Executive Secretary. Membership is by invitation and recommendation only. The joining fee is $3.00. Dues are $5.00 per year in advance, which amount includes a subscription to the "Phylaxis" magazine for one year.

All rights reserved. No part of this work may be reproduced or transmitted in any form or by any means, electrical or mechanical, or retrival system, without written permission from the publisher.

1976 DUES
ALL 1975 MEMBERS ARE REQUESTED TO FORWARD THEIR 1976 DUES [$5.00]

INDEX

A Word from the President	166
Herndon and Holder Retire	166
The Masonic Address and Writings of Ira S. Holder, Sr., F.P.S.	167
A Speech by Joseph A. Walkes, F.P.S.	171
Notes, Queries and Information on Items of Masonic Research	173
Report of the Caucasian Grand Lodge F. & A.M. of Wisconsin	174
The Origin and Objects of Ancient Freemasonry	176
Welcome New Members	179

A WORD FROM THE PRESIDENT

The success of any organization depends upon numerical growth. Any organization that is satisfied with its present status and has no desire nor makes any effort for growth and usefullness is in a very poor condition and will soon be surpassed by those who exert effort for growth and development.

In planning the work of the Society, we have one definite premise to work upon and that, is that increased membership must be a result of the effort of all the members of the **PHYLAXIS SOCIETY** and that no one member or group of members could hope to make a substantial increase in membership without the utmost in cooperation from every member.

We can well draw the conclusion that the building of the membership in our Society can only be accomplished by the individual effort of all the members in each and every state in the entire country. This cooperation can be obtained by enthusiastic and inspirational work by all. From past experience we found that the most effective method of securing new members was by personal contact. For there will be but a few who will approach us voluntarily.

The other day, I spoke by phone with a Grand Master on the East Coast, who was upset over the lack of members from his Jurisdiction in the Society. My advice to him was "give us a hand, Grand Master!" And we ask all Grand Masters of Prince Hall Freemasons and all members of the Society, BRING IN A MEMBER.

JOSEPH A. WALKES, JR., FPS
President

HERNDON AND HOLDER RETIRE

James E. Herndon, FPS (Colorado), Executive Secretary and Charter Member of the Phylaxis Society has decided to step down as Executive Secretary citing over-commitment as reason. The President, Joseph A. Walkes, FPS (Kansas) will assume the office until a new Secretary can be appointed. Brother Herndon becomes Executive Secretary Emeritus.

Ira S. Holder, Sr., FPS (New York) has retired as Chairman of the Membership Committee due to poor health and a desire to complete the history of Prince Hall Memorial Lodge #100 F. & A.M., Barbados, West Indies. Appointment of a new Chairman is pending.

The Phylaxis Society thanks both of these dedicated Prince Hall Freemasons for their years of service to the Society.

THE MASONIC ADDRESSES AND WRITINGS OF IRA S. HOLDER, SR., F.P.S. [NEW YORK]

"TWO BLACKS INADVERTENTLY DISRUPTS WHITE AMERICA"

BY
IRA S. HOLDER, SR.

Tuesday, February 10, 1970

MASTER OF CEREMONIES
WORSHIPFUL MASTER FERGUSON,
GRAND LODGE OFFICERS (Past and Present)
SENIOR & JUNIOR WARDENS,
PAST MASTERS,
VISITING BRETHREN OF THE CRAFT,
MEMBERS OF MT. OLIVE LODGE #2

GOOD EVENING:

It is with extreme pleasure that I accepted the invitation to address you at this time, from my good friend and brother—Joseph Ferguson, Worshipful Master of this illustrious and outstanding Lodge. Since accepting the invitation however, I read with interest where the late Harry A. Williamson, Past Grand Historian and Masonic Scholar of world renown, received his first light in Masonry as an Entered Apprentice in Mt. Olive Lodge #2 in January 1904, before becoming a member of Carthagian Lodge #47 in Brooklyn, N.Y. where he resided.

This lodge is outstanding because it was Warranted many years ago on October 11, 1858 and has withstood the ravages of time; when so many other lodges are now slumbering, and illustrious because it too can claim as its own a great Masonic Leader. It was may good fortune to meet and know this outstanding Masonic Scholar during his declining years, sometime prior to his passing.

This being Negro History Week, I think it not only fitting but appropiate that I bring you something of a historical nature. My subject should be of the utmost interest, significance, and importance to all of us as Prince Hall Masons.

It is entitled:

"TWO BLACKS INADVERTENTLY DISRUPTS WHITE AMERICA"

The happenings and ramifications which I am about to unfold, transpired in the year 1897 (73 years ago) the impact of which, at that time, not only startled, but shook the very foundation of the (White) Masonic Fraternity the world over, especially in the United States and Canada.

With this advanced bit of information, the stage is set for describing the inner workings of Freemason's Grand Lodge of the State of Washington, and the chain reaction of Grand Lodges the world over to this particular incident. The essence of this turbulent situation forms the subject title for this evening's address:

"TWO BLACKS INADVERTENTLY DISRUPTS WHITE AMERICA"

On Wednesday, June 9, 1897, Freemason's Grand Lodge of the State of Washington was in its Annual Session with M.W. Yancy Blacock, Grand Master presiding; at which time a Petition coming from two Negro Masons: Gideon S. Bailey, and Con A. Rideout was received, asking for the privilege of obtaining Masonic Fellowship with the Masons in the area.

Both of these brethren were of irreproachable character and standing in the community.

Gideon S. Bailey served at one time as a Justice of the Peace. He received his degrees in Masonry in a Lodge chartered by the Grand Lodge of Pennsylvania (Prince Hall) in 1815.

Con A. Rideout was a practicing attorney. He received his Masonic Degrees in a Lodge chartered by the Grand Lodge of Florida, owing its origin to Hiram Grand Lodge of Pennsylvania.

The presiding Grand Master accepted the Petition coming from the two distinguished brethren and immediately appointed a "Special Committee" of three (3) Grand Lodge Officers, instructing them to return a recommendation at the next Grand Session. The names of this Committee are as follows:

1. R.W. Thomas M. Reed
2. R.W. James E. Edminston
3. R.W. William H. Upton

Before proceeding further, I deem it important that you be given a brief outline on the background and qualification of this important history making "Special Committee."

THOMAS M. REED was born in Kentucky and made a Mason there. He moved to the Pacific Coast in his early manhood and was prominent in its history, especially in California, Idaho and Washington. He held several public offices and was the last Territorial and the first State Auditor of Washington. He was

167

chiefly instrumental in organizing the Grand Lodge of Washington in 1858 and had been its Grand Secretary ever since its organization, except during three (3) years in which he was Grand Master and one (1) year he was absent in Idaho. He also was a Republican.

JAMES E. EDMINSTON was born in Arkansas and was made a Mason there, after having in his youth served in the Confederate Army. He received a college education, became a practicing attorney, filled many positions of honor and trust and had been a Democratic candidate for Superior Judge. He became Grand Master in 1890; and at the time of his death had been for eight (8) years consecutively, Chairman of the Committee on Jurisprudence. In that position he established a high reputation for the breadth and accuracy of his knowledge of Masonic Jurisprudence, cogency of reasoning, conservation and invaring candor and frankness.

WILLIAM H. UPTON was at that time a Grand Warden and installed Grand Master in 1898—was born in California and educated in New England. After residing some years in the south, he returned to the Pacific Coast in 1880. He was a Republican, a lawyer by profession and when appointed to the Committee he had completed his second term as Judge of the Superior Court of the State. He edited "The Masonic Code of Washington," published by the Grand Lodge in 1897.

During the following year, the Committee lost no time in gathering, examining and evaluating every piece of information where ever found, relative to the origin and status of Prince Hall Masonry; overlooking nothing that would tend to support their effort. Their findings complete, the Committee prepared their report based on the following two (2) conclusions:

1. Authentic evidence of the origin and status of Prince Hall Masonry.
2. Undisputed Grand Lodge Jurisdiction.

With such facts, the Committee completed its work and submitted their report ot the Grand Lodge Session on Wednesday, June 15, 1898, with the M.W. Archibald W. Frater, Grand Master presiding. The report is as follows:

"RECOMMENDATION:
Having thus set forth our views upon the import subject submitted to us, your Committee now submit to this M.W. Grand Lodge four (4) Resolutions, and recommend that they be adopted, to wit:

"RESOLVED, that in the opinion of this Grand Grand Lodge, Masonry is Universal; and, without doubt, neither race nor color are among the tests proper to be applied to determine the fitness of a candidate for the degrees of Masonry.

"RESOLVED, that in view of the recognized laws of the Masonic Institution, and the facts of History apparently well authenticated and worthy of fu credence, this Grand Lodge does not see its wa clear to deny or question the right of i constituent Lodges, or of the members thereof, t recognize as Brother Masons, Negroes who hav been initiated in Lodges which can trace the origin to Prince Hall #459, organized under th Warrant of our R.W. Bro. Thomas Howard, Earl Effingham, acting Grand Master, under th authority of H.R.H. Henry Fedrick, Duke Cumberland, etc., Grand Master of the Mo Ancient and Honorable Society of F. & A.M Masons in England, bearing date September 2 A.L. 5789 or to our R.W. Prince Hall, Master said Lodge; and in the opinion of this Grand Lodge for the purpose of tracing such origin, the Africa Grand Lodge of Boston organized in 1808—subse quently known as Prince Hall Grand Lodge Massachusetts, the First African Grand Lodge North America in and for the Commonwealth Pennsylvania, organized in 1815 and Hiram Gran Lodge of Pennsylvania may justly be regarded a legitimate Grand Lodges.

"RESOLVED, that while this Grand Lodg recognizes no difference between brethren base upon race or color, yet it is not unmindful of th fact that the white and colored races in the Unite States have in many ways shown a preference t remain in purely social matters, separate an apart. In view of this inclination of the two races— Masonry being pre-eminently a social institution this Grand Lodge deems it to the best interest o Masonry to declare that if regular Masons o African descent desire to establish, within th State of Washington, Lodges confined wholly o chiefly to brethren of their race, and shall establis such Lodges strictly in accordance with the "Land marks of Freemasonry" and in accordance wit Masonic Law as here-to-fore interpeted by Masoni Tribunials of their own race, and if such Lodge shall in due time see fit in like manner to erect Grand Lodge for the better adminstration of thei affairs, this Grand Lodge having more regard fo the establishment of such Lodges or Grand Lodge as an invasion of its Jurisdiction, but as evincing disposition to conform to its own ideas as to th best interests of the Craft under peculia circumstances; and will ever extend to our colore brethren its since sympathy in every effort t promote the welfare of the Craft or inculcate th pure principles of our Art.

"RESOLVED, that the Grand Secretary be s instructed to acknowledge receipt of th communication from Gideon S. Bailey and Con A Rideout, and forward to them a copy of the printed

168

Proceedings of this Annual Communication of the Grand Lodge, as a response to said Communication."

Fraternally Submitted,
Thomas M. Reed
William H. Upton
James E. Edminston
Committee

The effect of this Report recognizing the legitimacy of the Prince Hall Grand Lodge, not only shocked but stunned and incensed many Grand Masonic Bodies through the United States, to the extent that between October 1898 and June 1899 no less than sixteen (16) of them severed all Masonic intercourse with the Grand Lodge of Washington, in the following order: Kentucky, Arkansas, Texas, Alabama, South Carolina, Florida, New Jersey, Tennessee, Mississippi, Louisiana, Indiana, Nevada and Wisconsin—possibly "reflecting with horror on the atrocity of their course, recanted prior to May 1900 and re-entered what Robert F. Gould called "The Harmonious Family of Grand Lodges", the others, so far as known, appeared to have persisted in their design.

In 1898 William H. Upton, one of the members of the "Special Committee" became Grand Master, and in order to justify the stand taken in the Committee's Report, wrote to many Grand Lodges throughout the Masonic World, sending them copies of the Report and asking for their opinion and advice in dealing with the matter. He also wrote a book entitled "Negro Masonry" by William H. Upton, (a copy of which I have in my possession) based on the facts which prompted the Report. His reason for writing this outstanding volume (which is now out of print) in support of his convictions is best explained in his own words. (quote)

"I have not be particularly intimidated by the knowledge which had come to me, not merely by what appeared in print, but by abusive letters, that the undertaking would subject me to scurrilous abuse and cowardly vituperation; for since I have learned how thin the veneer of Masonry and civilization is upon some men who have held high places in Masonic Councils; and that, as one eminent brother has expressed it, men whom I had been want to look up to as leaders, are fifty years behind the times and a thousand years behind the principles they profess," I have become indifferent to their abuse: as Lawrence Burmott expressed it, "I do not find that the calumny of a few Modern Masons has done me any real injury."

"I write for four (4) classes of readers: FIRST, the little band of Masonic Scholars who, in diverse climes, pursue their studies for the sake of truth alone—the most of these already know and declare that the Grand Lodge of Washington is right; SECOND, that large class of brethren who have neither time nor opportunities for personal investigation, and are compelled to take their information second hand; THIRD, a determined and implacable and well organized band of men who have determined that, right or wrong, Mason or no Mason, come what may, the Negro shall not be recognized by American Grand Lodges; and LASTLY, the members of our own Grand Lodge, who may be called upon to act upon matters which I shall discuss, and who have a right to feel sure of their ground, before acting.

I feel that the first and the last of these classes know me well enough to rely implicitly on the frankness and candor with which I shall address them. I feel quite as certain that the discordant and milignant cries of the third class will so drown my voice that for the present it will not reach the ears of the second; and possessed of this conviction, I am content to address the few of today, the many of tomorrow—to appeal to posterity and a future age." (end of quote)

There are many comments both pro and con that I could bring you concerning this Report, but time will not permit me to do so, I will curtail my remarks.

This prepared address is intended both for your enlightenment and also that you too may see for yourselves, the treachery, hypocrisy and deceitfulness that has prevailed for so long a time in many Masonic Lodges and Grand Lodges, especially by those in high places who profess and practice the principles of Freemasonry, down to this day. One is prone to wonder just how far has Masonry travelled towards its objective, the Brotherhood of man?

In final conclusion it must be stated that our Illustrious Bro. William H. Upton, although severely abused and critized for his convictions, remained firm in his beliefs to his dying day. Prior to his death he had the following recorded in his last will and testament: (quote)

"I desire no monument except the most simple headstone to mark my grave until such time as the Grand Lodge F. & A.M. of Washington, or some other Masonic Grand Lodge now recognized by it, shall unite with some organization of those Masons commonly known as Negro Masons...or at least with representative members of some such organization... in erecting near my grave a monument to the memory of myself and my late wife." (end of quote) Proceedings of M.W. Grand Lodge F. & A.M. Washington. Vol. XVI, Part II, 1907 p302

Thus my brothers I have attempted to give you a vivid account of how:

"TWO BLACKS INADVERTENTLY
DISRUPTED WHITE AMERICA."

Thank You

57th SESSION — CONFERENCE OF GRAND MASTERS — PRINCE HALL MASONS

Front Row: Clarence J. Groves, New Jersey; Charles H. Jenkins, Iowa; Samuel T. Daniels, Maryland; I.H. Clayborn, Texas; Jno. G. Lewis, Jr., Louisiana; David L. Holliman, Colorado; Dr. X. L. Neal, Georgia; William Reynolds, Missouri; Horace Kelly, New Mexico; H.M. Thompson, Mississippi; Robert L. Alston, Ohio; John D. Howard, District of Columbia.
Second Row: James E. Taylor, Massachusetts; James H. Black, Illinois; Lomas Gist, South Carolina; Wendolyn G. Terrell, Michigan; Johnnie Cato, Wisconsin; Rev. H. J. Evans, Arkansas; Eugene B. Penn, Nebraska; James M. Landers, Indiana; Judge C.P. Houston, Jr., Delaware; Charles McGarrah, New York.
Third Row: Herbert J. Turner, Alaska; Allie S. Carr Sr., Kentucky; James W. Davis, Washington; James E. Morley, Bahamas; Erskine R. Nunn, West Virginia; Jessie B. Thompson, California; Landon H. White, Virginia; Enoch A. Parker, Sr., Connecticut; Clarence J. Groves, New Jersey; Rudolph Bradley, Florida and T. Roosevelt Butler, Kansas.

**A SPEECH BY
JOSEPH A. WALKES, JR.
F.P.S. [KANSAS]
President
The Phylaxis Society**

**TO THE CONFERENCE OF
PRINCE HALL GRAND MASTERS
Colorado Springs, Colorado
May 5-7, 1976**

It is a pleasure, though an awesome one, to address such an honorable and august body of Freemasons, which combined, represent one of the major institutions founded by Blacks for the benefit of our race, which has sustained us for 200 years.

My purpose is to attempt to explain the role of a small body of Prince Hall Freemasons who have organized themselves into a research society and their relationship to you, to Freemasonry in general, and to Prince Hall Freemasonry in particular.

Understanding, that there is more to Masonry than the four walls of our individual Lodges. That there is more to Masonry than the combined efforts of our Districts. That there is more to Masonry than the yearly gatherings of our Grand Lodges. That there is infact, a whole world of Masonry outside our individual circle of influence, and that the knowledge that can be gained is awesome. It is an adventure within itself. It is an education within itself. And this is my theme...Education...Masonic education.

Today's world is one that is hectic, of hustle and bustle, of going here and there, of doing this and that, of television, pocket calculators, CB radios, massive entertainment, travel, of putting it together.

It is also a time of keen competition, where everything is geared to compete for the individual's time. Masonry likewise competes for our time, and for our fraternity this competition for our time, is often for our very survival.

Caucasian Freemasonry, which publishes such figures, recorded for the year 1973, a total membership in the United States at 3,611,448. With seven Grand Lodges showing a gain of 3,662 and 43 Grand Lodges showing a loss of 53,721 for a total net loss of more than 50,000. Prince Hall Masonry is likewise in a decline.

I would not attempt to suggest that I have a solution, I don't, and others much more qualified than I, have tackled this problem. But, we must look at all of our options.

We raise the Master Mason, then often sit him in the Lodge with no designs upon the Trestle Board. When a man knocks at the door of Masonry and is admitted, it is only natural that he wants to learn everything that a candidate should know.

He has a right to expect that his Lodge will discharge its obligation to him—not merely by teaching him the forms and ceremonies he is to go through when taking the degrees but also he has a right to expect that someone will teach him all he must know and answer the many questions that occur to him, and not leave him to flounder around in a sea of darkness when Masonic light is supposed to be his for the asking.

Interest must be generated to motivate the Craft. And to raise this level of interest, one option that is open to us, is through Masonic education and information, which will open the doors to that wide world of Masonry, that awaits to be rediscovered by this generation, and then to bask in its knowledge and beauty.

To look not only towards the future, and the present, but to the past as well. For as the author James Baldwin says, the past is all that make the present coherent.

I spoke of options, and I spoke of a small body of Freemasons, and I have also spoke of Masonic education, which as a combination is the ingredients of the society of Light. A society for Prince Hall Freemasons who seek more light, and who have light to impart! A society based on education, on history, on literature, on research, and also on pride. A society of challenge.

I present to you an ancient Grecian idiom, Phylaxis, which translated means to preserve and to safeguard. Let's briefly explore its meaning.

To preserve and to safeguard to this society means to preserve not only the historical heritage of our Masonic past, the 200 years of our Masonic existence, but to honor ourselves and to bask in the Masonic glory that is ours.

To safeguard our existence from our enemies, from those who mean us harm, from those who would distort our image with falsehoods and untruths. To safeguard our fraternity by the use of the most powerful weapon at our disposal, which Lord Byron called "Things, and a small drop of ink, falling like dew upon a thought, produces that which makes thousands, perhaps millions think!"

The written word! For there is no more powerful weapon against the sword of distortion, then, the unbias pen of truth coupled with the undeniable verification of facts.

We are reminded of the great Prince Hall Historian, R.W. Harry A. Williamson, of the Prince Hall Grand Lodge of New York and his attempt to form a Research Lodge chartered by that Grand Lodge in the 1940's, with the blessings of Louis Fair, Jr., then Grand Master, which was established to encourage and promote the study and research into Ancient Craft Masonry.

Its name, which is similar to ours, was Phyloran. It was a bold step forward, and we, who have followed in their footsteps have taken it one step further.

Not as a Masonic body with limitation of active membership to one Jurisdiction, but as a research society which limits its active membership to Prince Hall Freemasons.

Not as a chartered research Lodge which search for Light would be jurisdictional, but as a International society which dispenses its light to the entire Masonic community.

Not as the research Lodge which Bro. Williamson hoped that Freemasons everywhere would become deeply interested in and would join with the Craft in New York for the pursuit of Light, but as the Phylaxis Society, which joins with the entire world Masonic community, in that endeavor.

The Society is better known by the magazine that it publishes each quarter for its membership. **THE PHYLAXIS!**

And those who receive it can attest to the fact that it is the most unique magazine published within Prince Hall Masonry, and that within its pages is to be found that Masonic adventure we simply proclaim as Light.

The fact that it has received praise and acceptance through out the entire Masonic community, on these shores of North America as well as Europe, and that it is on file and display in Masonic libraries and museums, that it is discussed in research Lodges and Grand Lodges outside of our immediate Prince Hall family, and the fact, that for many it is the first time that they have come into contact with our fraternity, and it is for the first time their introduction to our history, our literature, and our lectures is proof of a measure of success of one of our programs.

In our search for input, we have dusted off the shelves of Masonic libraries and museums, here and abroad; we have searched Grand Lodge archives, as well as the archives of the United States of America. We have searched Black Historical Associations and Societies, their libraries and their collections, and in the process have built a worthy collection of our own.

And not content with this, we invite and encourage our members to do likewise. Not to be content to merely attend Lodge, but to seek and explore the entire breath of Masonry, thereby strengthening themselves, their Lodges, their Grand Lodges, and the entire Prince Hall Fraternity.

The very essence of the Society is not found only in its name, which means to preserve, to safeguard, to educate, but can be seen in its symbol, which often mystifies so many with its bold number of 15, which in reality represents Prince Hall and the 14 Fellows raised with him March 6th, 1775.

Notice if you will, I mentioned Fellows. For within the structure of the Society is the honored title of Fellow, which we limit to 15 in total. An honor which must be earned, as our certificate reads, in recognition for service to the Society, Humanity and Prince Hall Freemasonry. The receipient being elected to this honor on the 6th of March each year.

At the present time there are only a handful of members who carry this honored title. I will not name those so honored, but you, who are there, Grand Masters are aware of their names.

The resources of the Society for the most part, has not been fully tapped by our fraternity. It is not only a tool for Masonic education, it is a bureau of information, it is an instrument of Public Relations for Prince Hall Masonry, it is an investigation agency aimed at those who would imitate us, it is a monitoring service for those Masonic organizations who publish papers on our fraternity, it is a sounding board to let our Masonic views known throughout the Masonic community, it is an answering service for those who would distort the truth and level attacks at our solidarity, it is all of these things and more, and with your help we hope to see it grow. We desire each and every Grand Master, each and every Prince Hall Lodges, each and every Master Masons to join with us in this great work, by becoming members of this honorable society of light.

As a Society of Prince Hall Freemasons we have let it be known to the entire Masonic community, that, in the words of Samuel W. Clark, Past Grand Master of Most Worshipful Prince Hall Grand Lodge of Ohio, proclaimed at the 50th Annual Communication of its Grand Lodge, that...

As Negro Masons, we need expect no recognition from white American Masons; I plead for none; I care for none at the sacrifice of honor and dignity. I stand as just, as true, as pure a Freemason as ever trod God's green earth.

My title is as perfect as that of the Prince of Wales or the President of the United States; as he who travels with the caravan over the desert or he who dwells on the plains of the far west.

Where ever he may be upon the continents of the land or the islands of the sea, if he be a Freemason he is my Brother and cannot deny me if he would!

NOTES, QUERIES AND INFORMATION OF ITEMS OF MASONIC INTEREST
By The Phylaxis Society, P.O. Box 3151, Ft. Leavenworth, Ks. 66027

THIS SECTION IS PRESENTED TO OUR READERS, and relates to matters pertaining to Prince Hall Masonic history, biography and tradition.

We invite our readers and members to send such material that is appropriate for use in this column. It must be stressed that this page is for EXCHANGE of information and opinions concerning Prince Hall Masonry and does not pretend to provide the final answers to any query.

7) 1/6-5(2/3-3. WHAT IS THE MEANING? It is rather amusing but our friend Jerry Marsengill, Associate Editor of the Philalethes Magazine and Honorary Fellow of the Phylaxis Society; Grand Master Grand Council of Royal and Select Masters of the State of Iowa (Caucasian), Secretary of Research Lodge No. 2 of Des Moines, Iowa and noted Masonic author failed to recognize these numbers. It would be interesting to see how many members of the Phylaxis Society know what their meanings are. Drop us a line.

LODGE REGALIA AND MASONIC SUPPLIES, Drew Sales; 723 West 111th Street, Chicago, Illinois 60628. Phone (312) 995-6807. Bro. Drew is a member of Jachin Lodge No. 133, Chicago. A Prince Hall Mason on the move.

A BICENTENNIAL TRIBUTE TO PRINCE HALL Masonry—1775-1976 October 7, 1976 at the New York Hilton Hotel. It will be a Testimonial Dinner to Dr. Jno. G. Lewis, Jr., Grand Master of Prince Hall Masons of Louisiana and Sovereign Grand Commander, Southern Jurisdiction; who has given more than fifty years of his life to Prince Hall Freemasonry. Grand Master Lewis was recently re-elected for the 36th consecutive year as Grand Master of Masons for the State of Louisiana. Dr. Lewis is a member of the Phylaxis Society.

WREATHS PLACED ON TOMBS OF OUTSTANDING PRINCE HALL MASONS IN NEW ORLEANS. The Prince Hall Grand Lodge of Louisiana recently visited the gravesites of two outstanding Prince Hall Freemasons; Oscar J. Dunn and P.B.S. Pinchback. Both Brother Dunn and Pinchback served as Lieutenant Governor of Louisiana and Bro. Pinchback filled the office of Governor. Bro. Dunn served as Grand Master of Prince Hall Masons of Louisiana from 1864 to 1867, while Bro. Pinchback was Worshipful Master and Secretary of Stringer Lodge No. 3. JET Magazine (Aug. 26 issue) reported that the Ku Klux Klan interrupted ceremonies honoring Bro. Pinchback in the chambers of the Louisiana House in Baton Rouge. America may be celebrating its Bi-centennial but the old problems remain.

MIDDLE-CLASS BLACKS IN A WHITE SOCIETY, Prince Hall Freemasonry in America by William Alan Muraskin is a most interesting book and should be read by all Prince Hall Freemasons. The Society will print a complete review of it in a later issue. For those interested the book can be purchased from The University of California Press, 1414 South Tenth Street, Richmond, California 94804. Cost $14.95.

CONFERENCE OF GRAND MASTERS PRINCE HALL MASONS OF AMERICA will meet in the following cities the following years:
    1977 — Washington, D.C.
    1978 — Seattle, Washington
    1979 — Cincinnati, Ohio
    1980 — Bahamas (Massachusetts Yielded)
    1981 — South Carolina
    1982 — Virginia
    1983 — Florida (Miami)
    1984 — Wilmington, Del.
    1985 — Arkansas

TRANSACTIONS OF THE PHYLAXIS SOCIETY. Copies of the Transactions of the Phylaxis Society can also be purchased from the President Joseph A. Walkes, Jr., F.P.S., P.O. Box 3151, Ft. Leavenworth, Kansas 66027. Cost $2.00.

BACK ISSUES OF THE PHYLAXIS MAGAZINE: Volume I Number 3 (August 1974) and Volume II Number 3 (September 1975) are available. Only a limited number. $1.25 each. Make check payable to the Phylaxis Society, forward to the President.

PRINCE HALL MASONIC YEARBOOK. The official list of Prince Hall Masonic Lodges around the globe can be received from Thomas G. Waldon, P.G.M., Executive Secretary-Treasurer Conference of Prince Hall Grand Masters, 2322 Tippecanoe, Terre Haute, Indiana 47807. Cost $2.00, allow about three weeks for delivery.

GRAND MASTER LEWIS listed in latest edition of Who's Who in America, page 1892, Volume 2 of the 39th edition, 1976-77 of Who's Who in America. Along with the usual biographical information given on persons included in the edition, we quote the last sentence of the listing as follows: "Any success I may have achieved can be summed up in these words: I have tried to so live that no one will regret having done me a favor."

Cont. on Page 179

REPORT OF THE CAUCASIAN GRAND LODGE F. & A.M. OF WISCONSIN

TO THE MOST WORSHIPFUL GRAND MASTER, CARL W. SKOOG, AND TO THE GRAND LODGE, F. & A.M. OF WISCONSIN:

The "Committee to Study Nonrecognized Grand Lodges" herewith submits its final report concerning the question whether the Grand Lodge of Prince Hall Masons of Wisconsin, Inc. (for convenience hereinafter referred to as "Prince Hall") shall be recognized by the Grand Lodge of Wisconsin (hereinafter for convenience "Grand Lodge").

As was true with respect to the investigation and study conducted by the Committee prior to its initial report, dated June 11, 1974, the Committee has found no occasion to concern itself with the subject of admission of black candidates to membership in Masonic Lodges operating under the jurisdiction of the Grand Lodge, because it is clear that the Grand Lodge makes no distinction between men on the basis of race, color, or creed.

In its study the Committee has considered:
(a) The history of Prince Hall Masonry in the United States, and, in particular, the manner in which it was established.
(b) The history of "Prince Hall."
(c) The permissibility under the Masonic Code of the Grand Lodge, as amended, of two Grand Lodges co-exisiting within the State of Wisconsin.
(d) Conformity on the part of "Prince Hall" to Masonic Doctrine and Ritual, as embraced and practiced by the Grand Lodge.
(e) What the practical consequences of "recognition" would be in terms of fraternal relationship and in terms of any changes in the status of the Grand Lodge before the public at large.

In its initial report the Committee included a resume of the history of Prince Hall Masonry, as obtained from a variety of sources which the Committee deems authoritative. It is assumed that such historical resume will be considered a part of this report, and appended as an addendum to this Report.

The Committee, nonetheless, pursued further its investigation regarding the history of Prince Hall Masonry, and found of particular value the work of Harry E. Davis, entitled **"A History of Free Masonry Among Negroes in America."** Because the "History" by Harry E. Davis, a member of the Cleveland, Ohio, Bar, and the Special Deputy for Foreign Relations of the Supreme Council, Northern Jurisdiction (Prince Hall Affiliation) was carefully reviewed prior to publication by members of the Supreme Council of the Ancient Accepted Scottish Rite for the Northern Masonic Jurisdiction of the United States, including the then Sovereign Grand Commander, Ill. Melvin F. Johnson, 33°, and Supreme Council Historian and Grand Secretary General, Ill. Samuel H. Baynard, Jr., 33°, both of whom were recognized Masonic scholars, and after reference to the Committee on Foreign Relations of the Supreme Council, an appropriation by the Supreme Council for financial aid in publishing the book was made, the Committee considers it desirable to further append to this report a compendium of excerpts from the "History" to supplement and expand upon the origin and development of Prince Hall Masonry in the United States. The members of the Committee are in agreement that Prince Hall Masonry constitutes a legitimate Masonic organization, and is entitled to be treated accordingly.

The Committee undertook, in particular, to trace the origin and basis for establishment of the Grand Lodge of Prince Hall Masons of Wisconsin. In the year 1878 Brown Lodge No. 25 was organized, and later became Widows' Son Lodge No. 1, Milwaukee. In 1894 Triangular Lodge No. 53 was organized in Superior, Wisconsin. In 1906 Capitol City Lodge No. 75 was organized in Madison. In 1906 W.K. Kennedy Lodge No. 106 was organized in Beloit, and in 1924 L.F. Palmer Lodge No. 115 was organized in Milwaukee and later became Blazing Star Lodge No. 4. On June 29, 1925, the Grand Lodge of Prince Hall Masons, F. & A.M. of Wisconsin was created by Charter by the then existing Grand Lodge of Prince Hall Masons of Illinois. As was true in the case of our Grand Lodge, the Illinois Lodge of Prince Hall Masons had previously been created as the Masonic Order moved westward from the eastern portion of the United States. Thus your Committee has concluded that the Grand Lodge of Prince Hall Masons of Wisconsin was organized and exists on substantially the same basis as has been true of various recognized "white" Grand Lodges throughout the United States.

The next point of inquiry pursued was whether the Masonic Code of Wisconsin contains any provision which would preclude the recognition of the Grand Lodge of Prince Hall Masons of Wisconsin. The Masonic Code provides that the territorial jurisdiction of the Grand Lodge shall embrace the State of Wisconsin (Section 3.01), and that it is the supreme Masonic authority in the State of Wisconsin subject only to the Ancient Landmarks (Section 3.02). Particularly worthy of note is Section 37.03, relating to "recognition of other Grand Lodges" which is set forth in full:

"37.03 **Recognition of Other Grand Lodges**
Recognition of other Grand Lodges is the exclusive perogative of this Grand Lodge and the following shall be the rules of guide in the fraternal recognition of

other Grand Lodges of Free and Accepted Masons:

"Rule 1. Such Grand Lodges must be sovereign, independent and supreme—the sole governing body over its constituent lodges."

"Rule 2. It must be in possession of and exclusively control the work of the Entered Apprentice, Fellow Craft and Master Mason degrees in the lodges under its authority."

"Rule 3. It must display the volume of the Sacred Law on its altars; requiring a belief in diety; make Masons of men only; exclude religious and political questions and discussions from its lodges; and must conform to, abide by, and uphold the Ancient Landmarks of Ancient Craft Masonry."

"Rule 4. Lodges forming a new Grand Lodge must be at least three in number and must trace their descent from regular sources recognized by this Grand Lodge."

"Rule 5. Recognition will not be extended to a new Grand Lodge that shall have been formed in occupied territory against the wishes of a recognized Grand Lodge in that territory.

"Rule 6. Recogniton will not be extended to a Grand Lodge that shall warrant lodges in territory occupied by a regular Grand Lodge against the wishes of that Grand Lodge."

"Rule 7. In countries where the doctrine of exclusive territorial jurisdiction does not apply, two or more Grand Lodges occupying the same or overlapping territory, recognizing each other as regular and conforming in all other respects to our requirements, may be recognized.

"Rule 8. Grand Lodges of Scottish Rite Descent, having renounced allegiance to any other superior authority, and having since had a long established and continous existence during which they have conformed to all our requirements, may be recognized."

"Rule 9. Although the original formation of a Grand Lodge may have been irregular, if it has had a long continuous and uninterrupted existence and otherwise conforms to our requirements, it may be recognized."

It is the determination of the Committee that the foregoing provisions do not in any manner proscribe the recognition of the Grand Lodge of Prince Hall Masons of Wisconsin. Moreover, on the question of exclusive territorial jurisdiction, the observation of Harry E. Davis in his "History" is considered fair comment. He argued

"***the territorial doctrine should not be used to challenge the legitimacy of Masonic establishments which were in existence long before the doctrine obtained respectable sanction, even though it has gained such general acceptance in America that today it has the force and effect of law." (page 127)

In the view of the Committee, the sole remaining consideration was whether the Grand Lodge of Prince Hall of Wisconsin and its constituent lodges require observance of and conformity to establish and accepted Masonic Ritual and Doctrine. While this area of investigation presented some practical problems, particularly the obligation of secrecy to which of Grand Lodge subscribes and to which the Committee has been informed the Grand Lodge of Prince Hall Masons of Wisconsin in like manner subscribes, it is nevertheless true that rather full and complete documentation of Masonic Ritual and Doctrine is available in most major libraries throughout the United States, and is, in fact, available in the Milwaukee Public Library. The Grand Master of the Grand Lodge of Prince Hall Masons of Wisconsin has provided the Committee with a statement substantiates the fact that the Grand Lodge of Prince Hall Masons of Wisconsin observes and conforms to the Ancient and Accepted Rules and Practices applicable to the conduct of Masonic Proceedings.

The Committee suggests that, it may be entirely possible that, within the world of Masonry, there are some insignificant variances in procedure. Any such minor variation should not militate against recognition of the Grand Lodge of Prince Hall Masons of Wisconsin, other considerations aside, any more than would be true in the case of any presently recognized Grand Lodge.

Finally, the Committee is of the opinion that recognition will make possible the opportunity for visitation by members of constituent lodges of the Grand Lodge of Wisconsin to constituent lodges under the jurisdiction of the Grand Lodge of Prince Hall Masons of Wisconsin, and, conversely, by members of constituent lodges of the Grand Lodge of Prince Hall Masons of Wisconsin. We hasten to add that such right of visitation would be subject to the same, but not different, restrictions as exist in the case of visitation by a member of one constituent lodge of the Grand Lodge of Wisconsin to another constituent lodge of the Grand Lodge of Wisconsin to another constituent lodge of the Grand Lodge of Wisconsin. Additionally, such recognition may well provide the means by which the Grand Lodge of Wisconsin and the Grand Lodge of Prince Hall Masons of Wisconsin may collaborate in those areas of activity in which they have mutual and common interests.

The Committee respectfully recommends that the Grand Lodge reproduce this Report, together with the addendums thereto, and distribute the same through the Grand Secretary's office to the Masters and Wardens of each constituent lodge in order that the information compiled by the Committee may be made available preliminary to formal consideration of any

175

action on the subject by the Grand Lodge in the future.

Respectfully submitted,

GEORGE R. CURRIE, Chairman
FLOYD W. McBURNEY
KENNETH M. KENNEY
PERRY A. SAITO
STEWART HONECK

PHYLAXIS NOTE: This Committee was chaired by Brother George R. Currie, former Chief Justice of the Supreme Court of Wisconsin and is hereby reprinted without comment.

THE ORIGIN AND OBJECTS OF ANCIENT FREE MASONRY

(Cont. from Previous Edition)

The three great attributes of Deity—omniscience, omnipotence, and omnipresence—were recognized by the ancients, and represented in the character given to their ruling god—as above mentioned—as presiding over the universe of eternal space—of celum, terra, and tartarus—answering to the Christian doctrine of three persons in one—Father, Son and Holy Ghost.[3]

Man, then, to assimilate God must, in his nature, be a trinity of systems—morally, intellectually and physically. This great truth appears to have been known to King David, who with emotion, exclaims, "We are wonderfully and fearfully made."

To convince man of the importance of his own being and impress him with a proper sense of his duty to his Creator were what was desired, and to effect this would also impress him with a sense of his duty and obligations to society and the laws intended for his government. For this purpose was the beautiful fabric of Masonry established, and illustrated in the structure of man's person.

Man, scientifically developed, is a moral, intellectual, and physical being—composed of an osseous, muscular, and vital structure; of solid, flexible and liquid parts. With an intellect—a mind, the constituent principles of which he is incapable of analyzing or comprehending, which rises superior to its earthy tenement, with the velocity of lightning, soars to the summit of altitude, descends to the depth of profundity, and flies to the wide-spread expanse of eternal space. What can be more God-like than this, to understand which is to give man a proper sense of his own importance, and consequently his duty to his fellows, by which alone, he fulfills the high mission for which he is sent on his temporary pilgrimage.

While the Africans, who were the authors of this mysterious and beautiful Order, did much to bring it to perfection by the establishment of the great principles of man's likeness to Jehovah in a tri-une existence, yet, until the time of King Solomon, there was a great deficiency in his government, in consequence of the policy being monopolized by the priesthood and certain privileged classes or families.

For the purpose of remedying what was now conceived to be a great evil in the policy of the world, and for their better government to place wisdom within the acquirement of all men, King Solomon summoned together the united wisdom of the world, —men of all nations and races—to consider the great project of reducing the mystic ties to a more practical and systematic principle, and stereotyping it with physical science, by rearing the stupendous and magnificent temple at Jerusalem.[4] For the accomplishment of this masterpiece of all human projects, there were laborers or attendants, mechanics or workmen, and overseers or master-builders. Added to these, there was a designer or originator of all the schemes, an architect or draughtsman, and a furnisher of all the materials for the building—all and every thing of which was classified and arranged after the order of trinity, the building itself, when finished, being composed of an outer, an inner, and a central court.

After the completion of this great work, the implements of labor having been laid aside, there were scattered to the utmost parts of the earth, seventy thousand laborers, eighty thousand workmen, and three thousand and three hundred master builders, making one hundred and fifty-three thousand and three hundred artizans, each of whom having been instructed in all the mysteries of the temple, was fully competent to teach all the arts and sciences acquired at Jerusalem in as many different cities, provinces, states or tribes. At this period, the mysteries assumed the name of Masonry, induced from the building of the temple; and at this time, also commenced the universality of the Order, arising from the going forth of the builders into all parts of the world. This then, was the establishment of Masonry, which has been handed down through all succeeding ages.

For a period of years after the destruction of the temple and the sacred or mystic records, there was some slight derangement in the Craft; men were becoming ungovernable both in church and state owing to the want of proper instruction, and their consequent ignorance of the relation they bore to their Creator and society. For the purpose of again bringing back the "prodigal son" to the household of his father, the "stray sheep" to the rich pastures of the fold of Israel, and repairing the somewhat defaced, honored monument of time, Prince Edwin of England, in 930 of the Christian era, being nine hundred and twenty-two

176

years ago, summoned together at York, all the wise men of the order, where the rites were again scientifically systematized, and preserved for coming time. At this point, the Order, in honor to Prince Edwin, assigned to itself the title of York Masonry.

THE STAGE OF MAN'S HISTORY

We have here the history of man's existence from Adam to Solomon, showing three distinct periods, fraught with more mystery than all things else, save the ushering in the Christian era by the birth of the adorable Son of God: his origin in Adam's creation, his preservation in Noah's ark, and his prospects of redemption from the curse of God's broken laws by the promises held out in that mysteriously incomprehensible work of building the temple by Solomon. Adam, Noah, and Solomon, then, are the three great types of the condition of man—his sojourn here on earth, and his prospects of a future bliss.

Founded upon the similitude and consequent responsibility to his Creator, the ancients taught the doctrine of a rectitude of conduct and purpose of heart, as the only surety for the successful government of man, and the regulations of society around him. Whether Gentiles, Greeks or Jews, all taught the same as necessary to his government on earth—his responsibility to a Supreme Being, the author and Creator of himself. But the mythology of those days, not unlike the scientific theology of the days in which we live, consisted of a sea of such metaphysical depth, that the mass of mankind was unable to fathom it. Instead, then, of accomplishing the object for which this wise policy was established, the design was thwarted by the manner in which it was propagated. Man adhered but little, and cared less, for that in which he could never be fully instructed, nor be made to understand, in consequence of his deficiency in a thorough literary education—this being the exclusive privilege of those in affluent circumstances. All these imperfections have been remedied, in the practical workings of the comprehensive system of Free and Accepted Masonry, as handed down to us from the archives at Jerusalem. All men, of every country, clime, color or conditon, (when morally worthy,) are acceptable to the portals of Masonic jurisprudence.

In many parts of the world, the people of various nations were subject to lose their liberty in several ways. A forfeiture by crime, as in our country; by voluntary servitude for a stipulated sum or reward, as among the Hindoos; and by capture in battle and being sold into slavery, as in Algiers. Against these Masonry found it necessary to provide, and accordingly the first two classes were positively proscribed as utterly unworthy of its benefits, as they were equally unworthy of the respectful consideration of the good among mankind. In this, however, was never contemplated the third class of bondees; for none but him who voluntarily comprised his liberty was recognized as a slave by Masons. As there must be a criminal intention in the commission of a crime, so must the act of the criminal be voluntary; hence the criminal and the voluntary bondsmen have both forfeited their Masonic rights by willing degradation. In the case of the captive, and entirely different person is presented before us, who has greater claims upon our sympathies than the untrammeled freeman. Instead of the degraded vassal and voluntary slave, whose prostrate position only facilitates the aspect of his horrile deformity, you have the bold, the brave, the high-minded, the independent-spirit, and manly form of a kindred brother in humanity, whose heart is burning, whose breast is heaving, and whose soul is wrung with panting aspirations for liberty—a commander, a chieftain, a knight, or a prince, it may be—still he is a captive and by the laws of captivity, a slave. Does Masonry, then, contemplate the withholding of its privileges from such applicants as these? Certainly not; since Moses, (to whom our great Grand Master Solomon, the founder of the temple, is indebted for his Masonic wisdom,) was born and lived in captivity eighty years, and by the laws of his captors a slave. It matters not whether captured in actual conflict, sleeping by the wayside, or in a cradle of bulrushes, after birth; so that there be a longing aspiration for liberty, and a manly determination to be free. Policy alone will not permit of the order to confer Masonic privileges on one while yet in captivity; but the fact of his former condition as such, or that of his parents, can have no bearing whatever on him. The mind and the desires of the recipient must be free; and at the time of his endowment with these privileges, his person and mind must be unencumbered with all earthly trammels or fetters. This is what is meant by Free and Accepted Masonry, to distinguish it from the order when formerly conferred upon the few, like the order of nobility, taking precedence by rank and birth, whether the inheritor was worthy or not of so high and precious privileges.

In the three great periods as presented to view, you have the three great stages of man's existence—Adam, with childlike innocence in the Garden of Eden, turned out for disobedience, as a youth upon the world, without the protecting hand of his Omnipotent Parent—Noah, as in adventurous manhood, in constructing and launching his great vessel (the Ark) "upon the face of the great deep"; and Solomon, as in old age, in devising, planning and counseling, and heaping up treasures in building the temple of Jerusalem; all of which are impressively typified, in the cardinal Degrees of Masonry. The Entered Apprentice as a child, and as in youth the Fellow

177

Craft; the Master Mason, as in mature and thinking manhood; and as an old and reflective man of years of wisdom, the Royal Arch completes the history of his journey of life.

ITS INTRODUCTION INTO THE UNITED STATES

Masonry was introduced into the United States by grant of a warrant to Henry Price, Esq. of Boston, on the 30th of July, 1733, as Right Worshipful Grand Master of North America, "with full power and authority to appoint his Deputy," by the Right Honorable and Most Worshipful Anthony Lord Viscount Montague "Grand Master of Masons in England." Cole's Lib. p. 332. I do not conceive it necessary to prosecute the history of Masonry farther in this country; but let it suffice to say, that hostilities which commenced between Great Britian and America in 1775, absolved all Masonic ties between the two countries, and left American Masons free to act according to the suggestions of the peculiar circumstances in which they were then placed. With the independence of the country, commenced the independence of Masonic jurisdiction in the United States.[3]

The Grand Lodge of Massachusetts was formed in 1769; Maine, New Hampshire, 1789; Rhode Island, 1791; Vermont, 1794; New York, 1787; (another being established in 1826, which has recently been denounced by England and all other legal Masonic jurisdictions throughout the world;) New Jersey, 1786; Pennsylvania, 1734, under England, to which she remained attached until September, 1786, when the connection was absolved; Deleware, 1806; Virginia, 1778; N. Carolina, 1787; S. Carolina, 1787; Georgia, 1786; Ohio, 1808; Kentucky, 1800; Louisiana, Mississippi and Tennessee, the data not being given. Cole's Lib. 363 to 375. This gives a fair history of the introduction of Masonry into the United States of America.

AMONG COLORED MEN IN THE UNITED STATES

In the year 178—, a number of colored men in Boston, Massachusetts, applied to the proper source for a grant of Masonic privileges, and this being denied them, by force of necessity they went to England, which at that time not recognizing the Masonic fraternity of America, the then acting Grand Master, (recorded on the warrant as the Right Honorable, Henry Frederick, Duke of Cumberland) granted a warrant to the colored men to make Masons and establish Lodges, subject, of course, to the Grand Lodge of England. In course of time, their ties became absolved; not before it was preceded by the establishment of an independent Grand Lodge in Philadelphia, Pa., by colored men, and subsequently, general Grand Lodge of North America.

In the year 1832, another Grand Lodge was established by a party of dissatisfied colored Masons in the city of Philadelphia, known as the "Hiram Grand Lodge of the State of Pennsylvania".[6] There was, also for many years, a small faction who rather opposed the F.I.A.G.L. still adhering to what they conceived to be the most legitimate source—the old African Lodge of Boston, among whom was the colored Lodge of Boston, and a very respectable body in New York City, known as the "Boyer Lodge." In December, 184- by a grand communication of a representative body of all the colored Lodges in the United States, held in the city of New York, the differences and wounds which long existed were all settled and healed, a complete union formed, and a National Grand Lodge established, by the choice and election, in due Masonic form, of Past Master, John T. Hilton, of Boston, Mass. Most Worshipful Grand Master of the National Grand Lodge, and William E. Ambush, M.W.N.G. Secretary

Cont. Next Edition

FOOTNOTES

3. One of the old doctrines of the priesthood was, that God the Father presided over heaven, the Holy Ghost on earth and Christ the Son in hell; hence, his descent into the grave is called a descent into hell, where some believe, or affect to believe, he ever remains; and this is the foundation of the belief of that Christian sect whose doctrines teach purification and redemption in the grave,—purgatory, a place of purging or purification—or hell.

4. Here the Trinity is again typified: three times fifty thousand, three times one thousand, and three times one hundred.

5. It is said, that at that early period of its existence in this country, entertaining a kind of superstitious idea of its sacredness, the Masonic warrant was kept closely in some secret place, prohibited from the view of all but Masons; consequently when General Warren—who was the Grand Master of Massachusetts—fell in the Revolutionary struggle, the warrant was lost, and with it, Masonry in Massachusetts. All Masons are familiar with the fact that Grand Master Warren was raised from his grave and search made, doubtless, supposing that the warrant might have been found councealed about his person.

6. This Grand Lodge dissolved in 1847, after an existence of fifteen years, becoming convinced that they had no just nor legal foundation for an independent existence; and none contributed more to the accomplishment of so desirable an end, than the then acting Grand Master of the Hiram Grand Lodge,—Mr. Samuel Van Brakle, an upright, intelligent, and excellent man.

WELCOME TO NEW MEMBERS

Dr. G. Wesley Allen, Fayetteville, North Carolina 28302. Recommended by James A. Mingo, M.P.S.

M. Brooks Waters, Baltimore Maryland 21217. Recommended by James A. Mingo, M.P.S.

Percy E. Norris, Columbia, South Carolina 29210. Recommended by James A. Mingo, M.P.S.

Col. West A. Hamilton, Washington, D.C. 20011. Recommended by James A. Mingo, M.P.S.

Stanford J. Hughes, Sr., Hyattsville, Maryland 20785. Recommended by James A. Mingo, M.P.S.

Augustus Finley, Jr., Washington, D.C. 20017. Recommended by James A. Mingo, M.P.S.

Dr. Hildrus A. Poindexter, Clinton, Maryland 20735. Recommended by James A. Mingo, M.P.S.

Burton W. Johnson, Washington, D.C. 20019. Recommended by James A. Mingo M.P.S.

Attorney DeLong Harris, Washington, D.C. 20001. Recommended by James A. Mingo, M.P.S.

Robert R. Childs, Jr., Washington, D.C. 20012. Recommended by James A. Mingo, M.P.S.

Rev. Milton Johnson, Washington, D.C. 20012. Recommended by James A. Mingo, M.P.S.

J. Henry Evans, Jr., P.G.M., Emporia, Virginia 23847. Recommended by James A. Mingo, M.P.S.

William R. Washington, Kansas City, Missouri 64130. Recommended by Maurice C. Davis, M.P.S.

Leslie Bowen, Kansas City, Missouri 64109. Recommended by Joseph A. Walkes, F.P.S.

Wendall T. Fagin, Washington, D.C. 20011. Recommended by James A. Mingo, M.P.S.

Carl C. Burton, Vandenberg AFB, Ca. 93437. Recommended by Herbert Dailey, M.P.S.

William David Robinson, Offutt AFB, Nebraska 68993. Recommended by Herbert Dailey, M.P.S.

Edward Jackson, Moses Lake, Washington 98837. Recommended by William D. Green, M.P.S.

Walter H. Howell, Queens Village, New York 11429. Recommended by Ira S. Holder, Sr., F.P.S.

Donald G. Sherwood, M.P.S., Cape Girardeau, Missouri 63701. Recommended by James Walker, M.P.S.

Thomas E. Puckett, St. Louis, Missouri 63136. Recommended by James Walker, M.P.S.

Chester W. Closson, St. Louis, Missouri 63121. Recommended by James Walker, M.P.S.

Charles P. Smith, St. Louis, Missouri 63133. Recommended by James Walker, M.P.S.

Clayton Williams, St. Louis, Missouri 63133. Recommended by James Walker, M.P.S.

Calvin L. Thomas, St. Louis, Missouri 63133. Recommended by James Walker, M.P.S.

James Joy, St. Louis, Missouri 63113. Recommended by James Walker, M.P.S.

Leroy Gill, St. Louis, Missouri 63130. Recommended by James Walker, M.P.S.

Glen A. Gates, St. Louis, Missouri 63115. Recommended by James Walker, M.P.S.

Tommie L. Penson, Jenning, Missouri 63136. Recommended by James Walker, M.P.S.

Martin A. Hayott, New York, New York 10037. Recommended by Ira S. Holder, Sr., F.P.S.

James C. Moose, Sr., St. Louis, Missouri 63107. Recommended by Joseph A. Walkes, F.P.S.

Milton R. Chatham, Englin AFB, Florida 32542.

Jessie P. Rice, St. Louis, Recommended by James Walker, M.P.S.

Zoll Ramsey Randolph, University City, Missouri 63130. Recommended by James Walker, M.P.S.

Horace M. Walters, Jr., St. Louis, Missouri 63136. Recommended by James Walker, M.P.S.

Warfield V. Clay, St. Louis, Missouri 63147. Recommended by James Walker, M.P.S.

St. Julian F. Devine, Charleston, South Carolina 29403. Recommended by Herbert Dailey, M.P.S.

David C. Johnson II, Tacoma, Washington 98405. Recommended by Herbert Dailey, M.P.S.

Leroy Trent, Tacoma, Washington 98445. Recommended by Herbert Dailey, M.P.S.

Elmer Johnson, Tacoma, Washington 98404. Recommended by Herbert Dailey, M.P.S.

NOTES, QUERIES AND INFORMATION ON ITEMS OF MASONIC INTEREST — cont. from Page 173

FROM THE PRINCE HALL MASONS LEGAL RESEARCH DEPARTMENT. As of May 15, 1976 there were 5,636 Prince Hall Masonic Lodges with 266,508 members. Estimate in assets including buildings, land equipment $57,057,999.63.

PRINCE HALL BICENTENNIAL MEDALLIONS. The Iowa Masonic Library is collecting them for a display in the Masonic musuem. Grand Lodges who have not been contacted by the library please contact Bro. Keith Arrington, Assistant Librarian; Grand Lodge of Iowa, A.F. & A.M., Box 279, Cedar Rapids, Iowa 52406. Bro. Arrington is an Honorary Fellow of the Phylaxis Society.

Credo

I BELIEVE IN GOD — Grand Architect of the Universe. The Alpha of unreckoned yesterdays, the Omega of the inpenetrable tomorrows. The beginning and the end.

I believe in Man, potentially God's other self often faltering on his way upward — but irrepressible in the urge to scale the spiritual Annapurnas.

I believe in Freemasonry — that corporate adventure in universal brotherhood, despising kinship with no child of the All-Father.

I believe in Prince Hall Masonry — a door of benevolence, securely tiled against the unworthy, but opened wide to men of good report, whether Aryan or Hottentot.

I believe in Masonic vows — the truths of true men plighted in their better selves.

Scripsit L Sherman Brooks 1976

THE PHYLAXIS SOCIETY REQUEST CARD

Mail to: Joseph A. Walkes, Jr. F.P.S.
President
Post Office Box 3151
Fort Leavenworth, Kansas 66027

Joining fee: $3.00/yr.
Subscription rate: $5.00/yr.

Gentlemen:

☐ I am a Prince Hall Freemason in good standings and interested in becoming a member of the Phylaxis Society, please forward application for membership.

☐ I am not a prince Hall Freemason, but would like to receive copies of the Phylaxis Magazine. Enclose find my check for $5.00 for a year's subscription.

Name:..

Address:..

City:... State......................... Zip Code:..........

A SOCIETY FOR PRINCE HALL FREEMASONS WHO SEEK LIGHT AND WHO HAVE LIGHT TO IMPART.